Discovering
HISTORY
Junior Certificate

Patsy McCaughey

MENTOR
BOOKS

Mentor Books Ltd.,
43 Furze Road
Sandyford Industrial Estate
Dublin 18
Republic of Ireland

Tel: +353 1 295 2112/3
Fax: +353 1 295 2114
e-mail: admin@mentorbooks.ie
www.mentorbooks.ie

A catalogue record for this book is available from the British Library

The paper used in this book is made from the wood pulp of managed forests. For every tree
felled, at least one tree is planted, thereby renewing natural resources.

ISBN: 978-1-906623-48-7

Cover: Kathryn O'Sullivan
Typesetting and layout: Kathryn O'Sullivan
Editor: Treasa O'Mahony

Printed in Ireland by ColourBooks Ltd
1 3 5 7 9 10 8 6 4 2

YEAR 1

YEAR 2

YEAR 3

ACKNOWLEDGEMENTS

The Publishers would like to thank:

AKG Images; Alamy; Archives of the Evangelical Lutheran Church of America; Bridgeman Art Library; Corbis Images; Jamil Dar; Terry Fagan, Director of the Dublin North Inner City Folklore Project, for the extract by Mary Foran on page 473; John Frost Newspapers; Getty Images; *The Irish Times*; National Army Museum; National Gallery of Ireland (*Cast of Death Mask of Theobald Wolfe Tone, United Irishman, 1798*; *The Visit of the Queen of Sheba to Solomon, c.1600* by Lavinia Fontana, 1552-1614; *The Marriage of Strongbow and Aoife, c.1854* by Daniel Maclise, 1806-1870; *The Taking of Christ, 1602* by Caravaggio, 1571-1610: Courtesy of the National Gallery of Ireland and the Jesuit Community who acknowledge the generosity of the late Dr Marie Lea Wilson); National Library of Ireland; National Museum of Ireland; Clive Limpkin; Michael Phillips; Royal Society of Antiquaries; RTÉ Stills Library; Tim Keefe, Digital Resources, Trinity College Library; Ulster Linen Hall Library; Ulster Museum; www.CartoonStock.com

Author's Acknowledgements

The author would like to acknowledge the following people's help, support and inspiration:

My parents, Ohna and Terence; Sorley, Mary and Kevin McCaughey; Nicolas Marcoux; Sinead Duffy; Sheila Hoare; Treasa O'Mahony; Aidan Clarke; Niall MacMonagle; Shuna Hutchinson Egar; Oriole Cullen; Jonathan Forbes; Conor Brownlee; Hanna Kickham; Bobby Doyle; Evan Doyle; Sanja Pesek; and all my students at High School.

YEAR 1

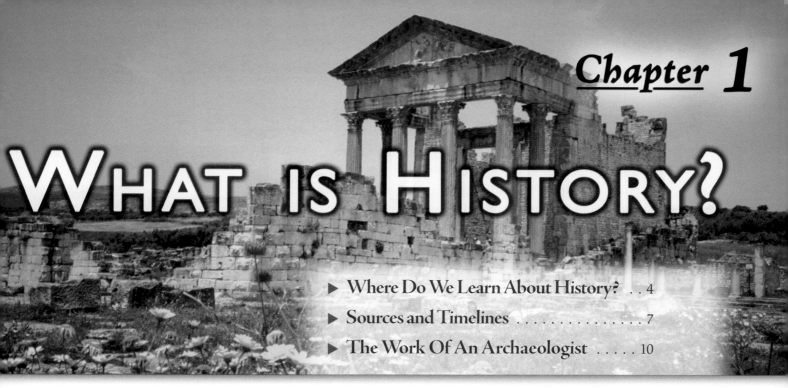

WHAT IS HISTORY?

● What is History?

History is the study of events and people from the past. Anything that has occurred up until this moment in time is history.

● Why Do We Study History?

We study history so that we can understand why things are the way they are now. Why do we speak English and Irish? Why do we live in Ireland? Even personal questions such as 'why are your eyes blue/green/brown' are part of history. Your surname is part of history. History is not only about kings, queens and army generals. It is also about everyday people like you, the student beside you and even your teacher. If we know our history, we know more about ourselves, the places in which we live and the world around us.

● Skills Needed To Be a Historian:

Historians learn about the past from many different places and in many different ways, including:

- Looking closely at items in museums
- Reading and checking books in libraries
- Researching (finding out about) information on the internet
- Interviewing people about events
- Examining photos, videos and films about events

Historians need to be very curious and ask lots of questions. The more information a historian can find out, the better an idea he or she can get about the topic they are researching. The information and evidence available to the historian allows him/her to form a clear account/report of a past event or person. If the information is incorrect, then the historian's account /report is also incorrect.

Where Do We Learn About History?

Historians learn about history from **sources**. These sources are like pieces of evidence or jigsaw pieces. If they are put together properly, a historian can understand what happened in history and why. Sources can be stories, photos, songs, newspapers, films, books, paintings or documents. Sometimes, historians examine objects from the ancient past that were buried underground. These historians are called **archaeologists.**

Newspapers are ▶ excellent sources.

▲ As the South Tower of the World Trade Center collapses, smoke billows from the top of the North Tower. 11 September, 2001. This photograph is a source as it is a piece of evidence showing what happened on that day.

▲ This old photo of the Claddagh in County Galway was taken in 1870. Old photos can be very helpful in showing us how people worked, dressed and relaxed in the past.

● Sources

It helps to think of historians as detectives of the past. They take pieces of evidence (sources) and put them together to build up a picture of a particular time in the past. Sometimes these pieces of evidence are very straightforward. For example, after the attacks on the World Trade Center on 11 September 2001 there were TV and radio reports as well as hundreds of eye-witness accounts. Other times, it is more complicated or there are very few clues. For example it is difficult to find sources for the assassination of Julius Caesar in 44 BC as so few accounts still exist today.

There are different types of sources: primary and secondary.

PRIMARY SOURCES

Primary sources are sources directly from the past. For example, if you wanted to examine sources from today, you would look at the newspaper from today. You might also watch the television from today. Anything that is from the day or time in question is a primary source. A historian may be interested in what you think about living during this time. If you talked or wrote about today, in 20 years' time it would be a primary source because you were there – you experienced that time.

Examples of primary sources:

1. **Newspapers:** They report on political, social and sporting events.

2. **Government records:** Data from the **Central Statistics Office** gives us information on births, deaths and much more in Ireland. This information is collected from a national **census** that takes place every six years.

3. **Diaries:** If someone keeps a diary, they keep a record of their day-to-day lives and events.

4. **Correspondence** (e.g. letters/ emails): When people write emails and letters, they comment on events that are happening around them.

5. **Speeches:** Political speeches made in parliament or at events are often recorded.

6. **Interviews:** A recorded conversation with someone about their lives and their experiences.

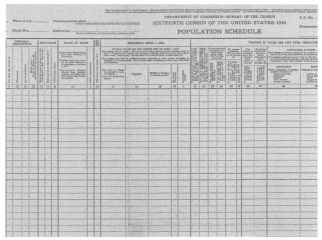

▲ A census form in which citizens of a country fill in personal details.

▲ A photograph of Vladimir Lenin, leader of Russia, giving a speech whilst Leon Trotsky stands beside the podium surveying the crowd. Later, for political reasons, Trotsky was removed from the photo.

▲ Anne Frank's diary

7. Photographs: Historians can see exactly what happened by looking at photos of events. Photos also show how people dressed at that time.

8. Paintings and posters: Before the camera was invented, people had to paint what they saw. Therefore, paintings are very useful because they often show important events allowing historians to see what happened and who was involved.

9. Autobiographies: Famous figures – political and otherwise – sometimes write an account of their lives. This can be a very useful primary source as the person was present for all of the events that took place in his/her life.

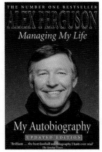

▲ Alex Ferguson's autobiography: this book is a primary source.

SECONDARY SOURCES

Secondary sources are evidence from a later time than the event in question. For example, if someone was to write a book about a famous person, that would be a secondary source because they were not present at all the events. This textbook is a secondary source because the author was not present in the Stone Age or in World War II. These sources can be of interest but they are not as reliable as primary sources.

Here is a list of secondary sources:

▲ Alex Ferguson's biography: this book is a secondary source.

1. A biography: A book about a famous figure written by someone who has examined primary sources.

2. History books: These contain accounts of historical events and people but they are written after the events described in the books took place.

3. TV or radio documentaries: Programmes on television or radio that describe what happened in the past.

Questions

1. How are historians like detectives?
2. Give three examples of a primary source.
3. Give three examples of a secondary source.
4. Examine the following list and state if they are primary or secondary sources:

   (a) a newspaper from 1945

   (b) a photograph of Hitler

   (c) this textbook

   (d) an interview with your teacher about schools today

   (e) an interview with your teacher about World War I

   (f) a recent book about Jesus

   (g) an autobiography by Irish President Mary McAleese

Sources and Timelines

● Problems with sources

A historian must examine his/her sources very carefully. A primary or secondary source can sometimes be biased and choose to present a person or an event in a certain way in order to make someone or something look better or worse than they really were. A historian needs to be determined to find the truth, look at each source and follow certain steps:

1. Ask where was the source created, when was the source created, who created it and why was it created?

2. Is it a primary source or a secondary source?

3. How reliable is the source? Can the historian believe what is being written? For example, a book about the former American President George W Bush written by someone who worked for him and admired him greatly may not include any reference to any unpleasant actions that he took.

4. Does the source agree with other sources about the same event? If they don't, why don't they?

THE RELIABILITY OF SOURCES

Many sources – both primary and secondary - suffer from a lack of reliability:

Bias: This is a form of prejudice (an unfair preference for or dislike of somebody or something). For example, if you like someone, you might highlight only their good points. If you dislike someone, you might point out only their faults. They remain the same person but your opinion of them is biased.

Propaganda: This is information or rumours created and

▲ Spot the difference! The man at the back of the boat has been removed from the second photo - although if you look carefully his leg is still there.

◀ A famous headline that appeared in *The Sun* during a war between Britain and Argentina. The story celebrates the British navy's successful destruction of two enemy ships.

spread to influence people's views. During wars, it is common for governments to pretend that their armies are winning the battle even if this is not the case.

Exaggeration (stating that someone or something is more or less, bigger or smaller, better or worse than is really the case): In primary and secondary sources, it is common for people to exaggerate the number of people at events or the popularity of a ruler.

Accuracy (to be precise and avoid errors): Sources sometimes get things wrong. It is important that historians check their sources. Although the internet is a very useful research tool, some websites simply make up information. Some websites are reliable (e.g. bbc.co.uk) because they are written by experts and regularly checked. Others, such as Wikipedia, can be wrong because anyone can insert an entry even if they are not entirely sure of their facts. This does not mean the entry is always incorrect, but historians must be very careful and double-check information taken from the internet.

● Timelines

Time is very important to historians. Without time, it would be impossible to know when important events happened in history. Putting events in the correct order of time is called **chronology** (from the Greek for 'study of time'). When events are put in chronological order, they are put in the order in which they occurred.

By the way . . .
Because not everyone believes in Jesus, some people have begun to use BCE (Before the Common Era) instead of BC and CE (Common Era) instead of AD. Both labels are correct but BC and AD are used in this book.

To help with this, time is divided into seconds, minutes, hours, days, weeks, months and years. Years are grouped into periods called **decades** (10 years), **centuries** (100 years) and **millennia** (1,000 years). To work out when an event happened, we look at the date. For example, if an event happened on 6 April 1975, we know it was on the sixth day of the fourth month 1,975 years after the birth of Christ.

In most western countries, the year of an event is worked out from the year Jesus Christ is supposed to have been born, Year One. Therefore, an event that occurred in 1975 took place 1,975 years **Anno Domini** (from the Latin for 'in the year of our Lord'). If something happened in the years before Jesus, the date would be BC (Before Christ). This can be confusing as you must count down to Year One (the year Jesus was born) if something happened BC, and then you count up if something happened <u>after</u> Year One.

- The century (100 years) directly before Jesus is known as the first century BC. So the years 1 to 99 BC are the first century BC.
- The century after Jesus was born is the first century AD. Therefore, the first 12 months from Jesus' birth in Year 0 AD to 99 AD are the first century AD.
- This means that 1975 AD is the twentieth century AD as it is between 1900 and 1999.

This may seem a little confusing, but do not worry – you will get used to it!

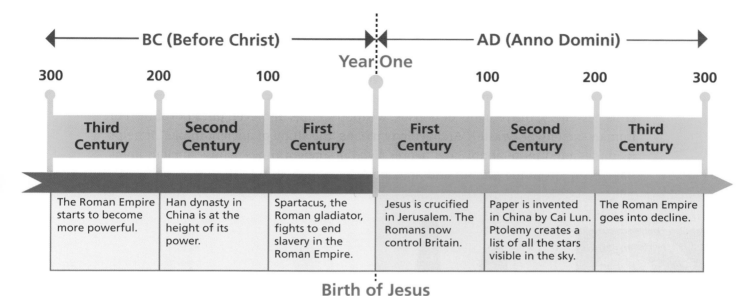

Birth of Jesus

PERIODS

Some events in history continued for so long that they are referred to as a **period** or an **age**. This means that this period of time has a common link. For example, the Stone Age lasted from about 2,500,000 BC to 2,000 BC. The reason this period is known as the Stone Age is because the people who lived during this time used stone weapons and tools. In the same way, the Bronze Age was roughly between 2,000 BC and 500 BC and is referred to as the Bronze Age because people used bronze tools.

By the way . . .
It is now thought that Jesus of Nazareth was more likely to have been born between 8-4 BC.

Questions

1. Outline the steps a historian must go through to be sure a source is reliable.

2. Explain the following terms:

    (a) Bias   (b) Accuracy   (c) Exaggeration

3. What does the term 'chronology' mean?

4. Give the correct term for the following periods of time:

    (a) 100 years   (b) 10 years   (c) 1,000 years

5. What does the term AD stand for and what does it mean?

6. Give the correct century for the following dates, e.g. 1862 is in the nineteenth century.

    (a) 1975 AD   (b) 1066 AD   (c) 480 BC   (d) 333 BC   (e) 32 AD

7. Give the correct dates for the following centuries, e.g. the eighteenth century AD is from 1700-1799 AD.

    (a) twenty-first century AD   (c) sixteenth century AD

    (b) first century BC   (d) eighteenth century BC

The Work of an Archaeologist

One of the ways in which we can discover more about history is by examining objects from the past. These objects are sometimes buried deep in the ground. These pieces of evidence from the past are known as **artefacts**. They can be anything: cups, jewellery, the remains of houses, weapons, coins and even piles of rubbish or human excrement (waste). Archaeology means 'the study of ancient things'. It helps us understand more about how people lived in ancient times. These ancient items have been left in the ground and archaeologists dig them up.

▲ Coins, tools and jewellery are artefacts sometimes found by archaeologists.

● How Did They Get Into The Ground?

The artefacts find their way into the ground in a number of ways:

1. People may lose them. They fall out of carts, are left behind during a move or stored somewhere safely and then forgotten.

2. People may hide them. People often bury treasure or important things. Something may happen to the people before they can dig up their buried goods.

3. Items may be buried alongside people. In ancient times it was common for people to place a dead person's favourite objects alongside their bodies when they were burying them. This could be jewellery, weapons or sometimes even their wives or slaves who were still alive!

4. Whole towns are sometimes lost. Disease or natural disasters such as volcanoes can force people to flee towns. Over time these towns are then covered in soil and forgotten.

When Mount Vesuvius, which is near to the Roman town ▶ of Pompeii, erupted in AD 79, it happened so quickly that archaeologists later unearthed bodies of people who had been shopping, playing chess or baking bread when they were suffocated by the ash from the volcanic eruption.

• How Do Archaeologists Find These Artefacts?

1. Often archaeologists are simply lucky. Items like the Ardagh Chalice were found by chance in a bog in Ireland by a farmer.

2. Archaeologists can use **geophysics** to look underneath the soil. Using metal detectors and electronic probes, they can see if there are any remains or artefacts in the soil.

3. When a new building or road is about to be built, it is possible for archaeologists to examine the area. This happened when the motorway past the hill of Tara was being built. This is called **rescue or salvage archaeology**.

4. Some sites are found after listening to old stories. The story of the siege of Troy led a German archaeologist called Heinrich Schliemann to a location in northern Turkey. Here he found the remains of the ancient city of Troy that existed 1200 BC.

▲ The Ardagh Chalice was found in a bog.

5. Other sites can be seen from above – using an aeroplane or helicopter. Shapes in fields can often show if ramparts or walls existed there in the past. Look at the picture below and see if you can work out the shape of the old fort.

▲ An aerial view of Hod Hill in Dorset, England. Note the circles in the ground surrounding the ancient fort.

THE EXCAVATION

When the archaeologists have found a location they want to investigate, they have to plan the **excavation** or **dig** very carefully to make sure nothing is broken. They also have to preserve the site from bad weather or from people destroying the site. After the top layer of soil has been removed by a digger or by pickaxes, the archaeologists begin work.

They use a large number of tools:

Pick-axes loosen the soil.

A **trowel** can remove smaller amounts of soil.

Brushes allow soil to be very delicately removed from an artefact.

Sieves are used to make sure no artefact, no matter how small, is thrown away with the soil.

During a dig, **drawing frames** are used to record the position of each artefact found.

The dig is constantly photographed and drawings are also made to make sure that the archaeologist does not forget where everything was located.

Each artefact is catalogued into a **site book** and a **computer**.

As the artefacts are being catalogued, they are numbered and sorted before being sent to the laboratory.

Finally, the artefacts are brought to a **museum** where they are kept and sometimes displayed to the public.

▲ Archaeologists excavate an ancient residential site in Askum, Ethiopia.

Questions

1. What are artefacts? Give an example of an artefact.

2. Explain what an archaeologist does.

3. List some of the ways in which artefacts may end up in the ground.

4. List the tools that an archaeologist would use at a dig and explain how each one is used.

● How Can Archaeologists Tell How Old Things Are?

There are a number of ways for an archaeologist to tell how old an artefact is:

1. STRATIGRAPHY

Stratigraphy is a method that dates artefacts by the other objects found at the same level in the ground. The older the artefact, the further down it is likely to be. For example, if you dropped something, it would lie on the top of the ground or near the top. Over hundreds or thousands of years, new things may fall on top of it and it is pushed further down.

2. CARBON DATING

Every living thing contains a chemical called Carbon-14 while it is alive. When it dies, it begins to slowly and steadily release Carbon-14. The older the object, the less Carbon-14 it has in it.

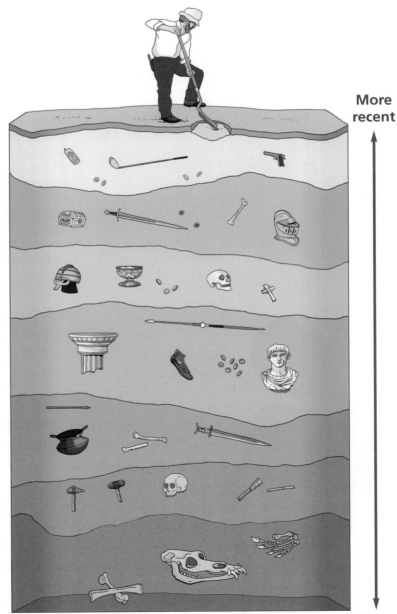

More recent

More ancient

▲ Archaeologists use stratigraphy to date artefacts found buried in the ground.

3. DENDROCHRONOLOGY

This method is used to date any wooden object. Each year a tree adds a layer of wood to its trunk and branches. When it is a good summer of growth, the ring is much wider. The tree rings create a sort of pattern that can be compared to other trees. Archaeologists have created a record of the pattern going back thousands of years. Whenever a wooden artefact is found, it is possible to work out when it was alive from the pattern in its rings.

◀ The Giant Sequoia of Yosemite Park, USA. This section was cut from the giant sequoia in 1919, when the great tree was felled by a storm. At that time the tree was 996 years old – a baby compared to some of the trees in Yosemite National Park which are 3,000 and 4,000 years old. Naturalist A.F. Hall is measuring the span of life of the tree for tourists visiting the park. The various markings show the time of life of the tree at various historical events, such as the discovery of America, the signing of the Declaration of Independence and others.

4. THE BONES OF A SKELETON

▲ The remains of a male skeleton found preserved in a bog in Clonycavan, County Meath in 2003.

Just like in modern TV programmes, archaeologists use modern methods such as reconstructions and **DNA** to find out more about skeletons they have found. By examining a skeleton, it is possible to discover much more about the person.

Pelvis: This allows archaeologists to tell if the skeleton is that of a man or a woman.

Teeth: Depending on how worn they are, the skeleton's age can be estimated.

Bones: If there are any broken bones, it may be possible to tell how the person died.

Thigh: The length of the thigh bone (the femur bone) shows how tall the person was.

Body hair or skin: Scientific analysis can tell what the person ate and drank.

Questions

1. How does stratigraphy help to date an artefact?
2. Explain the term carbon dating.
3. Explain how dendrochronology allows wood to be dated.
4. Give two facts that an archaeologist can learn from a skeleton.

Chapter 1 Questions

1. Pictures

Examine the picture above and answer the following questions:

(a) What work is Archaeologist (1) doing in the picture?

(b) What work is Archaeologist (2) doing?

(c) List five different tools that the archaeologist is using in this picture.

(d) What difficulties might an archaeologist face when they are digging at a site?

2. Documents

Read the following pieces written about the Ireland versus England soccer game in Stuttgart in 1988 and answer the questions that follow:

(a) It was at once the longest day and the greatest day; a day of deep passion and towering courage. It was the day that the Republic of Ireland took its place among the aristocracy of international football and beat England for the first time in a competitive game in front of 53,000 incredulous [not believing] supporters in Stuttgart yesterday afternoon. Ray Houghton's goal after only six minutes, exploding like a giant fire-cracker in the bow shaped Neckarstadion lit the way to Ireland's finest win and from that point, the men in green were men inspired.

(b) England were stuffed like Fourth Division nobodies. It wasn't just a defeat, it was a national disaster... it was humiliation on a grand scale, by the boyos from their own backyard. At the end, England scurried down the tunnel, their heads surely bowed in shame... what hope is there for a team beaten by a fairly average Irish side.

(i) Give two examples of bias in the extracts above.

(ii) Give an example of exaggeration in either of the pieces above.

(iii) One of these pieces was written by Peter Byrne of *The Irish Times* newspaper and the other by Patrick Barkley from the *Independent* newspaper in Britain. Can you guess which one is by which author? Give reasons for your answer.

3. Short-Answer Questions

(a) Name two methods of dating an object.

(b) Give an example of a primary source and an example of a secondary source.

(c) Give one skill that a historian must have.

(d) What would you expect to find at a museum?

(e) What is a drawing frame?

(f) Explain why it is important for historians to obtain information from more than one source.

(g) How does geophysics help archaeologists?

(h) What does the word archaeology mean?

(i) What is rescue archaeology?

(j) Explain the term propaganda.

4. People in History:

Imagine you are an archaeologist working on a dig. Write a brief account about your work. Use the following headings as a guide:

- How the site was discovered
- The preparation of the site
- The tools used in the dig
- The methods of dating the objects found.

Key Terms to Summarise Chapter 1: What is History?

Sources Pieces of evidence used by historians to explain why and how events in history happened.

Archaeologist A person who studies ancient civilisations by examining items buried in the ground, such as tools, bones and the remains of buildings.

Primary source A source that comes directly from the past, e.g. an eye-witness account of an event, a newspaper from the day in question, a photo of an event or an autobiography.

Central Statistics Office (CSO) The organisation that keeps all the information collected at each census about each citizen.

Census An official count of the population.

Secondary source Evidence taken from a later date about an event. Examples of a secondary source include this history book, television documentaries about a historical event or a biography written about someone's life by someone else.

Bias A form of prejudice, an unfair preference for or dislike of something.

Propaganda Information or rumours created and spread to influence public views about people or events.

Exaggeration Stating that someone or something is more or less, bigger or smaller, better or worse than is actually so.

Chronology The order in which events happen.

Decade A timespan of 10 (ten) years.

Century (plural: centuries) A timespan of 100 (hundred) years.

Millennium (plural: millennia) A timespan of 1,000 (thousand) years.

Anno Domini (AD) Latin phrase meaning 'in the year of our Lord'.

Artefact An object, e.g. a tool, that is of interest to a historian or archaeologist.

Geophysics A method that allows archaeologists look under the soil for artefacts.

Rescue or salvage archaeology
When archaeologists excavate an area because a new building or motorway is about to be built in that area.

Excavation/ dig The location of an archaeologist's work.

Museum A building in which artefacts are kept in safe conditions.

Stratigraphy A method of dating artefacts by dating the objects found at the same level in the ground.

Carbon dating A method of dating an object by measuring how much carbon the object has released.

Dendrochronology A method of dating wooden objects by examining the tree ring patterns and comparing them with other records.

DNA (Deoxyribonucleic Acid) The substance that carries every organism's genetic information. It can be used to find out more information about skeletons and bodies that have been found.

Stone Age Ireland

The first people in the world are thought to have lived in East Africa about 2.5 million years ago. Over time some travelled farther and farther from Africa in search of more land on which to live. These people used very basic tools and weapons made from stone. This period of history is therefore called the Stone Age. It is divided into three stages:

1. The Old Stone Age (also known as the **Palaeolithic** period).

2. The Middle Stone Age (also known as the **Mesolithic** period).

3. The New Stone Age (also known as the **Neolithic** period).

> ## By the way . . .
>
> *Lithos* is the Greek word for stone.

	(Approximate dates)
Old Stone Age (Palaeolithic) period:	**2,500,000 BC until 8000 BC**
Middle Stone Age (Mesolithic) period:	**8000 BC until 3500 BC**
New Stone Age (Neolithic) period:	**3500 BC until 2000 BC**

▲ A map showing Britain still connected to Europe

A boat made from a dug-out tree trunk ▲

● The Paleolithic Period

The Palaeolithic period lasted from 2.5 million BC to about 8000 BC. No one lived in Ireland during this time because the island was completely covered in ice. During the Mesolithic period the ice melted and trees and plants began to grow. Ireland was not an island at this time but was connected to Britain and even Europe.

Animals searching for food wandered onto what would become Ireland. As the ice continued to melt, the sea level rose and cut Ireland off from Britain, making it an island. The first evidence of people settling in Ireland dates back to about 7000 BC.

● The Mesolithic Period

Historians are not sure how people arrived in Ireland. It is likely they travelled over across the narrow straits between Ireland and Scotland or Wales. They may have travelled in dug-out tree-trunks or on pieces of wood strapped together and covered with animal hides to keep them water-proof.

Most of Ireland was covered by dense forest so they settled along the coast or along river banks. Archaeologists have discovered evidence of a Mesolithic settlement at **Mount Sandal** in County Derry. They found what appeared to be a pile of rubbish. In this pile there were bird and animal bones as well as shells of nuts, including hazelnuts. These items were carbon-dated and it was estimated that they date from 7000 BC.

There was no evidence of farming. These people were therefore known as **hunter-gatherers** as they hunted animals and gathered fruit and nuts for food. They did not plant crops or try to grow food themselves and they did not settle in one place. The Mesolithic hunter-gatherers used stone for axes and for making the dugout tree-trunk boats. They began to use sharpened wood, antlers and pieces of bone for weapons. They also put **micro-liths**

▲ A javelin head found in Kellysgrove, County Galway

(small sharp pieces of flint widely found in north-east Ireland) into wood to create spears for either fishing or hunting animals.

They did not yet have the skills to weave cloth and so their clothes were made from animal skins tied together.

◄ The remains of Mesolithic and Neolithic houses similar to these have been found at Mount Sandal in County Derry and Lough Gur in County Limerick.

HOUSES

Evidence shows that the Mesolithic hunter-gatherers lived in huts similar to a Native-American tepee. Young trees were cut, bent and then woven into a bee-hive shape, tied at the top. Grasses, rushes, animal skins and branches were placed over the frame to provide shelter. We know this because at Mount Sandal darkened circles in the ground were found in a pattern. These were the post holes of the young trees that had rotted there leaving this pattern. Blackened **hearth** (fireplace) stones were also found showing where they cooked and built fires.

Questions

1. Name the three periods of the Stone Age.
2. When do archaeologists think the first settlers arrived here?
3. Where did archaeologists find evidence of Stone Age man in Ireland?
4. Explain the term hunter-gatherer.
5. Explain the term microlith.
6. Using the images which appear above, describe what an early Stone Age home looked like.

● The Neolithic Period

FOOD

During the Neolithic period settlers to Ireland brought with them new skills. They cleared away some of Ireland's forest and grew **crops** like barley and wheat. They also brought **domestic animals** such as pigs, cattle, goats and sheep and had the

▲ Céide Fields, County Mayo

▲ An axehead and chisel from Neolithic times.

skills to weave and make pottery. These new **farmers** no longer had to move around looking for food. Instead they settled in one location. Remains of Neolithic sites have been found preserved in the bogs in the **Céide Fields** in County Mayo. Here they separated fields with stones they took from the ground. Using pollen analysis and carbon dating it is possible to date these remains to around 3000 BC.

TOOLS AND WEAPONS

These Neolithic farmers used new, more advanced tools. They still used stone **axes** to cut down the trees but now turned the soil using **mattocks** (a tool used to break up hard ground) and stone **ploughs**. Stone hide-scrapers were also used to get animal hides ready for use as clothes or hut linings. Small **needles** were made from bone. This shows that Neolithic people could sew and even weave their clothes using wool from their sheep. Pottery was also made at this time. Using local clay, pots were moulded and then put into extremely hot bonfires to fire (harden) them. These pots could then be used to store food, especially grain.

HOUSES

Their skill at building houses also improved. In **Lough Gur**, County Limerick, ruins have been found showing that houses were usually rectangular and made from local materials. Stone and timber were often used and walls were made by weaving sticks through vertical timbers to create a basket effect. These walls were then covered in a mixture of mud and straw to provide insulation. This method is known as **wattle** (the weaving) and **daub** (the mud). The roof was made of rushes or straw and the hearth was located in the middle of the house with a small hole in the roof to let the smoke escape.

BURIAL CUSTOMS

The burial tombs from this period of the Stone Age are fascinating and have long baffled historians. The main mystery is how did they manage to move such enormous stones and why did they build such elaborate tombs. There are over 1,000 of these tombs located

▲ Houses like this were built using wattle and daub.

in Ireland. These graves are known as megalithic tombs as the stones that were used were huge (mega = great and lithos = stone). Hundreds of people must have been used to move these stones and place them in their positions using only ropes and timbers to roll the stones.

1. The megaliths were moved using ropes and timbers.

2. When in the correct location, the megalith was lifted into place.

3. Finally the megalith was slotted into a hole in the ground.

There are three main types of Megalithic tombs:

Court-cairns

These were the earliest types of graves found in Ireland. There was an open entrance to the grave known as the **court** while a covered passageway led to a circular covered room called a **cairn.** The cremated remains or the body was placed in the cairn along with objects, known as **grave goods**, connected to the person. These grave goods could include tools or weapons. This suggests that Stone Age people believed in some form of afterlife in which the person would need these goods.

▲ Court-cairns like this one in Proleek, County Louth were the earliest types of graves found in Ireland.

Dolmens

There are over 150 dolmens located in Ireland. Three stones standing upright support a massive **capstone** weighing many tonnes. Earth or soil was then placed over these stones. Over the years this earth has been removed or eroded leaving the stones standing alone. The body or pottery jars containing the **cremated** (burnt) remains were then placed underneath the capstone. There are many examples of dolmens around Ireland. One good example is at **Kilclooney**, County Donegal.

◀ This dolmen is located at Proleek, County Louth.

Passage tombs

▲ Newgrange in County Meath is one of the finest examples of a passage tomb in Ireland.

By the way . . .

When Newgrange was excavated the corbelled roof was found to be completely intact. There was no need for any repair work as the chamber had stayed perfectly dry for 4,500 years!

Passage tombs are the most famous of the megalithic tombs in Ireland. There are many in the Boyne Valley in County Meath and also in County Sligo but **Newgrange** in County Meath is the most impressive. Newgrange is estimated to date from between 3000 and 2500 BC which makes it older than the Pyramids of Egypt or Stonehenge in England. Although discovered in 1699, Newgrange was not excavated properly until 1962. The remains of four bodies were found there. Newgrange has a 20-metre central passage that leads to a six-metre high central chamber with three sections. This central chamber has a domed roof made by placing rocks on top of each other, each one slightly closer to the centre until they met in the middle and a capstone was placed on top. This type of ceiling is known as a **corbelled roof**.

▲ A corbelled roof in Newgrange

▲ How a corbelled roof is made

The archaeologists were puzzled to find a **roof-box** at the entrance to the passage. For a long time they could not figure out the function of this roof-box. Finally one of the archaeologists discovered that on 21 December (the **winter solstice,** which is the shortest day of the year), the sun rises and shines directly through the roof-box, lighting up the central chamber for 17 minutes. This shows that the Neolithic people had a strong understanding of astronomy and engineering even though they could not read or write. It also suggests that they worshipped the sun and that they had some understanding of the seasonal calendar. Many other passage tombs were also built in line with the seasonal equinoxes or solstices.

Outside the tomb large stones called **kerbstones** were found with designs of zig-zags and spirals on them. There is no explanation for the designs but ones just like these have been found in Brittany in France. This suggests that the people who built Newgrange had some contact with those in France.

▲ Sun coming through the roof-box at Newgrange on the winter solstice (21 December)

Questions

1. What did Mesolithic settlers eat? Give three examples.
2. Name two new tools that the Mesolithic settler used to farm.
3. Give a location where archaeologists have found Mesolithic settlements.
4. Explain the term wattle and daub.
5. List the three types of burial tombs used by Mesolithic settlers. Give a description of one.
6. What type of burial tomb is Newgrange?
7. Explain the following terms:
   (a) Grave goods   (b) Capstone   (c) Corbelled roof

Bronze Age Ireland

▲ Bronze Age farmers used quern stones to grind grain into flour.

Around 2000 BC more settlers arrived into Ireland from Britain and Europe. They brought with them a new invention – bronze. Bronze is a metal made by mixing **copper** and **tin**. Copper was mined in Ireland at **Mount Gabriel**, County Cork and tin was imported from the south of England. To make bronze, copper and tin must be extracted from the rocks in which they are found. The ores of the copper and tin are heated to a very high temperature until the metals melt. This process is called **smelting**. The ores are then mixed together and this new piece of bronze can be reshaped or poured into a mould. Bronze is stronger than stone or bone and can be made much sharper. The Bronze Age lasted from 2000 BC to 500 BC.

● **Everyday life**

FOOD

Bronze Age people continued to farm as Neolithic farmers had done, growing wheat and barley to make flour using **quern stones** (grinding the grain into flour between two heavy stones). They used the flour to make bread, porridge and pancakes.

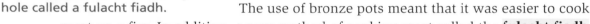

▲ Meat was cooked in a rectangular hole called a fulacht fiadh.

The use of bronze pots meant that it was easier to cook meat on a fire. In addition, a new method of cooking meat called the **fulacht fiadh** was invented. A rectangular hole was dug into wet boggy soil. After letting water pour into the hole, pieces of wood or stones were used to secure the walls around the hole. The water could be brought to the boil using stones that were heated in a nearby fire and placed into the water using pieces of wood. Meat was then covered in straw and placed into the boiling water. Wooden sticks were used to hold the hot stones.

TOOLS AND CRAFTS

People began to make much more delicate objects with bronze. **Sickles** were used for cutting grass, wheat and barley and the first **swords** were made during this time. Metal axes were popular tools as more forest was cut down to make way for the growing population.

Some gold was also found in County Wicklow and more was imported from abroad. Some of the most beautiful types of jewellery were gold **torcs, dress fasteners** and **lunulae** which were crescent moon-shaped necklaces.

▲ An example of a bronze sword from the Late Bronze Age

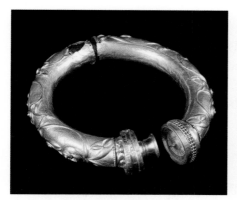

▲ Torcs were worn around the neck.

▲ Dress fasteners

▲ Lunulae were worn by women as necklaces.

HOUSES

Bronze Age people continued to build houses in the same way as in Neolithic times, i.e. a rectangular or circular building using wattle and daub with a roof covered in thatching (straw and grass). However, they also began to build walls around their houses for protection from animals and perhaps even from other people.

> **By the way . . .**
> Lunulae comes from the Latin word for moon – *luna*.

▲ An example of a Bronze Age home: Note the wall surrounding the houses which was built to protect the inhabitants from animals and maybe even other people.

BURIAL CUSTOMS OF THE BRONZE AGE

Wedge tombs

These tombs had vertical stones supporting a large flat stone at an angle. The tomb looked like an angular wedge from the side. The body or cremated remains was buried underneath these stones.

▲ An example of a wedge tomb located in County Cork

Cist graves

These were much simpler and therefore far more common. They consisted of a grave with stones around the edge into which the body was placed, usually in a crouched position. A large flat stone was then placed over the grave. In both the cist graves and the wedge tombs, grave goods were found alongside the bodies.

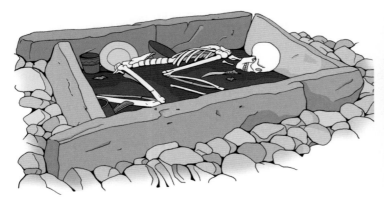

▲ A skeleton in a cist grave surrounded by grave goods.

▲ Drombeg stone circles located in Glandore, County Cork.

Standing stones

Some cist graves have been found under large **monoliths** (large single standing stones) or even in the middle of **stone circles**. These stone circles are usually aligned in some way with the sun and may have been part of some form of sun worship as in Newgrange.

Questions

1. Which two metals make bronze?
2. Give one benefit of using bronze rather than stone.
3. What was a fulacht fiadh? Explain the process of using one.
4. Give three examples of Bronze Age jewellery.
5. Why do you think that cist graves were the most popular method of burial during the Bronze Age?
6. What is a monolith?

Celtic Ireland

There are many opinions on how and why the Celts came to Ireland. Some believe that they came from southern Germany, Austria and Switzerland and conquered the Bronze Age people living in Ireland. However, there is no evidence to suggest there was ever an invasion. What we do know is that tribes from central Europe were known as *Keltoi* by the Greeks and *Gauls* by the Romans. Neither the Greeks nor the Romans could see any differences between the tribes in northern Europe and so they called all the tribes in the north *Keltoi* or *Gauls*. The artwork of the Celts from La Tène in Switzerland is the same as the spirals and floral designs typical of the Irish Celts. The Celts arrived in Ireland sometime after 500 BC and became the dominant culture. The main reason they became so powerful is that they used iron instead of bronze. Iron metal was as hard as bronze but it was much easier to find. Tin was quite rare and had to be brought in from southern England. Iron ore deposits (from which iron is made) were much

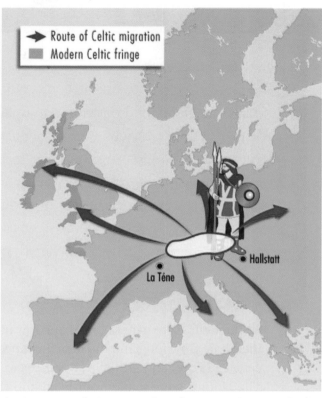

▲ A map of Europe showing La Tène and the modern Celtic fringe

more widespread. This meant that it was widely used throughout Europe. For this reason the period between 500 BC and AD 400 is known as the **Iron Age.**

● How do we know about the Celts?

1. Celtic myths and legends were recorded in much later writings after AD 400 by Christian monks.

2. Descriptions of Celtic tribes and warriors given by Roman writers such as Julius Caesar or by Greek writers such as Diodorus, Herodotus and Strabo are very useful.

3. Celtic remains are located all over Ireland. Archaeological sites provide further information about the lives of the Celts.

• What did the Celts look like?

SOURCE A

One ancient Greek source says:

The Gauls (Celts) are tall of body with rippling muscles and white of skin and their hair is blond, and not only naturally so for they also make it their practice by artificial means to increase the distinguishing colour which nature has given it. For they are always washing their hair in limewater and they pull it back from the forehead to the nape of the neck ...[and] the treatment of their hair makes it so heavy and coarse that it differs in no respect from the mane of horses. Some of them shave the beard but others let it grow a little; and the nobles shave their cheeks but they let the moustache grow until it covers the mouth.

–Diodorus , a Greek writer

So the Celts were generally tall and fair in complexion. Both the men and women let their hair grow long and the men grew beards or moustaches. The men wore trousers called **bracae** and all their clothes were colourfully dyed using berries and plants. The clothes were made from wool and they wore leather shoes. During the winter months Celtic men and women wore great woollen cloaks around them which could double as blankets at night. The Celts liked to wear jewellery. Golden torcs, necklaces and brooches for fastening their clothes have been found by archaeologists. When going into battle men liked to paint their bodies with a dye called woad and they brushed lime into their hair so it would become hard and spiky.

▲ Celtic man and woman

Lime
in hair

Torc

▲ A statue of a wounded Celtic Warrior

Food and drink

Like the Bronze Age people, the Celts were farmers. They continued to grow many of the same crops and breed the same animals as the Bronze Age farmers although cattle had become the most important of all their livestock as the number of cattle a person had showed how wealthy they were. The Celts were famous for having huge feasts at which beer and a drink from honey called **mead** were drunk. The greatest warrior at the feast would get the best part of the meat being served. This part was called the **hero's portion** and it often caused conflict between warriors who each believed they were the greatest.

Political society

Celtic society was far more developed than society in the Bronze Age. Ireland was divided into 150 **tuatha** (kingdoms) and each was ruled by a **rí** (king) who was head of the **derbfine** (royal family). When the king died he was replaced by a tánaiste (successor to the king) who was elected either by agreement or by defeating all other opponents. The next most important people were the **Aos Dána** (nobles). They were made up of landowners, warriors and educated and skilled people.

Aos Dána

The Aos Dána were made up of:

1. **Warriors** who were highly respected. The Celtic tribes in central Europe sacked the city of Rome in 387 BC and the Romans saw the Celts as a sort of bogeyman. In battle, the Celts covered themselves in war paint and spiked their hair. Roman writers recorded that these Celts cut off the heads of their enemies and carried them into battle. A Celtic warrior was seen as a wild and barbaric warrior by the Greeks and Romans.

2. The **brehons** (judges) who ensured the **Brehon Laws**, which had been in place for generations, were applied. They were responsible for settling any disputes in the tuath.

3. The **druids** (priests) who were responsible for performing any religious ceremony and for crowning the king. They were also responsible for making potions to heal the sick.

4. The **filí** (bards) who had to be able to recite very long poems about great heroes from memory. Their training took almost 20 years to complete and it was very difficult. Some of these stories, for example **An Táin Bó Cuailnge** (the

Derbfine

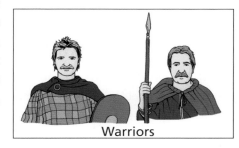
Warriors

Aos Dána

Slaves & Commoners

▲ Celtic society

By the way . . .

According to legend, when famous Celtic Irish warrior Cúchulainn went into his battle frenzy one eye grew as big as a plate while his other eye went so far back into his head that not even a stork could peck it out. He shook and spun within his skin and his knee-caps began to spin around. His hair would go hard and stick straight up.

Cattle Raid of Cooley), took days to recite! They composed poems praising warriors or kings but they could also cause great damage if they criticised someone in their poems. For this reason they were respected and even feared.

5. **Craftsmen** who were carpenters, smiths and metalworkers.

6. The rest of the tuath consisted of **commoners** and **slaves** (people captured during battles) who had very little say in the running of the tuath.

● Role of Women

▲ Queen Medb featured on the old Irish Pound note.

Women in Celtic society were well respected. As well as weaving, making clothes and bringing up children they could own property and were very independent. The rebellion of the female warrior **Boudicca** in Britain against the Romans in AD 61 shows that female leaders were acceptable to Celts. In Irish Celtic legends, **Queen Medb** of Connacht was a very famous and powerful queen while Cúchulainn was taught how to fight by the warrior witch **Scáthach**. Although there is no historical evidence to support these legends, they do show that women were respected within Celtic society.

▲ An example of a Celtic board game

● Leisure time

The Celts enjoyed many pastimes including hunting, a form of hurling called *báire,* story-telling, music and poetry. People sat together and listened to the *file* telling legends and stories of Cúchulainn, Fionn Mac Cuchaill and Na Fianna. They also had board games called *brandubh* and *ficheall* which are mentioned in the epic poem, *An Táin*.

Questions

1. From where do historians believe the Celts originally came?

2. Where do we get most of our information about the lifestyle and appearance of the Celts?

3. Give a description of the appearance and dress of a typical Celtic man.

4. What was the name given to the area ruled by the rí?

5. Explain the following words:
   (a) Mead   (b) Derbfine   (c) Brehons   (d) Tánaiste   (e) Ficheall

6. Who were the people who made up the Aos Dána?

7. Why were filí so powerful?

8. What kinds of pastimes did the Celts have? Give two examples.

• Where they lived

Many ancient Celtic sites have been excavated here in Ireland by archaeologists. As a result we know more about the places in which the Celts lived. As the wealth of each person was determined by the number of cattle they owned it was important that people built homes to protect their livestock. There are three main types of homes or forts that have been found:

> **By the way . . .**
> The lia fáil (stone of destiny) at the hill of Tara is said to scream if the true High King of Ireland sits on it.

1. RINGFORTS

These were the most common type of fort and are sometimes called a **rath** or a **lios.** A circular raised bank was built and a timber wall placed on top of the bank. A **fosses** (ditch) was dug around the bank for further protection from attack. Sometimes a **souterrain** was built. This was a tunnel underneath the fort and it was probably used for either storing food as it was dark and cold or for refuge if the fort was being attacked. In the west of Ireland these forts had stone walls instead of timber and are known as **caiseal** or **cathar**. A large ringfort was referred to as a **dún.**

Emain Macha in County Armagh is an example of a rath. ▲

Rath / Lios	**Timber walls, e.g. Rathfarnham / Rathdrum / Lismore**
Caiseal / Cathar	**Stone walls, e.g. Cashel / Cahirciveen**
Dún	**Large ringforts, e.g. Dundalk / Dunleer**

2. HILLFORTS

These forts were located on higher ground and were easier to defend. They had walls built on top of earthen banks around the houses as a defence against attack. Large stones were also placed in front of these banks to block any attackers on chariots. A good example of this kind of fort is the **Hill of Tara** in County Meath. Some hillforts were located beside cliffs and these are called promontory forts. The most impressive example of this in Ireland is the remains of the fort at **Dún Aengus** on the Aran Islands off the coast of County Galway. Dún Aengus and the Hill of Tara were very important Celtic sites. These two locations were mostly used for religious and political ceremonies rather than as dwellings.

▲ The Hill of Tara in County Meath: the fort here was used by the Celts for religious and political ceremonies.

▲ The remains of the fort at Dún Aengus on the Aran Islands show that it was an important Celtic site.

◀ A reconstruction of a crannóg near Clifden, County Galway

3. CRANNÓGS

These dwellings were very safe as they were located in the middle of a lake. Crannógs (from the Irish for a young tree) were built by bringing stones, rocks and pieces of timber to the middle of a lake and creating an island. Once the island was built, timber was used to construct a fort that could only be accessed by either a wooden bridge or a boat. It is possible to see reconstructions of a crannóg at **Craggaunowen**, County Clare and **Ferrycarrig**, County Wexford.

● Religion

The druids were very important in the lives of the Celts. They performed religious ceremonies and were thought to have magic powers. They sacrificed offerings to the gods, sometimes including human sacrifices. The Celts worshipped many gods. **Dagda** was the god of the afterlife and his wife was the river god **Boann** (Boyne). **Lug** was the warrior god and also the god of the sun. Throughout the year, druids celebrated many festivals.

Festivals

(a) Samhain (November)	Festival to honour all the spirits of the underworld.
(b) Imbolg (February)	Festival in honour of the goddess Brigid at the beginning of spring.
(c) Bealtaine (May)	Festival in honour of the goddess Bel for good crops and healthy livestock.
(d) Lughnasa (August)	Festival in honour of the god Lug for a bountiful harvest.

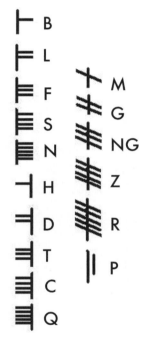

▲ This is some of the alphabet in Ogham.

The Celts believed in an afterlife called **Tír na nÓg** (land of the young). On the massive stones (monoliths) above cist graves they often carved decorations of spiral and floral designs. Sometimes they used **ogham** – the earliest form of writing in Ireland. Using a very simple alphabet they carved notches on the side of the stone. Ogham was read from the bottom up.

Questions

1. Explain the following words:

   (a) Rath   (b) Fosses   (c) Souterrain

2. Why were some forts located on hills or beside cliffs?

3. Where would you find a crannóg?

4. Give an example of a promontory fort in Ireland.

5. What jobs did a druid perform?

6. What was Ogham and where would you find it?

Early Christian Ireland

As we will see in the next chapter, the Roman Empire spread across all of Europe in the first centuries AD. As Britain was part of the Roman Empire Irish Celts came into contact with Christians in Britain. This contact through trading and raiding meant that by the fifth century there were Christians in Ireland. We know this because in AD 431 a bishop called **Palladius** was sent by Pope Celestine to the Irish 'who believe in Christ'. Unfortunately we know nothing of what happened to him when he reached Ireland. It is St. Patrick who is thought to have spread Christianity in Ireland.

• St. Patrick

▲ St. Patrick wrote an account of his life in a book called *The Confession*.

We know about the life of St. Patrick only through his own writings called **The Confession**. In this he explains why he came to Ireland. He tells of how he was brought to Ireland from somewhere in Britain. He was captured by Irish raiders at the age of 16 and forced to work as a shepherd. He escaped six years later, around AD 432, and returned to Britain. In his Confession, he wrote that he had a dream that he should return to Ireland and convert the Irish to Christianity. Sometime in the middle of the fifth century he returned to Ireland. He spent the remainder of his life converting and baptising people. He believed that if he converted the kings the rest of the tuath would then follow their king and also convert. He managed to convert some people but the druids did not like his new religion. St. Patrick states that he lived in 'daily expectation of murder'. So there must have been some resistance to this new religion but there is no further evidence that there was any killing of Christians. Over time more and more missionaries (people who want to convert people to their religion) were sent to Ireland such as St. Secundius and St. Auxilius. The power of the druids was slowly reduced. By the middle of the sixth century, Christianity was the main religion in Ireland.

• Celtic reaction

Celtic life continued throughout these centuries and for some time the daily life of the people remained the same. Over time, however, churches were built near old pagan sites and bishops, priests and monks took over the role of the druids. Traditional Celtic festivals were replaced by Christian ones, e.g. Imbolg became St. Brigid's day and Samhain became Halloween.

▲ Sceilig Beag with the early Celtic monastery island of Sceilig Mhichíl behind it – both islands lie off the coast of County Kerry.

▲ Clonmacnoise lies about 20 kilometres from Athlone on the eastern bank of the River Shannon. The monastery was founded in the mid sixth century by St. Ciarán.

During these early years of Christianity a new way of Christian life became popular among some people. Christians who wished to devote their lives entirely to God separated themselves from the rest of the population. They set up places called **monasteries** for men and **convents** for women. The first monastery in Ireland was set up by St. Enda on Inis Mór on the Aran Islands. Soon other monasteries were established: e.g. at Kildare by St. Brigid, at Clonmacnoise by St. Ciarán and at Clonfert by St. Brendan. Perhaps the most spectacular monastery was on Sceilig Mhichíl off the coast of County Kerry. This isolated location meant that the monks (the Christian men who lived there) could focus on praying and devoting themselves to God. They lived on milk, cheese and fish and if they wished to grow anything they had to bring the soil from the mainland. More convents and monasteries were built over the next 200 years and they became centres of learning and grew in importance. Monks and nuns lived very strict and simple lives. They spent their days praying and studying the Bible. Some monasteries became famous for their metalwork and beautifully illustrated Bibles.

Questions

1. How do we know about the life of St. Patrick?

2. From where was St. Patrick supposed to have come from?

3. Why were monasteries set up during this time?

4. Give two examples of monasteries that were established in Ireland during this time.

THE MONASTERY:

The monastery was designed like the rath that we looked at on page 31. A circular ramp of soil or a stone wall was built around the monastery. Inside the walls there was:

1. An **oratory** or church where monks attended mass and prayed.

2. The **refectory** where the monks ate their meals.

3. The cells in which the monks slept. These were made either from wattle and daub or stone. These huts were called **beehive huts** **or beehive cells**.

4. A **scriptorium** where **scribes** (people who wrote) copied manuscripts (books written by hand).

5. Some monasteries built **round towers** which could be used as a bell tower or a safe place in which to hide if the monastery was attacked. Two good examples of round towers are in Glendalough, County Wicklow and Ardmore, County Waterford.

6. The bigger monasteries had guesthouses for travellers and tradesmen.

Texts written by the monks and archaeological evidence tell us more about what life in the monastery was like.

By the way . . .

Manuscript comes from the latin *manus* = hand and *scribere* = to write.

THE WORK OF MONKS

Each monk had his own responsibilities given to him by the **abbot** (the head of the monastery).

1. Cooking and farming were necessary for the monks to feed themselves.

2. Scribes produced hand-written religious books **(manuscripts)**. Some of these beautifully written, illustrated and colourful manuscripts still exist.

By the way . . .

The name Cathach means 'battle book' as it was brought into battles for good luck by the O'Donnell clan.

   (a) The **Cathach**. This is the oldest surviving book in Ireland. It was written in AD 600.

   (b) The **Book of Durrow**. This was written about a century after the Cathach and can be found in the library of Trinity College, Dublin.

▲ Round Tower   Book of Kells ▶

   (c) The **Book of Kells**. This book is also kept in Trinity College library. It is a copy of the four gospels and each page is highly decorated.

These manuscripts were written on **vellum** (calf skin) or **parchment** (sheepskin). The monks made **quills** (pens) from goose feathers and they made ink from plants and powdered coloured stones.

3. Other monks were responsible for making objects from metal. They used the Celtic designs similar to those of La Tène. The most famous surviving pieces of metalwork are:

By the way . . .

These ornaments are now in the National Museum of Ireland

   (a) The **Ardagh** and the **Derrynaflan Chalices**. A chalice is the cup used during Mass.

   (b) The **Cross of Cong**. This was used in religious processions.

▲ Ardagh Chalice

▲ Ardagh Chalice details

▲ Cross of Cong

◄ St. Patrick's Bell Shrine from County Armagh

(c) **Reliquaries** were boxes that held important relics (objects) connected to saints. One important reliquary is **St. Patrick's Bell Shrine.**

(d) The **Tara Brooch** is a highly decorated brooch for tying a cloak of an important Celtic person. The decoration for these objects was made by twisting very thin wires of gold and silver into designs. This method of decoration is called **filigree**. The monks also used precious stones and gold leaf.

4. Stone masonry was also important. They carved very detailed crosses known as **High Crosses**. The population could not read or write so the masons carved scenes from the Bible onto the crosses. These images helped monks to explain the story of Jesus through pictures. Two of the most beautiful High Crosses are at **Clonmacnoise,** County Offaly and **Monasterboice,** County Louth.

▲ This High Cross is at Monasterboice, County Louth.

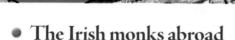

● The Irish monks abroad

During this time pagan tribes of the Huns and the Goths from central Europe conquered the Christian Roman Empire. The fall of the Roman Empire meant that mainland Europe entered what is known as the Dark Ages. Many Irish monks believed they should continue to spread Christianity. Some travelled to mainland Europe and established monasteries there. They went as far as Bobbio in northern Italy, Taranto in the south of Italy and Wurzburg in Germany. **St. Colmcille** of Donegal set up a monastery on the Scottish island of Iona. It is thought that the Book of Kells was first written there and then brought back to Kells at a later date.

▲ St. Colmcille set up a monastery on the Inner Hebridean island of Iona off the west coast of Scotland.

Chapter 2 Questions

1. Pictures

(a) What is the name given to these standing stones?

(b) Who made these stones?

(c) What pictures were carved into the stone?

(d) Why were these pictures carved into the stone?

2. Documents

The following is an extract from a Celtic epic poem called The Táin. It describes the great Celtic Irish warrior Cúchulainn. Read the extract and answer the questions that follow:

SOURCE A

This is what he wore: a fitted purple mantle, fringed and fine, folded five times and held at his white clear breast by a brooch of light-gold and silver decorated with gold inlays – a shining source of light too bright in its blinding brilliance for men to look at. A fretted silk tunic covered him down to the top of his warrior's apron of dark red royal silk. He carried a dark deep-red crimson shield – five disks within a light-gold rim – and a gold-hilted sword in a high clasp. On his chariot he had a tall grey-bladed javelin with a hard hungry point, riveted with bright gold. He held in one hand nine human heads and in the other hand ten, and he shook them at the armies – the crop of one night's warfare on the four provinces of Ireland.

Source: *The Tain*, translated by Thomas Kinsella, Oxford University Press

(a) List three weapons that Cúchulainn had with him.

(b) Name two items of clothing that Cúchulainn is wearing.

(c) How can we tell that Cúchulainn is a rich important warrior?

(d) What evidence do we have that Cúchulainn is a fierce warrior?

(e) Describe the brooch Cúchulainn is wearing.

(f) Name a highly decorated brooch that was made during the Early Christian period in Ireland.

3. Short-Answer Questions

(a) What was the main occupation of the Mesolithic people?

(b) What type of stone was used to make tools and weapons in the Mesolithic period?

(c) What was the name of the method of building walls that used wet mud and weaved sticks?

(d) Name three types of tombs/graves in the Neolithic period.

(e) What two metals are used in the making of bronze?

(f) What is smelting?

(g) What is the name given to a hole in the ground (usually in a bog) used for cooking?

(h) Name the two main methods of burial during the Iron Age.

(i) Name four types of dwellings used by the Iron Age Celts.

(j) What was the name of the round tool used for grinding grain?

(k) Describe the decorations the Celts used when making metal ornaments.

(l) In which buildings did monks live?

(m) In which building did the monks write their manuscripts?

(n) Name two famous manuscripts written by Irish monks.

(o) Name one monastic site in Ireland.

(p) Explain the term filigree.

(q) Which two materials were used to make the pages of manuscripts?

4. People in History

Write about the life of a monk in Early Christian Ireland. Use the following headings as a guide:

- The reasons why he wanted to become a monk
- The work he did in the monastery
- The buildings in the monastery
- The activities of the other monks

5.

(a) Give two sources of archaeological evidence used to gain information about the lives of Stone Age people.

(b) Name two locations in Ireland that have provided archaeological evidence and state which period of the Stone Age they are from.

(c) How did the arrival of monks who could read and write help historians in their studies of Ancient Ireland?

(d) Write an account of two of the following aspects of life in Celtic Ireland:

(i) Food and clothing

(ii) Housing

(iii) Work, art and craft

Key Terms to Summarise Chapter 2: Ancient Ireland

Palaeolithic The first period of the Stone Age between 2.5 million BC and 8000 BC.

Mesolithic The middle period of the Stone Age between 8000 BC and 3500 BC.

Neolithic The most recent period of the Stone Age between 3500 BC and 2000 BC.

Hunter-gatherers Term for the Stone Age people who hunted animals and gathered fruit and berries for food.

Microliths Small pieces of stone used to make weapons and tools, also known as flint.

Wattle and daub Method for making walls by weaving branches through upright sticks and then covering this in a mixture of clay and straw.

Court-cairns A burial tomb with an open entrance called a court with a covered passage leading to a chamber called a cairn.

Dolmens A burial tomb with three upright stones supporting a large capstone.

Capstone A very large stone on top of a cairn.

Passage tomb Burial tomb with a passageway that leads to the central burial chamber.

Corbelled roof Circular ceiling made from stones projecting out from the wall.

Kerbstones Large decorated stones found at the outside of passage tombs.

Smelting The process of making a metal by mixing melting metal ores.

Quern stones Stones used to grind wheat and other grains.

Fulacht fiadh A method of cooking meat in a pit full of water by placing heated stones into water.

Lunulae Half moon-shaped necklaces from the Bronze and Iron Age.

Wedge tombs A burial tomb with smaller stones supporting a large stone at an angle.

Cist graves Bronze Age burial site in which the body was placed in the grave and a large stone was placed on top.

Monoliths Single stones, usually very large.

Bracae Trousers worn by Celtic men.

Tuath The name for kingdoms in Celtic Ireland.

Rí A king in Celtic Ireland.

Derbfine The Celtic word for the royal family in Celtic Ireland.

Aos Dána The important members of the Celtic tuath who helped the rí make decisions.

Brehon Name for the legal judges of Celtic Ireland.

Druid Name for the Celtic priests who performed religious ceremonies and were believed to have magic powers.

Fíle Name for the poet or bard in Celtic Ireland.

Ringforts Celtic dwellings that had a circular wall for protection.

Hillforts Celtic dwellings that were located on top of hills for protection.

Crannógs Celtic dwellings located on man-made islands.

Ogham First type of writing used in Ireland with vertical marks etched onto the side of stones.

Monasteries A place where monks lived together to devote themselves to God.

Oratory The church in a monastery where monks prayed.

Refectory The room in a monastery where monks ate.

Beehive huts/beehive cells Small beehive-shaped huts in which monks lived.

Scriptorium The building where monks would write books or copy parts of the Bible.

Scribes Monks who copied manuscripts.

Round towers Tall circular towers used as a bell tower or for protection in monasteries.

Abbot The head of a monastery.

Manuscript Hand-written books.

Filigree Very detailed design using fine metal wiring.

High Crosses Tall stone crosses from the eighth century onwards with images from the Bible carved on them.

Web References

For further reading on topics mentioned in this chapter, view the following websites:

www.museum.ie

www.bbc.co.uk/wales/celts/

www.museumsofmayo.com/ceide.htm

www.inhp.com

www.ni-environment.gov.uk/places/monuments/navan.shtml

www.newgrange.com/

Women in History

St. Brigid

St. Brigid (her name means 'fiery arrow') is a patron saint of Ireland. It is thought that she was born around AD 453 near Dundalk, County Louth. Her mother, Broicseach, was a Christian and her father, Dubhtach, was probably a warrior. Renowned for her healing powers, she was supposedly able to cure lepers. As a young woman, she didn't want to marry and so she prayed to God to make her less beautiful. She felt her prayers were answered when she developed a disease that left one side of her face badly scarred.

St. Brigid wanted to set up a monastery and so she asked a chieftain for some land. It is said that the chieftain told her she could have only as much land for her monastery as her shawl would cover. She returned with a shawl that covered all of the Curragh in County Kildare when it was pulled by its four corners. The monastery at the Curragh in Kildare (from the Irish Cill Dara – 'the Church of the Oaks') was built and she became the abbess. During her life, she was famous for being a very good charioteer and travelled throughout Ireland converting people to Christianity.

St. Brigid died around AD 525 in Kildare. Her body was later removed and reburied in County Down alongside St. Patrick and St. Colmcille. The Celtic festival of Imbolg on 1 February is now St. Brigid's day and she is remembered by a simple cross made from rushes.

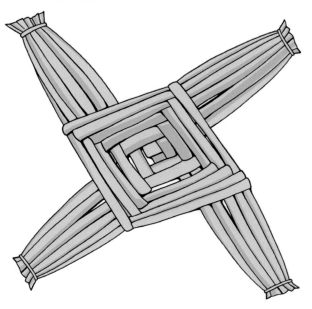

▲ St. Brigid's Cross

ANCIENT ROME — Chapter 3

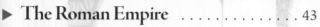

The Roman Empire

The Roman Empire was the greatest empire Europe has ever known. It stretched over Italy, Spain, France, England, Wales, Turkey, Greece, Germany and Belgium as well as most of North Africa and large parts of Iraq. What started as a cluster of villages around the river Tiber in Italy became a superpower that lasted for one thousand years.

● A short history of the Roman Empire

It is thought that Rome was founded around 753 BC. At first it was ruled by a line of kings, but in 510 BC King Tarquin was expelled and Rome became a **republic** (a country that elects its leaders).

A parliament called the Senate was created. Members of the Senate were called **senators**. Once a year two members of the Senate were elected by the public to become **consuls** . They could only be consuls for one year to ensure no individual was able to gain too much power. Consuls commanded the army and chose who could become senators. The Senate made decisions as to how to govern Rome and the lands it conquered. This system of government remained in place for the next 450 years.

Due to a mixture of attacking and making alliances with tribes living in the area, Rome managed to conquer all of Italy by 272 BC. Over the next 100 years the Romans moved into North Africa and Greece. The Romans wanted to conquer these lands because they needed more farmland to feed the population and they wanted to control all trade in the area around the Mediterranean.

▲ According to legend, Romulus and Remus' mother was killed and they were brought up by a she wolf.

By the way . . .

Legend has it that Rome was founded by the brothers Romulus and Remus. They were the twin sons of a priestess Rhea Silvia and the god of war Mars. They built the town but Romulus killed Remus after an argument and so gave his name to the new town.

In 49 BC a Roman general named Julius Caesar took control of Rome and civil war began. Caesar defeated his rivals and became dictator for life, which was against all rules of the Senate. After his assassination in 44 BC another civil war broke out as various powerful Romans tried to become ruler. In 31 BC Julius Caesar's nephew Augustus Caesar became the first Emperor of Rome.

▲ A map of the Roman Empire in 100 BC

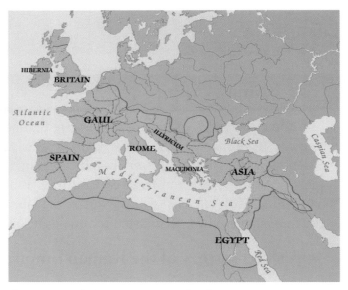

▲ A map of the Roman Empire in AD 198

The Roman Empire continued to expand for the next 200 years before slowly declining. It was sacked by the Goths (a tribe from Germany) in AD 410. However, for almost one thousand years the Romans dominated European political, social, economic and cultural life. As a result, they have had a large influence on our society today.

Questions

1. Name the legendary founder of Rome.
2. When did Rome become a republic?
3. Who were the consuls?
4. What position in Rome did Julius Caesar's nephew have?
5. What happened to Rome in AD 410?

● How do we know about the Romans?

1. ARCHAELOGY

Because the Romans dominated Europe for so long they left many different clues about their lifestyle and culture. They built many cities and towns all over the Empire and archaeologists have been able to excavate many of them to find out how they lived. In Roman times, these cities were full of buildings such as temples and shops, mosaics (pictures made from small pieces of coloured glass or tile), frescoes (paintings on walls that depict daily life) and artefacts (coins, pottery, pictures and monuments). These clues help us understand how they lived their lives.

Source A

▲ **Mosaic showing daily life**

Some towns have been discovered that are still almost perfectly intact. Ostia Antica, on the coast near Rome, was hit by a plague and so people left the town to escape catching it. The abandoned town slowly became covered in silt and soil and was forgotten about until 1801 when archaeologists began to excavate the site.

Another more dramatic event took place in AD 79.

Pompeii, a wealthy trading town near Naples, was situated on the side of Mount Vesuvius, a volcano that had been dormant for almost 1,000 years.

▲ Ostia Antica

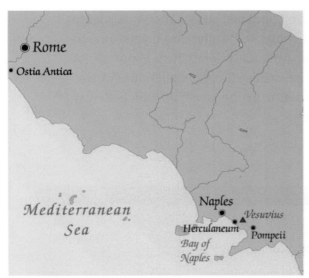

▲ A map of Southern Italy showing Rome, Naples, Herculaneum, Vesuvius and Pompeii

▲ Rome's Colosseum is a huge tourist attraction today.

▲ A streetscape of Pompeii with Mount Vesuvius in the background

▲ Archaeologists working on a street in Pompeii surrounded by the dust-caked bodies of people from the town who had no time to escape when Mount Vesuvius erupted.

In August of that year, Vesuvius erupted without warning and over two days the towns of Pompeii and Herculaneum were covered in lava, toxic ash and dust. The people had no time to flee and so in 1748 archaeologists found the city almost perfectly preserved under layers of ash. People were found in the same position as when the lava covered them. Archaeologists have made casts of their bodies.

The eruption happened so fast that meals were discovered preserved under the layers of ash. People had obviously been just about to sit down and eat when disaster struck. Bread was even found still in the oven in which it was being baked.

Source B

'A fearful black cloud was rent [split] by forked and quivering bursts of flame, and parted to reveal great tongues of fire . . . Darkness fell, not the dark of a moonless or cloudy night, but as if the lamp had been put out in a dark room.'

Pliny the Younger

2. WRITTEN ACCOUNTS

Most people in Rome could read and write so historians have found many written accounts of life at that time. The language they used is called Latin and it is still taught in some schools.

By the way . . .

The Italian, French, Spanish, Portuguese and Romanian languages all come originally from Latin.
The poems, plays and books written by Romans give us a very clear picture of the way of life people had at that time.

Source C

First, the priestess brought to this place four black bullocks. She poured wine on their foreheads, then snipped off the tops of the hairs growing between their horns and threw them into the fire as the first offering, calling aloud upon Hecate, mistress of heaven and hell. Others slit the victims' throats with their knives, and caught the warm blood in bowls … and put on [the] flames whole carcases of bulls and poured rich olive oil over their burning entrails.

From *Aeneid* by the Roman writer Virgil

Questions

1. List two sources from which we have learned about the life of a Roman.

2. Name two things that an archaeologist might find when excavating a Roman town.

3. Can you guess what these Latin words mean in English?

    (a) Aqua

    (b) Flora

    (c) Villa

    (d) Via

4. Look at Source A on page 45. This is a mosaic from Pompeii showing street musicians.

    (a) Is this a primary or secondary source?

    (b) Can you see two of the three instruments the musicians are holding?

    (c) What does the man on the right have on his head?

    (d) What can this picture tell us about the clothes that Romans wore?

5. What happened to Pompeii in AD 79?

6. Read Source C above and explain why this translation helps us to know more about Roman life.

The Roman Army

▲ A map of Europe at the height of Roman power

By the first century BC, the Roman Empire had expanded much farther than just the Italian peninsula. Rome now controlled much of modern-day Turkey, Egypt, Morocco, Britain, France, Spain and Germany. This growth was made possible by the success of its army, by far the most organised and powerful army in Europe. Every male was expected to fight in the army at some point in his life. Wealthier men were given positions of authority in the army (e.g. officer) while poorer Romans regarded the army as a job for life. They were paid while serving in the army and sometimes they were given land to farm when they retired.

● The organisation of the army

The Roman army was very organised which is why it was so successful at conquering much of Europe. The army had a very clear structure:

- Eight soldiers made up a contubernium.

- Ten contuberniums made up a century (under the control of a centurian).

- Six centuries made up a cohort.

- Ten cohorts made up a legion.

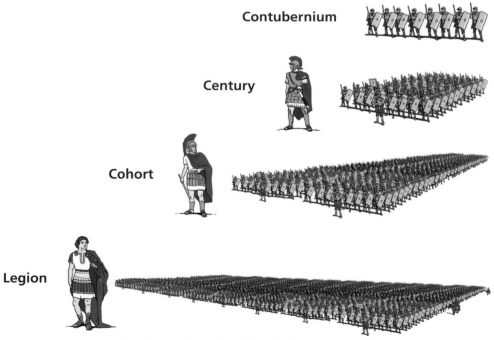

Contubernium

Century

Cohort

Legion

A Roman legion with each of its divisions ▲

Including all the messengers, cooks and other men that did not fight, each legion consisted of roughly 5,000 soldiers. Roman soldiers were known as **legionnaires.**

The army also had divisions of cavalry (soldiers on horseback) who fought but also acted as scouts and carried messages during battles. There were other groups called the artillery (soldiers in charge of missiles and siege machinery) who were needed when the Romans besieged a town.

Life as a soldier

Discipline was very strict in the Roman army. Different punishments were carried out depending on the offence. These punishments ranged from extra work to flogging. If a mutiny (a rebellion by the soldiers) occurred, the men involved were lined up and every tenth man was killed. This punishment was called **decimatio** (coming from the Latin word decimus meaning a tenth, giving us the word 'to decimate' in English.)

Soldiers had to be able to march 32 kilometres each day. They were expected to carry on their backs all the equipment they would need to survive in a battle or siege. This included weapons, tools, cooking pots, tents and enough food to last them for three days. In total this could weigh 40 kilograms. They ate a soup made from barley called gruel and drank either water or cheap wine.

Pilum

Greaves

▲ A Roman soldier

Each soldier had to pay for his own equipment and uniform. The uniform was different depending on the soldier's rank in the army. Soldiers wore chain-mail or metal vests over their tunics. They carried their shield, a sword, a dagger and a javelin called a **pilum**. They wore **greaves** (metal shin guards) and a helmet on their head.

When the legion stopped at night they set up camp and dismantled it completely the next morning. The camp was set up in exactly the same way in every legion so it was possible for a soldier always to find his way around any camp throughout the Empire.

Roman enemies

The Romans had many enemies throughout their Empire. The Gauls of France and Belgium were a very powerful tribe and in 390 BC they managed to capture Rome itself. Eventually Julius Caesar (100-46 BC) defeated the Gauls in France and captured their leader Vercingetorix at the battle of Alesia.

▲ Vercingetorix, leader of the Gauls, surrenders to Julius Caesar in 52 BC.

The Roman Empire was also often at war with the city of Carthage in North Africa. At the time, Carthage was a very important and wealthy city. The conflict between these two superpowers of the time were known as the Punic Wars. The Romans finally defeated the Carthaginians in 146 BC and razed the city to the ground. Legend has it that salt was ploughed into the ground so that nothing would ever grow there again.

Source D

Vergentorix (Vercingetorix), the supreme leader in the whole war, put on his most beautiful armour, had his horse carefully groomed, and rode out through the gates. Caesar was sitting down and Vergentorix, after riding round him in a circle, leaped down from his horse, stripped off his armour, and sat at Caesar's feet silent and motionless until he was taken away under arrest, a prisoner reserved for the triumph [in Rome].

From *The Fall of the Roman Republic* by Plutarch

Questions

1. What was a Roman soldier called?
2. Explain the following words:
   (a) Cavalry   (b) Artillery   (c) Mutiny   (d) Gruel
3. What was decimato?
4. Roman soldiers were sometimes called mules. Can you guess why?
5. What happened to the city of Carthage?
6. Give an account of the life of a Roman soldier using the following headings:
   (a) Organisation of the army and his position in the army
   (b) Equipment and weapons
   (c) Daily life
   (d) Enemies that he fought
7. Read Source D above and answer the following questions:
   (a) What was Vercingetorix's position in the army of the Gauls?
   (b) What preparations did Vercingetorix make before he came through the gates?
   (c) Why do you think he strips off his armour?
   (d) What does Caesar do with Vercingetorix?

Life in Rome

The population of Rome was divided into two groups: the **patricians**, the rich aristocrats who did not work, and the **plebeians**, who made up the rest of the Roman population. The plebeians were all the workers and tradesmen of the city. The more educated of these worked as doctors or lawyers. Others worked as bakers, butchers or carpenters.

The centre of the city was the Roman Forum. The ruins of this building still stand in the centre of Rome today and are a popular tourist site. The forum was the city's main marketplace and many of the most important temples and government buildings were close to it. This marketplace was where people bought their fruit, vegetables and meat. The Via Sacra (the Sacred Way) ran through the middle of the market. The armies of returning victorious generals passed along this road so that everyone could see them return after another victory.

● Houses

A patrician was wealthy enough to own a private house called a **domus**. Usually this type of house was built around an open square called an **atrium** which had a small pool (impluvium) to catch rainwater. The bedrooms (cubicula) and kitchens (culina) were located around the atrium. Most of these houses also had a **peristylium**, a small walled garden with columns and shrines to the family's favourite gods. The walls were decorated with frescoes and mosaics. If the patrician was very wealthy he might also have a villa (large house) in the countryside.

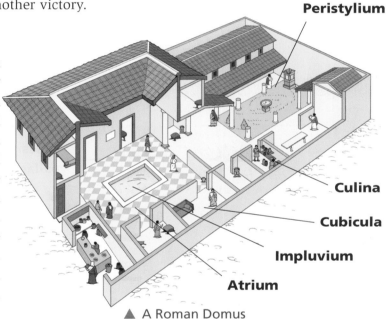

Peristylium
Culina
Cubicula
Impluvium
Atrium

▲ A Roman Domus

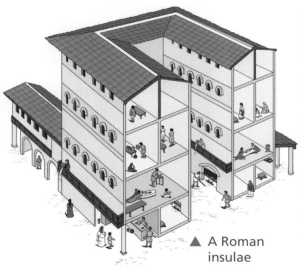

▲ A Roman insulae

The plebeians or poorer classes lived in **insulae** (apartment blocks) sometimes five or six storeys high. Families lived either in one room of an apartment or else they had an entire floor of the block, depending on their wealth. The sanitation was poor in these insulae and most waste was simply thrown out the window onto the narrow streets below. In the winter these buildings were kept warm by wood-burning stoves. As a result, there was always a risk of fire and in AD 64 most of Rome burnt down in a blaze.

Questions

Match the following words (1–7) with their meanings (A–G):

1. Patricians   A. Apartment blocks for the poor of Rome
2. Domus   B. Pictures made from small coloured pieces of glass or tiles
3. Culina   C. The private house of a rich person in Rome
4. Atrium   D. The rich or aristocrats of Rome
5. Plebeians   E. The kitchen in a private house
6. Mosaic   F. The workers and poor of Rome
7. Insulae   G. A small open square at the centre of a private house

▲ How to put on a toga – Stages 1 to 3

Stola   Palla   Tunic

▲ Different garments worn by men and women in Rome.

By the way . . .

Government assistance for unemployed people today is known as 'the dole'.

● Clothes

Men, women and children all wore a short-sleeved, knee-length garment called a **tunic**. Over this tunic wealthy Roman men wore long pieces of material called a **toga**. Important politicians such as senators or consuls wore white togas with a purple trim. Women wore ankle-length dress called **stolas** and then wrapped shawls called **pallas** around themselves.

● Eating

For the patricians, the main meal of the day was the **cena** and was taken in the evening. The meal had many courses and was often accompanied by entertainment.

Many of these dinners were very extravagant. The poor of Rome had much more simple meals. They often relied upon the free grain provided by the government called the **dole**. This grain was used to make breads or a form of porridge. Many insulae had no kitchens and so the plebeians had to buy their food at takeaways called **thermopolia**.

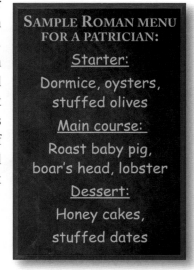

SAMPLE ROMAN MENU FOR A PATRICIAN:

Starter:
Dormice, oysters, stuffed olives

Main course:
Roast baby pig, boar's head, lobster

Dessert:
Honey cakes, stuffed dates

▲ A Roman feast for the patricians

▲ The poor of Rome often bought their food in thermopolias.

● Education

From the age of seven, young Romans from rich families attended a school called a **ludus**.

Here they learned the basics of reading, writing and arithmetic. Around the ages of twelve to sixteen, boys attended a Grammaticus where they studied Greek and Roman history, literature, grammar, geometry and more arithmetic. The works of Greek and Roman writers such as Homer, Horace, Virgil and Terence were studied and often memorised.

By the way...

Ludus comes from the Latin word 'to play' which also gives us the name of the board game Ludo.

It was important for young men to be able to speak well in public. Roman politicians were excellent public speakers and anybody who wanted to become a member of the Senate had to be able to hold the public's attention with his speeches. So the skills of **oration** (making speeches in public) and **rhetoric** (being able to make a point strongly and clearly either in writing or in speeches) were also taught.

Discipline was very strict and students were severely flogged (beaten with a stick) if they were disobedient. A sharp-pointed stylus was used to write on a tablet of wax that could be wiped clean and reused. Arithmetic was taught using an abacus.

▲ Students used equipment in school such as a stylus, tablet and abacus.

After the age of twelve, young girls stayed at home with their mothers and learned domestic skills such as spinning, weaving, embroidery and flower-arranging. They also learned how to order all the food for the house, organise the slaves' jobs and arrange the meals in a household. These duties prepared them for marriage when they became the matriarch (female head of the family) of the home.

▲ A Vestal Virgin tending the fire which constantly burned in the temple of Vesta.

Women in Rome

Women were not seen as equal to men in Roman society. A young girl was under the authority of her father until she was married and then authority switched to her husband. However, by the first century AD women had gained a little more freedom and were permitted to own and inherit property. They were not allowed to vote or stand for political office but a few women had their own businesses including lamp-making and hairdressing. A small number were even gladiators but these were very rare. Some wealthy women chose to become priestesses, the most important of which were the Vestal Virgins.

In the country

Many Roman patricians lived on farms outside the city. Slaves did most of the work on these farms. The owners lived in large villas. They grew grapes to produce wine, cereals to make bread and olives to eat and to make olive oil. The population in Rome was too big for these farmers to supply everyone so most of the cereal was imported from Sicily and North Africa.

By the way . . .

Vestal Virgins were women devoted to the goddess of the hearth (fireplace), Vesta. Her temple was regarded as one of the most lovely, and a fire constantly burned in it. This fire was tended by the Vestal Virgins, who took sacred vows to avoid all contact with men and devote their lives to Vesta.

Questions

1. Explain the following words:

   (a) Stola   (b) Matriarch   (c) Thermopolia

2. Examine the education of a Roman boy and girl. What are the similarities between them? Are there any differences?

3. What subjects did Roman children study at school?

4. What kind of produce would Romans living on farms grow?

5. Would you have liked to grow up in Rome? Give reasons for your answer.

Slaves

The use of slavery was widespread throughout all of the Roman Empire. Usually slaves were people captured during one of the many wars Rome fought and won. They were brought to Rome and sold in the marketplace to individuals. Slaves were regarded as pieces of property and their masters were permitted to do anything they wished to them, including kill them. Slaves did either manual work around the house and on the land or – if they were educated – they worked as doctors, teachers or secretaries.

In the houses of patricians there could be thousands of slaves. Even the poorer Romans had one or two. It is estimated that there were more than two million slaves in Italy at one point – about 20% of the population of Roman citizens.

Slaves were sometimes permitted by their master to marry other slaves. However, if they had children they would immediately become the property of the master of the house also. Many slaves tried to escape even though there were very severe punishments for those who tried and those who helped them. Professional slave catchers were sometimes employed to catch escaped slaves. When they were caught they were branded with a hot iron or crucified. It was possible for slaves to buy their freedom (manumission) but many slaves could not afford this or were refused it by their master.

▲ Roman slaves in the marketplace

Source E

Here's the way a slave who's worth his salt should act: the way I do. Quickly and obediently, follow orders cheerfully. For if a slave sincerely seeks to serve his master skillfully, he ought to do his master's business first and then his own. Even if he's sleeping he must serve his master in his dreams... He should learn to read his master's face and know his every wish. Faster than a speeding chariot a good slave hastens to his duties. And whoever's conscientious [hard-working] won't be feeling any leather, nor will he be forced to polish any iron around his ankles.

From *Pot of Gold* by Plautus

In 73 BC a gladiator called Spartacus attempted to revolt against these harsh conditions and raised an army of 90,000 slaves who fought the Roman army. After three years of warfare all across the south of Italy, Spartacus and his army were defeated. As an example to other slaves thousands of slaves were crucified all along the main road into Rome called the Via Appia. The body of Spartacus was never found but historians believe he was probably killed in battle.

By the way . . .
A film called Spartacus was made in 1960 and won 4 Oscars. Its tagline was 'they trained him to kill for their pleasure . . . but they trained him a little too well.'

Questions

1. Read Source E on page 55. What does this extract tell us about how slaves were treated in Rome? Use evidence from the text.

2. Write a paragraph about the life of a slave focusing on:

    (a) the jobs they performed

    (b) how they were treated by their masters

    (c) their feelings about their masters.

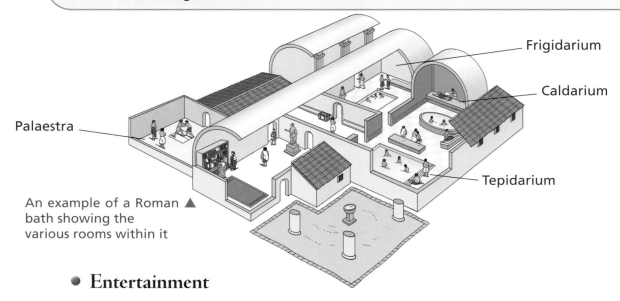

Palaestra

Frigidarium

Caldarium

Tepidarium

An example of a Roman ▲ bath showing the various rooms within it

● Entertainment

BATHS

Due to the number of slaves who did almost all of the hard work, Romans had more spare time to enjoy. One of the most popular pastimes for men was to attend the local baths. They could swim in the pool or move from a caldarium (hot room) to a tepidarium (warm room) to a frigidarium (cold room). The men were massaged with a mixture of oil and perfume and any dirt was then scraped off their bodies using a small curved rod called a **strigil.**

▲ Romans flocked to Circus Maximus to watch chariot races.

In places such as the massive Baths of Caracalla or Baths of Diocletian there were also areas for wrestling and exercise (palaestra), libraries, lecture theatres and gardens. The baths became important locations for Romans to meet and socialise. Women could attend during certain times when men were not there or else they could attend women-only baths.

CHARIOT RACES

Chariot racing took place at the **Circus Maximus** in the centre of Rome. This venue was built using marble and could seat over 200,000 people. The track length was almost 1,400 metres and a race was usually seven laps around the central spine of the track. The chariots of four horses each were divided into Reds, Blues, Greens and Whites. Supporters followed their team's colour with great devotion. Crashes were very common and could easily result in deaths. Successful charioteers were hugely popular and could become very rich, like modern-day footballers!

▲ Chariot racing was a very popular event among Romans, but it was a dangerous sport to take part in due to the high numbers of crashes, often resulting in death.

GLADIATORS

Another popular pastime was to attend gladiatorial fights at the **Colosseum**. It could hold over 70,000 people. Gladiators were usually criminals or slaves but sometimes they were professional fighters. They fought one another or fought wild animals such as bears and lions.

There were three main types of gladiator:

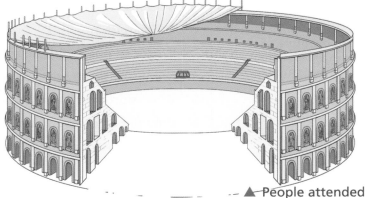

▲ People attended gladiatorial fights at the Colosseum.

1. The Thracian with a round shield and scimitar.

2. The Retiarius who had a net, a dagger and a trident.

3. The Samnite with an oblong shield, short sword and visor.

Depending on how a gladiator fought and how popular he was, a losing gladiator could ask the emperor to spare his life. The emperor listened to the crowd and then give him either a thumbs-up if he was to be spared or a thumbs-

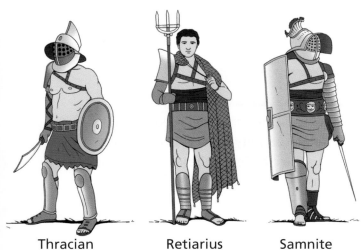

Thracian   Retiarius   Samnite

▲ The three main types of gladiator

down if he was to be killed. The day-long gladiatorial festivals were bloody and cruel but were also hugely popular among the Romans.

THEATRE

Playwrights such as Terence and Plautus were popular and their comedies were very successful. The Romans loved boisterous humour so violence was common in the plays of the time. The audience participated in the play by shouting, clapping and booing throughout. Only men could be actors. They wore brightly-coloured masks so people could recognise their character and also because it was easier to see from the back of the theatre. Being an actor was seen as a very lowly profession and Emperor Nero caused a scandal when he decided he wanted to perform in some plays.

▲ An example of a mask worn by actors in Rome

Questions

1. Explain the following words:
   (a) Strigil   (b) Palaestra

2. Match the following words with their correct meaning:

A. Frigidarium	1. Hot-room
B. Caldarium	2. Warm-room
C. Tepidarium	3. Cold-room

3. Where in Rome did the chariot races take place?

4. Name the three types of gladiator.

5. What sign did the emperor give if he wanted the gladiator to be spared?

6. Why did actors wear masks?

7. Write an account on the life of a Roman patrician using the following headings:
   (a) Daily life   (c) Where they lived
   (b) What they wore   (d) Their pastimes

The Gods and Customs of Rome

By the way . . .

Janus was the god of doorways and had two faces – one faced forwards and the other backwards. The month of January is named after him. Can you guess why?

The Romans were a very religious people. They believed in many gods and goddesses. This is known as **polytheism**. Every aspect of their lives was connected to their belief in these gods. They prayed to the gods to help them with warfare or the harvest. They even had gods for doorways and fireplaces!

Jupiter was the king of the gods. Juno was his wife and she was the goddess of marriage. Jupiter had two brothers, Pluto (god of the Underworld) and Neptune (god of the sea). Venus was the goddess of love and beauty and she often used her son Cupid to make people fall in love using his little bow and arrow.

▲ Jupiter, King of the gods, on his throne

▲ Neptune, the god of the sea

Minerva was the goddess of wisdom and Diana was the goddess of hunting. All soldiers prayed to the god of war, Mars (who has the month of March named after him). Apollo was the god of prophecy and music. Whenever anyone drank alcohol they gave thanks to the god of wine, Bacchus. When people harvested their crops they worshipped Ceres (this is where we get the word cereal). Some Roman Emperors were worshipped as gods and were believed to be divine.

In fact, whenever any Roman needed anything at all he would pray to one of the gods and ask for help. They prayed and gave sacrifices and gifts to these gods and goddesses in temples all around Rome. One of the most important temples, the Pantheon, still exists today and is used as a Catholic church. In fact, ever since it was built in 27 BC it has been in use either as a temple or a church, right up to today. In these temples, Romans often asked to have the insides of dead animals examined by augurs (people who could predict the future) as they believed signs of the future could be found there.

▲ The Pantheon is used as a Catholic church today.

▲ Cupid

The Underworld

Romans believed that when they died their souls went to the Underworld ruled by Pluto. When a person died, their body was laid out and a coin was placed either in their mouths or on their eyes. This allowed the soul to pay the ferryman (Charon) to bring them over the mythical river Styx and into the Underworld. It was also believed that the Underworld was guarded by a ferocious three-headed dog called **Cerberus**. In Pluto's kingdom, people who were good went to Elysium (heaven) and those who were bad went to Tartarus (hell). In Tartarus people were punished for crimes they had committed during their lives on earth.

▲ Cerberus, the ferocious guard dog of the Underworld

NAME OF ROMAN	PUNISHMENT
Tantalus	Condemned to be thirsty and hungry for ever, yet he had water and grapes always just out of reach. This is where we get the word 'tantalising'.
Tityus	He was tied to the ground. An eagle ate his liver and insides every day and they grew back every night.
Sisyphus	He had to push a rock to the very top of a hill, but it always rolled down again just before it reached the top.
The Danaids	Forty-nine sisters were forced to carry water from a well using a sieve for all eternity.

Roman Funerals

Romans believed in an afterlife, so most Romans were buried. After they had coins placed on their eyes they were wrapped in a toga and laid out on a bed. Some patricians were cremated (burnt) and their ashes were placed in pottery jars called urns. Funerals were very important as they showed how important the person was. A procession of relatives and friends and sometimes also professional mourners followed the body as it was brought to its grave. For health reasons everyone had to be

▲ A tomb on the Via Appia where rich Romans bought huge family tombs.

An example of a Roman funeral procession ▲

buried outside the walls of the city. Many rich people had huge family tombs called columbaria along the main road into Rome called the Via Appia. The family mourned for nine days. The plebeians had smaller funerals and were buried in far simpler plots of land, also outside the city.

● Christianity and Rome

In the first century AD, a new religion began to spread throughout the Roman world. It started in Palestine with Jesus of Nazareth. Many of its followers soon arrived into Rome. This new religion involved worshipping only one god, not the many gods of the Romans. As a result it was unpopular with the Emperors who wanted to be worshipped as gods by their subjects. This meant that Christians were often persecuted.

They were arrested, executed and often suffered horrific deaths at the Circus and the Colosseum, such as being thrown to lions and tigers. St. Peter and St. Paul were executed for being Christians and many other Christians became martyrs because they died for their religion. It is said that Emperor Nero (AD 56-68) even blamed the Christians for the great fire that destroyed Rome in AD 64.

This did not stop the spread of the religion. Despite persecution many Christians continued to practice their religion secretly. Over the next few hundred years, they created an underground network of tunnels and passages just outside Rome, called the **catacombs**. Here they held ceremonies and buried their dead in holes in the walls. In the fourth century AD Emperor Constantine converted to Christianity and made it the state religion. This helped Christianity to spread quickly throughout the whole Roman Empire. Today some of the temples of the Roman gods, such as the Pantheon, are Christian churches.

By the way . . .
When Christians were being persecuted they had to use secret signs to show if a house was Christian or not. They often used a symbol of a fish as a sign to other Christians.

▲ Emperor Constantine converted to Christianity in the fourth century AD.

Questions

1. Complete the four sentences using A–D:

1. Apollo was the god of	A. wisdom
2. Minerva was the goddess of	B. the Underworld
3. Neptune was the god of	C. prophecy and music
4. Pluto was the god of	D. the sea

2. What did augurs do?
3. What evidence do we have that the Romans believed in an afterlife?
4. Write an account of Roman burial customs.
5. Why were the Christians persecuted in ancient Rome?
6. What is meant by the word martyr?
7. What were the catacombs?
8. Name the Roman Emperor who first converted to Christianity.

The Legacy of Rome

1. Discoveries

The Romans were famous for their engineering (the building of roads, bridges and waterworks). They were the first people in Europe to discover concrete (by mixing lime, water and ash from volcanic soil). They also learned how to build arches. These discoveries meant that they were able to build very large buildings such as the Colosseum. They also built domes such as the famous one in the Pantheon in Rome.

2. Aqueducts

The aqueducts that the Romans built meant that they could bring fresh running water into towns. By the first century AD there was approximately 130 million gallons of water being supplied to Rome every day. That is almost 200 Olympic-sized swimming pools of water every day. Very high aqueducts were built throughout the Empire. Many still exist like the ones in Nimes, France and Segovia, Spain.

▲ The dome inside the Pantheon

▲ The aqueduct in Nimes, France

They allow the water to flow down from the mountains all the way into the cities.

3. Roads

The need to be able to travel throughout the empire resulted in 84,800 kilometres of major roads being built. That's about twice the distance around the world. The Romans used a foundation of large stones, sometimes bound by concrete, placed on a bed of sand and gravel. These paving stones were raised slightly in the middle and drains on either side of the road allowed rainwater to run off. Milestones were located along the road with distances between important towns written on them. The roads built by the Romans are of such excellent quality that many are still the basis for modern roads throughout Europe.

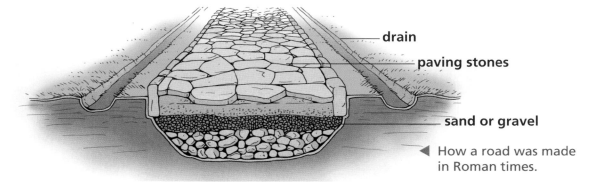

— drain

— paving stones

— sand or gravel

◄ How a road was made in Roman times.

4. Architecture

Roman buildings had many features that continued to be used down through the centuries. Pillars, arches and domes were common in Rome and this style was copied during the fifteenth and sixteenth centuries in Europe and sometimes even today.

▲ The Panthean in Rome. Can you spot its similarities with the GPO and St. Peter's Basilica?

▲ GPO, Dublin

▲ St. Peter's Basilica, Rome

5. The Latin Language

Latin became the language used throughout the Roman Empire. It had a huge influence on all the modern European languages. Italian, Spanish, Portuguese, French and Romanian are all based on Latin. Even in English it is estimated that almost a quarter of the words we use have a Latin origin.

6. Calendar

The original calendar used by the Romans had too few months. In 45 BC Julius Caesar introduced a 12-month year to fix this problem. The month of July is named after Julius Caesar and the month of August is named after his nephew Augustus Caesar.

I	=	1
V	=	5
X	=	10
L	=	50
C	=	100
D	=	500
M	=	1000

7. Numbers

The Romans introduced a method of numbering that we still use today. Roman numerals use letters instead of figures. For example, 3 is written as III, 9 is written as IX (10 – 1 = 9), 635 is written as DCXXXV (500 + 100 + 30 + 5), 2012 is written as MMXII (2000 + 10 + 2). These Roman numerals are often seen on buildings and at the end of films.

Using Roman numerals write the following: 27, 40, 162, 734 and 1975.

Chapter 3 Questions

1. Pictures

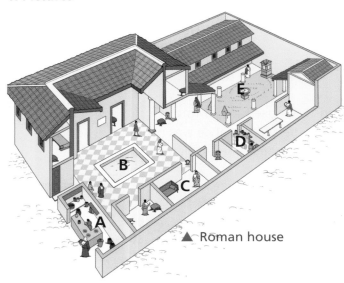

▲ Roman house

(a) Give the names for the parts of the buildings marked A, B, C, D, E.

(b) What is the name given to this type of house?

(c) Give two differences between the buildings patricians lived in and the buildings plebeians lived in.

2. Documents

The following is an extract from an epic poem by the Roman writer Virgil describing the arrival of the Trojan prince Aeneas to Italy. He enters the Underworld with the priestess of Apollo.

> Across the mouth of a cave lay the huge body of Cerberus, as he made the Underworld ring with the howls from his three throats. The priestess saw that the snakes on his neck were already beginning to bristle, so she threw him a titbit of honey and corn, doctored with sedative [sleeping] drugs. Crazy with hunger the animal opened all three mouths and gobbled down what she had thrown him. The great body flopped to the floor of the cave, sprawling from wall to wall. Aeneas sprang past the unconscious watchdog into the entrance, swiftly leaving the [river] bank to which no one ever returns.
>
> From *Aeneid* by Virgil

(a) How many heads does Cerberus have?

(b) How did the priestess know that Cerberus was angry?

(c) What did the priestess give Cerberus to fall asleep?

(d) State the name of the mythical river that Aeneas crossed.

(e) Why do you think the author states that Aeneas left the river 'bank to which no one ever returns'?

(f) List three Roman customs that suggest they believed in an afterlife.

3. Short-Answer Questions

(a) Name one town that was destroyed by Mount Vesuvius in AD 79.

(b) Where was the Roman Forum and what took place there?

(c) How many soldiers formed (i) a cohort and (ii) a legion?

(d) Explain the following words:

   (i) Peristylium   (ii) Patrician
   (iii) Plebeian   (iv) Pilum

(e) Name three items of clothing that Romans wore.

(f) What does the word manumission mean?

(g) Name the warm, cold and hot rooms in a public bath.

(h) Where in Rome did gladiators fight?

(i) What happened in the Circus Maximus?

(j) What were the following gods of:

   (i) Mars   (ii) Venus
   (iii) Apollo   (iv) Bacchus

(k) Name two ways in which the Romans have influenced us.

(l) Name one invention of the Romans.

(m) Name a month that is called after a Roman and state who that Roman was.

(n) How much is MCM?

4. People in History

Write about life as a young person in Rome. Use the following headings as a guide:

- Education
- Food and meals
- Clothing
- Pastimes
- Religion

5.

(a) Name one famous historical person from the Roman civilisation.

(b) Name two achievements of Roman civilisation.

(c) Give three ways in which historians and archaeologists have discovered information about the lives and customs of the people of ancient Rome.

(d) Write an account on three of the following:

   (i) Roman burial customs and religion
   (ii) Food and clothing in ancient Rome
   (iii) Roman work, arts and crafts
   (iv) Roman pastimes

Key Terms to Summarise Chapter 3: Ancient Rome

Republic System of government where the people vote for their leaders.

Consuls Elected leaders of the Roman Republic. They held the position for one year.

Senators Members of the Senate. They looked after the affairs of Rome.

Legionnaries A Roman soldier who was part of the 5,000 men in a legion.

Patricians The wealthy, aristocratic population of Rome.

Plebeians The poorer working class population of Rome.

Domus Large houses owned by patricians.

Insulae Four- or five-storey apartment blocks in which the plebeians lived.

Atrium The open square at the centre of a patrician's domus.

Peristylium A walled garden with columns surrounding it.

Tunic A short sleeved, knee-length garment worn by Romans.

Toga A long garment that Roman men draped over their tunics.

Stola The ankle-length garment a female Roman wore.

Dole Free grain given to the poor.

Cena The main meal of the day for a Roman.

Thermopolia Where plebeians bought their takeaway meals.

Circus Maximus The location of the chariot racing in Rome. It could hold over 200,000 people.

Colosseum The location in Rome where gladiatorial and other games took place. It could hold 70,000 people.

Polytheism When people believe in many gods rather than one god.

Catacombs Underground tunnels where Christians met and buried their dead.

Aqueducts Concrete structures designed to bring water from the mountains to the cities.

Web References

For further reading on topics mentioned in this chapter, view the following websites:

www.novaroma.org/

www.bbc.co.uk/history/ancient/romans/

www.historyforkids.org/learn/romans/games/circus.htm

www.ostia-antica.org/

www.marketplace.it/museo.nazionale/emuseo_home.htm

http://thehistoryofrome.blogspot.com/

Women in History

Eumachia

First Century AD, Priestess of Venus, Patron of the Fullers Guild

Roman women did not have much power. They were not allowed to hold political positions and were expected to be dutiful wives. There is plenty of evidence of virtuous women who did what they were told by their husbands or fathers. There is also evidence of women such as Queen Cleopatra of Eygpt who gained power by manipulating others. In Pompeii there is some evidence that women may have played a slightly more influential role in that city. Evidence of female weavers, butchers and doctors has been uncovered. One of the most important women was Eumachia.

Eumachia was born to a family who had become wealthy from brick-making. She married a very successful landowner and this gave her increased influence in society. She was a priestess to the cult of Venus (goddess of Love) and also an important woman in the cult dedicated to the Emperor Augustus. She became the patroness (donated money) of the fuller's guild, an association of craftsmen who made and dyed cloth. In AD 62 there was a great earthquake and there was much damage to the town. Eumachia paid for the construction of a large building in the middle of the forum (centre of the town). The building was given to the fullers and in return they erected a statue to Eumachia inside the building. She dedicated the building to her son which was of great advantage to him as he hoped to gain a political position in Pompeii at the time. A very large and expensive tomb was built by her for her family on one of the most important streets in Pompeii. Unfortunately, she was not buried there as she and the rest of Pompeii were caught by the dust and lava from the eruption of Mount Vesuvius in AD 79.

The Middle Ages

Chapter 4

● The Dark Ages

In the fifth century the Roman Empire collapsed due to successful and violent invasions by tribes such as the Huns and the Goths. Without the central power of Rome, Europe slowly divided into many smaller kingdoms. There was no powerful leader to enforce law and order and Europe quickly became a more dangerous place. Many of the advances in art and engineering made by the Romans were forgotten. This is why the period from about AD 500 up to the Renaissance in the 1400s is known as the **Dark Ages.** Historians also call it the **Middle Ages** or the medieval period.

A map of Europe in ▶ the Middle Ages

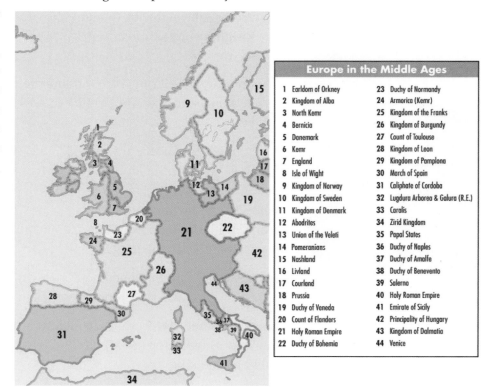

Europe in the Middle Ages

1 Earldom of Orkney	23 Duchy of Normandy
2 Kingdom of Alba	24 Armorica (Kemr)
3 North Kemr	25 Kingdom of the Franks
4 Bernicia	26 Kingdom of Burgundy
5 Danemark	27 Count of Toulouse
6 Kemr	28 Kingdom of Leon
7 England	29 Kingdom of Pamplona
8 Isle of Wight	30 March of Spain
9 Kingdom of Norway	31 Caliphate of Cordoba
10 Kingdom of Sweden	32 Lugdura Arborea & Galura (R.E.)
11 Kingdom of Denmark	33 Caralis
12 Abodrites	34 Zirid Kingdom
13 Union of the Veleti	35 Papal States
14 Pomeranians	36 Duchy of Naples
15 Nashland	37 Duchy of Amalfe
16 Livland	38 Duchy of Benevento
17 Courland	39 Salerno
18 Prussia	40 Holy Roman Empire
19 Duchy of Veneda	41 Emirate of Sicily
20 Count of Flanders	42 Principality of Hungary
21 Holy Roman Empire	43 Kingdom of Dalmatia
22 Duchy of Bohemia	44 Venice

Timeline:

Ancient Europe
2,500,000 BC ➜ 500 AD

Medieval / Middle Ages
500 AD ➜ 1400 AD

Modern Europe
1400 AD ➜ today

Medieval Society

Smaller kingdoms throughout Europe began to compete with each other for land and power. It was a dangerous time for the poor people of Europe. If they wished to be protected they had to look to the king of their land. This system was called the **feudal system.** This system existed in many countries in Europe, including Ireland, England, France, Germany, Spain, Italy and Portugal.

• The Feudal System

By the way . . .

The vassal had to kneel down in front of the king and swear, 'I will be your man from this day onwards'. The French for man is *homme* which is where we get the word homage from.

▲ Vassals swearing an oath of homage to their king

The king owned all the land in the country and could pass any law he wished. He granted portions of this land to **vassals** (rich and powerful men in the kingdom). Vassals then swore an oath of **homage** (loyalty) to the king.

These vassals were also called **nobles** or 'the nobility'. The nobles were given titles such as the Earl of Ulster or the Earl of Ormond. In return for renting the land from the king, the nobles promised to:

1. Provide money for the king.

2. Protect and fight for the king. To do this the noble provided **knights** (professional soldiers on horseback) if the king went to war.

3. Provide hospitality in his **demesne** (home) – pronounced de-main – to the king and his many followers if he came to visit.

These nobles, who were often **earls** and **bishops**, then rented some of their land to lesser nobles (e.g. **barons** and **knights**). These lesser nobles promised to fight for the earl or bishop whenever he asked. Therefore the noble became overlord to the knights and barons. With the money and knights he got from renting his land, he was able to pay the king.

Peasants (poor farmers) lived on the knight's or baron's land. They worked for him and paid rent and taxes to him.

This meant that the peasants were at the bottom of this pyramid. They had to work for the knight so he could pay the noble so he could pay the king.

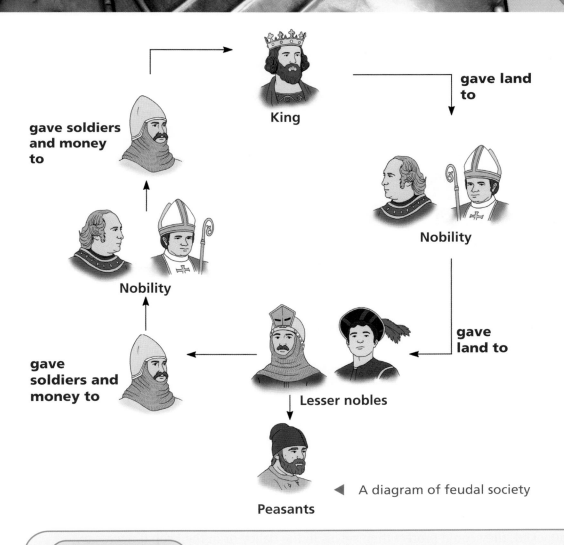

King

gave land
to

**gave soldiers
and money
to**

Nobility

Nobility

gave
land to

**gave
soldiers and
money to**

Lesser nobles

◄ A diagram of feudal society

Peasants

Questions

1. Explain the following words:

   (a) Vassal (b) Demesne (c) Homage

2. List the four levels within the feudal system.

3. Who were known as nobles?

4 Why do you think the Middle Ages are also called the Dark Ages?

The Medieval Castle

Kings and nobles spent much time and effort defending their lands from attack. These attacks came from other kings and nobles who wanted more land or who simply wanted to steal whatever treasures they could find. So once a noble or knight received land from the king, the first thing he did was build a castle on it. During an attack, the noble could defend himself and his people from within the castle.

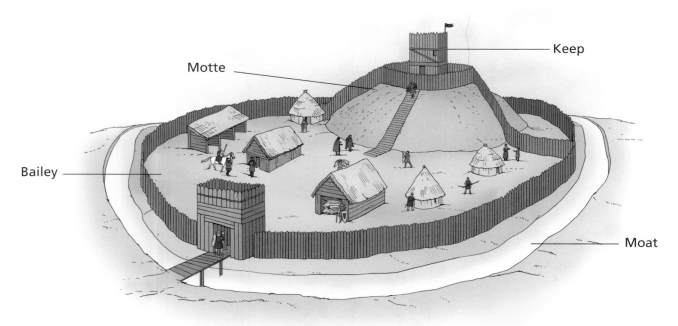

Motte

Keep

Bailey

Moat

▲ A motte and bailey castle

Wooden castles

The first type of castle was a **motte and bailey** castle. First a hill was built, often from a pile of rocks and soil. This was called the motte. On top of this hill a wooden tower called a **keep** was built surrounded by a wooden fence. Below the motte there was an area called the bailey. A wooden fence surrounded the bailey and a **moat** (ditch) was dug around the fence. In the bailey there were houses where the noble's soldiers and slaves would live. The noble and his family lived in the keep. If they were attacked, they could protect themselves in the bailey or in the keep if necessary.

Stone castles

Wooden castles could easily be destroyed by fire, either during an attack or else by accident. Therefore, many nobles built **stone castles**. However, these castles were more expensive to build so only very wealthy nobles could afford to do so.

In these stone castles, the **keep (1)** was where the noble and his wife lived. Their servants and some soldiers also had their quarters (where they lived) there. The stone walls of the keep were between three and six metres thick. For protection, the door was raised above ground level so it was difficult for attackers to get into the building. Windows were small slits so that **archers** (soldiers who used bows and arrows) could shoot out but it was difficult to shoot in.

The bailey or **courtyard (2)** was surrounded by **curtain walls (3).** These stone walls were about 5 metres thick and 15 metres tall. Along the top of the walls were **ramparts (4)**. Soldiers could walk along the ramparts and shoot arrows from them. When under attack, defenders threw boiling oil down from the ramparts onto the attackers and then set it on fire.

On top of the curtain walls and the keep, **turrets (5)** (towers) were built to allow soldiers watch for enemies.

A moat was dug in front of the walls. This could be filled with water. A **drawbridge (6)** from the gatehouse was raised or lowered using heavy chains.

The gatehouse had turrets on either side and a **portcullis (7)** (heavy iron gate) could be lowered to block the entrance when the castle was under attack.

The **latrines (8)** (toilets) were holes in the side of the keep or outer walls. Any waste simply fell into the bailey or the moat.

The bailey was where all the work of the castle took place. Most of the servants and craftsmen lived here. The blacksmith, the carpenter and the mason had their **workshops (9)** here. The **stables (10)** were also located here. A **well (11)** for fresh water and the **kitchen (12)**, where all the food was prepared, were also within the bailey.

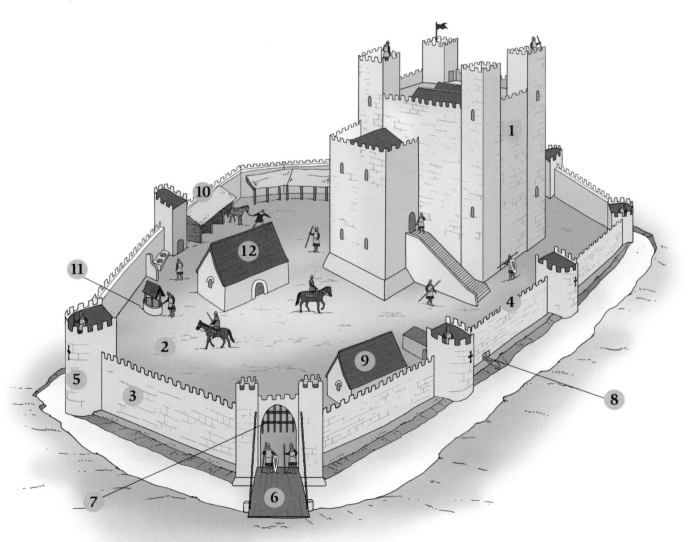

▲ Stone castles were more expensive to build than wooden castles but they provided better defence for the nobles who lived in them and they could not be as easily destroyed by fire.

• Life in the castle

Life in the stone castle was grim. There was no central heating so huge fires had to be lit to keep rooms warm. The windows were small slits and had no glass so rooms were dark and damp. Coloured **tapestries (1)** (large pieces of fabric with scenes or designs embroidered onto them) were hung on the walls to make the rooms more pleasant.

The interior of a stone castle ▲

The **great hall (2)** was located on the middle floor. This was where the noble and his wife ate. During the day, the noble carried out any business he had in the hall. He met with his bailiffs (people responsible for collecting taxes from anyone living on his land) or the estate steward who was responsible for managing the noble's lands.

Under the great hall there were **dungeons (3)** where food was stored and prisoners were held.

On the top floor there was a **chapel (4)** (a small church) so the noble and his family could pray and attend mass. The noble's **apartments (5)** were located on this floor along with his wife's **solar (6).** The solar was a south-facing room where the lady could sit and weave tapestries and listen to musicians.

Questions

1. What work took place in the bailey of the castle?

2. Match the following words (A–F) with the correct definitions (1–6):

A Chapel	1. South-facing room where the lady of the castle would weave and listen to music.
B Keep	2. Ground-floor room where food and prisoners were kept.
C Solar	3. Pieces of fabric decorated with embroidered designs and hung on walls.
D Latrine	4. Small church where the noble could pray and attend mass.
E Dungeon	5. The building where the noble and his family lived.
F Tapestries	6. A toilet in a castle.

3. Name four parts of the castle used for protection and explain how each was used to protect the castle.

4. What activities occurred in the Great Hall of a castle?

● Food

Big feasts took place in the great hall. The noble, his family and other important people sat at the top table. Meat was the main dish. Boar, rabbit, hare, pork, beef, lamb, goose and pheasant were all eaten. Very few vegetables were eaten. The meal was served on a **trencher** (a large stale piece of bread). People used knives and spoons to cut and serve the food but ate with their fingers. The noble and his wife drank wine while the rest of the diners drank mead or ale. The meat was often rotten so the cooks covered up the smell and taste with spices. During the feast, entertainment was provided by musicians or jesters (clowns).

FIRST COURSE

BEEF MARROW FRITTERS
EELS IN SPICY PURÉE
ROAST OR BOILED MEAT

SECOND COURSE

BROTH WITH BACON

THIRD COURSE

VENISON · PHEASANT · GOOSE

A typical dinner menu in a castle in the Middle Ages ▲

▲ Nobles sometimes used a trained hawk to hunt birds.

● Pastimes

Apart from eating, nobles enjoyed hunting deer, boar and foxes. They sometimes used a trained hawk, who sat on the noble's arm, to hunt birds. Nobles attended tournaments where knights showed their skills at fighting or riding. Sometimes mock (pretend) battles were held for the amusement of the noble.

● The noble's family

The main role of the lady of the castle was to have as many male children as possible. Her family arranged her marriage when she was about 14 years old. The marriage had little to do with love but was simply a business arrangement. Important families offered the noble their daughter and a large **dowry** (money or gifts) in the hope that he would marry her. As lady of the castle, she spent her time weaving, spinning and embroidering. She made sure there was always enough food and wine in the castle and looked after the children.

Handmaidens helped her to carry out these duties. Her clothes were made from silk bought from merchants or with wool from the area. Her clothes were brightly coloured using dyes made from plants, fruits and ground stones.

The male children were educated until they were about seven. The lady of the castle taught her daughters the skills they needed to be a good wife and to run a castle.

◀ Medieval lord and lady

Questions

1. List four types of food that were eaten in the castle.

2. Why did cooks use spices in their dishes?

3. What did nobles do to entertain themselves?

4. Why do you think a dowry was important for a young girl?

5. Write about life as a lord in a medieval castle. Use the following headings as a guide:

   (a) The castle

   (b) The feudal system

   (c) Food and clothes

   (d) Entertainment

▲ A castle under attack

● Castle under attack

Attacking a castle was very difficult. Most armies laid **siege** to the castle (i.e. surround the castle and wait for the people inside to starve). If an army wished to capture the castle more quickly they had to use weapons to get over the walls or to break them down.

Soldiers used **scaling-ladders (1)** to climb up the walls and get over the top. This was very dangerous as the defenders could shoot arrows at them as they climbed.

Siege towers (2) were towers on wheels. They were covered in animal skins for protection and had ladders inside them.

Battering rams (3) were used to break down the door of the castle.

Catapults (4) fired boulders and fireballs at the wall and into the bailey. Sometimes human and animal excrement was fired in to spread disease in the castle.

Ballistas (5), similar to a large crossbow, were able to fire huge arrows at the wall and the defenders.

Attackers sometimes dug underneath the walls of the castle and then collapsed the tunnel bringing the outer wall down with it. This was called **undermining (6)** the walls.

• A knight's life

To protect himself from such attacks the noble had many **men-at-arms** to defend him. **Foot soldiers** carried swords and shields. There were also **archers** who used bow and arrows. **Knights** rode on horseback and were the most important soldiers.

It took 13-15 years for a boy to fully train to become a knight.

These were the two stages of training before he became a knight:

1. **Page:** When he was seven years old he was sent to a noble's castle to be a page. Here he learned how to read and write and also how to behave in a polite manner. He acted as a servant to the nobleman and the lady of the castle. He was given basic training in horse-riding and how to use a sword.

2. **Squire:** At around 14 years of age he became a squire. He carried and looked after his knight's armour and horse. He practised archery and how to fight on horseback.

If he was ready, at 21 years of age he was **dubbed** a **knight**. The squire spent the night before praying. In the morning he went to the ceremony dressed in his armour. He knelt in front of the noble and swore to uphold the code of **chivalry**. The code of chivalry demanded that all knights should be loyal to their nobleman and to God, brave in battle, generous to the poor and honourable and courteous to women. The noble then tapped the squire on his shoulder with his sword and said, 'Arise, Sir Knight'.

▲ A medieval knight

CLOTHING

A knight carried a long wooden pole called a **lance (1).** This was used in battle to knock other riders off their horses. He also used a sword **(2)** weighing between 20 – 30 kilograms, an axe **(3)**, a mace **(4)** and a hammer **(5)**. To protect his head he wore a helmet **(6)** and to protect his body he wore **chain mail (7)** (a garment made from small ringlets of metal) or metal armour. A **visor (8)** allowed him to see out of his helmet. He carried a shield **(9)** (weighing 16 kilograms) made from wood and metal. In the centre of his shield was his family crest (coat of arms). His hands were protected by metal gloves known as gauntlets **(10)**.

TRAINING

Knights spent much of their time practising their skills. They took part in competitions called tournaments attended by both nobles and peasants. Mock battles called **tourneys** were held for the amusement of the nobles. Due to the number of deaths at these battles they were stopped. **Jousting** was developed instead. Two knights would ride towards each other on either side of a **tilt** (a small fence). Each would try to knock the other knight off his horse using his lance. The winner was allowed to keep the armour and horse of the loser.

◄ Jousting competitions were popular during the Middle Ages.

Questions

1. Name four methods of attacking a castle and describe how they worked.

2. Name the three different men-at-arms during the Middle Ages.

3. What were the duties of a page?

4. What weapons did a knight use?

5. Explain the following terms:

    (a) Jousting   (b) Tilt   (c) Chain mail   (d) Tourney

6. Describe the process of dubbing.

7. Would you like to have lived in a castle in the Middle Ages? Give reasons for your answer.

8. Write about life as a knight in the Middle Ages. Use the following headings as a guide:

    (a) Training

    (b) Weapons and armour

    (c) Rules of chivalry

    (d) Tournaments

Life in the Countryside

During the Middle Ages, almost three quarters of the population of Europe lived in the countryside. Most of these lived in villages. Nobles who were not wealthy or powerful enough to own a castle lived in a manor house **(1)**, a smaller version of the stone castle. This was situated on the edge of a village. The village and the land surrounding it were known as the **manor** or **grange**.

Manor house and its surrounds ▲

The nobleman was called the **lord of the manor**. The land that he kept for his own use was called a demesne.

The lord's **bailiff (2)** lived beside the manor house. He made sure all rents and taxes were collected. If there were any crimes in the village, the bailiff brought the accused to the lord for punishment.

Around the manor there were small **houses (3)** where the peasants lived. The houses were made from wood or wattle and daub and had a thatched roof. They had two rooms: one for the family and the other for the animals.

There was a **church (4)** at the centre of the village.
The grassy area in the village was known as the **commons (5)**. This was where the peasants grazed their animals.

There was usually a **forest (6)** near the village where peasants fed their pigs, gathered berries and nuts and collected firewood. This area was called the **pannage.**

If there was a **river (7)** close to the village, it provided water for drinking, cleaning and washing clothes.

Local **craftsmen (8)** had shops in the village. A blacksmith's forge, an alehouse for drinking beer and a carpenter's workshop were also located around the village.

The peasant's **farmland (9)** was very close to the village and was divided into three open fields.

Life of a peasant

There were two types of peasant: a serf and a freeman.

> **By the way . . .**
> If a serf managed to escape and was not caught for a year and a day he became a freeman.

A **serf** was owned by the lord. He had to work on the lord's land two to three days each week whilst also trying to grow enough food for himself and his family on the other days of the week using whatever amount of land the lord allowed him to have. As he was owned by the lord, he did not receive any payment for helping the lord. If he wished to go anywhere or even marry, he had to ask the lord for permission.

A **freeman** had to rent land from his lord. He also had to work on the lord's land without any payment. Otherwise he was free to do as he wished. Compared to a serf, he worked for far less time on the lord's land.

Both serfs and freemen had to pay one tenth of their crops to the local priest. This payment was called a **tithe**. They also had to pay **rent** to the lord of the manor. This was paid either in money or in goods from the farm, such as eggs. A bailiff appointed by the lord checked that each peasant was paying the correct rent.

HOUSING

▲ Typical peasant living conditions in a wattle and daub house.
Note the animals living in the house also.

Peasants lived in small wattle and daub houses of one or two rooms. They used thatch (dried straw tied onto the rafters of the house) on the roof. The whole family cooked, ate and slept in one room. When the weather was bad they brought the animals inside the house for warmth. The house was very dark and smoky because there was no chimney for the fire and very small windows.

EATING

Dark bread with broth

Sometimes cheese

Bowl of curds (from milk)

▲ Typical menu of a serf

Food was very simple. Wheat, barley or rye was mixed with beans to make **pottage** (a thick vegetable soup). They used milk from cows that grazed on the commons. From this they could make butter and cheese. Chickens provided eggs. They could not afford meat except on very special occasions like Easter or Christmas. Nuts and berries were collected from the forest. Onions and cabbage were the only vegetables they ate and they were grown beside the house. Ale was their main drink. Food was difficult to preserve as there was no such thing as fridges then. People used a great deal of salt to try to keep food fresh. All the food they collected and harvested in the summer and autumn had to last until the spring. This meant that peasants lived in constant fear of hunger and famine.

Work

The land around the manor was divided into three open fields. Each peasant had a long strip of land within each field. To make sure they did not take all the nutrients from the soil, they rotated (changed) what they grew in each field.

Because they had no fertilisers, every third year they left the field **fallow** (did not plant anything). This meant that the soil could refill with minerals and nutrients. This system of farming is called **open-field crop rotation.**

Serfs at work throughout the year ▲

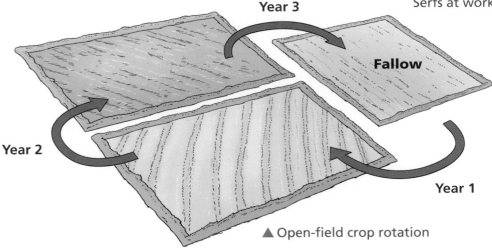

▲ Open-field crop rotation

They ploughed fields using oxen and gathered the crops using a **sickle (1)** or a **scythe (2)**. A **flail (3)** was used to divide the wheat kernels (the grains) from the stalks. Any tools they used were usually made from wood from the forest. For a few days each week peasants had to work on the lord's land. During busy times of the year women and children were also expected to help with farm work. At harvest time peasants were expected to do even more work on the lord's land. This extra work was called **boon work.**

Clothes

The peasants made their own clothes using wool from their sheep on the commons or rough linen from flax that they grew. Dyes were made from berries or plants. Shoes were made from animal skins.

Entertainment

Sundays were holy days and the peasants did not have to work. They spent time wrestling, playing board games like chess and draughts, singing and watching cockfighting.

Questions

1. What was the job of the bailiff?
2. What was the function of the commons?
3. What is the difference between a serf and a freeman?
4. Why did peasants rotate the crops they grew in each field?
5. Explain the following terms:
   (a) Fallow   (c) Grange   (e) Pannage
   (b) Pottage   (d) Tithe
6. What type of food did peasants eat in the Middle Ages?
7. Write about life as a peasant farmer in the Middle Ages. Use the following headings as a guide:
   (a) Housing   (c) Work throughout the year
   (b) Food and clothing   (d) Pastimes

Life in a Medieval Town

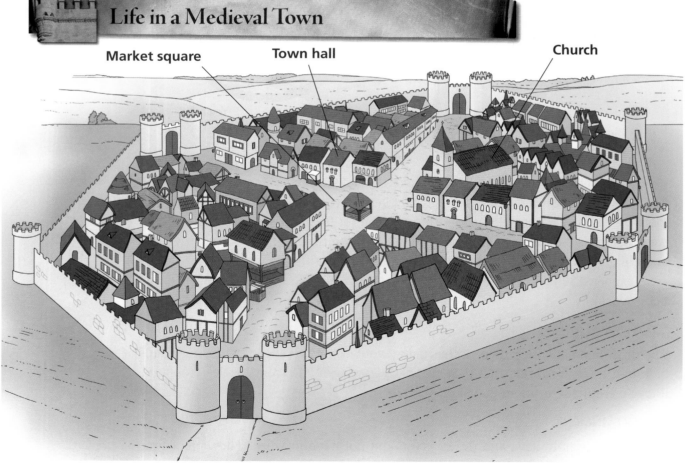

Market square   Town hall   Church

▲ Medieval towns were centres of trade. They were usually located at important trading points, e.g. close to river mouths, at crossroads.

In the Middle Ages, about one quarter of the population lived in towns. They were centres of trade and were usually located at a point where trading was important, e.g. river crossings, along the coast near river mouths, at crossroads and close to monasteries or castles. Some towns became very important and wealthy because of their location along a busy trade route. As more people came to work and live in the town, it became bigger and wealthier. Opportunities for work further encouraged other craftsmen to come to the town. Slowly the town became more and more important.

● The running of the town

Sometimes when a town became too big for the local lord to govern (or when wealthy merchants in the town gave money to the lord), he would grant a **charter** to the town. This charter gave the town the power to run its own affairs. It also made every man living in the town a freeman, so he no longer had to do any work for the lord. The townsmen elected a town council. The council then elected a mayor. All punishments and laws were decided by the council and mayor. They were also responsible for the defence of the town.

A town was surrounded by large walls for protection. **Sentries** (soldiers who watch for attackers) patrolled the walls and guarded the gates. The gates were closed from sunset until dawn the next morning.

Anyone arriving at a gate was asked why they wanted to enter. If they wanted to sell goods they had to pay a **toll** (tax) to enter.

The houses and shops were built very close together. They were made from wood and thick plaster. Houses could be up to three storeys high. The only buildings made from stone were the **town hall** and the **church**.

Two main streets led from the four main gates of the town.

Where these streets met there was a small square. This was the **market square**. Once a week peasants from the surrounding countryside came to the square to sell their produce. Fruit, vegetables and meat were sold at this market.

● Fairs

Once a year a large **fair** took place. Spices and silk from Asia, exotic food and cloth from Italy and jewellery and new fashions from other lands were bought and sold at the fair. Craftsmen bought new tools and everyone was entertained by jesters, jugglers and musicians. The fair took place just outside the walls of the town and could last for up to three weeks.

▲ Fairs were held annually in medieval towns – some could last for up to three weeks!

▲ London burning in 1666

● Threat of fire

As the houses were made of wood, it was easy for them to catch fire. To stop any fires, a **curfew** (from the French phrase *covre le feu* meaning cover the fire) was imposed. This meant that all fires in homes had to be put out after dark. London suffered a great fire in 1666. A fire in a bakery quickly spread and resulted in 13,000 houses being burnt over four days.

● Hygiene

The small size of medieval towns meant that streets were very narrow and winding. Streets were not paved and could become very muddy in bad weather. There were no drains or rubbish collections. Household rubbish was thrown out onto the street. People used **chamber-pots** instead of toilets. Waste and the contents of chamber-pots were thrown out of windows onto the streets below. This meant it could be dangerous for passers-by.

The narrow width of the streets, the dirt and the waste meant there was much disease in medieval towns. Diseases such as **typhoid, cholera** and **leprosy** were common. Leprosy resulted in open sores all over the body. If someone developed it, they had to leave the city. Lepers ended up living in colonies near to the town.

▲ Waste being thrown out of the window onto the street below.

▲ York, England – a medieval town

● The Black Death

Rats were everywhere in these dirty cities. In 1347 fleas from Asia were carried to Europe on rats in merchant ships. These fleas brought a terrible plague. The fleas caused black boils to swell in your arm-pit and then spread all over the body. A fever followed and usually resulted in death. This plague became known as the **Black Death** or sometimes the **Bubonic Plague**. It spread all over Europe and killed about one third of Europe's population (25 million people).

> ### By the way ...
> People thought the Black Death was spread through the air so they covered their mouths with handkerchiefs. Church bells were rung to clean the air too.

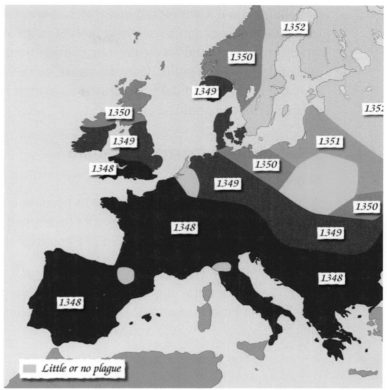

▲ The spread of the plague in Europe (1348 – 1352)

Questions

1. Who governed a town if the local lord granted a charter?
2. What might you find for sale at the annual fair in a town in the Middle Ages?
3. What does the term curfew mean? Why was it so important?
4. List three diseases common in medieval towns.
5. Why were the towns so dirty?
6. How did you know if you had the Black Death?

● Craftsmen and guilds

Many craftsmen lived in towns. These included bakers, carpenters, blacksmiths, millers, butchers and tailors. Most craftsmen had a shop on the street and lived directly above it. Often a particular group of craftsmen or businesses had shops beside each other, e.g. Fishamble Street and Winetavern Street in Dublin and Baker's Lane and Cook Street in Cork.

A craftsman in a town was required to be part of a **guild**. Each trade formed a guild to ensure high standards were kept in their particular craft. Prices and opening hours were set by the guild to ensure fair competition. Any disputes between members were settled by the guild. They also gave money to help sick members or families of members who had died. In return, craftsmen had to pay a **yearly fee** to remain a member of the guild.

● Becoming a master craftsman

Stage 1: Apprentice

At the age of 12 a boy who wanted to become a craftsman became an **apprentice** to a master craftsman. For seven years he learned all about the trade. While he was learning he practised his trade but did not get paid.

Stage 2: Journeyman

After seven years, the apprentice could offer his work for payment. He got paid by the day (the French word for day, *journée*, is where we get the term **journeyman**). He could travel anywhere and seek work.

▲ Stocks

▲ A ducking stool

Stage 3: Master

To join a guild, the journeyman had to become a **master craftsman**. To do so, he had to make a **masterpiece**. This piece of work was shown to the guild to prove he was good enough to become a member and open his own shop. If he was accepted he paid a sum of money to the guild and become a master craftsman.

● Crime and punishment

Punishment was very severe in medieval towns. Town councils decided if someone deserved to be punished. Thieves could have one of their hands cut off or they could even be hanged. People were put into **stocks** (planks of wood with holes cut into them for the person's feet) or a **pillory** (holes cut for the head and hands while the person stood) and had rotten food or sometimes even rocks thrown at them. If a craftsman was caught selling a bad product he was dragged through the streets on a **huddle** (a wooden sleigh) holding his produce. Women who gossiped were tied to a **ducking stool** and lowered repeatedly into water.

1. Name three crafts that you would find in a medieval town.
2. How did guilds help their members? Give three examples.
3. What did a craftsman have to do to become a member of a guild?
4. List two crimes and their punishments during the Middle Ages.
5. Where does the word journeyman come from?

Medieval Churches

● Spread of Christianity

During the Middle Ages the Christian Church grew in power, wealth and influence. Christianity was the main religion in Europe. People feared they would go to hell if they did not do exactly as the Church told them. Some members of the Church used this fear to influence kings to do as they wished.

THE CRUSADES

When Muslim armies captured the city of Jerusalem in 1070, Pope Urban II asked the kings of Europe to fight to recapture it. Between 1096 and 1270 many Christian armies travelled to Jerusalem and other places to fight the Muslims. These wars were known as the **Crusades.** Jerusalem was recaptured for a short period in 1099 AD. Eventually, however, the Muslim leader Saladin defeated the Crusaders.

● Organisation of the Church

The Pope was the head of the Christian church and lived in Rome. Throughout Europe areas called **dioceses** were ruled by **bishops.** In every diocese its bishop built a **cathedral** (the seat – cathedra in Latin – of the bishop). These were usually very impressive buildings to show the power of the church and the glory of God. Craftsmen such as stonemasons, carpenters and blacksmiths from all over the diocese were used to create these beautiful buildings. Inside these dioceses were smaller areas called **parishes**. These were run by **priests**. Parishes were usually made up of a village, town or manor town. The local priest performed all the marriages, baptisms and funerals and also said mass. He was usually the only person who could read and write in the parish.

▲ Crusader armies travelled to Jerusalem and many other places to fight Muslims.

By the way . . .

Even an army of children travelled on a crusade. They left from Germany and France in 1212 but were never heard of again.

• Church Architecture

▲ Romanesque church

▲ Romanesque door

▲ Interior of a Romanesque church

The first style of church was called **Romanesque** (meaning 'in the Roman style'). This was because they used arches – a Roman invention.

1. The doors and windows were rounded at the top.

2. The bell tower was square.

3. The walls were very thick.

4. The thickness of the walls meant that there were few windows. Any windows in the church were very small. As a result, the inside was very dark.

5. The columns inside the church were very big and rounded to support the roof.

The later style was called **Gothic**.

1. Advances in engineering allowed Gothic architects to build much thinner walls with thinner columns inside.

2. To support the walls, Gothic churches used supports on the outside. These were called **flying buttresses.**

3. The flying buttresses allowed the columns inside to be much thinner and more elegant.

4. As the walls were thinner, they could add more windows and make them much bigger.

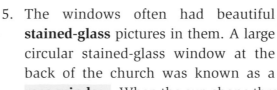

▲ Gothic church

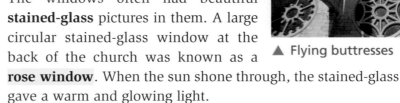

▲ Flying buttresses

5. The windows often had beautiful **stained-glass** pictures in them. A large circular stained-glass window at the back of the church was known as a **rose window**. When the sun shone through, the stained-glass gave a warm and glowing light.

6. The doors and windows were pointed at the top.

7. Gothic churches had tall **spires** that seemed to reach to heaven.

▲ Rose window

8. Gothic churches were decorated with horrible creatures called **gargoyles** to remind church-goers of hell.

Statues of gargoyles were ▶ used in Gothic churches to ensure church-goers were reminded of hell.

Questions

1. What jobs did the parish priest have?
2. Why did bishops build very impressive cathedrals?
3. Why were churches called Romanesque?
4. How did the architects of Gothic churches create thinner walls?
5. Name three differences between a Romanesque and a Gothic church.
6. What style are churches A and B? Give reasons to back up your answer.

B

A

By the way . . .

The name Gothic comes from the Goths who sacked Rome. It was a negative term used by Romanesque architects who disliked this new style of architecture.

Monastic Life

Medieval Christians sometimes wished to worship God away from the rest of the population. They created communities of men or women called monasteries and convents. Men in monasteries were called monks and women in convents were known as nuns.

These people lived very strict lives. They lived their lives according to the rules of St. Benedict written in AD 520. These strict rules allowed the monk or nun plenty of time each day to pray to God.

▲ The remains of Boyle Abbey, a medieval monastery which is located in County Roscommon.

● Becoming a monk

If someone wanted to become a monk he entered the monastery as a **novice**. He learned all the rules of the monastery. If he was suited to a monk's life and the **abbot** (the head of a monastery) believed he would be a good monk, he was accepted into the monastery. This usually took between one and two years. He then had to take **solemn vows** (promises).

The novice promised to live a life of:

1. **Poverty:** to give up all possessions. Everything he needed to live and worship God would be provided by the monastery.

2. **Chastity:** never to marry or have a family. This meant that he could concentrate all his energy into his prayers and worship.

3. **Obedience:** to vow to follow the rules of the monastery and to do whatever the abbot told him.

An older monk would then cut the novice's hair in a **tonsure** (the hair was shaved off around the top of the head). This meant everyone would immediately know he was a monk. He also gave up his normal clothes and wore a simple woollen **habit** (a plain tunic with a hood).

▲ Monk with tonsure and habit

Life in a monastery

Generally a monk's day was as follows:

Dawn:	Get up and perform **matins** (prayers).
	Lauds (Bible readings).
	Eat breakfast in complete silence.
6:00 a.m.	**Prime** (prayers)
	Do work around monastery.
9:00 a.m.	**Terce** (prayers and Bible readings)
	Mass.
	More work around the monastery.

Midday:	**Sext** (psalms and Bible readings)
	Eat simple dinner in silence.
	Sometimes a monk read aloud from a holy book.
	Work around the monastery.
3:00 p.m.	**None** (psalms and Bible readings)
	More work around the monastery.
Sunset:	**Vespers** (prayers)
	Light supper.
	Compline (prayers and Bible reading)
	Bed.

Some people wanted to live even stricter lives, such as living in total silence or having no contact with anyone from the outside world. These people set up new monastic orders (societies of monks) and followed slightly different rules.

● The buildings in a monastery

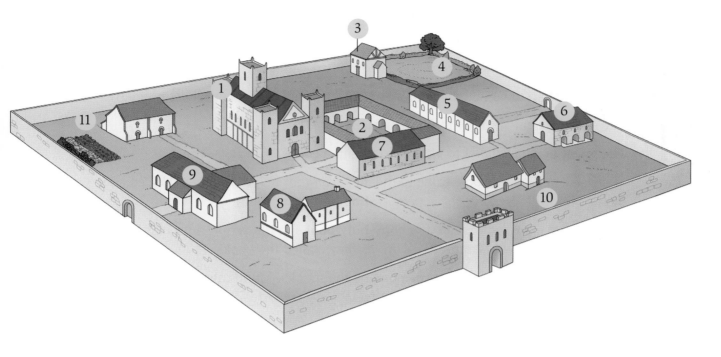

1. The church was the centre of the monastery. This was where the monks prayed. Monks sometimes prayed up to seven or eight times a day in the church.

2. The **cloister** was a walled courtyard in the middle of the monastery. Monks could walk, read or write in the fresh air.

3. The abbot (or abbess in a convent) had a house inside the monastery also.

4. Garden

5. Monks slept in the dormitory.

6. The Guest House was where visitors stayed when they came to the monastery.

7. All meals were taken in the refectory.

8. The **Chapter House** was where all the business of the monastery took place.

9. When monks were sick they went to the infirmary.

10. Manuscripts were written in the scriptorium and kept in the library.

11. Food was grown in the monastery.

• Jobs in a monastery

To avoid contact with the outside world, monasteries and convents provided for themselves. Each monk or nun had jobs to do.

The head of the monastery was the **abbot.** He distributed the jobs and organised the daily running of the monastery. His assistant was called the **prior.**

If anything had to be bought from merchants, the **cellarer** organised its purchase.

The sick were cared for by the **infirmarian.**

The **guest master** tended to visitors to the monastery.

Many sick and poor people came to the monastery for help. They were looked after by the **almoner**. He gave these people **alms** (money or food).

Monks were expected to read and **copy holy books** in the scriptorium and library. Some of them added beautiful artwork as they copied the books.

All **metal-work** or **carpentry** was done by the monks. Monks also grew their own food within the monastery. Fruit and vegetables were grown in the monastery and bees, sheep and cows were also kept.

• Other orders

Over the centuries new orders of monks and nuns were founded. Some of these orders kept their solemn vows but did not live in monasteries. Instead, they travelled around helping the poor and the sick. They also preached in towns and villages. The **Franciscans** and the **Dominicans** are two examples. They were also known as **friars** (after the French for brother, *frère*).

Questions

1. Explain the following words:

    (a) Novice   (b) Tonsure   (c) Habit

2. What solemn vows did a monk have to take? Explain what each one meant.

3. Explain what occurred in each of the following buildings in a monastery:

    (a) Infirmary   (c) Refectory   (e) Cloister

    (b) Scriptorium   (d) Chapter House

4. Write about life as a monk in the Middle Ages. Use the following headings as a guide:

    (a) Your training to be a monk

    (b) Your daily life

    (c) The buildings in the monastery

    (d) The jobs of people in the monastery

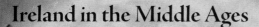

Ireland in the Middle Ages

The **Vikings** had been invading Ireland and plundering monasteries and villages along the coastline from around AD 795.

Over time Viking towns were founded along the coast and at river mouths. Towns such as Dublin, Wicklow, Wexford, Cork and Limerick were all Viking towns.

Vikings also settled in other places in Europe. They conquered Northern France which became known as **Normandy** (land of the men from the north or Norsemen).

Under **William I** (1028-87), the **Normans**, as they were now known, invaded England. At the battle of Hastings in 1066, William defeated and killed King Harold of England. We have wonderful evidence of this battle from the **Bayeux tapestry**. It was made by the Normans to celebrate the victory and tells the story of the battle. William is also known as William the Conqueror and became King of England.

From roughly AD 795, Vikings began raiding monasteries and villages along the coastline of Ireland. ▶

By the way...

The monastery at Clonmacnoise was attacked and burnt down 26 times between 547 and 1204!

◀ The Bayeux Tapestry shows the defeat and death of King Harold of England.

▲ This painting showing the marriage of Strongbow and Aoife is displayed in the National Gallery of Ireland.

Over the next 100 years all of England and Wales came under Norman control. In 1169 there was a dispute between the King of Leinster, **Dermot MacMurrough**, and the ard-rí, **Rory O'Connor.** MacMurrough travelled to England to ask the Norman King of England **Henry II** to help him get rid of O'Connor.

Henry agreed that MacMurrough could ask his Norman lords in Wales to help him. In 1169 Norman lords, led by the second Earl of Pembroke, **Richard de Clare,** arrived in Waterford. De Clare was also known as **Strongbow.** The Norman army easily defeated the Irish.

MacMurrough gave his daughter Aoife to Strongbow as a wife. He also promised that Strongbow could become King of Leinster on his death. Due to their well-equipped soldiers and organised way of fighting battles, the Norman lords now simply took over most of Ireland. In 1172 Henry II travelled to Ireland with 4,000 soldiers and 500 knights. He was declared **Lord of Ireland.**

By the way . . .
Strongbow's tomb is in Christchurch Cathedral in Dublin.

Questions

Examine the image of the Bayeux tapestry on page 93 and answer the following questions:

(a) Name two weapons that are being used by the soldiers in this picture.

(b) What advantage do the knights on the horses have over the foot soldiers?

(c) Is this a primary or secondary source? Give reasons for your answer.

(d) Is this source objective or subjective? Give a reason for your answer.

● Norman influence

Some areas of Ireland however, especially west Ulster, remained under Gaelic control. The Normans controlled the rest.

Norman lords built stone castles and manors all over the countryside. The castles built in Dublin, Trim, County Meath, and Carrickfergus, Co Antrim were particularly impressive. Other smaller tower-houses were also built throughout the island. Villages and towns grew around these castles, granges and manors, e.g. Manorhamilton, Grangegorman.

Gaelic farmers had focused mostly on tending herds of cattle. Under the new feudal system different farming methods were introduced. Now Norman farms grew crops such as wheat, barley and rye.

The Normans brought the system of parishes with them. The Irish church still uses this system today.

New names were introduced into Ireland. Many Norman names began with Fitz, e.g. Fitzgerald, Fitzmaurice and Fitzpatrick. Names like de Burke (Burke), de Butléir (Butler), de Brún (Browne) and de Barra (Barry) are also Norman names.

The Norman influence in Ireland is obvious from the number of people in Ireland with these names. Slowly the Normans began to mix with the Gaelic Irish. The Normans lived largely in towns but they married Gaelic Irish people and learned the Irish language. However, tensions between the Gaelic Irish and the Normans still remained.

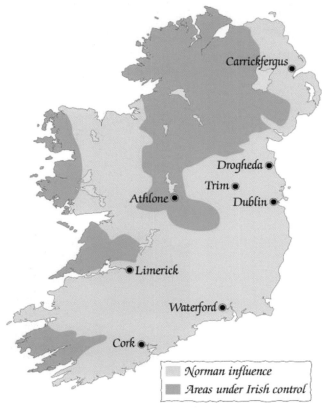

▲ A map showing Norman influence in Ireland

By the way . . .

In French 'de' means 'from' and 'fils' (from which we get 'fitz') means 'son of'.

▼ This castle at Carrickfergus was built by John de Courcy in 1180.

Chapter 4 Questions

1. Pictures

Picture A

◀ A - Trim Castle in County Meath

Picture B

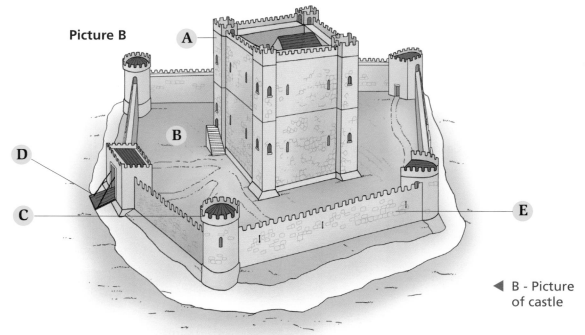

◀ B - Picture of castle

(a) Look at Picture A of Trim Castle in County Meath. Why do you think the castle was built at this location?

(b) Look at Picture B and answer the following questions:

   (i)   Name the features of the castle in picture B marked A, B, C, D, E.

   (ii) If you were to attack this castle, how would you do so? Name the weapons you would use.

   (iii) Why were the insides of castles very dark and damp?

2. Documents

The following is a contemporary (from that time) description of Strongbow. Read it and answer the questions:

> ### Source
>
> He had reddish hair and freckles, grey eyes, a feminine face, a weak voice and a short neck, though in almost all other respects he was of a tall build. He was a generous and easy-going man. What he could not accomplish by deed he settled by the persuasiveness (his ability to convince) of his words... When he took up his position in the midst of battle, he stood firm as an immovable standard (statue) round which his men could regroup and take refuge.
>
> Source: *A Story of Ireland* by John McCormack, Mentor Books

(a) Give a description of Strongbow's appearance.

(b) From this extract, what would make you think that Strongbow always succeeded in getting his way?

(c) Was Strongbow a good warrior? Give reasons for your answer.

(d) What was Strongbow's real name?

(e) How was Strongbow involved in the Norman invasion of Ireland? Give details.

3. Short-Answer Questions

(a) What was the feudal system?

(b) What was a demesne?

(c) Give an example of a title that a king might give to a noble.

(d) What took place in a solar?

(e) What was a trencher used for?

(f) What job did sentries have?

(g) Why did farmers leave a field fallow?

(h) Name three pastimes of a peasant farmer.

(i) How could a serf become a freeman?

(j) What was pottage?

(k) Name three things that happened at a medieval fair.

(l) What was the cause of the Black Death?

(m) Name two monastic or religious orders.

(n) Who were known as friars and what made them different from other monks?

(o) Who was the head of a convent?

(p) Name two things that the Normans introduced into Ireland.

(q) What does the word 'Fitz' mean in the name Fitzpatrick?

(r) Name one Norman castle in Ireland.

4. People in History

Write about life as a craftsman in a medieval town. Use the following headings as a guide:

- Name your craft
- Training and tools
- The guild of the craft
- Describe the town you live in
- Your workshop and home

5.

(a) Describe briefly two sites where medieval towns may have developed.

(b) Why did some medieval towns become wealthier and more powerful?

(c) Explain the following terms:
   (i) Portcullis   (iii) Turret
   (ii) Ramparts   (iv) Drawbridge

(d) Outline the main stages in the training of a knight in medieval times.

(e) Write an account of a lord in a manor.

(f) How have the Normans influenced Ireland? Give three examples.

Key Terms to Summarise Chapter 4: The Middle Ages

Feudal system A social system in which vassals (nobles) were granted land by the king in return for money and a promise to supply knights to defend the king in times of attack.

Vassal A wealthy person who promised loyalty and 'homage' to the lord or king in return for using the lord's land.

Knight A soldier on horseback who served as a page and a squire for 13 – 15 years before being dubbed a knight.

Demesne The section of land that a noble or lord kept for his own use.

Motte and Bailey A fortified courtyard (bailey) overlooked by a wooden castle built on a mound of earth.

Keep The building inside the castle walls where the lord and his family lived.

Turret Towers built on top of the curtain walls of castles to allow soldiers watch for enemies.

Portcullis Heavy iron gate which could be lowered to block the entrance if the castle came under attack.

Siege When an army surrounds a castle and blocks all access to the outside to force surrender.

Jousting A game during which knights on horseback galloped towards each other and tried to unseat the other knight from his horse with his lance.

Manor A noble's house and land.

Bailiff The person employed by the noble to look after his land, collect rent and taxes and enforce law and order.

Commons The area in the village where peasants let their animals graze.

Serf A farm worker on a lord's land who could be bought or sold.

Tithe Serfs and freeman had to give one tenth of their crops to the local priest. This payment was called a tithe.

Pottage A thick vegetable soup peasants ate.

Charter Permission given by the king or lord to a town to elect its own mayor and council; all town citizens were freemen.

Market square The centre of the town where the weekly market took place.

Curfew To prevent fires breaking out in medieval towns, all fires in homes had to be put out after dark.

Black Death A plague spread by fleas on rats. It killed a third of Europe's population between 1347 and 1351.

Guild An association of master craftsmen who helped their members and ensured high standards were maintained in their trade.

Apprentice The first stage for someone to become a master craftsman.

Journeyman When the apprentice had learnt his trade and could demand payment for his work.

Mastercraftsman When a journeyman produced a masterpiece that the guild believed was good enough, he became a mastercraftsman and could join the guild.

Stocks A punishment device used in medieval towns. Planks of wood had holes cut in them into which the person being punished had to place their feet.

Pillory Another punishment device. Planks of wood had holes cut in them for the head and hands while the person was standing.

Cathedral An impressive church where the bishop of the diocese celebrated mass.

Romanesque A style of architecture that used round arches.

Gothic A style of architecture that used pointed arches, flying buttresses and high, well-lit interiors.

Flying Buttresses The method used in Gothic churches to support the walls from the outside.

Rose windows Circular stained-glass windows at the back of a Gothic church.

Novice Someone who has entered a monastery but has not yet taken their final vows.

Tonsure Hairstyle used by monks – the hair was shaved off around the top of the head.

Cloister A covered walkway around an open courtyard where monks could read or pray in quiet.

Chapter House The building where the business of the monastery was discussed.

Almoner The monk in a monastery who looked after sick or poor people who came to the monastery for help.

Vikings People from Scandinavia who raided Ireland and Europe between the eighth and eleventh centuries.

Normans Name given to the Vikings who settled in northern France, now called Normandy.

Bayeux Tapestry An embroidered wall hanging showing images from the Battle of Hastings in 1066.

Web References

For further reading on topics mentioned in this chapter, view the following websites:

www.mw.mcmaster.ca/intro.html

www.hastings1066.com

www.notredamedeparis.fr/-English-

www.fordham.edu/halsall/sbook.html

www.bbc.co.uk/history/british/normans/

www.castles.org/Kids_Section/Castle_Story/

Women in History

Gormlaith

955 – 1042, High Queen of Ireland

Gormlaith was born in Ireland during the Norman conquest of Ireland. At that time many political alliances were being made between Gaelic Irish, Viking and Norman kings. Gormlaith's father was the lord of north Leinster. As a teenager she married the Viking King of Dublin Olaf Cuarán. She had five children with him. Her favourite son was Sitric Silkbeard. Soon, Olaf became ard rí (high-king of Ireland) and so Gormlaith became ard bean-rí (high-queen of Ireland).

In 980 Olaf's position was threatened by Malachy, the young king of Meath. Gormlaith decided to side with Malachy and used her influence in north Leinster and Dublin to turn her family against Olaf. Olaf fled to Scotland and Malachy married Gormlaith. Therefore she became ard bean-rí for a second time. Malachy also made her son, Sitric Silkbeard, king of Dublin in 994.

Around this time, Brian Ború, king of Munster threatened Malachy's lands and power. Gormlaith was not going to be caught on the losing side. She asked her brother Mael Mordha, now king of north Leinster, and her son Sitric to attack Malachy. After some confusion Brian accepted Gormlaith's aid and defeated Malachy. Brian became ard-rí and also took Gormlaith as his wife. Gormlaith became ard bean-rí for a third time! After twenty years of marriage, Brian grew tired of Gormlaith's meddling in his efforts to rule. So Gormlaith asked her son and brother to attack Brian. Sitric gathered a large Norse and Viking army in Dublin while Brian allied himself with her ex-husband Malachy. The battle took place in Clontarf in 1014 and Brian's army was victorious. However Brian was killed during the battle. Gormlaith spent the rest of her life in a convent and died in 1042. She lived to 87 years of age!

Chapter 5
THE RENAISSANCE

What was the Renaissance?

In the last chapter we looked at the Middle Ages between AD 500 – 1400. The modern history of Europe begins in **1400**.

The period from approximately 1400 to 1600 is known as the **Renaissance**. People began to: (1) revive many ideas of the ancient Greeks and Romans and (2) question the world around them much more than during the Middle Ages.

Renaissance means rebirth, in other words the rebirth of interest in ancient times. People studied ancient Greek and Roman art, architecture, engineering, writing and science. Many of the great achievements of the Greeks and Romans had been forgotten during the Middle Ages. However, during the Renaissance, scientists, scholars and artists used many of the ancient ideas and developed them further.

By the way . . .

The term renaissance is a French word first used by the Italian poet Petrarch when he described another Italian poet Dante's work as being as good as anything written in ancient Rome.

This interest in the ancient world led people to look more closely at the world around them. Beliefs people held without question during the Middle Ages were examined. Scholars wanted to understand how the human body worked. Could humans build flying machines? Did the sun and the stars really revolve around the earth? Everything was questioned. It was a time when people believed there was no limit to what humans could discover and explain about themselves and the world around them.

● Italy in 1400

The Renaissance began in Italy and spread to France, Germany, Belgium, Holland and England. It began in Italy because:

1. Italy was not a united country. It was made up of many different **city-states**

such as Milan, Venice, Florence, Genoa and Naples. These city-states ruled themselves and had large armies. They became very wealthy because Italian merchants brought spices, silks and other exotic goods from Asia and then sold them to northern Europeans. To deal with the large amount of money they earned as a result of trading, large banks were established in these city-states. These wealthy merchants and bankers enjoyed spending their money on beautiful art. They paid artists, writers and architects to create beautiful pieces of art. These people were known as **patrons**.

2. Italian traders came into contact with advanced civilisations such as the Chinese and Arabs. They brought home new ideas and ways of doing things.

3. The Italian language was based on Latin so most Italians could read the manuscripts of the ancient Romans. From these manuscripts they were able to learn more about the past and develop new ideas using old knowledge.

4. Ruins from ancient Rome were scattered throughout Italy. The Colosseum and the Forum in Rome, the many theatres and aqueducts that existed all over Italy reminded the Italians of their past and made them proud. It also made them want to discover more about their past.

5. Rome was the centre of the Christian Church. The Pope was very wealthy and owned a large part of central Italy.

6. In 1453, Muslim Turks captured **Constantinople** (modern Istanbul). Many Greeks who were living there fled to Italy. They brought with them ancient Greek manuscripts and were able to read the ancient Greek language. This added to the knowledge of the Italians.

▲ A map of Italy with city-states labelled and arrows showing different goods coming from Asia and Constantinople

By the way . . .

The people of each city-state believed their city was the richest and the most beautiful. Wealthy patrons were willing to spend vast sums of money to hire the best artists, sculptors and architects to create works of art for their city.

Questions

1. What does the term Renaissance mean?
2. How did the Colosseum and other Roman ruins contribute to the Renaissance?
3. How did the reading of ancient Greek and Roman manuscripts inspire people?
4. Why were the Italian city-states so wealthy?

Renaissance Florence

▲ The city-state of Florence was at the centre of the Renaissance.

● The Medici family

The city-state of Florence was at the centre of the Renaissance. Skilful weavers in Florence made silk and wool cloths. Merchants from Florence sold these cloths all over Europe, making huge amounts of money this way. With all this money, it was necessary to have banks. These banks soon became the biggest and richest banks in Europe. The largest bank in Europe was the Medici bank in Florence, owned by the Medici family.

The city-state of Florence elected its own government. However, the Medici family used their money to have friends elected to the government. So, in effect, the Medicis were the real rulers of Florence for more than a century.

● Cosimo de Medici (1389-1464)

▲ Dome of Santa Maria del Fiore, the Cathedral in Florence

Cosimo de Medici was the head of the Medici bank at the beginning of the fifteenth century. He was interested in collecting old manuscripts from ancient Greece and Rome. He housed all these manuscripts in the Medici Library and encouraged people to come and read them. He also set up the Platonic Academy named after the Greek philosopher Plato. He was patron to many great artists. He also hired the architect Brunelleschi to finish the dome of **Santa Maria del Fiore**, the enormous cathedral in Florence. When he died, the people of Florence gave him the name *Pater Patriae* (father of the city).

▲ Cosimo De Medici's collection of ancient Greek and Roman manuscripts helped to spark a revival of interest in that era.

● Lorenzo the Magnificent (1449-1492)

Cosimo's grandson, Lorenzo de Medici, took over the family business in 1469. Lorenzo was not particularly good at the business of banking. He was more interested in art and learning. During his rule, Florence became the centre of Renaissance art and culture. He expanded the library that his grandfather had begun and paid the scholars and writers of the Platonic Academy. Some of the greatest artists of the time were employed by Lorenzo: Michelangelo, da Vinci and Botticelli. Lorenzo was very close to these artists and Michelangelo even lived with Lorenzo's family for some time. Because of his patronage and love of art, he earned the title 'the Magnificent'.

▲ Lorenzo the Magnificent, Cosimo's grandson, was not very good at running the family's banking business.

Unfortunately his abilities as a banker were not so magnificent. The Medicis lost much of their wealth during his reign. Only two years after his death at the age of 43, the French invaded Florence and the Medici family lost all their power. After the fall of the Medicis, the artistic centre of the Renaissance moved to Rome. However, the Medicis continued to have a great influence on the Renaissance. In Rome Lorenzo's son, Giovanni, became Pope Leo X and Lorenzo's nephew, Giulio, became Pope Clement VII.

Questions

1. What is a patron?
2. How did the city of Florence become so wealthy at the beginning of the Renaissance?
3. How did the Medici family become so powerful?
4. How did Cosimo de Medici contribute to the Renaissance in Florence? Give three examples.
5. How did the Medici family lose their power in Florence?

By the way . . .

There was a lot of fighting between rival families in Florence. In an attack by the rival Pazzi family in the Cathedral in Florence, Lorenzo's brother was killed and Lorenzo just managed to escape.

Renaissance Art

● Art evidence

The reason why we know about the Renaissance is because we have many sources of evidence, including:

1. The **paintings** and **sculptures** of the Renaissance are on show in galleries and museums around the world, e.g. the Mona Lisa is on show in the Louvre in Paris. Buildings from this period also still exist, e.g. St Peter's Basilica in Rome. We can view how the style of the Renaissance is different to that of the Middle Ages by comparing paintings from these two periods.

2. Many artists' **notebooks** and **letters** are in libraries and museums. In these notebooks artists drew sketches and made notes about their work. Scientists and physicians (people who practise medicine) wrote books about what they studied and discovered. Some of these books were printed using the newly-invented **printing press**.

3. An Italian artist named **Giorgio Vasari** (1511-1574) wrote a book called *Lives of the Artists*. In this book he wrote biographies of many of the most famous artists of the Renaissance. This is a particularly good contemporary (in the same period of time) source.

The differences between Medieval art and Renaissance art

1. Subjects

▲ Portrait of Catherine de Medici

During the Middle Ages, paintings and sculpture mostly showed religious images. Renaissance artists continued to paint and sculpt religious images but due to a revival of interest in stories from ancient Greece and Rome, they also included Greek and Roman myths and legends. Also, wealthy patrons wanted to have individual or family portraits painted.

▲ Botticelli's *Birth of Venus* (c. 1486)

2. Realism

Renaissance artists wanted to show human beings as they really were. Their art was far more **realistic**. People began to look like human beings rather than the cartoon-like figures of the Middle Ages. This was helped by the interest in the 1400s in the **anatomy** (cutting open and examining an animal or plant). Renaissance artists used light, shadow and shade in a picture to make it more true to life.

▲ Medieval picture of a religious procession

▲ *The Taking of Christ* by Caravaggio is displayed in the National Gallery of Ireland.

By the way . . .

Brunelleschi invented the **vanishing point** . This is the point where all lines of perspective come from. It can also be described as the point at which parallel lines meet.

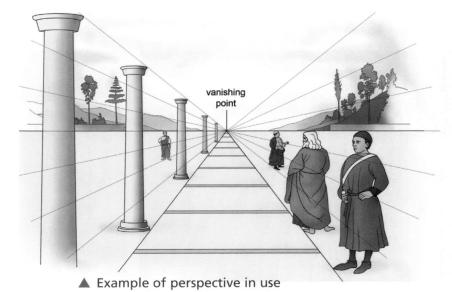

▲ Example of perspective in use

3. PERSPECTIVE

The images in medieval paintings often looked unreal. This was sometimes due to the two-dimensional images they painted, i.e. people/objects at the front and back of the picture were of the same size. However, Renaissance painters used **perspective** to help pictures look more realistic and give depth to the painting. This made the pictures look more three-dimensional, i.e. people/objects at the front of the painting were bigger than those at the back.

(Look closely at *The Last Supper* on page 108 and *The School of Athens* on page 115 to see if you can notice the use of perspective.)

4. MATERIALS

The **materials** used by Renaissance artists changed too. They began to use canvas instead of wooden panels on which to paint their pictures. They also used oil in their paints. Oil paint took longer to dry so artists could make corrections if they were not happy with their painting. It also gave a richer colour than the paint mixed with egg-yolk or water which was popular in the Middle Ages. Many artists also painted **frescoes**, i.e. painting pictures on walls of wet plaster.

5. ROMANESQUE STYLE

▲ Villa Rotunda by Andrea Palladio

As we learnt in the previous chapter, medieval churches were built in a Gothic style. This style used spires and pointed windows. However, Renaissance **architecture** returned to the style of the ancient Greeks and Romans. Columns, domes and pediments last seen in Ancient Rome came back into fashion.

6. SCULPTURE

The **sculpture** of figures during the Renaissance period was far more realistic. In the Middle Ages sculptures were usually attached to churches. Pieces of sculpture were now free-standing (they were not connected to anything else).

▲ Statue columns at Chartres Cathedral in France

◀ David by Donatello who was one of the greatest sculptors of the Renaissance.

Questions

1. Give three ways in which we know about the Renaissance and the lives of the artists and scientists.

2. (a) What were the new subjects that Renaissance artists began to paint and sculpt?

   (b) Why do you think they began to use these new subjects?

3. Give three differences between the medieval picture of a religious procession and *The Taking of Christ* by Caravaggio on page 105.

4. How did Renaissance artists make their art more realistic than medieval art?

5. Explain the following words: (a) Anatomy   (b) Fresco   (c) Perspective

6. Look at the image of David above. Does this statue appear to be more realistic than a statue from the Middle Ages? Give two reasons why.

Artists of the Renaissance

• Leonardo da Vinci (1452- 1519)

THE EARLY LIFE OF LEONARDO

Leonardo was born in the town of Vinci near Florence in 1452. Even as a young boy he showed great ability at painting and drawing. When he was fourteen he was sent to be an apprentice to an artist named Andrea Verrocchio in Florence.

▲ Leonardo da Vinci

Verrocchio was working on a painting called *The Baptism of Christ* and asked Leonardo to paint an angel in the corner of the picture. Leonardo's angel was so beautiful that Verrocchio decided that his student was better at painting than he was. Verrocchio decided to quit painting and from then on he worked only as a sculptor.

▲ *The Baptism of Christ* by Verrocchio (1475)

LEONARDO AS AN INVENTOR

Leonardo was brilliant at many different activities, including inventing. He recorded ideas in his notebook, drawing buildings, flowers, parts of the body and sketches of inventions. His sketches of inventions such as large catapults, cannons and tanks were for use in war. However he also had ideas about submarines, bicycle chains, parachutes and aeroplanes – hundreds of years before anyone else managed to create any of these things! In 1482 Leonardo left Florence and asked the Duke of Milan, Ludovico Sforza, if he could work for him.

▲ Da Vinci's plans for creating a parachute

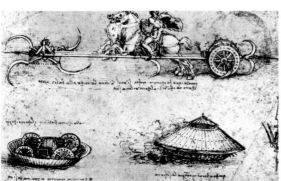

▲ Da Vinci's ideas of how to build a tank

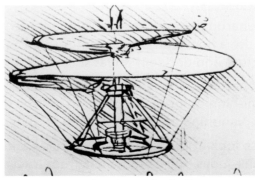

▲ Da Vinci's drawing of a helicopter

Source A

I can design portable bridges and cannon-proof ships. I can also make gun carriages and catapults. In times of peace I can paint anything you want. I can work as an architect or an engineer and I can make statues in marble, bronze or clay. I am also good at philosophy, poetry, mathematics, physics, chemistry, botany and mechanics.

(Letter from da Vinci to Sforza)

By the way . . .

The fresco of *The Last Supper* was damaged when the monks in the monastery cut a doorway through the picture.

LEONARDO AS A PAINTER

The Duke of Milan agreed to employ him. Once there, Leonardo painted one of his most famous paintings, *The Last Supper*, on the wall of a church.

▲ *The Last Supper* (1498) – one of Leonardo da Vinci's most famous paintings.

Questions

1. Leonardo painted *The Last Supper* onto the wall of a church in a convent. He tried to use a new method of painting frescos using oil paint. Look at the quality of the picture and decide if it was successful. Give a reason for your answer.

2. Leonardo uses perspective to great effect. Try to find where the vanishing point of the painting is. Why do you think he placed the vanishing point where he did?

3. Also look at Leonardo's use of shade and light. Why do you think Judas (third on the left from Jesus) is in shade?

In 1499 Leonardo moved back to Florence because Milan had been invaded by the French army and the Duke had been imprisoned. In Florence he painted a portrait of the wife of a Florentine merchant. This painting is called the *Mona Lisa* and it took Leonardo two years to paint. It is now in the Louvre Museum in Paris and is probably the world's most famous painting.

The *Mona Lisa* is quite a small painting as it measures only 77 centimetres in height x 53 centimetres in length.

▲ The *Mona Lisa* was painted using a technique that made the skin of the woman appear soft. This is called sfumato which means smoky in Italian.

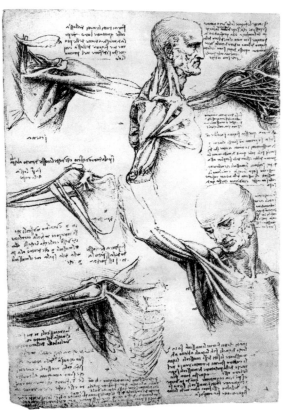

▲ Anatomy of a man – Leonardo da Vinci was very interested in finding out how the human body worked.

LEONARDO'S OTHER INTERESTS

Leonardo wrote all his thoughts and ideas into notebooks and so we still have over 5,000 pages of his writings. He studied the stars and planets (astronomy), the rocks in the earth (geology) and the life of flowers (botany). He was also interested in how the body works (anatomy). He cut open (**dissected**) over 30 bodies in his lifetime which helped him to understand how the muscles in the body worked. As a result he was able to paint more realistically.

By the way . . .

To achieve the soft glow on the faces of his subjects, Leonardo painted at dusk with a linen sheet over his head.

By the way . . .

Leonardo, who was left handed, was worried his ideas would be stolen so he wrote everything in his notebooks from right to left. You can only read his notes by looking at them in a mirror.

LATER LIFE

In 1513, Leonardo moved to Rome to work for Pope Leo X for three years. He was then invited to the royal court of France by King Francis I. Leonardo died in France in 1519 aged 67. Amazingly he died believing he had offended God because he felt he never fully achieved his potential.

Questions

1. When and where was Leonardo da Vinci born?

2. Many people have argued about Mona Lisa's smile. Do you think the woman is happy or sad? Give a reason for your answer.

3. Explain what the term sfumato means?

4. Leonardo da Vinci is regarded as a genius. Do you agree? Give reasons for your answer.

5. What type of information did Leonardo write in his notebooks?

6. Write an account on Leonardo da Vinci using the following headings:

   (a) His early life   (d) His inventions

   (b) His paintings   (e) His later life

   (c) His artistic methods

● Michelangelo (1475-1564)

EARLY LIFE

Michelangelo Buonarroti was born in the small village of Caprese in 1475. He grew up in the city of Florence when it was the centre of the early Renaissance. He preferred drawing to schoolwork. At age 13, he became an apprentice to a Florentine artist. In 1490, Lorenzo de Medici saw Michelangelo's work and asked him to study at his own private sculpture school. For two years he learnt much by being surrounded by some of the greatest artists, poets and scholars of the time. In 1494 Michelangelo moved to Rome.

▲ Michelangelo

MICHELANGELO'S SCULPTURE

In 1497 a French cardinal asked him to sculpt a statue of Mary and Jesus. The statue is called *The Pietà* (which means sorrow). The statue of white marble shows Jesus in the arms of Mary after being taken down from the cross. The realism of the Renaissance can be seen clearly in this statue. The folds of Mary's clothes and the body of Jesus are very detailed.

▲ *The Pietà*, Michelangelo's most famous sculpture

By the way . . .

After some confusion over who sculpted *The Pietá*, Michelangelo sneaked into St. Peter's and carved his name onto it.

In 1501 Michelangelo entered a competition in Florence to create something out of a large block of white marble. He won the competition, even defeating da Vinci in the process. The result was a five-metre tall statue of David from the Biblical story of David and Goliath. Michelangelo's interest in anatomy resulted in a statue of great beauty and detail. The statue was placed in the centre of the Palazzo della Signoria (the central square of Florence). It is now in a museum for safety.

THE SISTINE CHAPEL

Pope Julius II asked Michelangelo to paint frescoes on the ceiling of the Sistine Chapel in Rome. Although he preferred sculpture, he took the job, hoping that Julius would permit him to return to the job of creating sculptures for the pope's tomb once he finished painting. The two men had very strong personalities and frequently came close to blows over the design for the frescoes in the Sistine Chapel. Michelangelo was eventually allowed to do as he wished and Julius's original plan to show the 12 Apostles was enlarged to show more than 300 figures. Michelangelo did not allow any visitors into the Sistine Chapel while he worked.

▲ Michelangelo's statue of David: David's hands and head are over-sized to show that it was his head and hands that defeated Goliath.

◀ The ceiling of the Sistine Chapel in Rome

Perched on top of scaffolding he designed himself, he painted scenes from the book of Genesis in the Bible, e.g. the creation of the world, Adam, Eve and Noah. He covered the ceiling with 300 figures. He worked for four years on these frescoes. It is thought to be one of the greatest pieces of art ever created.

Thirty years later Michelangelo was asked by Pope Clement VII to paint a large wall in the Sistine Chapel. The picture he painted is of *The Last Judgement*. In this he shows Jesus sending people to heaven or hell.

▲   The wall of the Sistine Chapel showing *The Last Judgement* in which Jesus is depicted sending people to either heaven or hell.

St. Peter's Basilica

Michelangelo's skills extended to architecture also. Saint Peter's Basilica in Rome was designed by an architect called Bramante but he died before it was completed. Pope Julius II then asked Michelangelo to finish the work. He re-designed parts of Bramante's plan, including the **dome**. In fact, the whole design is very similar to the ancient Roman buildings in Chapter 3, Ancient Rome. From the inside of the basilica it is possible to see that Michelangelo's dome is also a masterpiece in architectural beauty.

Michelangelo died in 1564 aged 89. Although he preferred to sculpt, he was also a great painter, architect and poet. He is thought to be one of the greatest artists of all time. His life is summarised by the epitaph on his tomb: he was simply *Il Divino Michelangelo* (the divine Michelangelo).

◀ Michelangelo took over the design of St. Peter's Basilica when the original architect, Bramante, died.

▲ The interior of the dome in St. Peter's Basilica

Questions

1. Look at Michelangelo's *The Pietà*. How would you know that this is a Renaissance sculpture?

2. What material is *The Pietà* made from?

3. Art historians have put forward many theories regarding the expression on Mary's face in *The Pietá*. What expression do you think she is showing on her face?

4. How can you tell that Michelangelo was interested in anatomy?

5. Why do you think his statue of David on page 111 is thought to be so beautiful?

6. Look at the statue of David by Donatello on page 106 and then look at the statue of David by Michelangelo on page 111. What are the differences between the two statues?

7. What was the subject of the painting on the wall of the Sistine Chapel?

8. What architectural work did Michelangelo do?

9. How is St. Peter's Basilica similar to the buildings of ancient Rome? Give two examples.

10. What are the words written on Michelangelo's tomb? Do you agree with them?

● Raphael (1483-1520)

Raphael's full name was Raffaello Sanzio. He was born on 6 April 1483 in Umbria between Florence and Rome. He painted the *Marriage of the Virgin* in 1504. This typical Renaissance painting shows his expert use of *sfumato* and perspective. It also includes Renaissance architecture in the background.

Raphael painted this self-portrait c. 1506 – 1508. ▶

▲ *Marriage of the Virgin* which was painted by Raphael in 1504 shows his excellent use of *sfumato* and perspective.

In 1508, Pope Julius II hired Raphael to paint a fresco in the Vatican Palace in Rome. It was here that he painted his most famous piece of art. *The School of Athens* shows all the great ancient philosophers. Plato and Aristotle are in the centre of the painting. Raphael decided to paint the faces of his fellow artists on the different characters. Plato has the face of da Vinci while Heraclitus's face is that of Michelangelo and Raphael himself appears on the right in the black hat. The painting is thought to be a masterpiece in the use of perspective. It also shows how highly the Renaissance artists regarded the works of the ancient Greeks.

Raphael died of a fever on his birthday at the age of 37. He asked for his body to be buried in the Roman Pantheon.

By the way . . .

Michelangelo and Raphael were great rivals. They both lived in Rome and competed for work from the Pope, the wealthiest patron in Rome. However, before Michelangelo finished painting the frescos, Raphael made a secret visit to the Sistine Chapel and was so impressed by what he saw that he added Michelangelo's face to *The School of Athens* as a mark of respect.

Socrates

Pythagoras   Heraclitus   Plato   Aristotle

Raphael

▲ *The School of Athens* (1510) by Raphael

Questions

1. List three features that show the *Marriage of the Virgin* is a typical Renaissance painting.
2. Examine *The School of Athens*.
   (a) Where is the vanishing point in this picture?
   (b) Why do you think Raphael located it here?
3. How does *The School of Athens* show the interest in ancient Greece during the Renaissance?

● Artists outside Italy

The Renaissance spread outside Italy. Artists from all over Europe were inspired to use the methods and style of the Italian painters and sculptors.

REMBRANDT (1606-1669)

Rembrandt Harmenszoon van Rijn was a Dutch artist of the Renaissance. He is particularly famous for his paintings of groups of people and his use of light and shadow.

Rembrandt is famous for his use of light and shadow in his paintings. ▶

Early Life

He was born in Leiden in the Netherlands. He studied at the University of Leiden before moving to Amsterdam in 1631. In 1634, he married Saskia van Uylengurg, a cousin of a successful art dealer, and had four children with her. In many ways he was a very unlucky person. Three of his children died soon after birth and Saskia also died in 1642. His only surviving son, Titus, died almost a year before Rembrandt's death in 1669. He was declared bankrupt in 1656 and had to sell all his antiques and art collection along with his house. Rembrandt died in 1669 and was buried in an unmarked grave in Amsterdam.

▲ *Belshazzar's Feast* (1635) shows Belshazzar, King of Babylon, serving wine in sacred vessels which had been stolen from the Temple in Jerusalem when a divine hand appears and writes a stern warning from God on the wall.

He created roughly 400 paintings and over 1,400 drawings and etchings. He also painted about 60 **self-portraits** (pictures of himself). Many of these were attempts to capture different facial expressions.

Many of his paintings were portraits and religious scenes. These often showed scenes with many people and great drama. This painting, *Belshazzar's Feast*, shows a Biblical scene. How can you tell it is a Renaissance painting?

The Night Watch, ▶ 1642 is possibly Rembrandt's most famous painting.

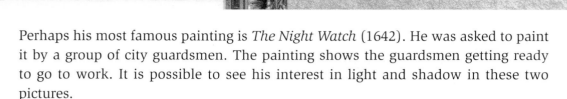

Perhaps his most famous painting is *The Night Watch* (1642). He was asked to paint it by a group of city guardsmen. The painting shows the guardsmen getting ready to go to work. It is possible to see his interest in light and shadow in these two pictures.

The Night Watch was originally called *The Shooting Company of Captain Frans Banning Cocq*. However, by the eighteenth century the painting had become covered in dirt and grime. This dirt meant that it was mistakenly thought to show a scene at night and so it was called *The Night Watch*. In 1715 the painting was cut to make it fit a wall in Amsterdam's town hall. As a result, three characters from the original painting are missing.

There were many other great artists from outside Italy. **Albrecht Dürer** (1471-1528), a German artist, visited Italy from Germany many times. He is particularly famous for his **engravings** and **woodcuts**. These were done by sketching on to a copper plate (engraving) or a piece of wood (woodcuts). This could be dipped in ink and numerous copies could then be made.

Pieter Bruegel (c.1525-1569) and Jan van Eyck (c.1390-1441) were Dutch painters who were also very influenced by the Renaissance.

> **By the way . . .**
>
> The Chester Beatty Library in Dublin has a number of Dürer engravings.

Questions

1. What aspects of Rembrandt's painting style is he most famous for?
2. What happened to Rembrandt in 1656?
3. What is the correct name for *The Night Watch*?
4. How did *The Night Watch* get this incorrect name?
5. Why are there three people missing from the original painting of *The Night Watch*?
6. What is the difference between an engraving and a woodcut?
7. Name three artists of the Renaissance from outside Italy.
8. Write an account of a Renaissance artist you have studied from outside Italy. Use the following headings as a guide:
   (a) The name of the painter and where he came from
   (b) Early life
   (c) Artistic techniques and subjects
   (d) Name one of his paintings
   (e) Describe one of his paintings

The Printing Press

The invention of the printing press in the 1400s had a massive influence on the history of Europe from that point onwards. Most people in the Middle Ages were **illiterate** (they could not read or write). Manuscripts were copied by monks in monasteries. These manuscripts sometimes took years to complete. This all changed when a man called Johann Gutenberg came up with the idea of a printing press.

▲ Johann Gutenburg, inventor of the printing press

● Johann Gutenberg (1398-1468)

The Chinese had been printing documents since the second century AD. They invented paper in AD 105 and this allowed them to print. In Europe, manuscripts were written on **papyrus** (made from pressed papyrus plant) and **vellum** (the skin of calves). These materials were not suitable for printing. However, paper produced in the Middle East was brought to Europe from about the 1200s onwards. In 1450 Johannes Gutenberg is thought to have invented the **moveable-type printing press**. He did this by placing small letters made of metal into a frame. This frame could then be pressed onto the paper producing the same page again and again. He produced his first book which is known as the **Gutenberg Bible**. It was written in Latin and was decorated with hand-drawn designs. Only 47 copies of this book still exist and of these only three are in perfect condition.

Metal letters being put into frames

Letters being arranged to form the words of the book

Sheets drying

Ink being spread onto page

The letters being pressed onto page

Sheets being bound into books

▲ This image shows the various activities that took place in a printing room.

Soon many other printers sprang up. Aldus Manutius in Venice and William Caxton in England were two very important printers. Between 1450 and 1500 over 6,000 books, documents and pamphlets were printed. Venice alone had 417 printers in the city by 1500.

RESULTS OF THE PRINTING PRESS

The explosion of printing in the fifteenth and sixteenth centuries had huge consequences:

1. Printed books became much cheaper to produce than hand-written manuscripts. This meant more people could buy books.

2. Because more people had access to books, more learned to read and write.

3. As more people read books, they were introduced to new ideas. So if someone wanted to spread a new idea it was possible to do so very quickly using printed pamphlets and leaflets.

4. Up until the fifteenth century it was usually the Church that wrote and owned most of the manuscripts. This meant they could control what was read. Books now allowed ideas to spread that were sometimes against the teachings of the Church.

5. During the Middle Ages most books were written in Latin. Only educated people could speak and read Latin. This changed during the Renaissance. Writers such as **Petrarch** in Italy, **Cervantes** in Spain and **Shakespeare** in England began to write in the **vernacular** (the everyday language of the local people). Their writings became very popular as so many people could read and understand them, not just people who understood Latin.

By the way . . .

The first book in Irish was printed in Dublin in 1550. It was a book of common prayer.

Questions

1. Explain the process of printing a book using a moveable-type printing press.

2. What was the first book that Gutenberg printed?

3. Name two important printers in Europe apart from Gutenberg.

4. What happened in places such as Venice and England to allow the number of books printed to increase to over 6,000 between 1450 and 1500?

5. How did the invention of the printing press help to increase literacy?

6. What does the term vernacular mean?

Writers of the Renaissance

▲ William Shakespeare became very wealthy and famous during his lifetime due to the plays he wrote.

● William Shakespeare (1564-1616)

One of the most famous of the Renaissance writers was an Englishman named William Shakespeare. He was born in Stratford-on-Avon in 1564. He married Anne Hathaway at the age of 18 and they had three children. He moved to London, became an actor and wrote poetry and plays.

He quickly became very popular as a playwright and his first play *The Comedy of Errors* was performed in 1594. He became part owner of a theatrical company called **The King's Men**. This company was very successful and even performed at the royal court. In 1599 the company opened a theatre called **The Globe** on the south bank of the River Thames. Plays were not seen as literature by the public. People saw them as entertainment, like the cinema today. The audience shouted and cheered if they liked the play. If they disliked it, they jeered and threw things at the actors.

Shakespeare wrote 38 plays and they were all performed in The Globe. His plays were performed at the royal court more than any other playwright at the time. These plays were popular enough for Shakespeare to become very wealthy and famous. With this new wealth he was able to buy property in London and Stratford.

▲ The Globe Theatre where all 38 of Shakespeare's plays were performed.

By the way . . .

The Globe Theatre had a large globe on its roof bearing the quote 'All the world's a stage'. In 1613, during a performance, a cannon set the roof on fire and the theatre burnt down. It was rebuilt in 1614 but was destroyed again thirty years later. The Globe was rebuilt in 1997 and was the first building allowed to have a thatched roof since the Great Fire of London in 1666.

Shakespeare is still very popular and his plays are performed all over the world. His plays deal with problems that people still face today. His plays are often divided into three different types:

Comedies, e.g. *A Midsummer Night's Dream*, *The Comedy of Errors* and *Twelfth Night*

Histories, e.g. *Julius Caesar, Henry V, Henry VIII* and *Antony and Cleopatra*

Tragedies, e.g. *Romeo and Juliet, Hamlet, Othello, King Lear* and *Macbeth*

He also wrote 154 sonnets and a number of poems. These **sonnets** (rhyming poems of 14 lines in length) are mostly about love.

▲ Stratford-on-Avon, the town in which Shakespeare was born.

Shakespeare moved back to Stratford and died in 1616. Many of the phrases we still use today in everyday language were invented by Shakespeare.

By the way . . .
It is estimated that one-third of all well-known English phrases were coined by Shakespeare.

▲ Niccolò Machiavelli

Niccolò Machiavelli (1469-1527) was an Italian writer from Florence. His book *The Prince* (1513) explained ways in which rulers could get and keep power. He felt it was more important for rulers to be feared than to be loved. He dedicated the book to the Medici rulers of Florence in the hope they would employ him. He also wrote *On the Art of War* in 1521 and *A History of Florence* (1525). Because of the books he wrote, the word **Machiavellian** now means using sneaky methods to get what you want.

Questions

1. Where was Shakespeare born?
2. What was the name of Shakespeare's theatre company and where did they perform?
3. Why do you think that Shakespeare's plays are still performed all around the world?
4. Briefly describe what it was like to attend a play during the Renaissance.
5. Name one of Shakespeare's comedies, histories and tragedies.
6. What is a sonnet?
7. What is *The Prince* by Machiavelli about?
8. What does the term 'Machiavellian' mean?
9. Write an account about a writer from the Renaissance you have studied. Use the following headings as a guide:

   (a) His name and where he was from.   (c) What kind of works he wrote.

   (b) His early life.   (d) Some examples of what he wrote.

Science and Medicine

Medicine

All understanding of medicine in the Middle Ages was based on the writings of ancient Greek philosophers and **physicians** (someone who practises medicine). A Greek physician from the second century AD was named **Galen** and he was the most famous and respected physician of his time.

▲ Galen was a Greek physician who dissected animals in an effort to understand more about the human body.

He dissected animals and gave public lectures. He based his understanding of the human body on what he discovered by dissecting animals. This meant that not all his findings were correct. He believed that blood came from the liver and that the liver pumps it around the body. He also thought that mental illness was due to the imbalance of four fluids in the body: black bile, yellow bile, blood and phlegm.

> **By the way . . .**
> One of the most common ways of curing a patient was **bloodletting**. This involved making a cut in their bodies and releasing some of the 'bad blood' in the body.

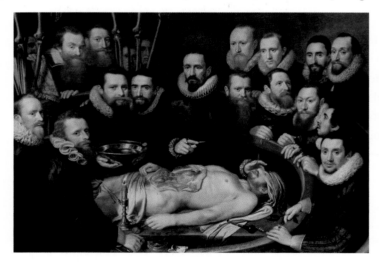

The Catholic Church thought it was wrong for physicians to dissect bodies. This meant that during the Middle Ages there was very little examination of bodies and therefore little advance in medicine. During the sixteenth century these views changed.

◄ *The Anatomy Lesson of Doctor William van der Meld* by Pieter van Miereveldd

Andreas Vesalius (1514-1564)

Vesalius was born in Brussels, Belgium in 1514. He studied medicine in the University of Paris before going to Padua, Italy to lecture on surgery at the very young age of 23. It was here that he showed that the

Andreas Vesalius had to resort to stealing dead bodies in order to dissect them and find out more about how the human body worked. ▶

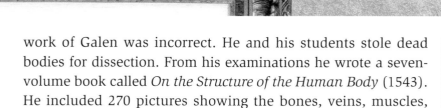

work of Galen was incorrect. He and his students stole dead bodies for dissection. From his examinations he wrote a seven-volume book called *On the Structure of the Human Body* (1543). He included 270 pictures showing the bones, veins, muscles, heart and brain of a human.

The book is thought to be one of the greatest medical books of all time. His work meant he was appointed as a physician to the royal court of Charles V of Spain. Vesalius is often thought to be the father of modern anatomy.

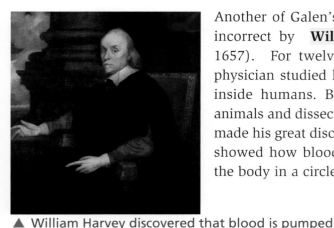

Another of Galen's beliefs was proved incorrect by **William Harvey** (1578-1657). For twelve years the English physician studied how the blood flows inside humans. By operating on live animals and dissecting dead humans he made his great discovery. In his book he showed how blood is pumped around the body in a circle by the heart.

▲ William Harvey discovered that blood is pumped around the body in a circle by the heart.

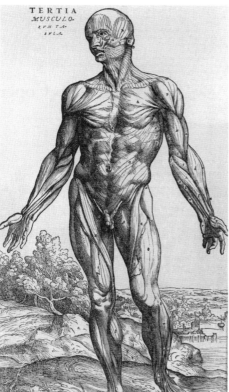

▲ An image from Vesalius's book on anatomy.

Questions

1. Who was Galen?
2. Give two examples of mistakes made by Galen.
3. Why did people not dissect human bodies during the Middle Ages?
4. Name the book that Vesalius wrote on anatomy.
5. What did Vesalius include in this book?
6. What is William Harvey famous for discovering?
7. How did Harvey prove that Galen was incorrect?

• Science

Astronomy (the study of the movement of the stars and planets) has always been of interest to people. Newgrange in Ireland, Stonehenge in England and the Pyramids in Egypt all have connections to astronomy. An Egyptian astronomer named **Ptolemy** wrote a manuscript called *Geography* in the third century AD. In it he wrote that the sun, moon and planets all moved around the earth. This belief continued through to the Middle Ages. This also fitted into the Church's beliefs. The Church thought the earth had to be the centre of the Universe because God had made it first. They based this belief on what it said in the Bible.

In the sixteenth century these beliefs were challenged. From reading the works of Aristotle and other Greek astronomers, people began to think that perhaps the earth circled the sun.

● Nicolaus Copernicus (1473-1543)

A Polish astronomer and priest named **Copernicus** studied the movement of the sun, moon and stars. He believed that the earth and the other planets in our solar system circled the sun. He also believed that the earth rotated on its own axis. He wrote a book called *On the Revolution of Heavenly Bodies* outlining his thoughts. It was only published near the end of his life because he was afraid that the Church would dislike his findings.

▲ Nicolaus Copernicus discovered that the earth circled the sun and rotated on its own axis.

● Galileo Galilei (1564-1642)

Galileo was born in Pisa, Italy in 1564, the same year as Shakespeare was born and Michelangelo died. He taught mathematics at the Universities of Pisa and later Padua, Italy. Galileo believed all things in nature could be explained by mathematics.

▲ Galileo Galilei was persecuted by the church because he did not believe that the sun orbited the earth.

FALLING BODIES

During his time in Pisa, he proved that all objects fell to earth at the same speed. This went against medieval opinion that the heavier the object the quicker it fell. Legend has it that he proved this by dropping two objects out of the leaning tower of Pisa.

GALILEO'S TELESCOPE

▲ The Tower of Pisa from which Galileo is said to have dropped two objects.

In 1608 a Dutchman named **Jan Lippershey** invented the **telescope** (a lens that magnifies objects so they appear to be much closer than they actually are) and upon hearing about the invention – and without ever seeing it – Galileo made his own telescope. Using this telescope he saw:

1. That the moon had mountains and craters.

2. The Milky Way was made up of many stars.

3. There were four moons circling around Jupiter.

These discoveries led him to believe that Copernicus was right.

▲ Having heard about Jan Lippershey's invention of a telescope, Galileo promptly made his own.

GALILEO'S TRIAL

His book called *Dialogue on the Two Chief World Systems* (1632) supported Copernicus's views. Galileo was asked to appear before the **Inquisition** (a court set up to question those who held views different to the Church) in Rome. The court claimed his beliefs were 'foolish and absurd'. The trial lasted several months and Galileo was worried he might be burnt at the stake if he was found guilty. He reluctantly agreed to say that his views were wrong. He was sent back to his house in Florence and was not allowed to leave it nor have any guests for the rest of his life. He went blind in 1637 and died five years later. In 1997, the Catholic Church officially recognised they had made a mistake in condemning Galileo.

▲ Galileo facing the Inquisition in Rome at which it was decided that he would be placed under house arrest for the rest of his life.

Questions

1. What did Ptolemy write about in *Geography*?

2. Why do you think the Church supported Ptolemy's views?

3. What was the new belief that Copernicus wrote about in his book?

4. Why did he only publish his book at the end of his life?

5. What was Galileo supposed to have proved when he dropped two objects from the tower in Pisa?

6. What invention allowed Galileo see the moon and the stars better?

7. What discoveries did Galileo make about the moon, stars and planets?

8. What did these discoveries lead him to realise?

9. Why was Galileo asked to go to Rome and what happened to him there?

RESULTS OF THE RENAISSANCE

1. New Discoveries

During the Renaissance people began to question the accepted beliefs of the Middle Ages. This questioning led to many new discoveries particularly in medicine, science and geography. These new discoveries spread to other parts of the world due to the invention of the printing press. These advances resulted in greater knowledge and new inventions. As we will see in the next chapter, people began to use these advances to explore the world around them more.

2. The idea of 'humanism'

In the Middle Ages people greatly feared death and viewed their lives simply as preparation for the afterlife. In the Renaissance people began to question this way of living. Greater importance was given to personal independence, enjoying life and expressing feelings whether through art or writing or sculpture. This new belief was called **humanism**. An important result of this new belief was people's questioning of the teachings of the Church. Some became unhappy with simply accepting what kings and popes told them to believe. In Chapter 7, The Reformation we will see the results of this unhappiness with the Church.

3. Spread of knowledge

During the Renaissance the printing press was invented. Books became cheaper and more widely available. This meant that more people learned to read and write. The increase in **literacy** (being able to read and write) helped to spread knowledge and ideas quickly across Europe.

4. Spread of ideas

Many of the ancient philosophers of Greece and Rome became popular during the Renaissance. Their ideas were spread throughout Europe in books. In this way, old ideas like democracy, republicanism and **liberty** (freedom) were revealed to more people than ever before. In Chapter 9, The Age of Revolutions we will see how these ideas resulted in huge changes throughout the eighteenth century in Europe and America.

5. Masterpieces

The Renaissance also gave us some of the most famous and beautiful works of art of all time. Artists and writers became admired, famous and sometimes wealthy. Da Vinci's *Mona Lisa*, Michelangelo's *David*, the Sistine Chapel and many more pieces of art are still viewed and admired by millions of people today.

Chapter 5 Questions

1. Pictures

(a) From this painting, give two pieces of evidence to show that it is a Renaissance painting

(b) Name one painter from outside Italy and two of his works.

2. Documents

Here the question arises: is it better to be loved than feared, or vice versa? I don't doubt that every prince would like to be both; but since it is hard to accommodate these qualities, if you have to make a choice, to be feared is much safer than to be loved. For it is a good general rule about men, that they are ungrateful, fickle, liars and deceivers, fearful of danger and greedy for gain . . . People are less concerned with offending a man who makes himself loved than one who makes himself feared: the reason is that love is a link of obligation which men,

because they are rotten, will break any time they think doing so serves their advantage; but fear involves dread of punishment, from which they can never escape.

From *The Prince* by N. Machiavelli

(a) What is the main question that Machiavelli is asking?

(b) What is the answer Machiavelli gives to this question?

(c) What does Machiavelli think about the character of men?

(d) Do you agree with Machiavelli's opinion of men?

3. Short-Answer Questions

(a) How did trading by Italian merchants contribute to the beginning of the Renaissance in Italy?

(b) How did the fall of Constantinople in 1453 influence the beginning of the Renaissance?

(c) Name a patron from the Renaissance that you have studied.

(d) How can paying visits to galleries and museums provide you with more information on the Renaissance?

(e) Name two differences in materials used by artists in the Renaissance and the Middle Ages?

(f) Give an example of the ways in which Renaissance artists made their paintings more realistic.

(g) What is the term for painting onto wet plaster on walls or ceilings?

(h) Name two pieces of art by Leonardo da Vinci AND two pieces by Raphael.

(i) What was the subject of Michelangelo's paintings on the ceiling of the Sistine Chapel?

(j) Name one other writer of the Renaissance apart from William Shakespeare.

(k) What is a telescope?

4. People in History

Write an account of a named **scientist** or **physician** during the Renaissance. Use the following headings as a guide:

- Name of person and early life
- His discoveries
- His beliefs and books he published

5.

(a) Give two results of the Renaissance.

(b) Some people believe that Gutenberg's invention of the moveable-type printing press was the greatest invention in Europe of all time.

Do you agree? Give reasons for your answer.

(c) Give a consequence of the invention.

(d) Write an account of two of the following aspects of the Renaissance:

(i) Painting

(ii) Science/ Medicine

(iii) Literature

(iv) Sculpture

Key Terms to Summarise Chapter 5: The Renaissance

Renaissance The period in Europe between the fourteenth and sixteenth centuries that saw a rebirth of art, literature and learning.

City-states Cities in Italy in the fifteenth century which ruled themselves and were very wealthy, e.g. Milan, Florence.

Patron A wealthy person who supported artists by commissioning paintings and sculpture.

Anatomy The study of the structure of humans, animals and plants.

Perspective A technique to show space and distance between objects in a painting.

Vanishing point The point in a painting from where all lines of perspective come.

Fresco A method of painting directly onto wet plaster.

Philosophy The study of how and why people exist in the world.

Botany The study of plants.

Sfumato A painting technique that blurs lines to create a 'smoky' effect.

Dissected To cut open a corpse (dead body) in order to examine it.

Dome A rounded roof built on a circular base.

Engraving Sketches on a copper plate.

Woodcuts Sketches on a piece of wood.

Moveable-type printing press Method discovered in 1450 of printing books by placing small letters made of metal into a frame which was then pressed onto the paper.

Vernacular The everyday language of people in each country.

Sonnets Rhyming poems of 14 lines in length. Shakespeare wrote 154 of them.

Machiavellian Able to use clever yet dishonest/deceitful ways to achieve a goal.

Bloodletting An ancient 'cure' of cutting a sick person's body to release 'bad blood'.

Telescope: A magnifying lens invented in 1608 by Jan Lippershey.

Humanism: A popular belief developed during the Renaissance that involved enjoying life, having personal independence and expressing emotions through art.

Web References

For further reading on topics mentioned in this chapter, view the following websites:

198.62.75.1/www1/sistine/0.Tour.html

www.rembrandthuis.nl

www.gutenbergdigital.de

www.the-tech.mit.edu/shakespeare/

https://www.nmwa.org/collection/profile.asp?LinkID=243

www.museoscienza.org/english/leonardo

Women in History

Lavinia Fontana (1552-1614)

The Visit of the Queen of Sheba to Solomon by Lavinia Fontana

In the sixteenth century it was very difficult for women to train to be artists. Despite this lack of training, there were some wonderful female artists during the Renaissance, such as Lavinia Fontana and Artemisia Gentileschi from Italy and Judith Leyster and Rachel Ruysch from the Netherlands.

Lavinia Fontana was born in Bologna in the north of Italy. She was the daughter of a leading artist of the city. In 1577 she married another wealthy artist named Gian Paolo Zappi. It soon became obvious that Lavinia was much more talented than her husband. He gave up being an artist and instead began to paint some of the backgrounds of his wife's paintings.

Most of her work was of portraits. One of her most famous paintings is called The Visit of the Queen of Sheba to Solomon (1600). It consists of a family portrait of the Gonzagas – the ruling family of Mantua, Italy. It is now in the National Gallery of Ireland. Her fame grew and she was soon asked to paint an altarpiece called Holy Family (1589) for the church in the Spanish royal palace. In 1603 she moved to Rome after Pope Clement VIII asked her to become the official painter to the Papal court. In Rome she continued to be employed to paint portraits and religious subjects.

During all this, Lavinia still managed to find time to have 11 children!

YEAR 2

Age of Exploration

A Europe in 1400

In 1400 people in Europe believed the world was much smaller than it really was. Most people, including sailors, believed that Europe was at the centre of the world and that one great sea surrounded the entire world. People thought huge monsters capable of swallowing whole ships existed in this sea. They also thought that the sea began to boil the farther south you travelled. Another fear was that the world was flat like a saucer and it was possible for a ship to simply fall off the edge of the world.

▲ A modern satellite image of the Nile Delta

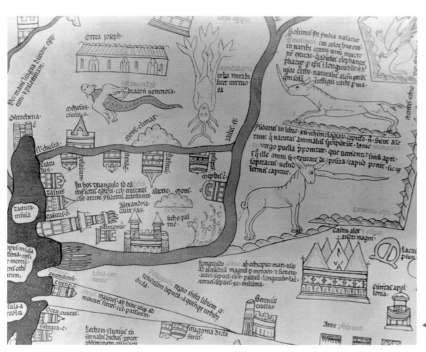

◀ A map of the Nile Delta drawn in the thirteenth century

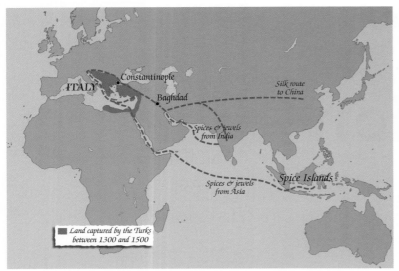

▲ The Great Silk Route before the Turks took over Constantinople. The Spice Islands was one of the best places to get the various spices used to preserve and flavour food in Europe.

Even though there was no accurate map of the world in existence in 1400, there were stories of journeys of many people to new lands. Between 1400 and 1750 Europeans travelled farther and learnt more about the world they lived in than ever before.

There were many reasons for this increased travelling, including:

1. Trade in Europe centred around the Mediterranean coast. Italian cities such as Genoa, Florence and Venice had made lots of money by trading with the Arabs. For many centuries products such as spices, jewels and silks were brought back from India and China along the **Great Silk Route**. Spices such as pepper, nutmeg, cloves, ginger and cinnamon were widely used in Europe to preserve and flavour food and also as medicines. The best place to get these spices was the **Spice Islands**, also known as the **Moluccas**, but these islands were on the other side of the world (see map). Traders were willing to bring the spices across many lands to get them to the populations of Europe because they were very profitable. However, after the Turks took over Constantinople in 1453 and expanded into neighbouring regions, this Great Silk Route became a very dangerous path for traders. This meant that Europeans were eager to find other routes to the Spice Islands, routes that did not go through hostile lands.

> **By the way . . .**
> Cloves were very popular in the Middle Ages as sucking on them numbed the mouth, helping to relieve the pain of toothaches. Even today the gel dentists rub onto patients' gums to numb them contains clove oil.

2. Many European rulers and Church leaders wanted to defeat the Muslims who lived in North Africa and the Middle East. This desire to spread the Christian religion meant that the explorers were ready to conquer and then convert any people they found in new lands. There was also a legend that a Christian king called Prester John lived in a kingdom on the other side of Arab lands and that if it was possible to find him a great alliance could be created among Christians against the Muslims.

3. The **monarchs** (royal leaders) of Europe also wanted to conquer more land. It was expensive to fight wars against other European countries, so it was easier to seek out new lands that had not yet been explored by Europeans and claim them for themselves. They also hoped that the explorers would find wealthy lands full of gold and goods with which to trade.

4. Previous explorers such as **Marco Polo** had written about their travels. The journeys and adventures they experienced seemed very exciting. As a result, many others wanted to follow in their footsteps.

1. Describe **two** things that sailors in the fifteenth century feared.
2. Name **four** items that were traded along the Great Silk Route and Europe.
3. Why did European monarchs want to find new lands?
4. Why did the Great Silk Route become so dangerous in the fifteenth century?
5. Who was Prester John and why did European monarchs want to find him?
6. True or False: (a) Europeans believed the world was much bigger than it really is.
   (b) European rulers wanted to conquer the Muslims living in North Africa.
   (c) The Moluccas were also known as the Spice Islands.
7. Name **two** purposes for spices in the 1400s and give examples.

Advances in Travel

● Maps

At the beginning of the fifteenth century, **cartographers** (people who draw maps) produced more detailed maps of Europe and the known world. The Portuguese used maps called *portolan* (which means harbour-finding) maps which were very detailed about the coastline. These *portolan* maps gave details about currents, sea depths and the best places to harbour a ship. This allowed sailors to plan their journeys better and therefore be more confident about reaching the places they wished to explore.

● Navigation

Sailors used compasses to show the direction in which they were sailing but old compasses were not always reliable. Even slight mistakes could result in a ship being miles out of position. New developments from this time allowed sailors to be far more accurate in their navigation (the guidance of ships from place to place).

▲ A *portolan* map of the Spice Islands

Sailors began to work out their latitude (their distance north or south of the equator) using instruments called **quadrants** and **astrolabes**. Both instruments measured the height of the sun or the north star above the horizon.

It was not until the seventeenth century that a **chronometer** was invented. This instrument can read the **longitude** of the ship (how many degrees east or west the ship is from a geographical point, usually the Greenwich Meridian in England).

▲ A quadrant measured the height of the sun or the north star above the horizon to work out their latitude.

To measure the speed of the ship, a sailor would throw out a piece of wood with a rope tied to it. A **knot** was tied in the rope at equal intervals and after one minute, the sailor would count how many knots had gone through his hands. Even today, a ship's speed is measured in 'knots per hour'.

If a ship was coming close to land, it had to be careful not to become grounded in shallow waters. Sailors would hang over the side and drop a line with a heavy lead weight into the water and measure the depth. The distance between two knots was known as a **fathom** (six feet or two metres in length) and this measurement is still used today.

Experience was also vital. Captains and sailors who had travelled certain routes understood the strength of the currents and winds. To help others, captains would write down the speed, distances and direction of the route they had travelled in a **logbook.** These logbooks were important in the spread of knowledge of newly explored areas.

▲ An astrolabe located and predicted the location of the sun, planets, moon and stars. This helped navigation.

Questions

1. What does the word *portolan* mean and why were these maps so important to sailors in the 1400s?

2. Explain the following words: (a) Longitude (b) Latitude (c) Fathom (d) Knot.

3. Match the instrument or development with the correct function:

   A Astrolabe   1 To record the movements of the ship

   B Logbook   2 To measure the longitude of the ship's position

   C Chronometer   3 To measure the latitude of the ship's position

By the way . . .

The opening lines of every episode of sci-fi series *Star-Trek* is 'Captain's log . . .' and then the date.

▲ Measuring the speed of the ship in 'knots per hour'

● Ships

At this time in the fifteenth century, there were also important improvements in shipbuilding. Around 1400, most ships built in Portugal and Spain had to be sturdy as they sailed in the rough Atlantic Ocean. One way of ensuring the ships were solid enough to withstand these rough seas was to make sure all ships were **clinker-built** which means that the wooden boards on the side of the ship overlapped. The wood used in these ships was very strong and the sails were all square in shape. As a result, these types of ship were strong but unable to turn quickly.

▲ A clinker-built ship had square sails and was built to withstand high seas.

The Italians were more interested in their ships being quick and agile to allow them to get into harbours in the calmer waters of the Mediterranean more easily. These ships had triangular sails called **lateens** to allow for quick changes in direction.

▲ A lateen ship used triangular sails for agility in the Mediterranean Sea.

Finally, the Portuguese brought the best of both these types of ship together into a **caravel**. The body of the ship was strong and durable but they used both square sails for power and triangular sails for manoeuvrability. After this breakthrough, ships were made bigger and stronger and finally a ship that was big enough to be used for storage was developed called a **carrack** or a **naos**.

▲ A caravel ship used both triangular and square sails.

Type of ship	Country that first used it	Sea in which it was used	Type of sail	Advantages
Lateen	Italy	Mediterranean	Triangular	Agile
Clinker-built	Portugal and Spain	Atlantic	Square	Strong
Caravel	Portugal	Anywhere	Triangular and square	Strong and agile
Carrack or Naos	Portugal	Atlantic	Triangular and square	Strong, agile and big for storage

Study this picture of a caravel used during the Age of Exploration and answer the questions below.

Questions

1. State how you can tell that this ship is a caravel.
2. Give **one** reason why it was more suited to longer voyages than other ships built during the Middle Ages.
3. Mention **two** dangers that faced sailors on journeys during the Age of Exploration.

● Life on the ship

Even with all the advancements in navigational skills there were still many dangers for sailors. Life was so difficult that captains brought more sailors than they needed because they knew many would die during each voyage. The new instruments were more accurate but they could still result in being hundreds of miles off course, especially in seas that had never been mapped. Shipwrecks due to storms or crashing into rocks were common and sailors were often washed overboard during bad weather.

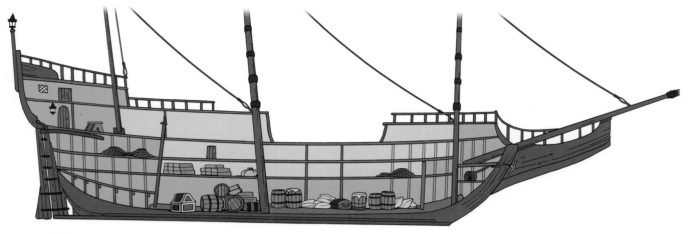

Sailors were expected to live in the hull of the ship with the cargo and so living conditions were very cramped. All cooking was done on deck in a **firebox** to stop the ship catching fire. On long journeys the food that wasn't dried or salted usually went bad. Often water became putrid (foul smelling and infected) and all fresh vegetables and fruit rotted. Even the **ship's biscuit** (a hard bread that didn't go stale) could become infested with worms. This poor diet meant that the crews regularly suffered from diseases such as **typhoid** (from bad water) and **scurvy** (from a lack of vitamin C – Read Source A below).

A chaplain (priest who travelled with the ship) on a seventeenth century ship describes the illnesses affecting the sailors:

Source A

During the winter, an illness attacked many of our people. It is called land-sickness, otherwise known as scurvy… There developed in the mouths of those who had it, large pieces of excess fungus flesh which caused a great rot. This increased to such a degree that they could hardly eat anything except in very liquid form. Their teeth barely held in place, and could be removed with the fingers without causing pain.

This excess flesh was often cut away, which caused them to bleed extensively from the mouth. Afterwards, severe pain developed in the arms and legs, which became swollen and very hard and covered with spots like fleabites. They could not walk due to the tightness of the nerves.

Consequently, they had almost no strength and suffered unbearable pain. They also had severe cramps in the loins, stomach and bowels, together with a very bad cough and shortness of breath. Unfortunately, we could find no remedy with which to cure these symptoms.

Voyages du Sieur de Champlain, Volume 1

Questions

1. Before the invention of the caravel, what type of ship did Portuguese sailors use and for what reason?
2. Give **one** reason why the lateen sail was more suitable for Italian sailors.
3. Describe **three** features of a caravel.
4. Read Source A.
   (a) What is the other name for scurvy according to the author?
   (b) Give **three** symptoms of scurvy.
5. Explain the following words:
   (a) Scurvy　　(b) Firebox
6. Imagine you are a sailor on a caravel ship in the fifteenth century. Give a description of what life was like on board. Mention the following:
   - The dangers you faced at sea.
   - The excitement of and the reasons for exploration.
   - The diseases from which some sailors suffered.

Portugal begins . . .

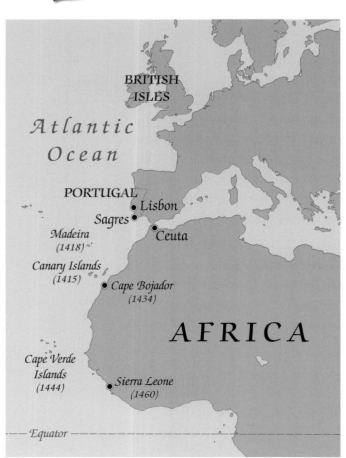

The Portuguese led the way in exploration for a number of reasons.

1. Portugal faces out towards the Atlantic Ocean making it more difficult to trade with the countries along the Mediterranean coast.

2. The Portuguese had been in conflict with the Moors (North African Muslims who had invaded Portugal) and had heard stories from the Moors of great wealth in Africa and also rumours of the legendary kingdom of Prester John. As a result, after driving the Moors from Portugal, the Portuguese became greatly interested in exploring further down the African coast.

3. The advances made by the Portuguese in navigation and ship-building enabled them to travel longer distances at sea.

◀ A map of Portugal and North Africa showing the locations in Africa which the Portuguese reached during the time of Henry the Navigator.

● Henry the Navigator (1394-1460)

Henry was the third son of King John I of Portugal. When he was made governor of the Algarve in Portugal, he decided to set up a navigational school at **Sagres** in 1420.

▲ Henry the Navigator

This school brought together the best mapmakers, shipbuilders and tradesmen in order to find a route to the east and to the Spice Islands by sailing around Africa. Many ships were sent along the African coast on exploratory missions by Henry. Each one kept records about the distances they travelled and mapped the coastline. The crews of these ships traded with the locals they encountered on their travels. When the crew got to the end of their journey, they placed **padroas** (large stone pillars) on the coastline for the next explorer to see.

By the time Henry died in 1460, Portuguese ships had travelled farther than ever before. They had passed **Cape Bojador** and sailed on towards the Senegal River and Sierra Leone. All along this coastline, the Portuguese were able to trade with the natives. Henry had to build warehouses in Sagres to store all the gold and slaves being brought back from newly discovered lands. Although Henry himself never travelled nor found the route around Africa, his explorations provided Portugal with great wealth and this encouraged more men to follow his example.

● Bartholomew Diaz (1450-1500)

The Portuguese named places along the African coast after the things they found there and this is how countries such as the Ivory Coast, the Grain Coast (now Liberia), the Gold Coast (now Ghana) and the Slave Coast (now Benin) got their names. In 1487 a sailor named **Bartholomew Diaz** set off with the intention of finding the southern cape of Africa. He sailed as far as the Orange River but he was then blown off course by a bad storm. He sailed eastwards to try to find land but when he found only open sea, he sailed northwards and eventually located a coastline. He realised he had found the cape and named it **The Cape of Storms**. When Diaz returned to Portugal, King John II decided to rename the cape **The Cape of Good Hope** as he hoped that this would be the route to the Spice Islands and did not want to discourage other sailors from using this route.

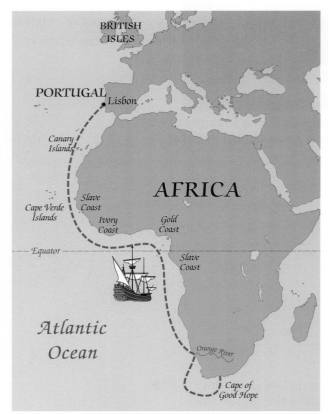

▲ A map of Bartholomew Diaz's trip on which he discovered the Cape of Storms, renamed by King John II as the Cape of Good Hope.

▲ Bartholomew Diaz sailed around the African Cape.

Questions

1. Give **three** reasons why the Portuguese were so eager to send out explorers to find lands.
2. Why do you think the Portuguese put *padroas* along the coast?
3. Explain how Henry the Navigator's School of Navigation influenced the exploration of the African coast.
4. List **two** items that Portuguese explorers brought back from Africa.
5. Why do you think the country of the Slave Coast changed its name?

● Vasco da Gama (1469-1524)

In 1497 another Portuguese sailor set out to find the route to the Spice Islands. His name was **Vasco da Gama** and he set sail on 8 July with four ships – a caravel (*Berrio*) and two naos (*San Gabriel* and *San Raphael*) and an even bigger boat that was abandoned along the African coast. Using the accurate maps that existed from Diaz's journey, da Gama was able to sail to the Cape of Good Hope very easily and landed on Christmas Day in a place they called Natal – which is Portuguese for Christmas. Da Gama and his crew travelled up the coast to modern-day Mozambique where they met an Arab trader whose name is thought to have been Ibn Majid.

▲ Vasco da Gama founded a route as far as Calicut in India.

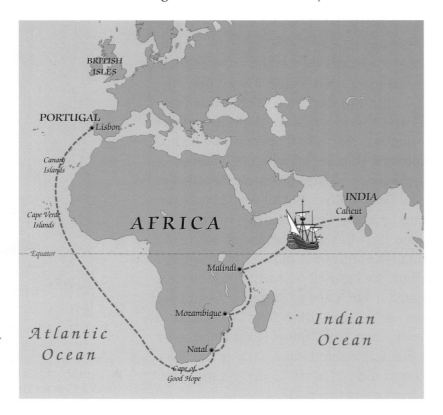

Vasco da Gama and his crew ▶ were the first to sail from Portugal to India via the Cape of Good Hope.

This trader knew the route to India and was able to give da Gama details of the sea-route. Da Gama and his ships arrived in Calicut in India on 20 May 1498. After purchasing many spices and precious jewels he headed home. After a very difficult journey that lasted more than three months da Gama returned to Portugal to a hero's welcome. During the voyage over half of his crew had died of scurvy and they had destroyed the *San Raphael* as there were not enough men to sail it. It had been a long and dangerous journey but after 80 years, Portugal had found the route to the East.

RESULTS OF THE PORTUGUESE EXPLORERS

1. The Portuguese travelled to the Spice Islands and became one of the wealthiest countries in Europe. They traded not only with the East but also with all the African countries along the route. Grain, gold, slaves, spices and jewels flowed into Portugal and this allowed them to finance more explorations.

2. Using superior weapons and soldiers, Portugal established an empire as many of the newly-discovered lands became Portuguese **colonies** (foreign lands that are owned by one country).

3. These explorations meant that other countries also wanted to create empires and gain great wealth. As we will see, one of the most successful countries to do so was Portugal's neighbour – Spain.

Questions

1. Match the discovery with the correct explorer:

   A Natal   1 Bartholomew Diaz

   B Calicut and India   2 Vasco da Gama

   C Cape of Storms

   D Orange River

2. Explain what a colony is and give an example.

3. Why did King John II of Portugal change the name of the Cape of Storms to the Cape of Good Hope?

4. Give two ways in which the explorations of the fifteenth century made Portugal a wealthier country.

5. Explain why Portugal's explorations inspired other countries to begin their own explorations.

Spain follows

▲ Christopher Columbus

● Christopher Columbus (1451-1506)

Columbus was born in the Italian city of Genoa in 1451. He grew up in a city that had an important **maritime** (something connected with the sea) tradition and was inspired by the journeys of another Italian – Marco Polo. After studying a map made by a cartographer named Toscanelli, Columbus estimated that **Cipangu** (Japan) and **Cathay** (China) were between 4,000 and 5,000 kilometres from Europe.

However, both Columbus and Toscanelli made a couple of mistakes. They estimated that the world was more than three times smaller than it really was and that nothing lay between Europe and Asia. Look at the maps below and examine how Columbus and Toscanelli got it wrong.

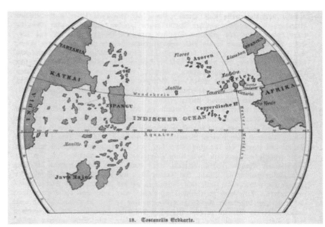

▲ Columbus used Toscanelli's map to plan his route to the east.

Columbus began to seek financial sponsorship for a trip to find a route to the east. Due to Portugal's advanced navigational skills and recent successes at discovering new lands, the obvious choice at that time was King John II of Portugal. However, John II turned Columbus down as he was more interested in finding the route to Asia by going around Africa. Columbus also asked the King of England but was again rejected. Columbus then turned to King Ferdinand and Queen Isabella of Spain. Initially they were not interested as Spain was involved in trying to beat back the occupation of Spain by the Moors of North Africa. Finally in 1492, after victory over the Moors, the king and queen agreed to finance a voyage westward.

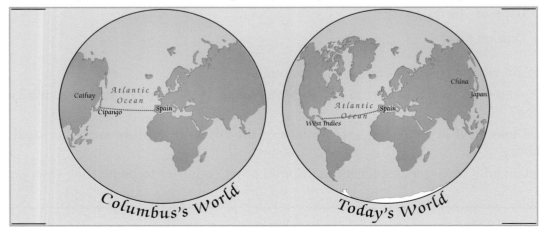

▲ Compare the world that Columbus believed existed with today's world. What are the differences?

Columbus began preparing for this adventure. He was given three ships – two caravels called the *Pinta* and the *Nina* and a nao called the *Santa Maria* which was to carry most of the provisions. Columbus was the captain of the *Santa Maria* while two brothers – Martin and Vincent Pinzon – captained the other ships. There were almost 90 crew members between the three ships. The supplies they brought included salted dried bread, strong wine, salted meat and fish. They set sail on 3 August 1492 from Palos in Spain and made their way to the Canary Islands where they took on board fresh food and water.

As Columbus headed westward he used the coordinates that Marco Polo had given for Cipangu. He hoped that it would not take too long to arrive at his destination and with favourable winds the ships made good speed. However, the crews were very nervous. Many were worried that they would meet dangerous sea creatures or fall over the edge of the world. Others thought they would find nothing and end up dying from starvation or scurvy. Columbus tried to keep their spirits up by telling them of the great riches they would find and by using two different logbooks. In one log he recorded the true distance they had travelled and in the other he recorded a shorter distance to make the crew less worried about how far from dry land they had travelled.

By the end of the fourth week without seeing any land, the crew demanded that they return to Spain. Columbus had to promise to return if no land was sighted in the next couple of days. On 11 October 1492, almost 70 days after leaving Spain, land was sighted and the next day Columbus went ashore on an island that he named **San Salvador** (which means Holy Saviour in Spanish). Columbus landed first and he placed a crucifix on the beach. He thought he had arrived in Cipangu and was confused when he did not find the great cities and civilisations that he had expected. He was met by friendly locals who wore gold necklaces and were fascinated by the Spanish sailors. He referred to these natives as Indians as he believed he had landed in India. He did not understand that he had landed on a new continent completely. In fact, Columbus had landed on the modern-day Caribbean Islands.

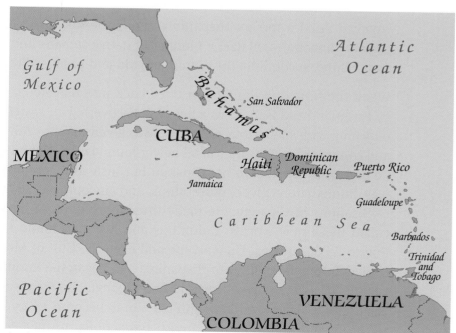

▲ A map of the Caribbean: Columbus first landed on the island of San Salvador, believing he had arrived in Cipangu.

Questions

1. Study Toscanelli's map and answer the following questions:
   (a) Why was the map of the west coast of Africa so detailed?
   (b) Mention **two** errors on the western side of the map.
   (c) Describe the principal fears of the sailors on Columbus's first voyage of discovery.
2. Why did Columbus think it was possible to reach the east by sailing west?
3. What mistakes did Columbus and Toscanelli make in their calculations?
4. Give **three** reasons why Columbus's crew were nervous about the voyage.
5. Why, do you think, did Columbus place a crucifix on the beach of San Salvador?

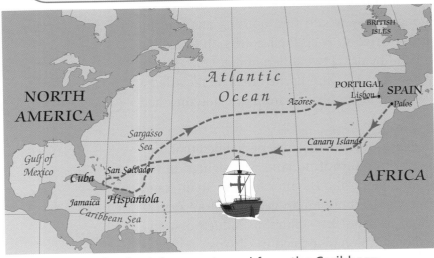

▲ A map of Columbus's journey to and from the Caribbean

He spent the following few months exploring the other islands around San Salvador including Cuba and **Hispaniola**, all the time under the impression that he had reached the East. He sent men into the interior of the islands searching for the great cities of Cipangu but found nothing. The *Santa Maria* was wrecked in a storm on Christmas Day 1492 and Columbus used the wood to build a fort on Hispaniola and made his way back to Spain with some parrots, pineapples, maize, a number of native Indians and a little gold. He left 40 men behind to continue the search for gold and promised to return within the year.

When the *Nina* and the *Pinta* arrived back into Barcelona, Columbus was greeted by Ferdinand and Isabella as a hero for discovering an eastern route to Cipangu and returning with such exotic riches. He was given the title 'Admiral of the Ocean Seas' and confirmed as Governor of all newly-found lands. Nobody realised that the lands he had discovered were not Cipangu but instead a completely new continent. He was immediately given more ships and encouraged to go back to find these civilisations of Cipangu. He made three more voyages back to the 'Indies' as he called these new worlds. Columbus and his crew found the islands of Trinidad, Puerto Rico, Jamaica, Guadeloupe and even the Gulf of Mexico. He brought many settlers from Spain to live in Hispaniola and began the farming of sugar cane on the island. He always hoped he would find Cipangu and the great wealthy cities of Asia. His desire to discover this wealth led him to become a very cruel man, mistreating, torturing and killing many natives. His actions meant he was removed from his position of Governor General of all newly-found lands and sent back to Spain in chains. He died in 1506 a very disappointed man.

RESULTS OF COLUMBUS'S JOURNEY

1. Columbus inspired more people to explore further. The prospect of new undiscovered lands encouraged explorers from all over Europe to join the expeditions.

2. The settlers he brought to these new lands were the first of many Europeans who would arrive in the New World with grave consequences for the native populations.

3. His voyage had shown the world that it was possible to head west and find land. Even though it was a new continent, his belief that you could sail west to reach the east would lead others to attempt it also. Columbus had discovered many new islands and lands in Central and South America. Years later, other explorers travelled up towards what is now the United States of America.

Questions

1. Why did the native people of the newly discovered lands become known as Indians?

2. Why was Columbus finally brought back to Spain in disgrace?

3. What influence did Columbus have on exploration?

4. What is your opinion of Columbus? Give reasons for your answer.

5. Imagine you are a sailor on Columbus's ship, the *Santa Maria*. Describe:
   (a) The difficulties you face and the fears you have about the voyage
   (b) The jobs you have to do
   (c) The excitement of the discoveries

6. Write a short account of Columbus's life including:
   (a) His early life
   (b) His attempts to get sponsorship
   (c) His first voyage westward
   (d) His later life

More explorers followed Columbus's route. An Italian called **Amerigo Vespucci** (1451-1512) worked for Spain. He travelled along the coastline of South America and realised that it was a new continent that Europeans had simply not known about. He wrote about his journeys and became famous. The continents of North and South America are named after his first name.

With this discovery, Spain came into conflict with the other great country of exploration – Portugal. To ensure that this did not end in war, Pope Alexander VI encouraged the two countries to sign an agreement. The **Treaty of Tordesillas** in 1494 agreed that a line would be drawn down the Atlantic Ocean 370 leagues west of the Cape Verde Islands. All land discovered west of this line was Spanish while all land

▲ Amerigo Vespucci, after whom America is named.

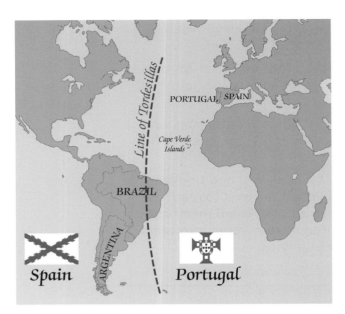

▶ A map of the world showing the Treaty of Tordesillas.

found east of this was Portuguese.

This meant that in 1500 when the Portuguese sailor Pedro Cabral (1467-1519) was blown off course near Africa and landed along the coast of South America, he was able to claim this part of the continent for Portugal. The land was full of brazil-nut trees and so the land was named Brazil. This explains why in Brazil the people still speak Portuguese while the rest of South America speaks Spanish.

Questions

1. Why were the newly discovered lands called after Amerigo Vespucci and not after Christopher Columbus?
2. What countries was the Treaty of Tordesillas between and what did it decide?
3. Why do the people of Brazil speak Portuguese and not Spanish?

▲ Ferdinand Magellan who led the longest and most difficult journey during the Age of Exploration.

● Ferdinand Magellan (1480–1521)

Columbus's expedition is probably the most famous of the period but the longest and most difficult was that of Ferdinand Magellan. Born the son of a Portuguese nobleman in 1480, Magellan fell in love with sailing. Prior to 1518, he had been part of a number of expeditions to the East and captained the first European ship to sail to the Spice Islands. He believed that it was possible to find a route by sailing westward and he proposed this idea to King Charles V of Spain. In 1518 Charles gave him the job of finding the Spice Islands of the East by sailing west. He was given five naos that were badly in need of repair. They were the *Santiago, Victoria, Concepcion, San Antonio* and his flagship the *Trinidad*. It took over a year to repair these ships but on 20 September, 1519 Magellan and his crew set sail from Seville.

His crew of roughly 270 sailors were mostly Spanish. Three of the other ships were captained by Spaniards. This resulted in a lot of tension between Magellan and these men as they were jealous and suspicious of a Portuguese man leading a Spanish expedition. However, he was able to trust the captain of the *Santiago*, Juan Serrano as he was also Portuguese. Magellan brought

▲ Magellan and his crew

with him food for two years, cannons, swords, crossbows and knives in case of battles and mirrors and bells for trading.

Magellan sailed along the coast of Africa and then turned westward and down the South American coastline. They wintered at the mouth of a river that they named Rio de Janeiro (river of January) before travelling further down to Port St. Julian. Here the Spanish captains **mutinied** (tried to take over the command of the expedition) but Magellan just about managed to keep control. Two of the captains who mutinied were killed while the third was left behind in Port St. Julian. The rest of the mutineers surrendered, the last one being Sebastian del Cano from the *Concepcion*.

Magellan now sent the *Santiago* down the coast of South America looking for *El Paso* (the passageway) to the Great South Sea. Unfortunately the ship was driven onto rocks and all the men had to swim to the shore before walking back to Port St Julian. Now with four ships, Magellan followed the coast along Patagonia (named after the **patagons** or 'people with big-feet' that inhabited the area) in the south of Argentina until they came to a wide estuary. Finally they found a small passageway through. The ships began a very slow and careful journey through the narrow strait and eventually they reached the Great South Sea. Magellan was so overjoyed that they had made it through the dangerous passageway that he named the end of the strait Cape Desire as it was what he had always desired. These straits are known as the **Magellan Straits** today in honour of his achievement. This joy was short-lived as he realised that the *San Antonio* had decided to desert the expedition and return to Spain. This was a blow as the *San Antonio* was the biggest ship and carried most of the food. Magellan decided to continue his exploration nevertheless.

After the rough weather that Magellan and his crew had endured they were delighted to find the Great South Sea was wonderfully calm. For this reason Magellan named it the **Pacific Ocean.** Unfortunately the ocean was so calm and peaceful that for three months they sailed without getting any wind. During this period many men died of starvation and disease, particularly scurvy.

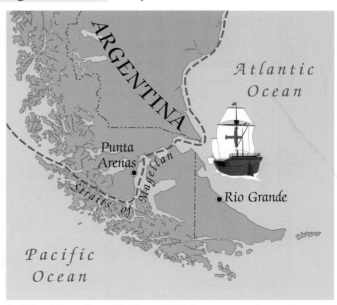

▲ The Magellan Straits provide a route from the Atlantic Ocean to the Pacific Ocean.

On board the ships was one sailor who kept a diary of the events of this voyage. His name was Antonio Pigafetta. From his diary we can follow the events of the journey.

Source B

We were three months and twenty days without any kind of fresh food. We ate what were supposed to be biscuits, but they were really powdered crumbs, swarming with worms and stinking of rats' urine. The water we drank had turned yellow. Nineteen men died of scurvy. I really think the likes of this voyage will be never be seen again.

By the way . . .

When some of the natives of an island were accused of stealing Spanish supplies, Magellan named the islands the Ladrones Islands (Islands of Thieves). They are now called the Mariana Islands.

Eventually, on 6 March 1521, they came to the island of Guam. They went ashore only to be attacked by natives. Next they came to a number of smaller islands that Magellan named the Philippines after King Charles' son Philip. As Magellan was trying to convert the natives of these islands to Christianity he found an island that refused to listen and attacked Magellan and his men as they landed. Magellan was wounded in the face as he retreated and then hit in the arm and leg before being killed by numerous blows. Pigafetta describes the incident:

Source C

*1500 natives of **Mactan** had formed three divisions on the shore. When they saw us coming they charged at us with loud cries, one division in front and one on either side of us. They fired arrows and bamboo spears, as well as pointed stakes and stones so that we could hardly defend ourselves...*

When our Admiral was shot through the right arm with a poisoned arrow, he ordered our men to retreat slowly. But the natives continued to attack us in the water, picking up the same spear five or six times and hurling it at us again and again...

The Admiral then tried to take out his sword, and when the enemy saw this they charged at him and wounded him in the left leg. This caused our leader to fall face downwards into the water. Then they charged at him again with bamboo spears and cutlasses until they had killed our mirror, our light, our comfort and our true guide.

▲ The death of Magellan

Questions

1. What weapons did the natives have?
2. Who was the 'Admiral'? Do you think that Pigafetta admired him? Give reasons for your answer.
3. How did the 'Admiral' die?

With their captain dead, the crew decided to leave the Philippines and find the Spice Islands. The *Concepcion* was no longer seaworthy and so they transferred all valuables into the two remaining ships. They finally landed on the Spice Islands in November 1521. They bartered for as much as they could and were about to leave when they realised the *Trinidad* was leaking. It was decided that the *Victoria*, with Sebastian del Cano – the former mutineer – as captain would return to Spain alone. Forty-seven men set sail, leaving the remainder in the Spice Islands. The journey home was very difficult as they sailed through Portuguese waters and many of the crew died of starvation and the heat.

On 6 September, 1522, the *Victoria* arrived into Seville. Of the five ships and 270 sailors that set sail over four years earlier, one ship and 18 men survived to tell the story of the voyage. This was one of the greatest and toughest sea voyages ever made. The first **circumnavigation** (going completely around) of the world had been achieved proving that the world was actually round rather than flat, as had previously been believed. Pigafetta wrote that 'coatless and barefooted and with lighted candles we went to the Shrine of Our Lady of Victory to give thanks. We had sailed 14,460 leagues (69,408 kilometres) and completed the circuit of the world.'

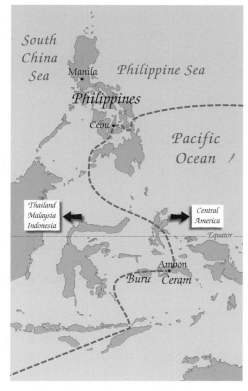

▲ After Magellan was killed near Cebu, the expedition travelled to the Spice Islands before sailing back to Spain.

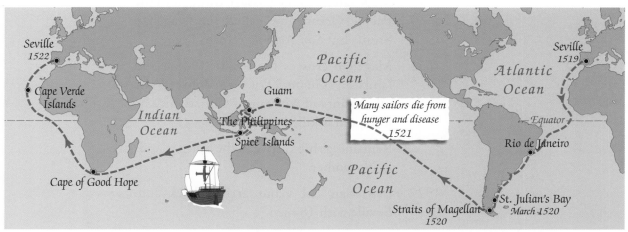

▲ A map of the full journey of the Magellan Expedition – the first circumnavigation of the world (1519–1522).

Questions

1. What difficulties did Magellan face when he decided that he wanted to sail westward to the Spice Islands?

2. Who was Antonio Pigafetta and why is he important to this voyage?

3. Give four problems Magellan had to deal with during the expedition.

4. Why was the Great South Sea renamed the Pacific Ocean?

5. What does the term circumnavigation mean?

6. Why was the success of Magellan's expedition so important?

FERDINAND MAGELLAN
⌦ EXPLORER ⌫

Born: 1480, Portugal

Died: 1521, Mactan

Key Events: 1518 – Charles V of Spain gives him the job of finding the Spice Islands by sailing to the east.

1519 – Magellan sets sail with five ships: *Santiago, Victoria, Concepcion, San Antonio* and *Trinidad*

1520 – Mutiny by Spanish captains at St. Julian's Bay. *Santiago* is wrecked as it looks for passage to the western ocean. Finally Magellan finds the passage through to the Pacific Ocean now called the Magellan Straits but *San Antonio* returns home.

1521 – Magellan crosses the Pacific Ocean and lands in Guam. Tries to convert the inhabitants of Mactan to Christianity by force and is killed in battle.

Remaining ships arrive in the Spice Islands in November

1522 – Sebastian del Cano arrives back into Seville with 18 men.

The Conquistadores

With so many stories of riches to be found in new and unexplored lands, there were many people in Europe who wanted to find adventure and wealth. These men who followed the first explorers became known as the *conquistadores*, which is Spanish for the conquerors. These men were ruthless leaders whose mission was to find the legendary cities of gold supposed to be on the South American mainland. There were many *conquistadores* but in this chapter we will examine the two most famous.

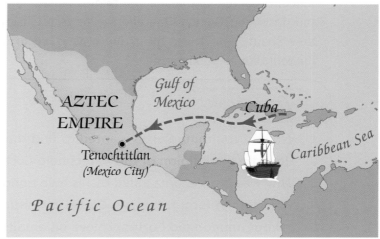

▲ A map of the Aztec Empire

● Hernando Cortés (1485-1547)

Cortés was a Spanish soldier who settled in the New World. He was living in Cuba when the opportunity arose to lead an expedition onto the mainland of Mexico. It was said that a mighty civilisation called the **Aztecs** existed in Mexico and Cortés wanted to find it. In February 1519 he landed on the coast of Mexico with 500 men and 16 horses. After burning the ships to show his men that there was no turning back, Cortés made his way inland.

▲ The Aztec city of Tenochtitlan

Cortés found a beautiful city called **Tenochtitlan** (pronounced te-noch-tee-tlahn) located on an island in the middle of a lake with canals, great temples and fresh water supplying almost 250,000 people. The Aztecs were able to read and write and were very advanced. Their religion demanded human sacrifices and for this they used people they captured from neighbouring tribes. They also believed that their god **Quetzalcoatl** (pronounced ket-sal-ko-aht-l) had prophesised that he would return to them one day.

▲ Hernando Cortés

When they saw Cortés on his horse, which they thought to be some form of monster, the king **Montezuma** (pronounced mont-e-zu-ma) greeted him as their god, Quetzalcoatl. This was very successful until Cortés's men began to steal any gold they found. The Aztecs realised what had happened and threw the Spanish out and killed their king Montezuma for letting Cortés into the city.

▲ The Aztec god Quetzalcoatl

Cortés returned in 1521 with an army of 100,000 men, mostly from local tribes that had been conquered by the Aztecs and disliked them. After a three-month siege, Tenochtitlan fell and heads and bodies filled the lake as Cortés massacred the Aztecs and destroyed Tenochtitlan and the Aztec civilisation. Cortés was made Governor of New Spain, which was the name now given to Mexico, and he decided to rebuild Tenochtitlan as Mexico City.

Questions

1. Why do you think Cortés wanted to find the Aztec civilisation?
2. How did the religion of the Aztecs help Cortés?
3. Why was Montezuma killed by his own people?
4. Why did the local tribes join Cortés in fighting the Aztecs?
5. In your opinion did Cortés achieve his ambitions?

▲ Francisco Pizarro

● Francisco Pizarro (1475-1541)

It was believed that another civilisation existed south of the Aztecs in the South American continent. The Incas of modern-day Peru were even more advanced than the Aztecs. They were a peaceful civilisation with a good system of government and administration. They had developed an advanced level of engineering, especially in terms of roads and buildings, and created beautiful and ornate art. Pizarro set sail for Peru with 180 men and 27 horses. Even with this small number Pizarro was able to defeat the peaceful Incas at Cajamarca and captured their leader **Atahualpa** using their superior weapons. Atahualpa was known as 'the Inca' and his people believed he was descended from the sun-god. The Incas offered to fill a room with gold and silver as a ransom for their leader but even when this was done Pizarro strangled and killed Atahualpa anyway.

Pizarro now marched on the capital city of Cuzco and easily defeated the remaining armies of the Incas. He established a new capital at Lima and the Incan empire was renamed New Castile. Later the Spanish discovered gold and silver in the Andes Mountains. This discovery helped Spain become one of the wealthiest countries in the world. Pizarro's success and his wealth made many people resent him and he was murdered by his own men in 1541.

▲ A map of Peru showing the extent of the Inca Empire.

RESULTS OF CONQUESTS

1. Many other men from other countries were inspired by the stories of discovering new lands. English explorers travelled to North America and later India, the Middle East and Australia and the French explored modern-day Canada and parts of Africa. The Dutch explorers also sought new lands, especially in the East Indies (Indonesia) and Africa. Over the next 300 years most of the world was explored, mapped and colonised by the European powers.

2. These European countries became very wealthy by creating these new empires. Spain, Portugal, France, Britain and Holland all increased their power and wealth through exploitation of the New World. Trading gold and silver, spices and silks, slaves and new produce like tobacco, pineapples, chocolate and potatoes made these countries extremely wealthy.

3. As these Atlantic-facing countries gained in wealth and power, the countries in the Mediterranean began to lose their importance. The Italian cities of Florence, Venice and Genoa became secondary to the huge ports of Amsterdam, Lisbon, London and Seville.

4. The European culture became dominant. Native languages died out as the European languages were used for government. Almost all the great civilisations of South America, Asia and Africa were destroyed by European exploration and exploitation. Millions of native Indians died over the next century as they were forced to work in the gold and silver mines. They were very badly treated and many died from the European diseases such as influenza that were brought over by Europeans. By the end of the sixteenth century, almost all of the native population of Mexico had died. Those who survived were encouraged to become Christian either through persuasion or by force.

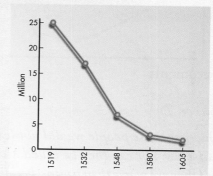

▲ Graph showing the decline in the size of the native population in South America.

5. Slavery became a huge business during this period. The farms of sugar beet, tobacco, cotton and coffee and the silver and gold mines of South America were worked by thousands of slaves, mostly from Africa. It is estimated that maybe 10 – 12 million Africans were sold into slavery to work on the farms and mines of the Europeans.

Chapter 6 Questions

1. Pictures

Study the map on the following page and answer the questions that follow.

(a) (i) Name the leader of each of the voyages of exploration marked A, B and C.

   (ii) Identify the straits marked X
Identify the cape marked Y
Identify the islands marked Z

  (iii) Name the civilisation in the area marked 1 that was conquered by Hernando Cortés in 1521.

  (iv) Name the civilisation in the area marked 2 that was conquered by Francisco Pizarro in 1531.

(b) (i) Give one reason why the voyage of exploration marked C took place some years after the voyage of exploration marked B.

  (ii) Name the rulers of Spain who sponsored the voyage of exploration marked B.

(c) Select one of the voyages of exploration A or B or C, or any other exploration of your choice, and discuss:

  (i) Why the exploration was undertaken.

  (ii) The main consequences/results of the exploration.

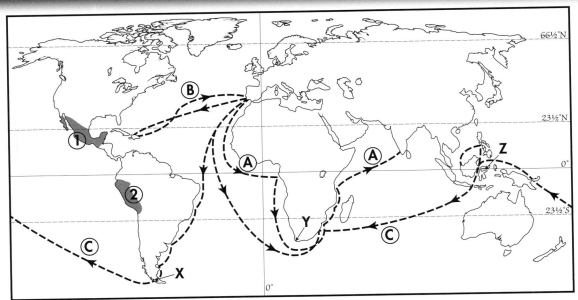

2. Documents

Source D

Amongst those people we did not learn that they had a law, nor can they be called Moors nor Jews and they are worse than pagans: because we did not observe that they offered any sacrifice: nor even have they a house of prayer: their manner of living I judge to be luxurious: their dwellings are in common: all over with palm-leaves, secure against storms and winds: and in some places [they are] of so great breadth and length, that in one single house we found there were 600 souls: and we saw a village of thirteen houses where there were four thousand souls: every eight or ten years they change their habitations: and when asked why did so: [they said it was] because of the soil which, from its filthiness, was already unhealthy and corrupted, and that it bred aches in their bodies, which seemed to us a good reason... in fine, they live and are contented with that which nature gives them.

The wealth that we enjoy in this our Europe is elsewhere, such as gold, jewels, pearls, and other riches, they hold as nothing: and although they have there in their own lands, they do not labour to obtain them, nor do they value them.

This is an extract from an account written by Amerigo Vespucci (1452 – 1512). It is about his first voyage in 1497. It describes one of the tribes living in the land that he had discovered. Read the extract and then answer the following questions.

(a) Give one reason why Vespucci said that the people whom he had discovered were 'worse than pagans'.

(b) Why did they change 'their habitations' every eight to ten years?

(c) What is the difference in attitude to wealth between the Europeans and the people described in the extract?

(d) Give two reasons why the rulers and merchants of European countries were prepared to sponsor voyages of exploration such as that of Amerigo Vespucci.

3. Short-Answer Questions

(a) Explain why there was such a demand for spices in Europe around the year 1500.

(b) For what purposes were two of the following used during the Age of Exploration?

   (i) Compass   (iii) Astrolabe

   (ii) *Portolan* charts   (iv) Log and Line

(c) Look at these three maps. Put them into chronological order.

(i)

(iii)

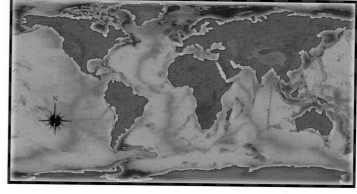

(ii)

Correct order:

☐ ☐ ☐

4. People in History

Write about a native of a land discovered by Europeans during the Age of Exploration using the following hints:

- Name the civilisation
- Outline the European invasion
- Describe the consequences of the invasion.

(d) Name the European country which discovered the sea route to India around the year 1500.

(e) Name the ruler who sponsored the first circumnavigation of the world.

(f) Name the captain who led that voyage around the world.

(g) From your reading of the conquests of the Aztecs and the Incas, what is your opinion of the Conquistadores? Give three reasons for your answer.

(h) What was the reason for the decline in importance of the ports of Genoa, Florence and Venice during the sixteenth century?

(i) Why, in your opinion, were the European explorers able to defeat the Inca and Aztec civilisations so easily?

(j) Name three products that explorers brought back to Europe from the New World.

(k) Give two reasons why the native population of South America declined during the Age of Exploration.

5. Exploration

(a) Give two reasons why rulers were prepared to sponsor voyages of exploration.

(b) Give one reason why the development of the caravel helped to make possible voyages of discovery.

(c) Name two instruments that helped sailors to navigate while at sea during the Age of Exploration.

(d) Write an account of Portugal's contribution to the Age of Exploration.

(e) 'Europe benefited, while the newly discovered lands and their peoples were exploited terribly.'

Do you agree? Write an account explaining your answer.

Key Terms to Summarise Chapter 6: Age of Exploration

Great Silk Route The main trading route between China and the East and Europe. This road passed through modern-day Turkey, Iran and Iraq.

Spice Islands Modern islands of Indonesia and the Philippines which were rich with spices and herbs.

Moluccas Another name for the Spice Islands.

Monarchs A royal leader of a country, e.g. a king or queen.

Cartographers People who draw and produce maps.

Portolan Maps of the coastline designed to help sailors find safe harbours

Quadrants & Astrolabes Instruments measuring the height of the sun or the North Star above the horizon.

Chronometer Instrument to measure the distance east or west from a geographical point. Invented in the seventeenth century.

Longitude The distance (east or west) something is from a fixed geographical point.

Knot The unit used to measure the speed of a ship.

Fathom The unit used to measure the depth of the water.

Logbook A daily diary kept by the captain of the ship detailing the journey of the ship.

Clinker-built A method of ship-building which used over-lapping wooden boards on the sides of the ship to provide strength.

Lateens Triangular sails used on ships to increase manoeuvrability.

Caravel A type of ship used originally by the Portuguese. It was clinker-built but it used both square and triangular sails.

Carrack/Naos A larger type of caravel that was developed to be used for storage.

Typhoid A disease associated with dirty water.

Scurvy A disease associated with the lack of vitamin C in the diet.

Sagres A town in the south of Portugal where Henry the Navigator established his navigational school.

Padroas Large stone pillars that were placed along the coast to mark the furthest distance travelled by explorers down the African coast.

Cape Bojador The most westerly point of the African coast; passed by the Portuguese in 1460.

Cape of Storms The name given to the most southerly point of Africa by Bartholomew Diaz.

Cape of Good Hope The replacement name given to the Cape of Storms by King John II of Portugal.

Colonies Foreign lands that a country claims to own.

Maritime Anything connected in some way to the sea.

Cipangu The name given in the 1500s to Japan.

Cathay The name given in the 1500s to China.

San Salvador An island in the Caribbean and the location of the first landing of Columbus in 1492.

Hispaniola The name given to the island of modern Haiti and the Dominican Republic; Columbus built a fort there before returning to Spain.

Treaty of Tordesillas An agreement made in 1494 between the Portuguese and Spanish dividing up the New World so as to avoid conflict. Spain took all new lands found west of this line and Portugal all lands east.

Mutiny When the crew of a ship try to remove the captain of the boat and take over its command.

Patagons This word literally means 'people with big feet' from the southern part of modern Argentina now called Patagonia.

Magellan Straits The name given to the route at the southerly cape of South America.

Pacific Ocean The name given to the ocean to the west of the American continents due to its calm waters.

Mactan The name of the island where Ferdinand Magellan was killed.

Circumnavigation To fly, sail or walk around something; to sail around the world.

Conquistadores A Spanish word meaning conquerors; the explorers who conquered large areas of Central and South America.

Aztecs People from the ancient civilisation of modern Mexico.

Tenochtitlan Capital of the Aztec civilisation.

Web References

For further reading on topics mentioned in this chapter view the following websites:

www.bbc.co.uk/schools/famouspeople/standard/columbus

www.mariner.org/educationalad/ageofex

www.nmm.ac.uk

www.aztecs.org.uk

//mexico.udg.mx/historia

www.pbs.org/conquistador

Women in History

Mary Henrietta Kingsley

(1862-1900)

Born in England, Kingsley stayed at home and looked after her invalid mother and father until they died in 1892. She then immediately set off for Africa, travelled along the African coast from Sierra Leone to Guinea and journeyed inland to modern-day Nigeria before returning to England. In 1894 she returned to Africa and became the first European to explore parts of Gabon and Congo, and also climbed Mount Cameroon, the tallest mountain in West Africa before returning to England the next year. In 1899 she returned to Africa for the last time as a nurse and journalist during the Boer War (between Britain and the Afrikaners of South Africa). During her explorations of Africa she wrote a book entitled *Travels in West Africa* in which, controversially for the time, she criticised the inhumane actions of many Europeans to the native populations. She died, aged 38, in 1900 from typhoid fever and was buried at sea.

▲ Kingsley's canoe on the Ogowe River in Gabon, west Central Africa.

The Reformation

The Church in Europe in 1500

The majority of the population of Europe at the beginning of the sixteenth century was Christian. At that time in Europe, being a Christian meant being a Catholic. There was no division within the Catholic Church – yet – and all Christians accepted that the leader of the Catholic Church was the Pope in Rome. The Church was very wealthy and had great power over the populations of Europe. However the Church faced many challenges. For example, although ordinary Christians carried out many good deeds throughout Europe (e.g. looking after the poor and sick) not all **clergy** (priests, bishops, archbishops, cardinals and monks) were as committed to doing good as they should have been. In this chapter we will examine the reasons why the clergy became so corrupt and why this corruption and abuse of power resulted in an important movement that hoped to reform the Church and improve it.

The changes that occurred during this period became known as the **Reformation** (the reforming or improving of something).

The Catholic Church is structured like a pyramid:

 The Pope: He is the leader of the Catholic Church on earth. He appoints cardinals, archbishops and bishops and makes decisions on how the Church is run. He is elected by cardinals and remains Pope until he dies.

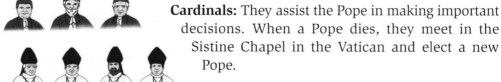 **Cardinals:** They assist the Pope in making important decisions. When a Pope dies, they meet in the Sistine Chapel in the Vatican and elect a new Pope.

Bishops: They are in charge of the administration and running of areas called dioceses. These are the administrative areas into which the Church divides countries, e.g. the Dioceses of Dublin, Kells etc.

Priests: Within each diocese there are different parishes. Each parish has a priest in charge of the day-to-day work of the Church, for example saying mass, carrying out weddings and funerals of the congregation.

Monks and **nuns** live in monasteries and convents and devote their lives to God. They often help with the poor and the sick of their neighbourhood.

● Reasons for the Reformation

1. THE WEALTH OF THE CATHOLIC CHURCH

By the sixteenth century the Catholic Church owned huge amounts of land throughout Europe. In fact, in Germany it was estimated that it owned approximately one third of all the land in that country. Many Church leaders (e.g. bishops, archbishops) lived in enormous palaces or monasteries. They received an annual tax from all farmers in their diocese, which amounted to one tenth of each farmer's harvest. This tax was called the **tithe**. This allowed many of the clergy to live in great luxury. Many ordinary people resented this luxury, while some of the monarchs of Europe were jealous of the power and wealth of the Church.

▲ A political map of Europe in 1500: As you can see, almost all of Europe was Christian and the Pope had a huge amount of political power.

2. ABUSES OF POWER WITHIN THE CHURCH

The priests, bishops and popes sometimes used the wealth of the Church to influence political life in Europe. They were even willing to go to war to gain more power and land. As a result, some people decided to join the Church in order to gain wealth and power rather than to serve God. In turn, this meant members of the clergy neglected their duties as they were more interested in becoming wealthy and powerful than in carrying out the duties of a priest or bishop. Some examples of this are:

(a) Absenteeism

Some of the priests did not live near their parishes and so the population of these parishes did not have any mass for months at a time. In addition, there could be no marriages or funerals until the priest chose to visit his parish.

(b) Pluralism

Each member of a parish was expected to pay a contribution towards the priest. So the more parishes a priest had, the more money he could earn. To priests who were corrupt, it did not matter that the distances between parishes meant that they could not physically visit their parishes very often and provide services.

> **By the way . . .**
> Nepotism comes from the Greek word **nepos** meaning nephew.

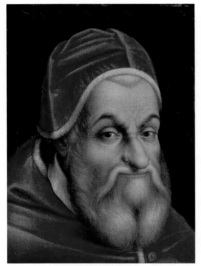

▲ Pope Sixtus IV appointed six of his nephews and cousins as cardinals.

(C) Simony

The potential wealth that could be earned by being a priest meant that the job became very sought after. Some people became priests even though they had no interest in religion at all. Bishops and even popes accepted money in return for giving someone a position in the Church.

(D) Nepotism

To help family members, men with power in the Church would often appoint their family or relations to positions within it.

(E) Indulgences

The Catholic Church believed that ordinary people's souls went to a place called **purgatory**. Purgatory was a place of great suffering for souls. When a soul had been cleansed through punishment it became fit for heaven. To speed up this process people could pray, go to mass or give money to the Church. This was called an **indulgence**. The more money a person gave, the less time their soul had to wait before entering Heaven. This meant that it seemed as if rich people, no matter what bad deeds they had done in their lives, could get to heaven before poor people.

▲ A member of the clergy, John Tetzel, seated at a table selling indulgences in a market square in Germany in 1517.

3. OTHER LOW STANDARDS

While the Church expected high standards of its **congregations**, many members of the clergy failed to live up to these expectations.

(a) Many lived with women and had families despite their vows of celibacy (not marrying). Pope Innocent VIII's son carried out his father's wishes by taking part in an arranged marriage to Lorenzo de Medici's daughter. Pope Innocent VIII also made Lorenzo's 13-year-old son a cardinal. This boy later became Pope Leo X.

(b) Other popes were interested mostly in gaining more land, and therefore power, for the Church. Pope Julius II spent so much time at war that he became known as the Warrior Pope.

▲ Pope Leo X was the son of Lorenzo de Medici.

4. THE RENAISSANCE

The influence of the Renaissance meant people in Europe began to question the accepted rules of the Church.

(a) Due to the translation of the Bible from Latin into different languages, anyone who was literate could read the Bible for themselves. Some people disagreed with interpretations of the Bible made by the Catholic Church.

(b) The invention of the printing press also meant that people could spread new ideas very quickly across Europe. These people decided that what was needed was a reform or improvement of the Church. One of these people was a German from Saxony called Martin Luther.

▲ Pope Julius II was also known as the Warrior Pope.

Questions

1. What duties did the parish priest have?
2. What was the tithe?
3. Explain the following words:
   (a) Absenteeism
   (b) Pluralism
   (c) Nepotism
4. What were indulgences?
5. According to the Catholic Church, what happened to people's souls in purgatory?
6. How could rich people's souls get to heaven before poor people's souls?
7. What influence did the Renaissance have on people's opinion of the Church?

Martin Luther (1483-1546)

Martin Luther was born into a Christian family in Eisleben, Saxony in Germany in 1483.

▲ Martin Luther

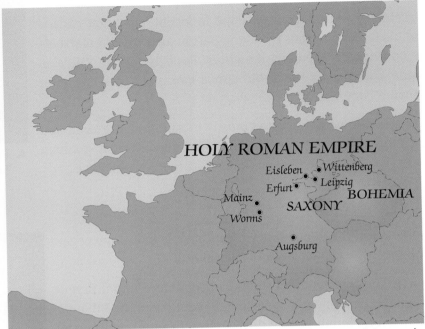

HOLY ROMAN EMPIRE

Eisleben • • Wittenberg
Erfurt • • Leipzig
Mainz • SAXONY BOHEMIA
Worms •

Augsburg •

▲ A map from the 1400s showing the main German cities and lands involved in the Lutheran Reformation.

By the way . . .

Luther became a monk after making a promise to St. Anne to save him from a terrible storm. When he survived it, he kept his promise and joined the Augustinian monks.

His father, a copper miner, was reasonably wealthy and so was able to provide his son with a good education. At the age of 17 Martin Luther went to study law at the University of Erfurt. He received his Bachelors of Arts degree one year later and then his Masters three years after that. Therefore, his family, who had hoped he would become a lawyer, was surprised when he announced that he wanted to become an Augustinian monk. He was sent by the Augustinian monastery to study **theology** (the study of God, religion and religious beliefs) in Wittenberg and soon became a Professor of Theology at the university there.

● Justification by Faith Alone

Luther's studies led him to question the teachings of the Catholic Church. He doubted that people could find **salvation** (go to Heaven after they die) simply by doing good deeds. While studying the Bible, Luther came across St. Paul's letter to the Romans that stated, 'The righteous shall live by faith' (Romans 1.17). Luther came to believe that it was not what you did in your life but rather the faith you had in God that would ensure your salvation. If someone had faith in God, their actions would always be directed by their faith and thus their actions would be good. This belief became known as **Justification by Faith Alone**.

The following is an extract from the writings of Martin Luther.

Source A

I was a good monk and . . . if ever a monk were able to reach heaven by monkish discipline I should have found my way there . . . if it had continued much longer I would, what with prayers, readings and other such works, have done myself to death.

Since works justify no one and it is necessary to be just before he does a good deed, it is most clear that it is faith alone which by the pure mercy of God . . . justifies and saves the person . . . the christian man needs no work and no law to be saved . . . by the grace of God and through his faith he has enough and is saved.

From *Religious Thought in the Reformation* by Bernard M. Reardon

▲ St.Peter's Basilica, Rome

By the way . . .
The difference between a Basilica and a Cathedral is that a Basilica must contain at least part of the body of a saint.

Meanwhile, as we saw in Chapter 5, The Renaissance, Pope Julius II had begun to rebuild St. Peter's Basilica in Rome.

A huge amount of money was needed to pay the great artists and architects working on it. In 1517 Pope Leo X decided to raise more funds for St. Peter's by selling indulgences across Europe. At the same time Archbishop Albrecht of Mainz in Saxony also wished to raise funds in order to repay some of the money he had borrowed to buy his Bishopric (an act of simony).

The Archbishop of Mainz sent a Dominican friar named **John Tetzel** to sell indulgences across Saxony. Half the money collected would go to the Archbishop to repay his debts and the other half would go towards the rebuilding of St. Peter's. John Tetzel told the people in Saxony that the souls of their relatives or their own souls would go straight to heaven if they bought indulgences from him. In fact, the more money they gave, the quicker the soul would gain salvation.

JOHANNES · TECELIUS · PIRNENSIS
Dominicanus, Nundinator Romani Pontificis, anno
1517. à μυχαλανδρη LUTHERO territus & in fugam versus,
uti talis ejus effigies visitur in templo Pirnensi.

Sobald der Gülden im Becken klingt,
Im Huy die Seel in Himmel springt.

▲ John Tetzel selling indulgences to ordinary people in Saxony.

▲ Luther nailing the theses to the door in 1517.

Luther did not like the idea that a person's soul could be saved simply by paying money and without any faith in God. He also believed the sale of indulgences was unfair because poor people could not afford to pay large amounts of money for these indulgences. He was angry that ordinary people were being frightened into handing over money (a) to pay off the debts of a man who was already very wealthy and guilty of simony and (b) to fund a building in Rome.

Luther wrote a list in Latin of his objections to this selling of indulgences and nailed these **95 theses** (statements of opinion for consideration) on the church door of **Wittenburg Castle** in 1517. He hoped that this notice on the door would spark debate among other scholars.

Here are some of the arguments Luther put forward:

No.	Theses
36	*Any truly repentant Christian has a right to full remission of penalty and guilt, even without indulgence letters.*
47	*Christians are to be taught that the buying of indulgences is a matter of free choice, not commanded.*
49	*Christians are to be taught that papal indulgences are useful only if they do not put their trust in them, but very harmful if they lose their fear of God because of them.*
53	*They are the enemies of Christ and the pope who forbid altogether the preaching of the Word of God in some churches in order that indulgences may be preached in others.*
54	*Injury is done to the Word of God when, in the same sermon, an equal or larger amount of time is devoted to indulgences than to the Word.*
62	*The true treasure of the church is the most holy gospel of the glory and grace of God.*

Luther's ideas became very popular among the German population and many agreed with his objections. The rapid spread of Luther's ideas was mainly due to two factors:

(a) The ideas were translated from Latin into German, meaning everyone in Saxony and further afield could read them.

(b) The invention of the printing press allowed copies of Luther's ideas to reach all the surrounding provinces.

> **By the way . . .**
>
> People had raised objections to the corruption in the Catholic Church before Martin Luther, but it was the widespread circulation of his ideas that made Pope Leo X sit up and take notice of the German monk!

Questions

1. Which universities did Luther attend and what did he study?
2. From Luther's early life what sort of person do you think he was? Give reasons for your answer.
3. In relation to salvation, what was the main difference in thinking between Luther and the Catholic Church?
4. Why was Luther angry at John Tetzel?
5. Read thesis number 36 and try to explain in your own words what Luther meant.
6. How do you think the invention of the printing press contributed to the Reformation?

Pope Leo X was not happy when he heard about the spread of Luther's theses and he quickly sent Cardinal Cajetan to meet Luther in Leipzig and persuade him to recant (take back) his objections. Luther refused and so Leo in 1519 sent a **theologian** (someone who studies religions) named **John Eck** to discuss the matter with Luther. During their debate Luther went as far as to question the Pope's power, stating that 'a layman with scripture is to be believed before a pope or church council without scripture'. As Luther's views gained popularity, Pope Leo X began to believe that Luther was very dangerous and so he issued a *papal bull* (a papal bull is a formal letter from the pope) entitled 'Exsurge Domine' which means 'Arise, O Lord'. This letter threatened Luther with **excommunication** (when a person is not allowed to take communion and so is damned to hell for all eternity).

> **By the way . . .**
>
> The wax seal placed on the pope's letter was called a **bulla**, which is where we get the term papal bull.

On 10 December 1520 Luther publicly burnt the papal bull and therefore was excommunicated from the Catholic Church. This did not stop Luther who continued to write pamphlets outlining his view that the only place Christians must look for guidance was in the Bible, not from the Pope.

▲ Luther burning the Papal Bull in 1520.

By the way…

This is the same Charles V who paid for Magellan's circumnavigation of the world from 1519-1522. See Chapter 6, The Age of Exploration, pages 148 – 152.

The Pope next turned to Charles V of Spain. Charles was the Holy Roman Emperor and so ruled over Spain and parts of Germany, Italy, Holland, Belgium and most of the New World. Pope Leo asked Charles to intervene and try to force Luther to recant his teachings. In April 1521 a **Diet** (a large meeting or parliament of many of the German princes and rulers) was organised at a town called Worms. Emperor Charles V promised that Luther would be safe if he came to the Diet to discuss a possible solution. Luther had a lot of support from the German princes and he refused to back down at the meeting, stating, 'I cannot and will not recant anything for to go against conscience is neither right or safe'.

After the Diet ended, Charles V issued the **Edict (order) of Worms** declaring Luther to be an outlaw. All his writings were to be destroyed and if he was caught he was to be burnt at the stake as an **heretic** (someone who has beliefs that differ from the beliefs of an established religion). His followers were also outlawed and no one was permitted to provide food or shelter to them.

As Luther was travelling away from the Diet he was 'captured' by soldiers of **Prince Frederick 'the Wise' of Saxony**. Frederick supported Luther's ideas and so he wanted to ensure his safety so he took Luther to Wartburg Castle where he spent the next year. During that time, Luther, along with a young follower named **Philipp Melanchthon**, translated the Bible from Latin into German so that everyone could read it, not just the educated minority.

Luther's key beliefs:

1. The Bible, and not the Pope, was the only way to find out about God. As it provided all the guidance a Christian needed, there was no need even for priests or a hierarchy of bishops.

2. Any member of the church could become a minister or clergyman. Furthermore, any minister could marry. Luther himself married a former nun named **Catherine von Bora.**

3. Latin was replaced by the **vernacular** (the language used by the local population). This meant that the congregation in any country would be able to read the Bible in their own language and understand the services that took place.

4. The Catholic Church had seven special sacraments but after reading the Bible, Luther found only two mentioned in it. Therefore, Lutherans only celebrated Baptism and Holy Communion.

5. The Catholic Church also believed that during communion the bread and the wine were transformed into the actual flesh and blood of Christ. This is called **Transubstantiation**. Luther on the other hand believed that bread and wine used by the priest during communion remained bread and wine whilst at the same time becoming the flesh and blood of Christ. This was called **Consubstantiation**.

In 1530, an outline of Luther's doctrines was published called the **Confession of Augsburg**. These beliefs spread and many princes and their populations supported Luther. These people came to be known as **Lutherans** and their belief as Lutheranism. As they were 'protesting' against the Catholic Church the Lutherans were also known as **Protestants**. Martin Luther died suddenly in 1546, just months before the states of Germany broke into warfare. It was not until 1555 that a peace deal was agreed called the **Peace of Augsburg**. This tolerated both Catholics and Lutherans within the Holy Roman Empire and permitted each ruler to decide which **denomination** (different churches within the Christian religion) their populations were to follow. This resulted in many Lutherans and Catholics having to leave their homes and move to Lutheran or Catholic states.

Ego sum Papa.

Look at the picture on the left and answer the questions below:

Questions

1. The words 'Ego sum Papa' mean I am the Pope. What point do you think the artist is trying to make?

2. Do you think the artist is for the Reformation or against it? Give reasons for your answer.

By the way . . .

Protestantism is made up of many strands of Christianity, e.g. Anglican, Presbyterian, Methodist. None of these branches recognises the Pope as head of their church. We will learn more about these denominations in the next section.

✄ Results of Luther's Protests ✄

1. Northern Germany became Lutheran and southern Germany remained Catholic. This divide created many tensions and another war called the **Thirty Years War** broke out in 1618 between the two groups.

2. Luther began what became known as the **Protestant Reformation**. As we will see in the next chapter, other religious leaders joined with Lutheranism in protesting against the Catholic Church.

3. Lutheranism remains the majority religion in countries like Sweden, Denmark, Finland and northern Germany. There are also large numbers of Lutherans in the United States. They are more commonly referred to as Protestants.

The differences between Lutheranism and Catholicism in the sixteenth century:

	Catholic Church	Lutheran Church
Where to find guidance about God	Through the advice and guidance of the priests and bishops and the direction of the Pope	Through reading, study and knowledge of the Bible
How to gain salvation	By faith in God and by good deeds and acts	By faith in God alone
Language of service/mass and Bible	Latin should be used at mass and the Bible should remain in Latin.	The services and the Bible should be in the language of the local population to allow for greater understanding.
Number of Sacraments	Seven: Baptism, Penance (Confession), Eucharist (Communion), Confirmation, Marriage, Holy Orders (becoming a priest) and Extreme Unction (the Last Rites)	Two: Baptism and Eucharist
Eucharist/ Communion	The bread and wine are fully changed into the flesh and blood of Christ.	The bread and wine remain present during the time they become the flesh and blood of Christ.
Clergy	Ordained priests cannot marry.	Ministers can marry.
Churches	Statues and pictures of saints and the Virgin Mary	Very plain and simple, no images at all

Questions

1. Outline the four ways in which the Pope tried to get Luther to change his mind.
2. What did Luther and his followers do with the papal bull sent by the Pope?
3. Why was Charles V involved in trying to persuade Luther to recant?
4. Why was Luther declared an outlaw by the Diet of Worms?
5. Why were the followers of Luther referred to as Protestants?
6. List four differences between Lutheranism and the Catholic Church.
7. What was the Confession of Augsburg?
8. What did the Peace of Augsburg decide?
9. How did the rebuilding of St. Peter's Basilica in some ways begin the Reformation?
10. Explain the following words:

    (a) Vernacular   (c) Eucharist   (e) Theology   (g) Diet
    (b) Edict   (d) Heretic   (f) Salvation

MARTIN LUTHER
✍ REFORMER ✍

Born:	Eisleben, Saxony 1483
Died:	1546.
Key events:	Wrote *Justification by Faith Alone*

1517 – Nails 95 theses on church door of Wittenburg Castle

1520 – Burns papal bull and is excommunicated by Pope

1521 – Summoned to Diet of Worms by Charles V but refuses to recant

1521-22– Spends year in Wartburg Castle of Frederick the Wise and translates Bible from Latin into German

1530 – Confession of Augsburg outlines his beliefs

▲ Martin Luther preaching to a small congregation during his period of voluntary 'imprisonment' at Wartburg castle.

John Calvin (1509-1564)

There were others across Europe who agreed with Luther's beliefs. They also wanted to reform the Catholic Church but had slightly different views to Luther. In Switzerland there were two important reformers: **Ulrich Zwingli** and **John Calvin**. Calvin and Zwingli were both important figures in the Reformation but in this section we'll concentrate on Calvin.

Calvin was born in Noyon in northern France in 1509. Although he initially studied theology in Paris, he switched to study law at the University of Orleans. He converted to Lutheranism in 1533 but it soon became very dangerous to be a Lutheran in Catholic France. To avoid persecution he fled to Basle in Switzerland in 1536. It was there that he wrote *The Institutes of the Christian Religion*, outlining his main beliefs. His followers became known as Calvinists or **Presbyterians** after the Greek word *presbyter* (minister).

▲ John Calvin also wanted to reform the Catholic Church but some of his ideas were different to Martin Luther's.

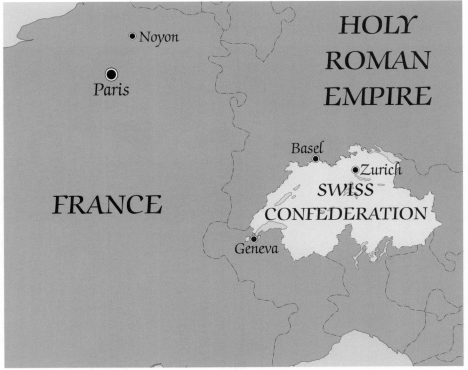

▲ A map of Switzerland and France showing land and cities associated with the Calvinist Reformation.

Calvin's main beliefs were similar to Luther's but there are some differences:

No.	Beliefs
1	*The Bible is the only authority that a Christian should follow.*
2	*There are only two sacraments: Baptism and the Eucharist.*
3	*The ministers of the church (presbyters) are elected by the congregation and they can marry. There are no bishops in the Calvinist church.*
4	*During the Eucharist the bread and wine remain bread and wine.*
5	*There is no place for unnecessary decoration in the church. Pictures and images were removed from Calvinist churches.*
6	*God, as He is omniscient (all-knowing), already knows those who are going to heaven. These people are called the **elect**. This belief is called **predestination**.*

• Calvin's Geneva

In 1541 Calvin was asked by the government of Geneva (which was a self-governing city-state in Switzerland) to set up a church and lead the Reformation in its city. He had complete control over the workings of the city and he set up a system of administration with four main groups or **orders**.

▲ Calvin arrives into Geneva – the government of the city-state invited him to set up a church there and lead the Reformation.

1. The **Presbyters** were responsible for the preaching of the word of God and baptising people.

2. The **Teachers** had control over the education of the young. All children were expected to have a good knowledge of the Bible.

3. The **Elders** were elected laymen (people within the church who were not ordained) who looked after the welfare of the congregation. They enforced many strict rules and ensured that all people were leading good Christian lives.

4. The **Deacons'** jobs included looking after the poor and the sick within the city.

▲ Calvin speaking at the Council of Geneva.

As all the positions within the Calvinist church were elected by the congregation, these jobs were spread out among the city's population. The city of Geneva had very strict laws. No gambling, dancing, theatres or unnecessarily fancy clothes were permitted, '... and anything approaching silliness' was forbidden. Sunday was the Sabbath. Everyone was expected to go to church and no work of any kind was allowed on that day. People who broke these rules were severely punished. Heretics were burnt at the stake. Geneva became known to people as the **City of God** as it was so well organised and people seemed so content and spiritual (Rome was thus known as the City of the Devil).

● Calvinism in Europe

John Calvin died in 1564 but his beliefs spread all across Europe. Many people visited Geneva and even studied at the University of Geneva. They were struck by its holiness. Many spread the teachings of Calvin when they returned to their home countries. A Scottish former Catholic priest, John Knox, was so inspired by Geneva that he returned to Scotland and spent the rest of his life ensuring the **Church of Scotland** adhered to Calvinist teachings.

▲ A former Catholic priest from Scotland, John Knox devoted his life to making sure the Church of Scotland obeyed Calvinist teachings.

In parts of France, **Huguenots** (as Calvinists were known in France) were persecuted by the Catholic French kings and there was an eight-year-war beginning in 1562 between the two sides. Eventually the **Edict of Nantes** in 1598 gave them equality with Catholicism in France but many sought safety in Protestant England and some were given land in Ireland. It is their descendents who are buried in the Huguenot cemetery on St. Stephen's Green in Dublin.

Calvinism is still very strong in the Reformed Church in the Netherlands. In England, Calvinism was known as **Puritanism** due to its strict rules about lifestyle. The English Puritans were persecuted by the state and by members of the Church of England. Many fled to North America as settlers in the New World.

◀ The Huguenot Cemetery just off St. Stephen's Green in Dublin was established in 1693.

Questions

1. Why did John Calvin have to flee France and where did he go to?

2. Why are Calvinists sometimes known as Presbyterians?

3. What was the name of Calvin's publication outlining his beliefs?

4. Give three of Calvin's beliefs that were different to the Catholic Church.

5. Why did Calvin go to Geneva in 1541?

6. Match the terms (A–D) with the duties (1–4):

   A Presbyter   1. Supervised the welfare of the congregation and upheld the laws.

   B Teacher   2. Cared for the sick and poor

   C Deacon   3. Preached the word of God

   D Elder   4. Looked after the education of the young

7. Why was Geneva referred to as the City of God?

8. Match the terms (A–E) to the correct locations (1–5):

   A John Knox   1 The Netherlands

   B Huguenot   2 Geneva

   C Puritan   3 England

   D John Calvin   4 France

   E Dutch Reformed Church 5 Scotland

JOHN CALVIN
∽ REFORMER ∽

Born:	1509	Noyon, France
Died:	1564	
Key Events:	1536-	Flees France to avoid persecution
	1537-	Writes *The Institutes of the Christian Religion*
	1541-	Is asked to go to Geneva and establish a Church there
	1541-64-	Is put in charge of the running of the city and creates what becomes known as the City of God

Henry VIII (1491-1547)

Henry VIII became King of England in 1509 aged 18. He was a devout Catholic. When Luther posted his 95 theses on the castle wall in Saxony in 1517, Henry strongly condemned this attack on the Pope's authority. Pope Leo X was so happy with Henry that he gave him the title **Fidei Defensor** (Defender of the Faith).

▲ Catherine of Aragon, who was the first wife of Henry VIII, begged him not to divorce her as she was a devout Catholic.

Henry's brother, Arthur, died in 1509 and Henry wished to marry his widow, Catherine of Aragon, the daughter of Ferdinand and Isabella of Spain. Pope Clement gave him permission to marry his brother's widow and they had one child who survived – Mary. However, Henry wanted a male heir so he planned to divorce Catherine and marry a much younger woman he had fallen in love with named Anne Boleyn.

▲ Henry VIII was Catholic until he was refused a divorce by Pope Clement.

▲ Anne Boleyn became Henry VIII's second wife.

He applied to Pope Clement VII for an annulment (cancellation) of his marriage to Catherine, stating that according to the rules of the Catholic Church he should never originally have been allowed to marry his sister-in-law. In other words Henry wanted the Pope to say the Catholic Church was wrong to have let him marry Catherine in the first place. Clement did not want to say this. In addition, the Pope was in some difficulty as King Charles V of Spain, Catherine's nephew, had recently captured Rome and was keeping Clement prisoner. Under pressure from King Charles, Clement refused to annul Henry's marriage. As a result, Henry simply appointed Thomas Cranmer as the new Archbishop of Canterbury, divorced Catherine and married Anne Boleyn in 1533. Henry's new marriage was not recognised by the Pope and he was immediately excommunicated from the Catholic Church.

● Henry's reforms

Henry decided to call a meeting of Parliament and forced its members to pass the **Act of Supremacy** in 1534 which recognised Henry as the 'supreme head on earth of the Church of England'. Furthermore, he passed an **Oath of Supremacy** which insisted that all his subjects recognise him as the head of the Church. Many refused and were hanged, drawn and quartered or simply beheaded. One of Henry's closest friends and advisors, Sir Thomas More, was beheaded when he refused, stating 'I am the king's good servant, but God's first'.

▲ Henry VIII and his six wives.

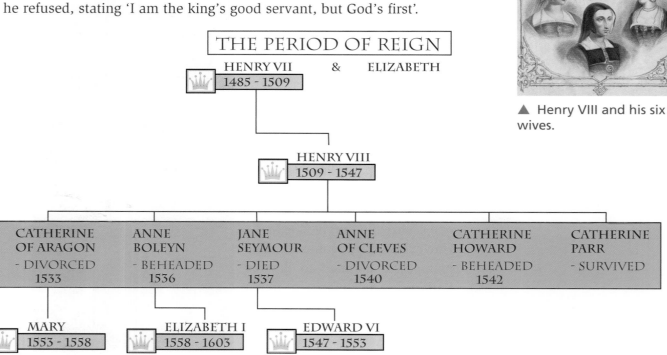

THE PERIOD OF REIGN

HENRY VII   &   ELIZABETH
1485 - 1509

HENRY VIII
1509 - 1547

CATHERINE OF ARAGON	ANNE BOLEYN	JANE SEYMOUR	ANNE OF CLEVES	CATHERINE HOWARD	CATHERINE PARR
- DIVORCED 1533	- BEHEADED 1536	- DIED 1537	- DIVORCED 1540	- BEHEADED 1542	- SURVIVED

MARY
1553 - 1558

ELIZABETH I
1558 - 1603

EDWARD VI
1547 - 1553

▲ The length of time for which each king or queen ruled during the Reformation and the fate of Henry VIII's six wives.

While Henry was prepared to be excommunicated by the Pope, he still did not believe in Luther's teachings and remained very Catholic in his faith. For example, he continued to attend mass. Nevertheless, Henry passed the **Act of Dissolution** in 1536 which closed down the Catholic churches and monasteries and took their land which he later sold. He also had the Bible translated into English so that ordinary people could read it. He regarded his marraige to Anne Boleyn as unsuccessful because she gave birth to a girl (named Elizabeth). Henry tired of Boleyn, accused her of adultery, had her executed and married Jane Seymour with whom he finally had a boy named Edward. Although he married three more times, he had no more children.

> **By the way . . .**
> Henry agreed to marry Anne of Cleves, his fourth wife, after seeing a painting of her. He divorced her within the year as he thought she was not as beautiful as the portrait made her out to be!

Questions

1. Why was Henry given the title Defender of the Faith by Pope Leo X?
2. What reason did Henry give to Pope Clement for wanting to divorce Catherine? Do you think it was the real reason?
3. Why would Pope Clement not annul Henry's marriage to Catherine of Aragon?
4. What position did the Act of Supremacy give Henry?
5. What did the Act of Dissolution of 1536 achieve?
6. Give an example of one reform which Henry made that was similar to Calvin or Luther.

The **Henrican Reformation** (the religious reforms made by Henry VIII) meant that England was officially no longer Catholic. However, Henry still attended mass and he retained most of the Catholic traditions. He did not agree with the Lutheran and Calvinist teachings that prevailed in parts of Europe. The future of this reformation in England was more complicated though. Mary, his child with the devoutly Catholic Catherine of Aragon, had been brought up as a Catholic whereas Elizabeth (daughter of Anne Bolyen) and Edward (son of Jane Seymour) were Protestants. When Henry died in 1547, Edward (aged 9) became King and he continued with the Protestant reforms.

▲ A cartoon of Henry VIII with his feet on Pope Clement

● Edwardian reforms

Edwardian Reforms were known as the **42 Articles**. They included:

1. The introduction of the Book of Common Prayer which replaced the Latin mass. The **Act of Uniformity** of 1552 made the use of these prayer books compulsory.

2. Many of the obviously Catholic images of the Church, such as statues and pictures of saints, were removed.

3. Penance (confession) was banned.

4. The sacrament of the Eucharist became more like that of a Calvinist mass.

5. Priests were allowed to marry.

6. A second Act of Uniformity made church attendance mandatory and imposed severe penalties on those who failed to attend.

▲ Edward VI who became King of England in 1547 at the age of nine.

▲ Bloody Mary returned England to Catholicism during her reign (1553 – 1558).

Edward died in 1553 aged 15 before these reforms could become permanent and was replaced by his Catholic half-sister, Mary. She returned England to Catholicism. Protestant services were banned and Protestants were deemed to be heretics. During her reign almost 300 Protestants were burnt at the stake or killed, giving her the nickname 'Bloody Mary'. She died in 1558 after only five years as Queen and was replaced by her sister Elizabeth.

● Elizabethan Reforms

Elizabeth I wanted to avoid the extremism of Edward and Mary so she established the **Anglican Church**. This was a mixture of Protestant and Catholic beliefs and traditions. Many of the Catholic vestments returned yet the vernacular services and married clergy also remained part of the Anglican Church. She also passed laws to ensure that England would remain Protestant. The Act of Supremacy of 1559 made her the Governor rather than the Head of the Church of England, thus allowing Catholics privately still to regard the Pope as head of

▲ Elizabeth I ruled for 45 years and established the Anglican Church.

the Catholic Church. She also reduced the fines and punishments imposed by the Act of Uniformity. Her rule lasted for 45 years and during that time England became firmly Protestant.

Questions

1. Examine the reforms made by Edward. Were his reforms similar to Luther, Calvin or his father's reforms? Give two reasons.

2. What were the reforms by Edward called?

3. Give three characteristics of the Anglican Church.

4. Examine the cartoon on page 179 and answer the following questions:

   (a) Henry VIII has his two feet resting on P. Clemens. What is the evidence in the picture that P. Clemens is Pope Clemens?

   (b) What message is the artist attempting to convey to the people by having Henry VIII's feet resting on P. Clemens?

   (c) What two other messages does the artist wish to give to the people by showing Henry VIII:
   (i) holding the sword in his right hand?
   (ii) giving the Bible to Cranmer, a reformation bishop?

   (d) Give one reason why the Catholic clergy on the right-hand side and in the forefront were right to be worried by the actions of Henry VIII.

HENRY VIII
∽ Reformation King ∾

1491-	Born in Greenwich, England
1509-	Becomes King of England
1521-	Given title of Defender of the Faith by Pope Leo X
1533-	Excommunicated by Pope Clement VII
1534 -	Act of Supremacy recognises Henry as Head of the Church of England
1536 -	Act of Dissolution closes down the monasteries and confiscates the Catholic Church's lands
1547-	Dies in London

EDWARD
∽ Child King ∾

1537-	Born in England
1547-	Becomes King of England at the age of nine
1549 -	Replaces Latin mass with The Book of Common Prayer
1552 -	The Act of Uniformity makes attendance at Church compulsory
1553-	Dies from tuberculosis

MARY
✧ 'Bloody Mary' ✧

1516- Born in England

1553- Becomes Queen of England

1553- Returns England to Catholicism killing almost 300 Protestants

1558- Dies in England

ELIZABETH
✧ The Virgin Queen ✧

1533- Born in Greenwich, England

1558- Becomes Queen of England

1559- Establishes the Anglican Church. Act of Supremacy makes her the Governor of the Anglican Church

1559- Reduces the fines and punishments of the Act of Uniformity.

1603- Dies in England

Results of the Reformation

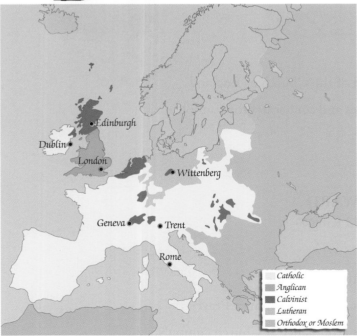

Catholic
Anglican
Calvinist
Lutheran
Orthodox or Moslem

▲ The religious divide in Europe as a result of the Reformation c. 1650.

So what were the consequences of the Reformation?

● 1. New Churches

During the sixteenth century, new varieties of Protestantism were established. Lutheran, Calvinist and Anglican churches (all connected to the Protestant religion) sprang up all over Europe. These churches continue to exist in the present day. Baptists, Methodists and many others are all branches of the Protestant church and many northern European countries have Protestant majorities.

2. Religious conflict

▲ Using over 100 ships, Spain tried to invade and conquer England in the sixteenth century. Amongst other reasons, the Catholic King of Spain, Philip II, wanted to destroy Queen Elizabeth's successful establishment of the Anglican Church. However, the Spanish attempt failed.

Religious conflict between Christian denominations continued after the Reformation. Between 1618-1648 Protestant countries in the north of Europe fought against the southern Catholic countries in the **Thirty Years War**. The wars between England and Spain in the late sixteenth century were heavily influenced by religious differences. Even up to recent times the tensions in Northern Ireland were partly a result of the religious conflict between Protestants and Catholics.

3. Increase in power and wealth of monarchs

As the Pope no longer had as much control over the politics of Britain, Germany and the Netherlands, the monarchs of these countries were able to increase their power. As there was no need to give the Catholic Church any money, the kings received more taxes and did not need to worry about the Pope's influence over the population. This was particularly obvious with Henry VIII who now owned all the land in England that had previously belonged to the Catholic Church.

4. Education

The use of the vernacular by the Protestant churches encouraged more people to read the Bible. Protestant churches promoted education for all so they could learn to read the Bible. An increased amount of literature and information was distributed by these churches. This was made possible by the invention of the printing press. As a result of the translation of the Bible into the vernacular, more people wanted to be able to read so that they too could find out what exactly was written in the Bible.

5. The Counter-Reformation

The Catholic Church also tried to reform itself. Many reforms within the Church took place during this time as well as measures to control the spread of Protestantism.

These included:

(A) NEW ORDERS WITHIN THE CHURCH

▲ St Ignatius de Loyola, ex-soldier and founder of the Jesuits

Many new religious orders (organisations or societies of priests, monks or nuns) were established to promote the Catholic Church's teachings among Europe's populations. The most important one was the **Society of Jesus**, or the **Jesuits** as they became known. They were founded by St Ignatius de Loyola. He was an ex-soldier and he organised the Order along military lines. All members are expected to follow rules without question and the leader is referred to as the general.

- Jesuits founded schools and colleges to educate the sons of the wealthy. Gonzaga College in Dublin, Clongowes Wood in Kildare and Cresent College in Limerick are examples of Jesuit schools in Ireland.

- The Jesuits hoped to spread the Catholic faith both in Europe and also across Africa and Asia. The most famous Jesuit missionary was St Francis Xavier (1506-52) who travelled to places like Japan and Malaysia to spread Catholic teachings.

(B) THE COURTS OF INQUISITION

In an attempt to stop the spread of Protestantism, Courts of Inquisition were established to try those accused of heresy (having beliefs that are in conflict with the teachings of a religion – in this case the Catholic religion). These courts were particularly important in Italy and Spain. Using torture, people were forced to confess to heresy and then had to wear a yellow garment called a San Benito. They could also be whipped. If people refused to confess, they were sometimes publicly executed by being burnt at the stake in the town square. This punishment was called an **auto-da-fé**. The methods of the Inquisitions were widely criticised by the Protestant churches but were reasonably successful in removing any opponents of the Catholic Church in these countries.

▲ The punishment called auto-da-fé whereby people who refused to confess to heresy were burnt at the stake in their town square.

Questions

Look at the image. The person on the right is Luther.

(a) Who is the person on the left?

(b) Do you think the artist is for or against Luther? Give reasons for your answer.

(C) THE COUNCIL OF TRENT

Between 1545 and 1563 Catholic cardinals and bishops met at Trentino in Italy to decide on reforms for the Catholic Church. These meetings looked at matters relating to Discipline (how the church was organised) and Doctrine (the beliefs of the church).

▲ The Council of Trent at which Catholic cardinals and bishops decided on how to reform the Catholic Church.

Discipline:

(i) Absenteeism, pluralism, simony and nepotism were outlawed.

(ii) **Seminaries** were established. These were places that ensured the proper training of priests.

(iii) A new **Catechism** (instructions on the religious beliefs of the church) was written which outlined the beliefs of the church in a question-and-answer format. All Catholics were to be taught through this method.

Doctrine:

(i) Faith and good works were necessary for salvation and indulgences cannot be bought with money.

(ii) There are seven sacraments.

(iii) Christ is present at the sacrament, i.e. the bread and wine at mass become the body and blood of Christ during the Eucharist. This is known as Transubstantiation.

(iv) Clergy must remain celibate, i.e. they cannot marry.

(v) The Pope and his bishops are appointed by God.

With these reforms the Church hoped to remove the worst abuses and faults of the Catholic Church. Together with the other changes within the Counter-Reformation, the Catholic Church hoped that they could halt the spread of Protestantism and even regain some of its followers.

Chapter 7 Questions

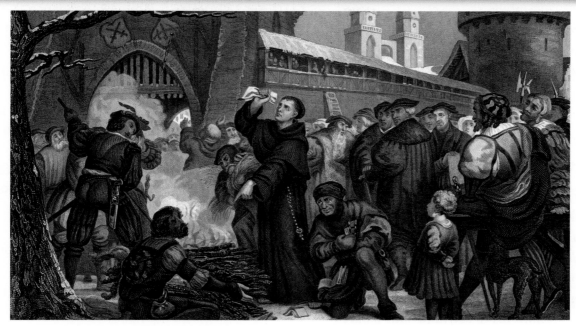

▲ Luther burning the Papal Bull in 1520.

1. Pictures

(a) What was a papal bull?

(b) Why is Luther burning this papal bull?

(c) What happened to Luther as a result of this action?

2. Documents

The following is a quotation from the speech Luther made at the Diet of Worms. Read the passage and answer the questions below.

> Unless I am convicted by Scripture and plain reason I do not accept the authority of popes and councils, for they have contradicted each other - my conscience is captive to the word of God. I cannot and will not recant anything for to go against conscience is neither right nor safe.

(a) What is the only way that Luther will accept his conviction?

(b) Whose authority does he not accept?

(c) Why can Luther not recant anything?

(d) From your studies, do you think Martin Luther was committed to his beliefs? Give reasons for your answer.

3. Short-Answer Questions

(a) List and explain three abuses of the Catholic Church.

(b) Explain what simony is.

(c) Name one sixteenth century religious reformer and one major belief of that reformer.

(d) Where was Martin Luther from?

(e) What did Martin Luther nail to the door of the church in Wittenberg?

(f) What is a Papal Bull?

(g) What was the Diet of Worms?

(h) Why were those who supported Luther and Calvin called Protestants?

(i) In which city did Calvin set up his church?

(j) Who founded the Jesuits?

(k) In which countries was the Court of Inquisition very successful?

(l) Name two results of the Reformation in Europe.

4. People in History

Write about a named religious reformer at the time of the Reformation.

Hints: • Name of the Reformer
• Main events in his life
• The main beliefs of his church
• The results of his reforms

5.

Petrarch, Letter to a friend.

> . . . Now I am living in France, in the Babylon of the West. Here reign the successors of the poor fishermen of Galilee; they have strangely forgotten their origin. I am astounded, as I recall their predecessors, to see these men loaded with gold and clad in purple, boasting of the spoils (riches) of princes and nations; to see luxurious palaces and heights crowned with fortifications instead of a boat turned downwards for shelter . . .
>
> Instead of holy solitude (silence) we find a criminal host (crowd) . . . instead of soberness, licentious (drunken) banquets, instead of pious pilgrimages, foul sloth (laziness); instead of the bare feet of the apostles, the war-horses of brigands (robbers) fly past us, the horses decked in gold and fed on gold, soon to be shod with gold, if the Lord does not check this lavish luxury.

From *Readings in English Social History from Contemporary Literature*, Vol. 4, 1603-1688 by R.B. Morgan

(a) Study the extract from a letter by Petrarch (1304-1374), a famous Renaissance writer, criticising the lifestyle of the popes in the fourteenth century.

(i) Who are the 'successors of the poor fishermen of Galilee'?

(ii) Did the writer approve of what he saw? Mention one piece of evidence from the extract to support your answer.

(iii) Explain any three of the following terms relating to the causes of the Reformation:

(a) Simony   (c) Nepotism
(b) Absenteeism   (d) Pluralism

(b) Write down the name of a Protestant reformer whom you have studied.

Outline three major differences between his beliefs and those of the Catholic Church.

(c) Write an account of one of the following topics:

(a) The Council of Trent

(b) The Society of Jesus (The Jesuits)

(c) Religious Wars in Europe, 1525-1648

Key Terms to Summarise Chapter 7: The Reformation

Clergy Members of the Church with authority, e.g. priests, bishops, cardinals.

Reformation A movement in sixteenth-century Europe aimed at reforming the Roman Catholic Church. This movement created a great divide within the Catholic Church and led to the establishment of Protestant churches.

Tithe A tax of one tenth of a farmer's harvest or income which had to be paid to the Church.

Purgatory The Catholic Church's belief that some souls spend time in purgatory where they are cleansed through punishment for their sins on earth.

Indulgence A method by which someone can either pay, pray or go to mass in order to reduce the amount of time a soul has to spend in purgatory.

Theology The study of God and religious beliefs; thus a theologian is someone who studies theology.

Salvation To be saved; in a religious sense, to go to heaven when you die.

Justification by Faith Alone Martin Luther's belief that only faith in God would ensure salvation.

Papal Bull A formal letter from the Pope.

Excommunication To be thrown out of the Church and refused communion, which for Catholics means being damned to hell.

Diet of Worms A large meeting in 1521 called to seek a solution to Luther's criticisms of the Catholic Church.

Edict of Worms The statement made by Charles V declaring Luther an outlaw after the Diet of Worms.

Heretic A person who holds beliefs/opinions that are contrary to the beliefs of an established religion.

Vernacular The language used by the local population of a region or country.

Transubstantiation: The Catholic belief that the bread and wine at mass become the body and blood of Jesus Christ.

Consubstantiation Luther's belief that the bread and wine remain bread and wine whilst being the flesh and blood of Jesus Christ at the same time.

Confession of Augsburg The publication of all of Luther's beliefs in 1530.

Lutherans The name for those who follow Martin Luther's teachings.

Protestants A more general name for Lutherans and for those who 'protested' against the Catholic Church at this time.

Peace of Augsburg A treaty agreed in 1555 tolerating both Catholics and Protestants living within the Holy Roman Empire.

Thirty Years War The conflict that broke out in 1618 between northern Germany (mostly Lutheran) and southern Germany (mostly Catholic).

Presbyterians The name given to followers of John Calvin. The term comes from the Greek word (presbyter) given to ministers of the Calvinist church.

Elect The name given by Calvin and his followers to the people who they believed were chosen by God to go to heaven.

Predestination The belief that God has already chosen those who will go to heaven.

City of God The name given to Geneva because the people who lived there seemed so spiritual and content.

Huguenots French name for Calvinists.

Puritanism The name given to Calvinism in England.

Act of Supremacy The Act passed by Henry VIII making him the head of the Church of England.

Oath of Supremancy Oath passed by Henry VIII forcing all his subjects to recognise him as the head of the Church of England.

Act of Dissolution Another Act passed by Henry VIII closing down all Catholic churches and monasteries in England and selling their land.

Anglican Church The church established by Elizabeth I (also known as the Church of England).

Society of Jesus A religious order established by St Ignatius de Loyola. This order is also known as the Jesuits.

Auto-da-fé Burning someone at the stake This punishment was common during the Catholic Inquisition in Spain and Italy.

Seminaries Places set up during the Counter-Reformation in which men trained to become priests.

Catechism A book outlining the main beliefs of the Catholic Church.

Web References

For further reading on topics mentioned in this chapter, view the following websites:

www.lutheran.co.uk

www.presbyterianireland.org

www.bbc.co.uk/history/british/tudors/english_reformation_01.shtml

www.jesuit.ie

www.ireland.anglican.org

www.vatican.va

Women in History

Caterina von Bora

(1499-1552)

Caterina von Bora was born in Lippendorf in Germany in 1499. After her mother died, she was sent to a convent at age 3. When she was 18 years of age she read about Luther's Biblical teaching. She and a number of other nuns decided they wanted to leave the convent. Luther heard about this and arranged for a friend of his to arrange an escape. His friend was a merchant called Kopp who delivered fish to the convent and after delivering herring to the convent, von Bora and 11 other nuns hid in the empty fish barrels. Most of the women returned to their families or found new lives.

Luther proposed to Caterina and married her in 1525. Luther was to write to a friend that 'There is no bond on earth so sweet' as marriage. She had six children with him. After Luther died she continued to look after her children and had to move to avoid wars and the plague. The lady whom Luther described as 'my lord Katie' died in 1552.

Chapter 8

THE PLANTATIONS

Ireland in the 1500s

The Reformation in England had a big impact on Ireland from the 1550s onwards. It led to an increase in tension between the mainly Gaelic majority and the English who lived in an area around Dublin called the **Pale.** The Pale was a protected area (i.e. English soldiers protected the English people who lived there from attacks by the native Irish) that stretched from Dundalk to Dalkey and out towards Trim, Kells and Tallaght.

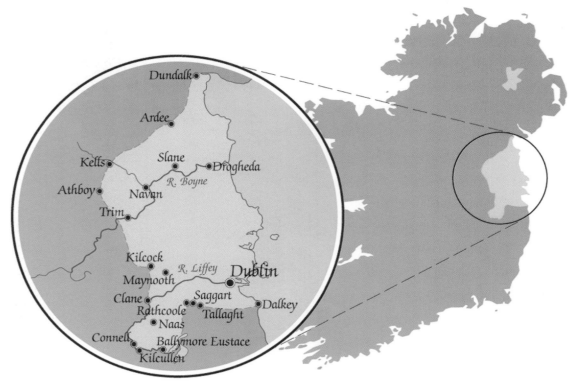

▲ The Pale was a protected area where most English people in Ireland lived.

In the early 1500s, before the impact of the Reformation was felt in Ireland, the population was made up of three main groups.

	Old English	Gaelicised Anglo-Normans	Gaelic Irish
Where they lived	Primarily in the Pale and in towns	In all parts of Ireland, especially towns	In all parts of Ireland, especially rural areas
Religion	Catholic	Catholic	Catholic
Laws and Customs	English	Gaelic and English	Gaelic
Examples of Names	Barnewall, Fleming, Plunkett	Fitzgerald, Burke, Butler	O'Neill, O'Donnell, McCarthy
Relations with English monarch	Trusted by the English	Not trusted by the English	Tension

▲ Table of population in Ireland in the early 1500s

O'More *Gaelic-Irish clans*
Dalton *Anglo Norman Lordships*
☐ *The Pale*
☐ *Areas loyal to England*

Family names in Ireland in the sixteenth century. Is your name on the map? ▶

Three groups in Ireland

- In the early 1500s, the people who lived in the Pale were mainly English merchants. The **Old English** were known as the 'king's loyal subjects'. They lived their lives according to English laws and were loyal to the English King. They held most of the administrative and judicial (legal) positions. They did not trust the Gaelic Irish who lived outside the Pale as these native Irish regularly attacked and raided the Pale stealing cattle and goods.

- The **Gaelicised Anglo-Normans** were descendents of the Norman settlers in Ireland. By 1500 they had adjusted to the Gaelic way of life and followed the Irish traditions and laws. They held important positions, including the position of **Lord Deputy of Ireland** (the English king's representative in Ireland). They remained Catholic during the Reformation.

- The **Gaelic Irish** were the **Catholic Gaelic chieftains** who followed **Brehon Laws** (see Chapter 2, Ancient Ireland). Many of the these families like the O'Neills and O'Donnells were located in Ulster, which was the most Gaelic of the provinces. They feared that they might lose power if the English King tried to expand his control in Ireland and as a result they disliked the English settlers.

▲ The Chief of the Mac Sweynes at dinner

The Causes of the Plantations

1. As we saw in Chapter 6, The Age of Exploration, Spain and Portugal created large empires in the New World (e.g. Mexico, Brazil). The English King, Henry VIII, also wanted to expand his kingdom and so wanted to control all of Ireland, not just the Pale.

2. During the English Reformation many people in England believed that the Catholic Irish should be forced to convert to Protestantism. They felt that Catholics could not be trusted as they might form an alliance with Catholic Spain or Catholic France and use Ireland as a base from which to attack England.

3. Occasionally there were attempts by Irish leaders to force the English settlers out of Ireland. To protect the settlers Henry VIII needed to keep a large number of soldiers in Ireland. Therefore Henry decided that it would be cheaper to 'plant' loyal Protestants in Ireland who would do that job for him. These 'planters' would live in Ireland permanently.

These factors led Henry VIII to come up with an idea called **Surrender and Regrant**.

▲ The Earl of Tyrone, Hugh O'Neill

By the way . . .

In Gaelic Ireland, when someone became the leader of his clan he received the title 'The'. For example Hugh O'Neill was known as The O'Neill.

Surrender and Regrant

This meant that Irish landowners would:

1. Recognise Henry as the King of Ireland (he had been declared King of Ireland by the Irish Parliament in 1540).

2. Acknowledge that as king, Henry had title (a legal right) over all land in Ireland.

3. Swear an oath of loyalty to him called the **Oath of Supremacy**.

In return Henry VIII would:

1. Allow Irish landowners to be tenants on his land.

2. Ensure the title of the land would be valid within English law.

3. Give some of the more important Gaelic Irish an English Peerage (title such as Earl). For example, The O'Neill of Tyrone became the Earl of Tyrone.

Surrender and Regrant meant that under the English legal system, Henry VIII could **confiscate** anyone's land if they did not behave appropriately.

Now look at the table below. By using Surrender and Regrant, the leader of each clan could increase the amount of land he owned and ensure his son became the next leader. This was known as **succession** (when the eldest son of the family 'succeeds' or takes over from his father).

▲ Surrender and regrant: Turlough O'Neill is shown surrendering to Sir Henry Sidney, Lord Deputy.

Brehon Laws	English system of Succession
• The land was owned by the whole clan.	• The monarch owned all the land.
• The leader (taoiseach) was elected by the whole clan.	• The landlord was a tenant of the monarch.
	• The eldest son of the landlord got everything.
• A new leader would often be the strongest person from the royal family (derbhfine). This sometimes led to large fights.	• Land was passed on from father to son.
	• This system resulted in increased wealth and power for one family instead of the whole clan.
• The taoiseach was only given a section of the land while he was leader.	

Overall, the policy of surrender and regrant was intended to deal with the Gaelic Irish by making them more English and part of the English legal system. This policy continued throughout the sixteenth century. However another more extreme policy was also used by the English government – the policy of plantation.

● The Policy of Plantation

(1) The English government knew that if any Gaelic Irish Lord tried to rebel, he could be evicted and his land confiscated by the king.

(2) Loyal English settlers could then be planted on this land.

(3) These planters would serve a number of purposes:
   (a) They would spread **English law and customs** wherever they were planted.
   (b) The **land would be defended** from the Gaelic Irish by the planters.
   (c) The planters could spread the **Protestant religion** among the Catholic Irish.

Questions

1. Name the three main population groups in Ireland in the early 1500s and describe the main characteristics of one of them.

2. What was the Pale?

3. What was the name of Henry VIII's plan to get all the Irish Chieftains to swear loyalty to him?

4. In your opinion, why were the Gaelic Irish not trusted by the English king?

5. Look at the picture on page 193 and answer the following questions:

   (a) Can you find the head of the family?

   (b) What are the two men on the left (at A) doing?

   (c) What jobs do you think the two people on the far right (at D) had in the clan?

   (d) The man at B is a priest. How do we know this?

The Laois-Offaly Plantation

Laois and Offaly are situated on the edge of the Pale and in the sixteenth century these two counties were ruled by two native Irish families, the O'Moores and the O'Connors. These families were enemies of English rule in Ireland and they constantly attacked and raided the Pale, despite charging residents of the Pale a 'mál dubh' (black rent) which was a form of protection money.

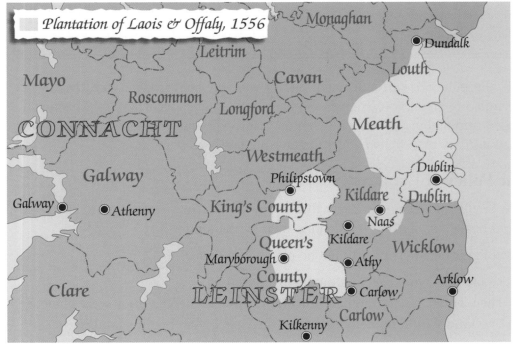

The 1556 Plantation of Laois-Offaly ▲

People living in the Pale were afraid of these attacks so the English government sent heavily armed soldiers into Laois and Offaly to find these Gaelic outlaws known as **woodkernes.** The O'Moore and O'Connor families then openly revolted against the English crown. As a result, their lands were confiscated.

> **By the way . . .**
> Woodkernes was the name given to the displaced members of any of the Gaelic Irish families who retreated to the woods for refuge.

▲ An attack by woodkernes carrying pikes as they begin to burn a farmhouse and drive off the horses and cattle.

In 1556 Queen Mary began the first **plantation** of English people into Ireland. By sending loyal English subjects to Ireland and giving them land on which to live and farm, she hoped to strengthen her control over this part of Ireland and bring an end to attacks by the O'Moores and O'Connors. Land confiscated from rebellious Irish families was given to these English planters, leaving the Irish with no home or land. Queen Mary hoped that this plantation would spread English control and laws beyond the Pale and protect the area from raids by controlling the native population.

How the Laois-Offaly Plantation Worked

1. Laois and Offaly were now known as **Queen's County** and **King's County**.

2. The county towns were renamed **Maryborough** (Portlaoise) and **Philipstown** (Daingean) after Queen Mary and her husband Philip II of Spain.

3. Each county had a **sheriff** who was in charge of introducing and enforcing English laws and customs, including the English language, within the counties.

4. The land was divided up into estates of varying sizes. Two thirds of the lands closest to the Pale was to be given to new loyal English planters and the rest of the land was to be given to loyal Gaelic Irish, i.e. those loyal to the English crown.

RESULTS OF THE LAOIS-OFFALY PLANTATION

1. The Laois-Offaly Plantation failed to achieve its aims for a number of reasons:

   (a) Due to the small size of the estates offered, very few English planters came to Ireland to take the land.

   (b) Only 80 out of the planned 160 land grants were given to English people living in the Pale.

   (c) The rest of the land ended up back in the hands of the Gaelic Irish so English customs, language and laws were not widely used in the two counties.

   (d) Those English planters who took up Queen Mary's offer immediately came under attack from the O'Moore and O'Connor clans who had lost their lands.

2. This plantation was seen as a failure but the English learnt from the mistakes they made in Laois and Offaly. As we will see, later plantations were much better organised.

Questions

1. Why did Queen Mary decide to confiscate the lands of the O'Moores and O'Connors?
2. What was the role of the sheriff in each county?
3. For what reasons did the Laois and Offaly Plantation fail?
4. What lasting consequences, if any, did the plantation have on the counties?

The Munster Plantation

The head of the Fitzgerald family of Munster was known as the Earl of Desmond. The Fitzgeralds were a very powerful Gaelicised Anglo-Norman family. However, Protestant Queen Elizabeth was now the English monarch and she wanted to spread the power of the crown more forcefully throughout Ireland. She proposed the appointment of **presidents** in Connacht and Munster to impose English law, language and the Protestant religion. She also encouraged Protestant Englishmen called **adventurers** to travel to Ireland and lay claim to land, particularly in Munster. Understandably the fact that these adventurers could come to Ireland and declare land as their own angered the Catholic Fitzgeralds. In 1569 the growing religious unease led to the first Desmond Rebellion.

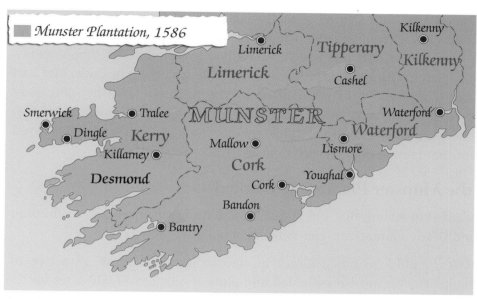

▲ The 1586 Plantation of Munster

The Desmond Rebellions

This first rebellion in 1569 was led by James Fitzmaurice Fitzgerald (the cousin of the Earl of Desmond) but it was easily put down. Fitzmaurice Fitzgerald fled the country and went to seek military help from the Catholic monarchs of Europe. He travelled to France, Spain and Italy and finally was promised soldiers by Pope Gregory XIII who regarded the conflict in Ireland as part of the Counter Reformation (see Chapter 7, The Reformation). Fitzmaurice Fitzgerald returned to Ireland in 1579 and began the second Desmond Rebellion. He was defeated and killed very early on in the rebellion but the Earl of Desmond then became involved and 600 troops sent by the Pope arrived in Smerwick Harbour, County Kerry in 1580.

▲ Ross Castle, the seat of the Desmonds in Killarney, County Kerry

English troops led by Lord Deputy Mountjoy surrounded the 600 soldiers as they landed. When they surrendered to the English, they were all massacred by Mountjoy's troops. The Earl was caught and killed by some of his Irish enemies who sent his head to Queen Elizabeth while his body was hung in Cork. The Earl of Desmond's lands were fully confiscated by the English crown in 1586. Very quickly the rebellion was over and most of Munster lay in ruins. It is estimated that 30,000 people were killed and most of the region's crops and cattle were destroyed which meant that famine gripped the countryside.

How the Munster Plantation Worked

Elizabeth wanted to ensure that the Munster Plantation was more successful than the Laois and Offaly Plantations. Her aims included the following:

1. The estates should be much larger in size so as to be more attractive to Englishmen. The estates were divided into plots of 4,000 to 12,000 acres each.

2. The planters were ordered to bring English tenants and staff with them as well as English craftsmen and livestock to ensure the spread of English language, customs and the Protestant religion. These planters were known as **undertakers** as they undertook (promised) to uphold the crown's conditions.

3. Elizabeth thought Spain might view Catholic Ireland as a good landing point for an invasion and so the undertakers also had to be ready to defend England from possible invasion.

WHO WERE THE UNDERTAKERS?

In estates of 12,000 acres they undertook to:
1. Remove all the Gaelic Irish from the land.
2. Bring with them from England:
   (a) Approximately 90 English tenants.
   (b) More than 70 household servants.
   (c) Craftsmen, e.g. carpenters and blacksmiths.
   (d) Sheep, cattle and horses.
3. Provide equipment for 15 horse soldiers and each tenant had to be able to equip one footsoldier.
4. Pay their annual rent to the crown. For estates that were less than 12,000 acres the requirements were smaller.

By the middle of the 1590s a number of problems had arisen. Only between one quarter and one third of the proposed 20,000 planters had come to Ireland. This meant that land had to be rented out to the Gaelic Irish. The planters had to live in fortified towns as they feared attacks from the Gaelic Irish in general and the Fitzgeralds in particular. Eventually many of the undertakers left Ireland and returned to England leaving their estates to be managed by someone else. These became known as **absentees** as they were literally absent from their land. By the end of the sixteenth century most of the planters had been killed or had fled the conflict.

RESULTS OF THE MUNSTER PLANTATION

This second phase of plantation in Munster had lasting consequences.

1. A number of new towns were set up in the region. Killarney, County Kerry, Lismore, County Waterford and Youghal, Mallow and Bandon, all in County Cork were established during this time. They became important economic centres and market towns for the region. English laws and customs were used in these places.

◀ A map of Bandon – one of the new towns established as a result of the Munster Plantation.

2. The introduction of new farming methods by the planters helped the local economy and many new trades sprang up and prospered, such as coopering (making casks or barrels to hold flour, gunpowder and milk) and the making of iron. Sir Walter Raleigh was one of the people who received land in Munster and he is credited with planting the first potato crop in Ireland.

3. A small number of Protestants remained even though not as many as Elizabeth had hoped. They were largely located in the towns where their numbers made them feel safer.

▲ Sir Walter Raleigh explored parts of North America and parts of South America. He is famous for introducing tobacco, potatoes and turkeys into Europe.

Questions

1. What were the causes of the Desmond rebellion?

2. Who was the leader of the first Desmond rebellion?

3. Why did he travel to Europe?

4. What happened at Smerwick Harbour in 1580?

5. Give three consequences of the rebellion in the province of Munster.

6. What were the main characteristics of the Munster Plantation?

7. Who were the undertakers and what did they undertake to do?

8. What, if any, were the lasting consequences of the Munster Plantation?

9. Was the Munster Plantation more or less successful than the Plantation of Laois and Offaly? Give reasons for your answer.

10. Had the English government learnt any lessons from the previous plantation? Give reasons for your answer.

The Ulster Plantation

▲ Hugh O'Neill, Earl of Tyrone.

Ulster had the strongest and most powerful chiefs in Ireland. The O'Neills of Tyrone and the O'Donnells of Donegal had not been affected by the Norman invasion of Ireland in the twelfth century and the English had never tried to fully conquer Ulster as it was a very remote region and difficult to reach. Elizabeth made attempts to ensure loyalty by appointing Hugh O'Neill, who had been educated in England, as Earl of Tyrone in 1582. He demonstrated his loyalty when he fought for the English during the Desmond Rebellion in 1579. However, during the early 1590s Elizabeth and Lord Deputy Fitzwilliam encouraged adventurers to lay claims to land and imposed sheriffs in Ulster. This made Hugh O'Neill and the leader of the O'Donnells, 'Red' Hugh O'Donnell, feel very threatened. In response to Queen Elizabeth's actions, in 1593 Hugh O'Donnell and the Archbishop of Armagh made an approach to King Philip of Spain for help to defend Ulster from Protestantism. Philip refused to send troops but despite this setback, O'Donnell and other Ulster leaders joined together to launch an attack on the English in 1594.

• The Nine Years War: 1594-1603

Hugh O'Neill employed a large number of Scottish **mercenaries** (soldiers for hire) called Gallowglasses. His well-trained army consisted of almost 10,000 men. He joined with O'Donnell and in 1598 defeated a significant English force at the battle of Yellow Ford. With this success, the rebellion spread through much of Gaelic Ireland. The rebels were further encouraged by the news that King Philip had changed his mind and decided that it was in the interests of Spain to help them fight the English. As a result, 3,500 Spanish soldiers arrived in Kinsale, County Cork in September 1601. O'Neill and O'Donnell, based in Ulster, had to decide how they would join with the Spanish, who were now besieged in Kinsale by a government army.

The Gaelic leaders marched the length of Ireland to free the Spanish. Upon their arrival in Kinsale on Christmas Eve 1601, they fought an unsuccessful battle against the English army.

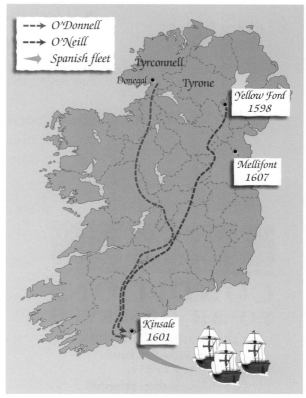

▲ A map showing the route of Hugh O'Neill and Hugh O'Donnell's armies from Ulster to Kinsale.

As a result of this defeat, the English allowed the Spanish to return home. O'Neill and much of his army escaped and continued to harass the English army. However, in 1603 O'Neill realised he had no hope of defeating the English army and so signed the Treaty of Mellifont. This Treaty allowed him to keep his Earldom and lands but over the next number of years he felt increasingly threatened by the English administration. In 1607 Hugh O'Neill and many of the Gaelic chieftains fled Ireland and went to other Catholic countries in Europe in what became known as the **Flight of the Earls**. While many of the Gaelic chieftains hoped to return, the Flight effectively ended all organised Gaelic resistance to English rule in Ireland.

Questions

1. Why did Elizabeth trust Hugh O'Neill?
2. Give two reasons why the Gaelic leaders in Ulster decided to revolt against the English crown.
3. Name two groups from outside Ireland who also fought in the Ulster Rebellion on the side of O'Neill.
4. What was the Flight of the Earls?

How the Ulster Plantation Worked

Elizabeth I died in 1603 and she was succeeded by her cousin James. He confiscated the lands of the Irish who had fled abroad and began to organise the Ulster Plantation. Having learnt some of the lessons of Munster, he applied stricter conditions to the Ulster **undertakers**. The plantation of six of the counties of Ulster in 1610 provided estates of 1,000, 1,500 and 2,000 acres and four different groups were allowed to have land.

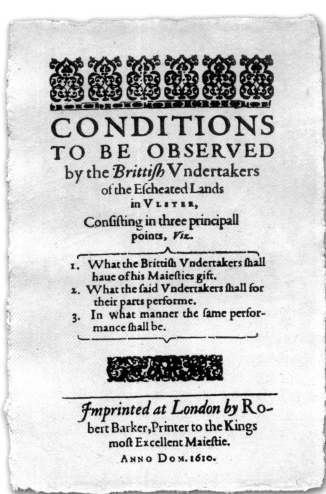

▲ Try reading the three principal points on the page. Notice how the 'f's and 's's are very similar and how 'u' is written as 'v'.

1. UNDERTAKERS

Many undertakers in Munster had not been able to pay the rents so the rent for this group in Ulster was very low to encourage people to come to Ireland. They could only have English or Scottish tenants. To ensure their safety, the undertakers undertook to have at least 24 men over the age of 18 on their land within three years. Depending on the size of the estate, they were expected to build a stone house or castle on their land for security and it was to be located close to other undertakers.

2. SERVITORS

The **Servitors** were soldiers who had 'served' in the English army during the Nine Years War. They were the second largest group and they were allowed some Irish tenants as long as they were supervised. Their rent was slightly more expensive than the undertakers if they chose to take Irish tenants.

3. LOYAL IRISH

Some Gaelic Irish were allowed to have estates. These were the Irish who had remained loyal to the English Crown during the Nine Years War. They paid almost twice the rent that the undertakers were charged. To ensure the safety of the plantation, it was decided that they should be located close to Servitors. Only 17 Gaelic Irish received large plantations; about 300 others received smaller amounts of land averaging about 300 acres each.

4. LONDON CRAFT GUILD

The area around the city of Derry was renamed Londonderry and the craft guilds of London were asked to provide members to settle in the area. King James wanted to ensure that the plantation was economically successful and so it needed new industries. Twelve different craft guilds sent planters to Derry. Using the map on the right, work out what each guild did.

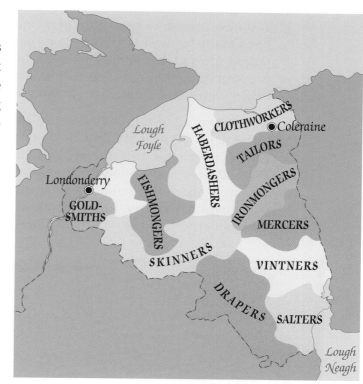

▲ A map showing the craft guilds into which the city of Derry was divided.

RESULTS OF THE ULSTER PLANTATION

1. The Ulster Plantation was far more successful than the previous two plantations. A large number of Protestant English and Scottish Presbyterians took up the estates and the Protestant population increased. By 1640 there were 40,000 Scots out of the total population of one million spread all across Ulster.

2. With the influx of Scottish Presbyterians and English Anglicans into Ulster, the numbers of Protestants in Ireland grew. This religious difference brought tensions in Ulster as many Irish Catholics resented losing their land and positions of power. At the same time, the new Protestant settlers feared for their lives as they travelled across Ulster. These tensions became more dangerous and within 40 years violent **sectarian conflict** (fighting or hostility between two or more religious communities) had broken out.

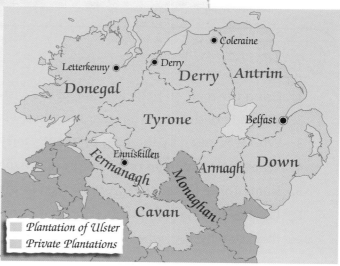

▲ The 1603 Plantation of Ulster and some private plantations.

3. The new industries created a great number of jobs. The production of linen made from Ulster flax became very successful and important to the region. Mills to weave the linen were built, and the new farming methods brought in by the Scots and English improved the Ulster farms. The new towns were full of merchants buying and selling new products.

4. New towns were established across Ulster on the site of existing Gaelic settlements. As well as Derry, or Londonderry as it was called then, towns such as Coleraine, Letterkenny and Enniskillen were planned and built. Over 20 were built following the same plan: a square called a 'diamond' with straight streets coming from the diamond and a large high wall surrounding the city for protection. The map below has a plan of Londonderry. Can you find the diamond and the city walls?

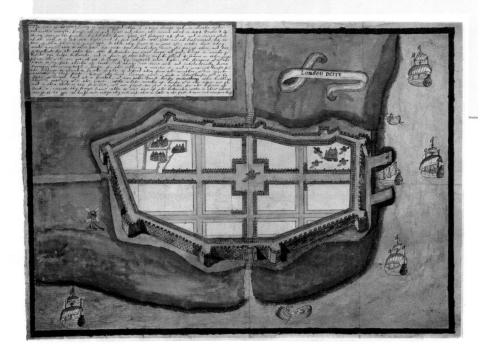

◀ A map of Londonderry

Questions

1. Using the map on page 205, name the Ulster counties that were planted.

2. Which English king organised the Ulster Plantation?

3. Who was asked by the king to 'plant' Derry?

4. What were the main religious groups involved in the Plantation of Ulster?

5. Name three trades that were located in the new town of 'Londonderry'.

6. (a) Was this Plantation more successful than the previous plantations?

   (b) If so why, (i.e. what made this plantation more successful than previous ones)?

7. What long-term consequences do you think the Plantation of Ulster had on the whole of Ireland?

The Cromwellian Plantation

Pulling them about the streets by the haire of the head, dashing the Childrens braines against the postes saynge these were the pigges of the English Sowes.

▲ English Protestants being killed by Irish Catholics.

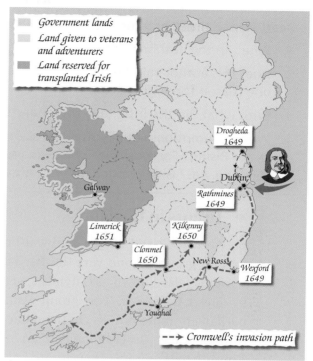

Government lands

Land given to veterans and adventurers

Land reserved for transplanted Irish

Drogheda 1649
Dublin
Rathmines 1649
Galway
Limerick 1651
Kilkenny 1650
Clonmel 1650
New Ross
Wexford 1649
Youghal

--▶ *Cromwell's invasion path*

▲ Cromwell's Path of Invasion in Ireland

The tensions in Ireland between the new Protestant settlers and the Gaelic Catholic Irish continued. In 1641 a rebellion broke out across all of Ulster. Between 10 to 15% of Protestants in Ulster were killed and many more fled either to Britain or to the safety of Dublin and towns. Fearing that the new Protestant English would associate them with the Gaelic Irish and persecute them for their religion, the Old English joined forces with the Gaelic Irish in an alliance called the **Catholic Confederacy** in 1642.

However, the Old English and the Gaelic Irish did not really trust each other and they fought two separate campaigns against the Protestant settlers rather than fully cooperating and fighting as one group.

By the way . . .

In the nineteenth century the Catholic Confederacy became known as the Confederation of Kilkenny.

Source A

In 1646, Sir John Temple wrote:

. . . All bonds and ties of faith and friendship were now broken; Irish tenants and servants. . . sacrifice[d]. . . their English Landlords and masters, one neighbour cruelly murdered by another; Irish children. . . fell to strip and kill English children; all other relations laid aside, and it was now esteemed [thought] a most meritorious work [a great deed] in any of them that could by any means or ways whatsoever, bring an English man to slaughter. . . The English well know they had given them [the Irish] no manner of provocation; they had entertained them with great demonstrations of love and affection. . . [the Irish had] their hearts enraged with malice and hatred against all of the English nation, breathing forth nothing but their ruin, destruction and utter extirpation [extermination]. From *The Irish Rebellion* by Sir John Temple

Questions

Read Source A and answer the following questions.

1. What, in the author's view, was the 'most meritorious work'?

2. Does this author think that the English did anything to deserve such a death? Give one reason for your answer.

3. With what did the Irish have their hearts enraged?

4. What assumptions could you make about the author of this report on the 1641 Ulster Rising? For example, where do you think he was from? What religion do you think he was? Give reasons for your answers.

● Events in England

Between 1642 and 1649 a civil war broke out in England. The civil war was fought by two groups – one was the **Parliamentarians**, which was largely made up of Puritans (also known as Calvinists, see page 173 of Chapter 7, The Reformation), led by Oliver Cromwell. This group wanted to reduce the power of the king and give parliament more power. On the other side, the **Royalists** supported the position of King Charles I. By 1649 the Parliamentary Army, known as the New Model Army or **Roundheads** due to their short haircuts, had defeated the Royalist forces. The English Parliament decided to behead Charles I. In 1649 Cromwell turned his attention to Ireland.

▲ Oliver Cromwell, leader of the Parliamentarians, who wanted to reduce the power of the King of England and give parliament more control.

▲ King Charles I, King of England, who was beheaded in 1649.

Cromwell in Ireland

The English Parliament believed that the defeat of the Catholic Irish would be of benefit to them because:

1. They needed to pay Parliamentary soldiers for their many years of fighting and they wanted to offer land in Ireland as payment. Also the Parliament had borrowed money from **adventurers** during the civil war which they needed to repay.

2. Many of the Parliamentarians were strict Puritans and so they wished to gain revenge for the killing of so many Protestants in the 1641 Ulster rebellion by the Catholic Irish. They also wanted to destroy all Catholicism in Ireland.

▲ A roundhead soldier

3. The English Parliament wanted to put down the rebellion to ensure no other Catholic European country (e.g. Spain, France) would use Ireland as a landing point for an invasion into England.

In 1649 Cromwell landed in Dublin with 12,000 well-trained and battle-hardened Roundheads. He immediately marched on the town of Drogheda and besieged it. Eventually the town fell and Cromwell killed all the defending soldiers as a warning to other towns that did not surrender. Dundalk surrendered and upon hearing the news of the massacre in Drogheda, the soldiers fled from Trim so fast they left their guns behind them. Cromwell now travelled south and besieged the town of Wexford which refused to surrender. It was captured and all its defenders and most of its population were killed. He took the towns of New Ross, Clonmel, Kilkenny and Youghal. Within a year Cromwell felt it was safe to leave Ireland in the hands of his son-in-law and return to England. By 1652 with the fall of Limerick and Galway, Ireland was fully under the control of the English forces.

▲ Oliver Cromwell's soldiers besiege Drogheda in 1649

Questions

1. Why did the Old English decide to join with the Gaelic Irish?

2. Explain the following words:

   (a) Royalist   (b) Roundhead   (c) Parliamentarians

3. What were the reasons for the Cromwellian invasion of Ireland?

4. Why do you think Cromwell and his New Model Army were so successful during their invasion?

5. Which side in this conflict do you think the artist of the image on page 209 supports? Give reasons for your answer.

RESULTS OF THE CROMWELLIAN PLANTATION

1. The country was devastated. After almost 12 years of warfare and bloodshed, many towns and farms were destroyed and there was widespread famine.

2. Some Catholic priests were captured and either executed or sent to islands such as Barbados to work on the sugar plantations. In some cases there was even a reward for capturing a Catholic priest. For this reason many priests fled to Europe.

3. Catholic prisoners of war, including women and children, and homeless vagrants were also sent to the West Indies as workers.

4. Approximately 30,000 Irish soldiers were allowed to leave Ireland and join the armies of other European countries.

5. Cromwell employed **William Petty** to survey the whole island of Ireland so that they would be able to distribute the land amongst his soldiers and the adventurers. As a result, Ireland became the best-mapped country in Europe until the nineteenth century. As the details of Ireland were written 'down', the survey became known as the **Down Survey.**

6. The Act of Settlement was passed in 1652. This act stated that:

   • Any Old English or Gaelic Irish who fought against England lost all their lands.

   • If a landlord had not fought but could not prove he or she was loyal to England, the choice was to go to 'Hell or to Connacht'. These people were transplanted to smaller amounts of land west of the Shannon with poorer soil. They were also forbidden to have any land within one mile of the coast as it was reserved for soldiers.

● How successful were the Plantations?

While the Laois-Offaly and the Munster Plantations had been generally unsuccessful, the consequences of the Ulster and Cromwellian Plantations lasted for a long time.

1. The land confiscated by the Cromwellian Plantation was used to pay three different groups:

   (a) The adventurers who had paid for the war.

   (b) The suppliers who had provided the ships, guns, boots, food and so on.

   (c) The soldiers.

   Very few of the adventurers and suppliers came to Ireland and only 20% of the soldiers were still in Ireland by 1670. Most of the land was bought by army officers and New English Protestants who had come to Ireland after the Reformation and were now able to expand their large estates. The Cromwellian plantation was more like a massive transfer of landownership than a plantation of new English planters.

2. The Ulster Plantation succeeded in bringing a large number of Protestants to that part of Ireland. The north of Ireland now had a majority of Scottish Presbyterians and English Anglicans but the rest of Ireland remained much as it had before the plantation. However, after the Cromwellian Plantation the number of Catholic landowners dropped dramatically. By 1703 there was only 14% of Ireland in Catholic ownership. It remained that way for almost another 200 years. Practically all the power, land and industry in Ireland were in the hands of a small minority of the total population of the island.

3. As Catholics lost their lands they were forced to become tenants on Protestant estates. In addition, Catholics were forbidden to live in towns and so could not own shops or trade with others. They became increasingly poor as their land was divided up into smaller plots after each generation.

4. Lack of land, wealth and opportunities drove Catholics to become **Tories** (from the Irish *tóraí* meaning an outlaw) or else they grew dependent on single crops such as potatoes to feed their families. Crops such as potatoes were popular as large numbers could be grown in small plots rather than cereals or livestock which needed large farms. This dependency on one crop was to have dire consequences over the next 150 years.

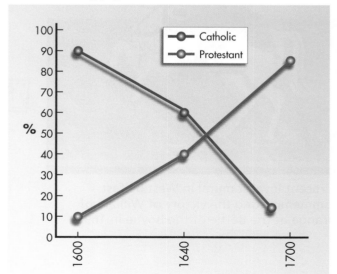

▲ Changes in the land ownership of Ireland 1600-1700

▲ A map of Ireland showing Catholic land ownership in 1703.

Percentage of land in
Catholic ownership, 1703
25 or more
11 to 24
10 or less

▲ A recent loyalist mural in West Belfast commemorating the victory of William of Orange at the Battle of the Boyne in 1690.

5. The attempts by each plantation to destroy the Catholic religion in Ireland largely failed. Apart from the Pale and the influx of Protestants – in particular Presbyterians into Ulster – Ireland remained strongly Catholic. Over the next 200 years there were many attempts to convert the population to Protestantism using both force and rewards. Despite this, Catholicism continued to be the religion of the vast majority of Irish people outside Ulster and cities.

6. The Catholic population was very angry due to the confiscation of its land. At the same time, the Protestant population was gripped with constant fear that the Catholics would rise up and kill them. This anger and fear resulted in lasting divisions between the two communities. The history of Ireland was affected by these divisions for hundreds of years and in parts of the island these divisions continued for almost the next 400 years.

7. Gaelic poets and writers in the period after the plantations wrote about the sufferings of their fellow Irishmen under the Cromwellian land system. An Englishman, Arthur Young, who visited Ireland over a hundred years later commented,

Source B

In Ireland a long series of oppressions, aided by many ill-judged laws, have brought the landlords into a habit of exerting a very lofty superiority and their vassals (tenants) into an almost unlimited submission.

From *A Tour of Ireland* by Arthur Young

Questions

1. Give two examples of restrictions Cromwell placed on Catholics after the conquest.

2. What differences in success were there between the Ulster and Cromwellian Plantations?

3. In terms of culture, religion and politics what disadvantages did the Irish Catholics suffer as a result of the Cromwellian Plantation?

Chapter 8 Questions

A  **B**  **C**

▲ Maps showing plantations of Ireland

1. Pictures

1. (i) Name the plantations connected with each of the maps above.

   (ii) Choose one of these plantations and give the following details:

      (a) The name of the plantation.

      (b) The leaders of the Irish rebellion or rising associated with the plantation.

      (c) The English monarch who ordered the plantation.

      (d) Was the plantation successful? Give two reasons for your opinion.

2. Documents

(a) A colonist from Nottinghamshire praises the Munster colony (1590):

> Their soil for the most part is very fertile and apt [suitable] for wheat, rye, barley... and all other grains and fruits that England anywise doth yield [produce]. There is much good timber in many places...There is very rich and great plenty of iron stone... also there is a great store of lead ore, and wood sufficient to maintain divers iron and lead works (with good husbandry) for ever.
>
> [From *A Brief Description of Ireland* by Robert Payne]

(b)

> Many of the Munster men now first about October, 1598 broke into rebellion and joined themselves with Tyrone's forces, spoiled [destroyed] the country, burnt the villages, and pulled down the houses and castles of the English, against whom they committed all abominable out–rages...The Munster rebellion broke out like a lightning, for in one month's space almost all the Irish were in rebellious arms, and the English were murdered, or stripped and banished.
>
> [From *An Itinerary* by Fynes Moryson]

(c)

> The cause of this original hate [among Irishmen] is that they were conquered by the English, the memory whereof is yet fresh among them and the desire both of revenge and also of recovery of their lands, is daily revived and kindled amongst them by their lords and counsellors; for which they both hate ourselves and our laws and customs.
>
> [From *A Brief Note of Ireland* by Edmund Spenser]

(i) From Document (a), mention one aspect of the Munster colony praised by the writer.

(ii) From Document (b), mention two actions taken by Munster men during the Munster Rebellion.

(iii) According to Document (c), what do the rebels desire?

(iv) From your knowledge of the plantations, give two reasons why the Munster Plantation failed.

3. Short-Answer Questions

(a) Where did the first policy of plantation of Ireland take place?

(b) Whose land was confiscated after the rebellion in Munster in the 1580s?

(c) Give two reasons why a rebellion occurred in Ulster in 1641.

(d) What was the Down Survey?

(e) What was meant by the phrase *To Hell or to Connacht*?

(f) What effect did the Cromwellian Plantation have on Catholic landowners?

(g) Why did Protestants fear the Catholic Irish in the years after the plantations?

(h) Why did the potato become more popular with the poorer Irish during the seventeenth century?

(i) Match the following plantations (A–D) with the correct terms (1–7):

A Plantation of Laois and Offaly	1	New Model Army
B Plantation of Munster	2	Earl of Desmond
C Plantation of Ulster	3	Hugh O'Neill
D Plantation of Cromwell	4	The O'Connor Family
	5	The Act of Settlement 1652
	6	James Fitzmaurice Fitzgerald
	7	The Battle of Kinsale

(j) Who in Ireland were known as Tories at the end of the seventeenth century?

4. People in History

Write about one of the following:

(a) A settler who received land during a **named** plantation in Ireland during the sixteenth or seventeenth century.

(b) A native Irish landowner who had his land confiscated during a **named** plantation during the sixteenth or seventeenth century.

In each case mention:

- The reasons for the plantation
- Why the person received or lost the land
- Where the planters came from
- The results of the plantation for the person

5.

How did the fortunes of the following religious groups in Ireland change throughout the period of plantation?

(a) Catholics

(b) Anglicans

(c) Presbyterians

Write about the changes in political power, land-ownership and religious freedom.

Key Terms to Summarise Chapter 8: The Plantations

The Pale A protected area in the sixteenth century where English laws and customs existed. It stretched from Dundalk to Dalkey and out towards Trim, Kells and Tallaght.

Old English English living in Ireland who were loyal to the English monarch.

Gaelicised Anglo-Norman Catholic descendents of the Norman settlers in Ireland who had adopted many of the Irish customs.

Lord Deputy of Ireland The English monarch's representative in Ireland.

Gaelic Irish The Catholic Gaelic chieftains who spoke Irish and used Brehon Laws.

Surrender and Regrant English policy to anglicise the legal and landowning system of Ireland.

Succession English system under which the oldest son inherits the land of his father.

Plantation English policy in Ireland that 'planted' loyal English in lands confiscated from disloyal Irish.

Woodkernes Gaelic-Irish outlaws who raided the area of the Pale.

Adventurers The name given to the people encouraged by the English monarch to lay claims on Irish lands.

Undertakers English planters who 'undertook' to fulfil certain conditions when they received land in Ireland.

Absentees Landlords who did not live on their estates.

Servitors Soldiers who had 'served' in the English army and were rewarded with land in Ireland.

Catholic Confederacy An alliance between the Old English and the Gaelic Irish against the Protestant English.

Parliamentarians Those who supported parliament against the king in the English Civil War.

Royalists Those who supported the king during the English Civil War.

Roundheads Soldiers of the English Parliamentary army.

Down Survey A survey of all of Ireland to help with the distribution of land to planters.

Tories (toraí) The name given to Irish Catholic outlaws during the late sixteenth and seventeenth centuries.

Web References

For further reading on topics mentioned in this chapter, view the following websites:

www.bbc.co.uk/history/british/plantation/

www.bl.uk/learning/histcitizen/uk/ireland/irelandintro.html

www.libraryireland.com/History.php

www.flightoftheearls.ie/

Women in History

▲ Elizabeth I ruled over England for 45 years.

Elizabeth I (1533-1603)

Elizabeth I of England was one of the longest reigning monarchs of the English throne. Having ascended the throne after her brother and sister both died at a young age, she showed great strength of character through her ability to control the different religious groups at the time. She created the Anglican Church and calmed the tensions between the Catholics and Protestants in England. Concerned about the possibility of Catholic threats to her throne, she was lucky to avoid the invasion of her country when the Spanish Armada was scattered as it tried to invade England in 1588. She never married and was known as the 'Virgin Queen'. She was succeeded by James VI of Scotland. Elizabeth reigned at one of the most turbulent and difficult periods of English history and saw the expansion of her empire into Ireland. She left a long legacy and perhaps defined the country of England in the post-Reformation Age.

Chapter 9

AGE OF REVOLUTIONS

Background to Revolution

Europe in the eighteenth century was ruled by monarchies. Spain, Portugal, France and the Netherlands all had kings or queens who ruled their kingdoms as they wished. They had absolute control over the people and over the right to raise taxes. This kind of royal rule is known as an **absolute monarchy**.

In Britain, King George III also had great powers but he had to consult with the British parliament before any new taxes or laws were passed. The parliament was made up of very wealthy landlords and aristocrats who supported the king in most decisions he made. This form of rule is called a **limited monarchy**.

However, both these types of monarchs believed in the 'divine right of kings'. They thought that God had specially chosen them to rule over their country and so what they decided must automatically be divine and correct. Over the eighteenth and nineteenth centuries, this view changed. The ordinary people in Europe and America began to question this assumption of the divine right of monarchs to do as they wished. These people began to demand that their views and opinions should be heard.

Many European thinkers argued that the people of Europe should demand more freedoms. **John Locke** (1632-1704) and **Thomas Hobbes** (1588-1679) were known as **contractarians** as they both believed that a type of contract should be made between the ruler and the ruled, outlining the rights and the responsibilities of the population and the ruler. If members of the population abused

▲ King George III ruled over Britain and Ireland.

▲ John Locke (1632–1704), English philosopher.

▲ Thomas Hobbes believed a form of contract should be made between ruler and people.

these rights and responsibilities, then the ruler could punish the culprits. Likewise, if the ruler broke any part of the contract then revolution by the population was acceptable.

Jean Jacques Rousseau (1712-1778), a French writer and philosopher, believed that there was no such thing as the divine right of kings and argued that a parliament, elected by the people, was the only acceptable way in which to rule a country. Finally, **Voltaire** (1694-1788), another French writer, argued that the power of the Churches was too great. He felt there should be much greater religious freedom and that each individual had the right to believe what they liked without fear of persecution. While these ideas may seem quite logical to us now, these concepts were revolutionary in the eighteenth century. These ideas spread across Europe and into the new colonies of America. By 1776 a British writer, **Thomas Paine**, had written a pamphlet called *Common Sense* which encouraged the American colonies to revolt and declare independence from Britain.

▲ Jean Jacques Rousseau was a French writer and philosopher.

▲ Voltaire believed the Church's power was too great.

▲ Thomas Paine wrote a pamphlet called *Common Sense* that influenced the American Revolution.

 ## Causes of the American Revolution

By the end of the sixteenth century, European powers had many colonies in the New World. Spain and Portugal divided up South America. North America was claimed by the British, the French, the Dutch and the Spanish. The French controlled modern-day Canada and all down the Mississippi to New Orleans and Louisiana. The Dutch owned New Amsterdam until 1664 when it was sold to the British and renamed New York. The Spanish took Florida and the British established 13 colonies along the east coast.

The first colony established by the British was in Virginia in 1607. Catholics fleeing religious persecution in Britain established a colony called Maryland in the 1630s. They were followed first by Puritans (English Calvinists) and then by Quakers led by William Penn. These people founded the colonies of Massachusetts and Pennsylvania.

Laws made in Britain were enforced in the American colonies by a **governor** who represented the British king and ruled over the population. The colonists were not allowed to elect an MP to the British Parliament so they had no one to argue on their behalf. This led to tensions between them and the British government.

These colonies were a great source of raw materials for Britain. Sugar beet, tobacco and cotton were important for British industries and in return the British protected the colonists from the native Indians and the French with whom the British had fought the **Seven Years War** (1756-1763). After the Seven Years War in which the British took control of Canada also, the British government kept large numbers of troops in America. This was expensive and King George III believed that the colonists should pay for this with their own taxes. In order to increase tax revenues, the **Stamp Act** was passed in 1765, which placed a tax in the colonies on all official documents such as wills, licences and college degrees, public documents such as newspapers and even playing cards and dice. The colonists resented these taxes and

riots broke out across the major towns. They felt that as they were not represented by any MPs in parliament in Britain, it was unfair for the British to impose taxes on the colonies. The slogan 'No taxation without representation' was shouted at these protests and riots and it was adopted by a group called the **Sons of Liberty** who attacked British officials and burnt their stamps.

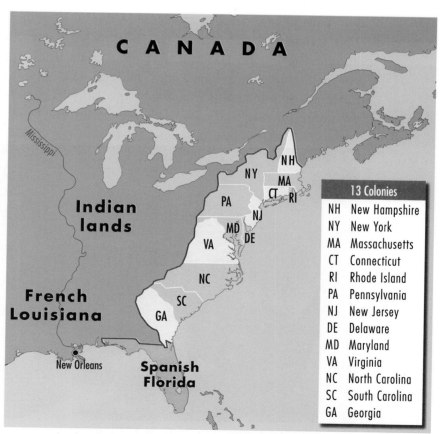

13 Colonies	
NH	New Hampshire
NY	New York
MA	Massachusetts
CT	Connecticut
RI	Rhode Island
PA	Pennsylvania
NJ	New Jersey
DE	Delaware
MD	Maryland
VA	Virginia
NC	North Carolina
SC	South Carolina
GA	Georgia

▲ The 13 British colonies on the east coast of America were an important source of raw materials for Britain.

▲ The Boston Massacre of 1770 by Paul Revere, patriot of the American Revolution.

The British government was very angry and insisted that it had every right to impose taxes. However, it **repealed** (officially withdrew) the Stamp Act but replaced it with another set of taxes. The **Townshend Acts** placed new duties (taxes) on items such as glass, paints, lead, paper and tea.

In a country that was building many new homes and towns, these taxes were particularly damaging. When more riots broke out, the British responded with force. In March 1770 five protestors were shot dead and another seven injured in Boston. This **Boston Massacre** increased the anger felt by the American colonists. Britain repealed the Townshend Acts to calm the situation down but then passed the **Tea Act** of 1773. This allowed the British East India Company to sell tea in the colonies without paying any import tax, making their price far cheaper than anyone else's. More protests occurred and in December 1773 American colonists disguised as American Indians boarded an East India Company ship and dumped its entire cargo of 45 tonnes of tea into Boston Harbour. This event was known as the **Boston Tea Party** and Britain's response was immediate. Boston Harbour was shut down until the East India Company was **compensated** (paid back) and **martial law** (the army was in control) was introduced. The conflict between the British and the American colonists had **escalated** (grown) and now there was no turning back.

▲ During the Boston Tea Party of 1773, American colonists disguised as American Indians boarded a British East Indian Company ship and dumped its cargo of 45 tonnes of tea into Boston Harbour.

1. Explain the following terms:

   (a) Absolute monarchy   (b) Divine right of kings   (c) Limited monarchy

2. Why were Hobbes and Locke known as contractarians?

3. What views did Voltaire hold about the church?

4. What did Thomas Paine suggest in his pamphlet, *Common Sense*?

5. What was the name of the first American colony set up by the British?

6. What was the role of a British Governor in the colonies?

7. Name three raw materials the colonies exported to Britain.

8. Name three items on which the Stamp Act placed taxes.

9. What does 'No taxation without representation' mean?

10. Why were the Townshend Acts so disliked by the colonists?

11. Examine the image of the Boston Massacre on page 220. Do you think the artist is pro- or anti-British? Give three reasons for your opinion.

The American War of Independence

The American colonists decided to call a meeting of all the colonies. In September 1774 they organised a large meeting called the **First Continental Congress** in Philadelphia to discuss how they were going to deal with the British. They were determined to remove Britain from the American colonies and were ready to use force if necessary. Guns and ammunition were collected and each colony prepared to go to war. The British Governor of Massachusetts, General Gage, heard about these plans and began to march with his troops to Lexington, Massachusetts, where he believed the American weapons were stored. Luckily for the Americans, a member of the Sons of Liberty named **Paul Revere** discovered this information and rode through the night to warn the people of Lexington. As a result some Americans were ready for the British troops when they arrived into Lexington. After a short skirmish (fight) the colonists fell back and the British were attacked again at the town of Concord where hundreds of Americans were waiting. The British were defeated and had to retreat to Boston. These small battles were the opening shots of the American War of Independence.

A **Second Continental Congress** was organised in May 1775. A new army called the **American Continental Army** was created with a wealthy landowner named **George Washington** as commander. The Battle of Bunker Hill followed a number of days later. Although the Americans were defeated, they inflicted a large number of casualties on the British. On 4 July 1776 the Second Continental Congress passed the **Declaration of Independence** written by **Thomas Jefferson**.

▲ Paul Revere riding to warn the people of Lexington.

The opening lines of the declaration are some of the most famous in history:

We hold these truths to be self-evident, that all men are created equal, that they are endowed by their Creator with certain unalienable Rights, that among these are Life, Liberty and the pursuit of Happiness.

With this declaration, the Americans showed their determination to separate themselves fully from Britain. However they still had a war to win as the British were not ready to let the American colonies – and their ready supply of raw materials for the British market – slip out of their control.

▲ Thomas Jefferson, author of the Declaration of Independence

George Washington was a wealthy landowner from Virginia. He had fought with the British and colonists against the French in the Seven Years War and been very successful. He retired to Virginia and married a wealthy widow named Martha Dandridge. He was elected as Virginia's representative at the First and Second Continental Congresses. When chosen to lead the American Continental Army, he was given the difficult task of turning a large band of farmers and tradesmen into a professional army to rival the best of the British troops.

A. American Continental Army: Advantages and Disadvantages

ADVANTAGES	DISADVANTAGES
1. They knew the countryside well.	1. The army consisted of farmers and tradesmen and many insisted on going home to take in their harvest.
2. They could use guerrilla tactics.	2. They had little experience fighting against professional soldiers.
3. They were fighting for their homes.	3. They had no supply routes as they had no navy.
	4. They had no money so had little equipment and could not pay the soldiers.

B. British Army: Advantages and Disadvantages

ADVANTAGES	DISADVANTAGES
1. They were a professional and experienced army.	1. The army was very far away from Britain so they were far from the source of their suppliers.
2. The army was four times bigger than the Americans and included a navy.	2. They did not know the countryside.
3. They were well equipped and supplied with cannons, weapons and ammunition.	

Questions

1. Why did the colonists call the First Continental Congress?

2. Read the opening lines of the Declaration of Independence written by Jefferson. Name the unalienable rights that are listed.

3. Give three advantages and three disadvantages the American Continental Army faced in their conflict with the British.

4. Which countries were involved in the Seven Years War?

5. Who was made Commander of the American Continental Army in 1775?

6. What disadvantages did the British face in their conflict with the colonists?

Initially the Americans were successful. They drove the British out of Boston and captured cannons and weapons, but they were unable to hold New York. The loss of New York was followed by a crushing defeat at the **Battle of White Plains** in September 1776. Two smaller victories at Princeton and Trenton helped but they then had to surrender the home of the Continental Congress – Philadelphia – to the British.

However, just as the Americans were losing hope, the American General **Horatio Gates** defeated a large British army at Saratoga. American optimism was further boosted by the arrival of men, weapons and ships sent by the French, Spanish and Dutch.

● Valley Forge

During the winter of 1777-1778 Washington and his army camped in **Valley Forge**, 20 miles from Philadelphia. His men suffered badly from the freezing cold and the lack of clothes and food. More than 2,000 of the 12,000 soldiers died mostly from disease. The remaining troops found some hope in the training provided by a Prussian army officer named **Frederick von Steuben** (from Prussia in Germany). He taught the troops new techniques and made them into an organised and well-trained army. George Washington's decision to remain with his troops and suffer the same as they did endeared him to his troops.

◀ Frederick von Steuben (on the left) training the American Continental Army at Valley Forge in the winter of 1777 – 1778.

▲ George Washington with his troops at Valley Forge in the winter of 1777 – 1778

Source A This is an account from a soldier at Valley Forge.

There comes a soldier — his bare feet are seen thro' his worn out shoes — his legs nearly naked from the tattered remains of an only pair of stockings — his breeches not sufficient to cover his nakedness — his shirt hanging in strings — his hair dishevelled — his face meagre — his whole appearance pictures a person forsaken and discouraged.

Battle Victories

Bunker Hill (1775)	British victory
Boston town (1776)	Americans capture the town
New York town (1776)	British capture the town
White Plains (1776)	British defeat the Americans
Trenton (1776) and Princeton (1777)	Minor victories for Americans
Philadelphia (1777)	British capture the town
Saratoga (1777)	Americans under Gates defeat British
Yorktown (1781)	General Cornwallis surrenders to Washington

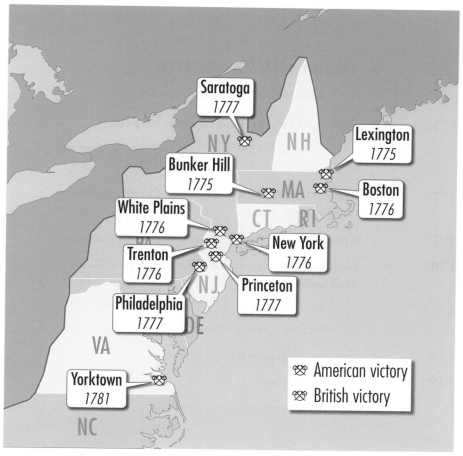

Saratoga
1777

NY

NH

Lexington
1775

Bunker Hill
1775

MA

Boston
1776

White Plains
1776

CT RI

Trenton
1776

New York
1776

NJ

Princeton
1777

Philadelphia
1777

DE

VA

Yorktown
1781

NC

⚔ American victory
⚔ British victory

▲ A map of the main battles of the American War of Independence,
1775 – 1781

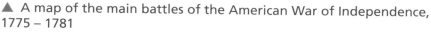

▲ The American flag in
1777 had 13 stars –
one for each colony.

▲ The current American flag
has 50 stars – one for each
state – and thirteen stripes
– one for each original
colony.

After that tough winter the supplies of ships, weapons and volunteers from France, Spain and the Netherlands began to have an effect. Slowly the Americans began to get the upper hand in the war. In 1781 Washington managed to defeat the British commander **General Cornwallis**. The British general was trapped in Yorktown in Virginia between Washington's army and the French fleet stationed along the coast. Cornwallis surrendered and the American War of Independence was over.

In 1783, the British government met an American delegation at Versailles in France to discuss terms. The **Treaty of Versailles** agreed to recognise the independence of the American colonies. George Washington returned to his plantation in Virginia after the war but in 1789 he was asked to become the first president of the new **United States of America.** He was president from 1789 to 1797 and died two years later.

▲ George Washington became the first president of the United States of America in 1789.

By the way . . .

George Washington is the only American President not to have lived in the White House as it was only completed in 1800 – one year after his death.

GEORGE WASHINGTON
✿ REVOLUTIONARY ✿

1732	Born in Westmoreland County, Virginia
1774	Sent as delegate for Virginia to First Continental Congress
1775	Made Commander of the New American Continental Army
1777	Spends the winter in Valley Forge with his men
1781	Cornwallis surrenders to Washington at Yorktown
1789	Asked to become the first president of the newly independent United States of America.
1797	Retires as president
1799	Dies in Virginia

Questions

1. List three victories achieved by the colonists against the British in the War of Independence.

2. Read the description of the winter spent at Valley Forge in Source A on page 224.
   What problems did the American Continental Army face?

3. How did Frederick von Steuben aid the American troops?

4. What other help did the American forces get and from whom?

5. Who was the Treaty of Versailles between and what did it recognise?

6. What position was George Washington given in 1789?

RESULTS OF THE AMERICAN REVOLUTION

➤ The revolution in America and its newly -won independence had an enormous effect on the world.

1. Erosion of the power of monarchy

During the eighteenth century the power of the monarchies began to decline. People now wanted to have a say in the running of the country and no longer accepted paying huge taxes to fund the king's expensive tastes. With the creation of a democratically elected government in America which had overthrown the British Empire, many people across Europe began to question the 'divine right of kings'. Instead, they expected their monarchs to serve their populations. When this did not happen, as we will see in France, the idea of removing the king or queen became acceptable.

2. Defeat of British

The defeat of the British Empire by a colony was a great shock to Britain and also to many Europeans. Britain, which was one of the great powers at the time, lost control of an area that provided raw materials and goods for its markets. The success of the American colonies inspired others to attempt revolutions of their own. Later in this chapter we will examine how Ireland was influenced by the American War of Independence.

3. The spread of new ideas

The ideas of Locke, Voltaire and Rousseau, which inspired many of the revolutionaries, continued to spread. The idea of democracy, although a very ancient concept, encouraged the Americans and when they achieved independence they put it into practice. Most parts of the world, although not all, now believe in democracy, equality and religious freedom. In fact, many use the American Declaration of Independence as an example to follow.

> **By the way . . .**
>
> Democracy means rule by the people. In Greek *demos* means people and *kratos* means to rule.

The creation of a free, democratic country that held the ideas of equality and liberty as important inspired others to believe in the same values. Many French fought alongside the Americans against the British. They learnt about the ideals that the Americans were fighting for and agreed with them. As we will see, on returning to France, these men began to push for similar reforms.

Chapter 9 Questions: American Revolution

1. Pictures

▲ A tax collector being tarred and feathered

(a) What is written upside down on the piece of paper on the tree?

(b) What do you think the men are pouring into the tax collector's mouth? Give a reason for your answer.

(c) Why do you think the man is being attacked?

(d) In what way did the collection of taxes contribute to the outbreak of the American War of Independence?

2. Documents

This is part of the letter sent by George Washington to his stepdaughter, Patsy, on being given the position of Commander of the American Continental Army:

> You may believe me, my dear Patsy, when I assure you, in the most solemn manner, that, so far from seeking this appointment, I have used every endeavour in my power to avoid it, not only from my unwillingness to part with you and the family, but from a consciousness of its being a trust too great for my capacity, and that I should enjoy more happiness in one month with you at home than I have the most distant prospect of finding abroad.

(a) What appointment does George Washington assure his stepdaughter, Patsy, that he has tried to avoid?

(b) Give one reason why he wished to avoid this appointment.

(c) Where does Washington say he would find more happiness?

(d) Does this letter give you the impression that George Washington wanted to get involved in the American War of Independence? Give a reason for your answer.

(e) From your studies, do you think Washington was a good Commander of the American Continental Army? Give reasons for your answer.

3. Short-Answer Questions

(a) Mention two causes of the American War of Independence.

(b) Give two reasons why the Americans defeated the British during the War of Independence.

(c) Why was the loss of Philadelphia such a blow to the American Colonists?

(d) Name two of the main military commanders on the colonists' side.

(e) Who surrendered to Washington at Yorktown?

(f) Give one example of how the ideals of the American War of Independence spread to Europe.

(g) How did the ideals of the American War of Independence conflict with the belief in the 'divine right of kings'?

(h) What was the name given to the newly independent America at the Treaty of Versailles?

(i) Abraham Lincoln described democracy as 'Government of the people, by the people, for the people.' Explain this statement in your own words.

4. People in History

Write about a named leader involved in the American Revolution during the period 1770-1781.

5.

(a) Write a paragraph about the following:
   (i) Boston Tea Party
   (ii) Winter at Valley Forge.

(b) Write an account on the lasting ideas of the American Revolution.

Causes of the French Revolution

By the end of the eighteenth century another revolution had broken out – this time in Europe. In 1789 the people of France revolted against their king and his government. This revolt provoked changes that influenced Europe for the next 200 years.

There were many reasons for this revolution.

● 1. Social Divisions

France in the 1780s was a very unfair country in which to live. The feudal system we looked at in Chapter 4 still existed in France. The country was ruled by King Louis XVI and the nobility. The king and the nobles were very rich and the peasants and ordinary people were very poor. This political system was called the ***ancien régime*** or 'old system'. Louis XVI had absolute power over the country. There was no parliament and he could pass any law he wanted. He even had the power to have someone killed.

However, Louis was a rather weak man who took very little interest in the politics of France. He preferred to go hunting on the land around his beautiful palace in Versailles. He married Marie-Antoinette, the sister of the Emperor of Austria, France's traditional enemy. She was distrusted and disliked by the French people because she was Austrian. They also believed she spent too much money on clothes and jewellery.

▲ King Louis XVI of France

▲ Queen Marie-Antoinette was originally from Austria.

The Palace of Versailles where King Louis and Queen Marie-Antoinette lived. ▲

Society in France in 1780 was divided into three different groups or 'estates'.

- The First Estate was the **clergy** (bishops and priests) of the Catholic Church. They did not pay any tax to the king.

- The Second Estate was the **nobility**. The nobility was made up of all the aristocrats in France. They were large landowners and they refused to pay tax.

- The Third Estate was made up of all the other people of France. Anyone who had to work for a living was part of the Third Estate. Some of them were quite wealthy and worked as lawyers or bankers, while others like farm labourers or peasants were very poor.

By the way . . .

Louis XVI seems to have disliked being King of France. When one of his ministers resigned, he was heard to remark, 'Why can't I resign too?'

The Three Estates of France: ▶ The Clergy, the Aristocrats and the Third Estate

First Estate	Second Estate	Third Estate
Clergy – Bishops/ Priests	Nobility (aristocracy – Lords, Dukes, Marquis etc.)	Everyone else – lawyers, merchants, peasants
Didn't pay taxes and decided who had to pay taxes	Refused to pay taxes	Had to pay taxes, e.g. tithes, tailles, gabelle, corvée
Approximately 100,000 men	Approximately 400,000 people	Approximately 25 million people
Owned 10% of land in France	Owned 60% of land in France	Most peasants still lived under feudal law

2. High Taxes

The First and Second Estates did not have to pay much, if any, tax even though they were some of the richest people in France. It was left to the Third Estate to pay most of the taxes.

▲ This political cartoon shows the First and Second Estate standing on the Third Estate.

There was a variety of taxes to be paid, including:

(a) The *Taille* – a land tax paid to the state.

(b) The **Tithe** – a tax of 10% of earnings or crops. This went to the Catholic Church.

(c) The *Gabelle* – a tax on salt that had to be paid by the Third Estate.

(d) The *Corvée* – members of the Third Estate had to work several days a year maintaining the roads across France without getting paid.

These taxes made many people in the Third Estate very unhappy. They believed that the First and Second Estates should have to pay taxes also. Some of the more educated and wealthy Third Estate (the middle class or **bourgeoisie**) believed they should also have some political power.

3. Influence of American Revolution

The French helped the Americans gain independence from the British. Many of the soldiers who had fought in America returned to France with the ideas of that revolution, e.g. democracy and equality.

4. Bankrupt State

France's military assistance to the colonists in the American War of Independence cost a lot of money. This left the French state almost **bankrupt** (had no money left). This meant that Louis would have to increase taxes on the three Estates. However, the First and Second Estate refused to pay any taxes. Louis would now have to put pressure on the Third Estate to pay even more tax.

5. The Estates-General

To organise this tax increase, Louis called a meeting of the three Estates. This meeting was called the **Estates-General**. It was like a large parliament as it had representatives of each of the Estates. This was the first time in 175 years that the King of France had called an Estates-General. On 5 May 1789 all the representatives met in Versailles. The First and Second Estates hoped they would gain more privileges, while the Third Estate was determined to gain some concessions and maybe even get the other Estates to pay some tax. Immediately there were problems.

The Third Estate was more numerous than the other Estates in France and so had 621 representatives. The First Estate had 308 and the Second Estate had 285. This meant that the Third Estate could out-vote the other two. Therefore the First and Second Estates believed that one vote should be given to each Estate so that they could out-vote the Third by 2:1. The Third Estate decided to create a separate **National Assembly** if it was given only one vote. The next day, when they were locked out of the Estates-General in Versailles the representatives of the Third Estate went instead

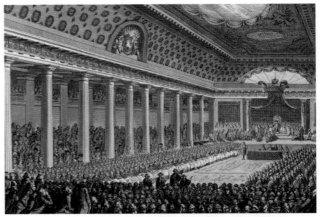

▲ The meeting of the Estates General in Versailles, 1789

to the Royal Tennis Court where they took an oath. They promised each other that they would not break up the National Assembly until a constitution was created for France that took into account all of their grievances. This oath became known as the **Tennis Court Oath**.

▲ The Third Estate swears the Tennis Court Oath.

Louis did not want to give in to the Third Estate, but there were rumours that 30,000 angry Parisians were ready to storm his palace, so he gave in and forced the First and Second Estate to join the National Assembly.

The tensions between the Estates and also between the king and the poor people of Paris meant that more dramatic events were about to unfold.

Questions

1. Explain in one or two sentences the following terms:

   (a) *Ancien régime*   (b) *Estates-General*   (c) Bourgeoisie

2. What were typical professions of the First, Second and Third Estates?

3. Name and explain two taxes that the Third Estate had to pay.

4. Look at the cartoon on page 231. What do you think the artist is saying in this cartoon?

5. Why did Louis XVI need to raise more money through taxes?

6. Outline the voting problems faced by the Estates-General.

7. Why did the Third Estate meet in the palace's tennis court?

8. What did the Third Estate decide to do in the tennis court?

Revolution in France

The people in Paris were worried that Louis might use the army to defeat the Third Estate or dissolve the National Assembly. Therefore, a mob of Parisians went in search of guns and ammunition with which to protect themselves from any attack. So on 14 July 1789 the mob turned its attention to the **Bastille**.

The Bastille was a huge prison in Paris to which many French people had been sent without trial. It symbolised everything that was wrong with the *ancien régime*. Over 100 people died in the attack on the prison. When they succeeded in breaking in, they found only seven prisoners, all of whom were set free. Nevertheless, the fall of the Bastille was of great symbolic importance to the poor of Paris. It is still celebrated every year on the French National holiday of Bastille Day on 14 July.

The storming of the Bastille in 1789 ▲

● Who was this mob?

The Parisian mob was made up of tradesmen, workers, shopkeepers and the poor of Paris who hoped that change would make their lives easier. They wanted to reduce their taxes and they also wanted the price of bread to be kept as low as possible so they could afford to feed their families. They were known as the **sans-culottes** (without trousers). They were called this because they could not afford the silk knee-length stockings that were fashionable among the rich. The sans-culottes supported change and were a very important part of the success of the revolution.

By the way . . .

One of the men released from the Bastille was mad and his family had put him there. When he was released he travelled all the way home whereupon his family put him straight back into prison.

▲ The sans-culottes played a very important role in the success of the French Revolution.

With the triumph of the sans-culottes at the Bastille a new **National Guard** (an armed force made up of the ordinary people of Paris) was formed under the leadership of **Marquis de Lafayette** – a noble who had fought in America and who supported the Third Estate. This National Guard was formed to ensure King Louis would be reluctant to use force against the revolutionaries.

<aside>
By the way . . .

Louis XVI had such little interest in politics that on 14 July 1789 he wrote in his diary that nothing important had happened that day!
</aside>

▲ A cartoon showing the Third Estate awakening much to the horror of the First and Second Estates.

Questions

1. Who stormed the Bastille and why?

2. On what date was the Bastille stormed?

3. From which city were the sans-culottes?

4. How did the sans-culottes get their name?

5. Who led the National Guard and why were they established?

6. Examine the picture above. Explain what is meant by 'The Third Estate awakens'. Give reasons for your answer.

The Rights of Man

On 26 August, the National Assembly passed a new law outlining the main beliefs of the revolution. This was called the **Declaration of the Rights of Man**. (See Source B below.) Many ideals of freedom and equality were enshrined in this law. The three main ideals of the French Revolution were summed up in the slogan, *Liberté, Egalité et Fraternité* (Liberty, Equality and Brotherhood).

▸ **Liberty** meant that all people should be free from slavery and oppression.

▸ **Equality** was the right of all to be treated equally regardless of how much you owned or who you were.

▸ **Fraternity** was the belief that all French men and women were as connected to each other as brothers or sisters.

Source B

Therefore the National Assembly recognises and proclaims the following rights of man and of the citizen:

▸ Men are born free and equal in rights.

▸ The purpose of all political associations is the preservation of the natural rights of man. These rights are: liberty, property and resistance to oppression.

▸ Liberty consists in being able to do whatever does not harm others. No man ought to be uneasy about his opinions, even his religious beliefs, provided that these actions do not interfere with the public order established by law.

▸ The free communication of thought and opinion is one of the most precious rights of man: every citizen can therefore talk, write and publish freely.

- An extract from the **Declaration of the Rights of Man and of the Citizen**

Reform Continues

By this point many thought that the revolution had been successful and that its objectives had been achieved. However others were still suspicious of the king and queen. In October 1789 Louis and Marie-Antoinette were forced to leave Versailles and move to Paris where they could be more easily controlled by the National Assembly. The flag of France dates from this time. The blue and red traditional colours of Paris were placed on either side of the white of the Bourbons (the French royal family) to illustrate this point. The flag was known as the **tricolore** and it inspired many other flags including Ireland's.

• The Civil Constitution of the Clergy

Further laws were then introduced. In December 1790, the **Civil Constitution of the Clergy** was passed. This law held that: (1) the pope could no longer appoint priests or bishops in France. Instead local assemblies would 'elect' the clergy; (2) all members of the clergy had to take an oath of loyalty to the revolution; (3) all the church's land could be seized by the National Assembly and sold. With this law, the Assembly hoped to make all clergy loyal to the revolution.

Pope Pius VI condemned the law, leading to deep divisions throughout France. About half of the clergy refused to take the oath and so were fired from their posts. Some were either exiled or imprisoned while others were even executed. The Civil Constitution had created as many problems as it had solved and the result was the Catholic Church was now willing to support any attempts to destroy the revolution.

▲ The French Tricolore and the Bourbon flag of the French royal family.

Questions

1. Name the three main ideals of the French Revolution and explain what each means.
2. Examine Source B on page 235. According to this extract, what are the natural rights of man?
3. What do the colours on the French flag stand for?
4. Give two reasons why you think the Pope was unhappy with the Civil Constitution of the Clergy of 1790.

• The Flight to Varennes

With the knowledge that he would find support from Marie-Antoinette's brother, Emperor Leopold of Austria, and the Catholic Church, Louis decided to try to escape from France. On the night of 20 June 1791 he and the queen began their journey to the Netherlands in a carriage. Although they were dressed in disguise as servants of a Baroness, they were caught near the border at a town called **Varennes**. They were brought back to Paris and placed under guard. Many people now thought that Louis must be in secret contact with foreign powers who wanted to crush the revolution.

▲ The Royal family's capture during the flight to Varennes in 1791.

Vive le Roi,Vive la Nation.

J SAVOIS BEN QU'JAURIONS NOT TOUR .

▲ A political cartoon showing the Third Estate being carried by the First and Second Estates.

Those in the Assembly who believed that there was no need for a king at all used Louis' attempt to flee as an excuse to push for the creation of a **republic** (a form of government without a monarch).

In September 1791 a new written French constitution was passed that limited the power of the king. The most he could do was delay for two years any law that a new parliament called the **Legislative Assembly** passed. France was now a **constitutional monarchy** (a type of government in which the monarch is the symbolic head of the state but has no power). This was a great step towards democracy, just like in America. However, voting was limited to males over the age of thirty who owned property. This limit on who could and could not vote did not fit in with the idea of fraternity enshrined in the Declaration of the Rights of Man.

After the royal family tried to flee, the Revolutionaries began to worry that the monarchies of nearby countries, in particular Austria and Prussia, might invade France. These countries feared that the Revolution could spread and endanger their thrones. Many aristocrats from France had fled abroad and were trying to organise an invasion to restore their positions. For this reason the National Assembly wanted to declare war on Austria to protect the changes that had occurred in France. Some also wanted to bring the new freedoms of the revolution to other people in Europe. On 20 April 1792, the National Assembly declared war on Austria.

Questions

1. Why did Louis XVI and Marie-Antoinette try to flee France?

2. Look at the image above. What is the artist saying in this cartoon?

3. Compare this image with the cartoon on page 231. Looking at both pictures, do you think the artist supports the revolution or not? Give reasons for your answer.

4. Explain the following terms:
   (a) Monarchy
   (b) Constitutional monarchy
   (c) Republic

The Revolution Continues

Outbreak of War Against Austria

While some in France thought the revolutionary soldiers would quickly win the war, their lack of experienced leadership and poor equipment meant that instead they suffered huge losses. Very quickly the war turned into a disaster as the Austrians, aided by the Prussians, closed in on Paris.

As French hopes of winning the war deteriorated, there was increasing anger towards Louis and Marie-Antoinette, both of whom, it was suspected, were hoping for an Austrian victory. People also feared that the French nobles would take action. Many of these nobles opposed the revolution as it had taken away their land and property. Some had already fled the country and were known as **émigrés**. Many émigrés had been leaders in the French army and were now assisting the invading armies. As the Austrians and the Prussians got closer to Paris, fear began to spread among the sans-culottes. This fear soon resulted in the most violent and bloody period of the revolution.

On 10 August 1792 the Parisian sans-culottes began to riot in Paris and demanded the right to vote and the dethronement of Louis. The mob attacked the Tuileries Palace where the royal family was staying and there was a very bloody battle. They eventually found and imprisoned Louis and Marie-Antoinette. The members of the Assembly agreed to the mob's demands to create a republic. A new assembly was set up called the **National Convention** and, on 21 September, France was declared a republic. However, the mob did not stop at that. During the month of September anyone suspected of not supporting the revolution was executed. Over 1,000 people died in these **September Massacres.**

France Becomes a Republic

As the revolution took this more violent turn, it wasn't long before there were calls for Louis and Marie-Antoinette to be tried as enemies of the revolution. In December 1792, Louis stood trial and on 14 January 1793 he was found guilty of treason by 387 votes to 334 and was sentenced to be executed. King Louis XVI of France was executed seven days later. This event caused great shock throughout Europe. Many monarchies feared that the revolution would spread to their countries.

▲ The execution of Louis XVI on 21 January 1793

In February 1793 England and the Netherlands joined Austria in the war against France. During this difficult time for the revolution, a group of very determined French men and women came to the fore.

▲ Maximilien Robespierre, nicknamed 'The Incorruptible'.

THE JACOBINS AND MAXIMILIEN ROBESPIERRE

A group of radical politicians was supported by the sans-culottes. These people were known as the **Jacobins** after the church where their first meeting took place. The Jacobins believed that their new freedoms could only be ensured by the killing of all people who were opposed to the revolution, inside and outside France. They were led by a lawyer from Arras in Northern France. His name was **Maximilien Robespierre** (1758-1794). He became president of the Parisian Jacobin club in April 1790 and was strongly opposed to the war with Austria. He believed the French army was not adequately prepared and that the revolution was not yet strong enough to be at war. He had been elected as a delegate for the Third Estate in 1789 and was very active in all political affairs.

His honesty and dedication to the cause of the revolution earned him the nickname 'The Incorruptible'. His opposition to the king, the nobles and the clergy, and his attempts to get lower food prices meant he was very popular with the sans-culottes: thus he had great power. In April 1793 the National Convention voted to create a 12-man group called the **Committee of Public Safety** to remove all counter-revolutionaries (i.e. those who opposed the revolution). Robespierre became its most influential member.

● The Reign of Terror

The Committee of Public Safety immediately introduced laws to ensure the safety of the revolution.

They passed the **Law of Maximum** which placed strict controls on the price of bread. This law was very popular with the sans-culottes and the poor of France. They then passed the **Law of Suspects** which allowed them to arrest and even execute anyone believed to be a counter-revolutionary. The number of prisoners was huge, totalling more than 4,500 by the end of 1793. The Committee also executed over 3,000 people using a method called the **guillotine** (named after Dr Joseph Guillotine) which cut off the prisoner's head. It was thought that this method was the most efficient and humane method of execution. In October 1793 Marie-Antoinette was one of the people sent to the guillotine.

▲ The guillotine was widely used by Robespierre and the Committee of Public Safety.

Over the next year it is estimated that over 40,000 people were executed. This period became known as the **Reign of Terror**. Some of those executed were against the revolution but many others supported its ideals. For example, some were revolutionary

By the way . . .

Sometimes killing people with the guillotine was too slow, so barges (boats) full of prisoners were sunk on the River Loire, drowning all on board.

leaders who simply believed the numbers being killed were too high. After a particularly vicious attack on the Catholic peasants of a region in France called La Vendeé, some in the Convention thought Robespierre had gone too far. When he attempted to increase the power of the Committee and allow for even more executions, some of the Convention knew they had to act.

By the way . . .

One woman made death masks out of wax of the people who were killed and she later exhibited these masks in England. Her name was Madame Tussaud.

▲ A cartoon of Robespierre cooking both French aristocrats and peasants.

Questions

◀ An English cartoon from the time of the sans-culottes relaxing after 'a day's work'.

1. Who are the people sitting at the table supposed to represent? Give reasons for your answer.

2. Who are they supposed to be eating? Give reasons for your answer.

3. Was the artist pro or anti revolution? Give three reasons to support your answer.

4. Is this a good cartoon, in your opinion?

5. The man with the axe is Thomas Paine. Why is he in this cartoon? (Hint: look at page 218)

On the night of July 28 1794, Robespierre and many of his supporters were arrested and sent to the guillotine. With the death of Robespierre the bloodiest period of the revolution came to an end and a new five-member committee called the **Directory** was set up to rule France.

Questions

1. Who were known as *émigrés*?

2. What was King Louis XVI found guilty of? Do you think his execution was justified?

3. How did the Jacobin political club get its name?

4. What was Robespierre's nick-name and how did he get it?

5. Name two laws that the Committee of Public Safety passed and explain what these allowed the Committee to do.

6. For what reason do you think Robespierre was executed?

7. Examine the cartoon on the top of page 240. Do you think the artist supports Robespierre? Give reasons for your answer.

8. Outline how the Directory came into power.

RESULTS OF THE FRENCH REVOLUTION

1. Across Europe there was an increased belief in the ideals of France. The political concepts of republicanism and democracy, the personal beliefs of liberty, equality before the law and national brotherhood all became commonplace.

2. These ideals also meant that other nations around Europe were inspired to achieve similar freedoms. Minorities in countries that had not been allowed to vote now demanded it as their natural right. As we will see, one of these countries was Ireland.

3. The French offered to militarily assist any nation that wanted to follow their lead. Ireland, among others, took up this offer in the 1790s.

4. The bourgeoisie (middle class) had gained a lot of power. Before the revolution all the power of France had been with the king and the rich but afterwards the bourgeoisie were far more important in politics.

5. Through the use of **conscription** (forcing all able-bodied men over the age of 18 into the army) a huge French army was created and won significant victories across Europe. As a result of these victories, a young general called **Napoleon Bonaparte** became very popular and eventually dissolved the Directory in 1799 and became France's new leader. In 1804 he crowned himself Emperor of France. Napoleon ruled over France's expansion throughout most of Europe. He was defeated at Waterloo, Belgium by the combined forces of Britain, Austria, Russia, Prussia and the Netherlands. Napoleon was captured and imprisoned on the island of St. Helena where he stayed until his death in 1821.

▲ French-controlled Europe at the height of Napoleon's expansion in 1812.

Questions

1. Name the countries that fought at the Battle of Waterloo.

2. Explain the term conscription and how it allowed France to defeat so many other countries.

3. How were other European countries influenced by the French Revolution?

▲ Napoleon Bonaparte became Emperor of France (1804) and oversaw France's expansion throughout most of Europe until the Battle of Waterloo.

Chapter 9 Questions: French Revolution

1. Pictures

◀ French Revolutionary poster

Examine this picture from the French Revolution. It states, 'Unity, Indivisibility [impossible to divide] of the French Republic; Liberty, equality, fraternity or death.'

(a) Who is depicted on the right of the picture? Give a reason for your answer.

(b) What does the picture mean by 'liberty, equality, fraternity or death'?

(c) What is the person on the left supposed to depict?

(d) What other revolutionary symbols are there in this picture?

2. Documents

This is a letter describing the execution of Louis XVI of France on 21 January 1793.

Paris, 23 January 1793, Wednesday morning. My dearest mother, I commend to you the spirit of the late lamented Louis XVI. To the very last he maintained the greatest possible courage.

He wished to speak to the people from the scaffold, but was interrupted by a drum-roll and was seized by the executioners, who were following their orders, and who pushed him straight under the fatal blade. He was able to speak only these words, in a very strong voice: "I forgive my enemies; I trust that my death will be for the happiness of my people, but I grieve for France and I fear that she may suffer the anger of the Lord."

From *The French Revolution; voices from a momentous epoch, 1789–1795*, edited by Richard Cobb, Colin Jones

(a) Mention one thing that happened when Louis tried to speak to the people.

(b) Why did Louis 'grieve for France'?

(c) Do you think that Louis met his death bravely? Give one piece of evidence from the letter to support your answer.

(d) What was the attitude of the writer to the execution of the king? Give one example of evidence from the text that supports your answer.

(e) Explain briefly why Louis XVI was executed during the French Revolution.

3. Short-Answer Questions

(a) What were the names of the King and Queen of France in 1789?

(b) Name two causes of the French Revolution.

(c) Who were the members of the Third Estate?

(d) What was the Tennis Court Oath?

(e) What was the function of the Bastille?

(f) Why was the Committee of Public Safety set up?

(g) Who was its leader?

(h) Name one consequence of Napoleon's reforms that still exists today.

(i) What title did Napoleon take in 1804?

(j) Name two results of the French Revolution.

4. People in History

Write about a named revolutionary leader in France in the late eighteenth century.

HINTS:

- Reasons for discontent • Aims of the revolution
- Battles fought • Results of revolution

5. Revolutionary Movements

Source B on page 235 is an extract from the Declaration of the Rights of Man and of the Citizen, which was passed by the National Assembly of France, 26 August, 1789.

(a) What are the 'natural rights of man'?

(b) From the Declaration, identify two freedoms enjoyed by the citizens of France.

(c) The Declaration was influenced by the ideas of Enlightenment writers. Name one famous Enlightenment writer.

Causes of the Irish Rebellion

In 1689 Prince William of Orange, a Protestant, was invited to become King of England in place of the Catholic King James II. The conflict that arose between these two men ended at the **Battle of the Boyne** in 1690.

By the way . . .

Prince William of Orange was asthmatic and when he attempted to cross the River Boyne, he had such a bad asthma attack that he had to be carried to the riverbank over the shoulder of a soldier from Enniskillen.

By the way . . .

King James II spent the whole of the Battle of the Boyne with hundreds of his cavalry two miles away on a hill and fled to Dublin even before the battle was over!

▲ William of Orange

▲ James II

This battle for the throne of England was to have a great impact on the Catholic Irish. William's forces defeated James' troops and soon afterwards James fled Ireland, leaving the throne of Britain and Ireland to the Protestant William. After this battle, Protestants in Ireland wanted to make sure that their position was never again threatened.

Protestant Ascendancy

During the beginning of the 1700s the Penal Laws were introduced to protect the Protestants in power – **Anglicans** who were members of the Church of Ireland, a branch of the Church of England (see page 180 in Chapter 7, The Reformation). These Anglicans became known as the **Protestant Ascendancy** in Ireland.

These Penal laws stated that:

1. No Catholic could build or attend schools or churches.

2. No Catholic priests, bishops or religious orders were allowed to stay in Ireland.

3. No Catholic could buy land from a Protestant and any Catholic land that was inherited had to be 'subdivided' among all the sons, making the size of the farms too small to be viable. However, if one of the sons converted to Anglicanism they could inherit the whole farm. This meant that by the last quarter of the eighteenth century Catholic land-ownership had fallen to around 5%.

4. No Catholic was allowed to become a solicitor, barrister or judge.

5. All Catholics had to pay a tithe (10% of their earnings) to the Anglican Church.

▲ The British government was afraid that Irish Catholics might ask France to help them fight the Protestant Ascendancy. So they used cartoons like this showing French soldiers attacking a Catholic priest to spread fear of the French amongst the Irish.

These laws, alongside a ban on Catholics living in towns, meant that the Catholic population in Ireland became even poorer. As each farm was subdivided among sons, the plots of land became smaller and so families were forced to rely on subsistence farming (to grow enough food only to feed your family to survive). Most Catholics by the middle of the 1700s were poor, **agrarian** (rural farmers dependent on agriculture to survive), persecuted and uneducated.

● Irish Population

At the beginning of the eighteenth century the Irish population was made up of three different groups.

1. Although 75% of Ireland was Catholic, they owned less than 15% of the land and had no political power.
2. About 15% of the people were Anglican but they owned almost all the land and had all the economic and political power.
3. The last group was the Presbyterians in Ulster who made up 10% of the population. They were involved in trade and were reasonably successful. The Presbyterians, or Dissenters as they were also called (as they 'dissented' against the Anglican Church), were not Anglican and so were forced to pay tithes to the Church of Ireland and were barred from being elected to Parliament and holding positions of power. This sectarian persecution began to annoy many Presbyterians. They became very angry when the British Parliament passed the Navigation Acts which placed limits on Irish exports of goods such as cattle, wool and linen. These export limits were intended to protect British industries from cheaper Irish exports.

● Spread of Revolutionary Ideas

Many Catholics throughout Ireland and more particularly the Presbyterians in Ulster found the ideals of the American Revolution and later the French Revolution inspiring. They believed that the concepts of liberty, equality and, very importantly, fraternity could also be achieved in Ireland. Some believed that with the support of revolutionary France it would be possible to create an Ireland in which all Irish people could prosper, regardless of religion. They saw the power of Britain over Ireland as the major threat to their hopes of religious tolerance, democracy and freedom. Gradually these people became prepared to use violence to achieve their aim of a free and equal Ireland. They were called the **United Irishmen** .

▲ The seal of the United Irishmen

Questions

1. What were the Penal Laws? Give two examples.

2. Who were the two leaders of the armies that fought at the Battle of the Boyne in 1690 and who won?

3. What was the tithe?

4. Match the correct population group (A–C) with the correct percentage for Ireland at the beginning of the eighteenth century:

A Anglican (Church of Ireland)	1. 75%
B Presbyterian	2. 15%
C Catholic	3. 10%

5. Explain the following words:

   (a) Dissenter   (b) Subsistence   (c) Agrarian   (d) Protestant Ascendancy

 ## Wolfe Tone and the United Irishmen

Theobald Wolfe Tone was born into an Anglican family in Dublin in 1763. He was a law graduate from Trinity College, Dublin, and by 26 years of age showed a great interest in the politics of the day. Inspired by the revolution in France he believed that political reform was needed and that the Catholics of Ireland should be allowed to take part in the political life of the country. In August 1791 he published *An Argument on Behalf of the Catholics of Ireland.*

Wolfe Tone supported the Revolution in ▲ France and believed that it should be an inspiration to the Catholics of Ireland.

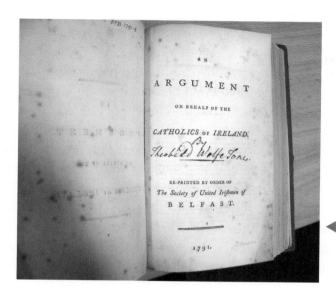

◀ The front of Tone's pamphlet –
*An Argument On Behalf of The
Catholics of Ireland*

He addressed it to those Presbyterians in Ulster who felt that
political reform should include Catholics. Soon after this he met with
a number of Presbyterians in Belfast to discuss proposed reforms. At
this meeting on 18 October 1791, with Henry Joy McCracken,
Samuel Nielson and Thomas Russell, the Society of the United
Irishmen was formed. Its founding principle was 'the complete and
radical reform of the representation of the people in Parliament' but
this would not be practical without including 'Irishmen of every
religious persuasion'. Soon branches of the Society of the United
Irishmen opened in Dublin and elsewhere throughout Ireland. In
January 1792 it began to publish its own newspaper called the
Northern Star edited by Samuel Nielson and William Drennan which
was distributed across Ireland.

By the way . . .

William Drennan, one of
the editors of the
Northern Star, wrote a
poem in which he was the
first to describe Ireland as
the 'Emerald Isle'.

▲ Samuel Neilson was one of the founders of
the United Irishmen and edited the *Northern
Star*.

▲ William Drennan was one of the editors of
the *Northern Star*.

Catholic Emancipation

Wolfe Tone was soon asked to work for the Catholic Committee, an organisation set up to campaign against the Penal Laws. The **Catholic Committee** sent representatives including Tone to Britain to ask for **Catholic Emancipation** (allowing Catholics to vote and sit in government). The king promised to introduce these reforms. By 1793 Britain was preparing for war with revolutionary France and many in Britain were worried that the Catholics of Ireland would form an alliance with the Presbyterians and that France would aid them. Many of the Penal Laws were abolished and Catholics were given the right to vote but they were still barred from being elected as MPs (Members of Parliament), becoming judges or holding positions of political power. The members of the Catholic Committee were satisfied but Wolfe Tone hoped for more. The United Irishmen still vowed to 'never desist in our efforts until we . . . subverted the authority of England over our country and asserted her independence'. However they still hoped that this would be possible through peaceful means.

Beginning of the Revolution

With the outbreak of war with France, Britain was now very concerned with the activities of the United Irishmen. A French spy named **William Jackson** was caught gathering information about the situation in Ireland from Wolfe Tone. The British government tried Jackson (an Anglican clergyman) for treason but Jackson committed suicide by taking poison while in the dock. Jackson's connections with the United Irishmen also allowed the government to outlaw the Society. In 1795 Wolfe Tone was forced to go into exile to America. After this setback, Wolfe Tone and the United Irishmen believed that the only way to achieve their aims was by force and with the help of the French. In 1796 Wolfe Tone travelled to France to enlist their support for a revolution.

Questions

1. (a) What pamphlet did Wolfe Tone publish in August 1791?
   (b) To whom did he address his pamphlet?
2. What were the founding principles of the Society of the United Irishmen?
3. (a) What was the name of the paper published by the United Irishmen?
   (b) Why do you think they wanted to publish a paper?
4. What aim did the Catholic Committee have?
5. What did Wolfe Tone mean when he wrote that he would not stop until the United Irishmen had 'subverted the authority of England over our country and asserted her independence'?
6. Why did Wolfe Tone have to leave Ireland?

The 1798 Uprising

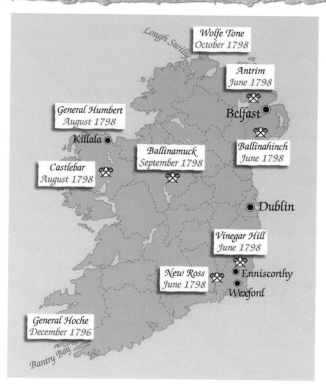

◀ A map of battle sites in Ireland during the 1798 Uprising

By the way . . .

Members of the United Irishmen and the Catholic groups were known as 'Croppies' because of the way they cut their hair. They cropped their hair short in the style of the French revolutionaries.

The British government now put measures in place to control any possible Irish rebellion. They:

1. Outlawed the Society of the United Irishmen.

2. Made it illegal to import guns.

3. Permitted British soldiers to search homes and arrest rebels without constraint.

The British government also organised loyal Catholics into militia and loyal Protestants into **yeomanry** (groups of armed volunteers). Other less legal groups were also formed like the sectarian **Peep-o-Day Boys** (so-called because they attacked at dawn). The Peep-o-Day Boys were a vigilante group who decided, without official approval, to protect and defend Protestants, usually by violent means.

Due to the harsh clampdown by the British government and without the hope of further reforms, thousands of Catholics now joined the United Irishmen. The organisation had to become a secret oath-based society. The illegal Catholic secret society called the 'Defenders' joined forces with the United Irishmen. The Defenders were a Catholic group that defended Catholic tenants and attacked Protestant landlords. There were frequent clashes between the Defenders and the Peep-o-day Boys. One particular battle resulted in over 20 people being killed at the Battle of the Diamond (the centre of the town) near Loughgall, County Armagh. It was after this clash that a new organisation called the **Orange Order** was formed in Loughgall by the Protestant population to protect themselves from Catholics.

▲ General Hoche led a fleet of 43 ships and 15,000 soldiers from France to Ireland. However, bad weather prevented the ships from landing and they had to return to France.

By the way . . .

▲ Cat o' nine tails

The phrase 'the cat's out of the bag' refers to the bag in which a particularly nasty whip called the cat o' nine tails was kept. When this whip was used, people tended to tell any secrets they knew.

● French assistance

Wolfe Tone's journey to France to ask for help was successful. In December 1796 a fleet of 43 ships and 15,000 soldiers set sail from France to Ireland. The expedition was led by **General Hoche**, one of France's greatest soldiers, and accompanying him was Wolfe Tone. However, bad weather separated the ships and only about 14 ships were able to make it to Bantry Bay. The storms were too bad to land and so eventually they had to return to Brest in France. Wolfe Tone wrote in his diary:

> 'Well, England has not had such an escape since the Spanish Armada, and that expedition, like ours, was defeated by the weather.'

By the time the ships returned to France, they had lost 11 ships and almost 5,000 men. Before Hoche could organise another expedition, he became ill and died. This failed invasion frightened the British government as they had only 15,000 soldiers in Ireland. They now increased their measures to put down any rebellion. A British official, **General Lake**, was sent to Ulster with orders to disarm the province. He was given new powers:

1. The death penalty was introduced for any person organising secret oath-based societies.
2. The *Northern Star* was banned and had its printing press physically removed.
3. The army could search houses, arrest people without any charges and punish anyone thought to be withholding information.

General Lake's tactics of burning houses, floggings (beatings), half-hangings (hanging someone until they almost die before releasing them), whipping, pitch-cappings (putting tar on someone's head and then setting it on fire) and killings were horrific but very effective. Thousands of weapons were found and hundreds of people arrested and imprisoned. However, the leaders of the uprising continued to plan for rebellion throughout Ireland even though many of the main leaders were captured before the uprising could take place, including the main organiser of the Dublin uprising, **Lord Edward Fitzgerald**.

▲ A walking gallows

▲ Pitch-capping

Fitzgerald was the son of the Duke of Leinster and had been educated in England and fought with the British army in America. As he was the leader of the planned Dublin uprising he had been evading capture for months. He was finally caught and fatally wounded on 19 May 1798. Despite all these setbacks, the United Irishmen decided that the uprising would continue and the date of 23 May 1798 was agreed.

▲ Lord Edward Fitzgerald was the leader of the planned Dublin Uprising.

Questions

1. After the capture of the French spy William Jackson what measures did the British government put in place to ensure there was no uprising?

2. Who did the following groups represent?

    (a) Defenders   (b) Peep-o-Day Boys   (c) Orange Order

3. What help did Wolfe Tone get from the French?

4. What new powers did General Lake have when he came to Ulster and were they effective?

▲ Rebels execute their Protestant prisoners at Wexford, June 20, 1798. The rebel flag's MWS stands for Murder Without Sin.

The Uprising

The Uprising took place in three different places:

1. WEXFORD

There were a large number of Protestants and Catholics living in Wexford and the tension between the two communities was high. On the 20 May, fearing a rebellion, the government began to hang suspects. By 27 May Protestant mobs began to join in and they attacked and killed 28 rebel prisoners at Carnew. Finally, the rebellion broke out with Father **John Murphy** and **Bagenal Harvey** (a Protestant landowner) leading the rebels. They won their initial battle at Oulart Hill and soon took Enniscorthy. By 31 May they had taken the town of Wexford and established a committee to take care of the lands they controlled.

In revenge for the massacre at Carnew, the rebels attacked Protestant prisoners at Scullabogue. They set fire to a barn and burnt 126 men, women and children. Later, 97 Protestants were piked to death at Wexford Bridge. The rebels attempted to take the town of New Ross but failed. The Battle for Arklow was a major turning point for the rebels. They failed to capture the town from British forces and lost 1,000 men in the attempt. They then fell back to Vinegar Hill. Here they took their last stand on 21 June. The rebels' long pikes were no use against the British cannons and muskets and the battle was over quickly. Father Murphy and Harvey were later captured. Both were hanged and beheaded (Harvey in Wexford, Murphy in Tullow). Their heads were put on spikes in Wexford Town.

2. ULSTER

On 7 June 1798 **Henry Joy McCracken**, a Presbyterian cotton manufacturer, led between 3,000 and 4,000 men against the British forces in the town of Antrim. The rebels managed to take the town but were quickly driven out by the artillery of the British. Although McCracken escaped and hid in Cave Hill overlooking Belfast, he was later captured and hanged on 17 June.

▲ A depiction of the massacre at Scullabogue, County Wexford

In County Down, **Henry Munro**, an Anglican linen manufacturer, led almost 7,000 rebels against the British at Ballinahinch but they were driven back by cannon fire. They also showed their inexperience when they heard the British bugler sound the retreat during the battle but thought that it was, in fact, the arrival of reinforcements. Fearing fresh British troops, they quickly began to retreat and lost both the initiative and, soon after, the battle. Munro was hanged and beheaded with his head put on a spike in Lisburn's marketplace.

3. CONNACHT

In August 1798 1,000 French troops led by **General Humbert** arrived in Killala, County Mayo. Humbert was a little disappointed in the number of Irishmen that joined with him but he captured the town of Ballina. When they attacked General Lake and his men in Castlebar, the British troops (who were largely Irish militia) were so surprised that they fled leaving all their guns behind. They left so quickly that the event became known as the Races of Castlebar. Humbert continued eastwards towards Dublin and were defeated by a far larger British army of 10,000 led by General Lake and Lord Cornwallis (previously mentioned on page 225) at Ballinamuck, County Longford. The French soldiers who were captured were allowed to return home to France but the captured Irish rebels were hanged.

Source C

From the blood of every one of the martyrs of the liberty of Ireland, will spring, I hope, thousands to revenge his fall... What will the French government do in the present crisis? After all, their aid appears to be indispensible: for the Irish have no means but numbers and courage...

From Wolfe Tone's diary, June 1798

Questions

Read Source C above and answer the following questions.

1. What does Wolfe Tone hope will happen when each martyr dies?

2. In your opinion, what kind of aid does Wolfe Tone hope the French will send?

3. What means does Wolfe Tone believe the Irish can offer?

4. From your reading of the uprising in Connacht do you think his belief was correct?

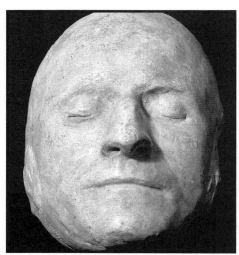

▲ Death mask of Wolfe Tone

● The death of Wolfe Tone

Unaware that Humbert had been defeated, another French expedition of 3,000 led by General Jean Hardy sailed into Lough Swilly, County Donegal with Wolfe Tone. They were met by a British fleet and after a long battle were defeated. Wolfe Tone was captured and charged with treason. He was found guilty and his request to be shot like a soldier was denied. He was to be hanged on 12 November but decided to cut his own throat that morning using the penknife he had for sharpening his quill. This injury did not kill him immediately and he died a week later on 19 November 1798. The leader of the 1798 uprising was dead and with his death came the end of the United Irishmen's Rebellion.

● Reasons for the defeat

The 1798 uprising that had promised so much failed for a number of reasons:

1. The British government managed to **infiltrate** (had spies among) the United Irishmen and other secret organisations. Their spy network meant that the British knew most of the plans that were made. The torture tactics of General Lake in Ulster and Leinster also provided them with information about the location of rebel leaders and weapons.

2. The capture of so many weapons and the arrest of rebel leaders meant that the uprising lacked organisation and equipment. The pike was of limited use against the cannons and muskets of the superior and stronger British armies.

3. The help from the French was insufficient. The only French to land in Ireland was General Humbert and he had only 1,000 men – hardly enough to take on the British army of 10,000 at Ballinamuck.

4. Bad luck also played a part. Poor weather scattered the French troops at Bantry Bay in 1796 and the wounding of Lord Edward Fitzgerald days before the uprising was to take place reduced the rebels' chances of success.

Questions

1. Name two leaders of the Wexford uprising.
2. Give two reasons for the failure of the Wexford uprising.
3. Name the leaders of the Ulster uprising.
4. Why, in your opinion, did the Ulster uprising fail? Give two reasons.
5. What were the Races of Castlebar?
6. Who were the leaders of the British army at the battle of Ballinamuck, County Longford?
7. What was Wolfe Tone charged with and what was his sentence?
8. How did Wolfe Tone die?
9. How did the death of Lord Edward Fitzgerald and the capture of other leaders cause difficulties for the planned uprising?
10. Give four reasons for the failure of the 1798 uprising.

RESULTS OF THE 1798 UPRISING

1. The ideals of Wolfe Tone and his commitment to the fight for Irish independence from England meant that he became an inspiration to many Irish nationalists. His desire to break the link with England and create a country in which all religions are tolerated was adopted by others over the next 150 years. The 1798 uprising was also seen as a very idealistic rising during which Protestant and Catholic Irishmen came together to seek independence.

2. After the rebellion, the British government believed it would be safer to dissolve the Irish Parliament in Dublin and for Britain to take direct control over Ireland's affairs. The two countries were to be united as one in the United Kingdom of Great Britain and Ireland. The **Act of Union** proposed that Irish MPs should sit in Westminster (the location of the British Houses of Parliament in London) with the other MPs from the rest of Britain. While it was initially rejected by the Irish Parliament in Dublin, through force and persuasion (but more often due to MPs accepting bribes), it became law on 1 January 1801. Ireland would not have its own parliament again until 1922.

3. One of the leaders of the United Irishmen, Thomas Addis Emmet, had a younger brother named Robert. In 1803, inspired by the 1798 uprising, Robert bought weapons and ammunition using the money that his wealthy Protestant father had left him. Due to poor organisation and support, his rising was little more than a drunken riot and was easily put down. Emmet should have escaped from Dublin but he chose not to. He wished to be near his fiancée, Sarah Curran, and he was soon caught when he tried to visit her. On 20 September 1803 this romantic rebel was hanged, drawn and quartered on Thomas Street, Dublin. No more rebellions took place in Ireland for almost 50 years.

4. In the early 1800s, a Catholic from Derrynane, County Kerry, called Daniel O'Connell campaigned for Catholic Emancipation (to allow Catholics to become MPs). He had seen the violence and bloodshed of failed rebellions and believed more peaceful methods were necessary. In 1823 he set up the Catholic Association to campaign for the right to sit in parliament and asked all Catholics to pay a penny each week to the Association. It was a huge success and by 1828 O'Connell had been elected to Westminster as an MP even though he was forbidden to sit because he was a Catholic. With growing support for Catholic Emancipation in Ireland, the British government decided to permit it and in April 1829 Catholic Emancipation was passed. O'Connell became known as **The Liberator**.

▲ Robert Emmet, the romantic rebel, asked that no epitaph should be written on his tombstone until Ireland 'takes her place among the nations of the earth'.

▲ Daniel O'Connell who became known as The Liberator after he successfully campaigned for Catholic Emancipation.

WOLFE TONE
✿ REVOLUTIONARY ✿

1763   Born in Dublin, Ireland

Key events:

1791   Publishes *An Argument on Behalf of the Catholics of Ireland*

1791   Sets up the Society of the United Irishmen in Belfast

1795   Goes into exile to America and then travels to France to get assistance for a rebellion in Ireland

1796   Sails with French fleet and 15,000 troops to Bantry Bay but cannot land due to bad weather

1798   Captured after sea battle in Lough Swilly. Convicted of treason but commits suicide while in jail in Dublin.

Chapter 9 Questions: 1798 Uprising

1. Pictures

Examine the image on page 252 depicting the massacre at Wexford Bridge and answer the following questions:

(a) What weapons are the rebels using?

(b) What does this picture tell you about the discipline of the rebels? Give reasons for your answer.

(c) Looking at the different images of the Protestants and the rebels, do you think the artist is in favour of the uprising?

(d) What do you call images that are designed to promote one opinion over another?

2. Documents

June 20: To-day is my birthday. I am thirty-five years of age; more than half of my life is finished, and how little have I yet been able to do... I had hopes, two years ago, that, at the period I write this, my debt to my country would have been discharged, and the fate of Ireland settled for good or evil. To-day it is more uncertain than ever. I think, however, I may safely say, I have neglected no step to which my duty called me, and, in that conduct I will persist to the last.

From *Journals of Theobald Wolfe-Tone*

(a) How old was Wolfe Tone when he wrote this letter and in what year was he born?

(b) What are the two hopes he had two years ago?

(c) Does he believe that he has realised those hopes?

(d) Has he, in his opinion, fully tried to achieve his hopes?

(e) In your opinion, was he successful in achieving those hopes? Give reasons for your answer.

(f) How did Wolfe-Tone die?

3. Short-Answer Questions

(a) Why did Wolfe Tone become an inspiration to other Irish nationalists?

(b) (i) What was the Act of Union of 1800?

(ii) What were its results?

(c) Where in London is the location of the British Houses of Parliament?

(d) Of what organisation was Robert Emmet's brother a member?

(e) Why did Emmet's rising fail?

(f) Why was he caught?

(g) Explain the term Catholic Emancipation.

(h) Why did Daniel O'Connell believe that peaceful methods were needed to achieve Irish independence?

(i) What was the Catholic Association and what did it hope to achieve?

(j) Why was O'Connell known as The Liberator?

4. People in History

Write about a named rebellion leader in Ireland in the late eighteenth century using the following headings:

•Reasons for becoming a revolutionary

•Political activities

•Revolutionary activities

•Success or failure of the revolution

OR

Write about a supporter of a named revolutionary leader during the period 1770-1803.

5.

Let no man write my epitaph [words written on a tombstone] . . . Let my memory be left in oblivion and my tomb remain uninscribed until other times and other men can do justice to my character. When my country takes her place among the nations of the earth, then, and not till then, let my epitaph be written. I have done.

From a report of the trial of Robert Emmet

Read the passage from Robert Emmet's trial and answer the questions below.

(a) What country is Robert Emmet talking about?

(b) When will he allow his epitaph to be written?

(c) What do you think he means when he says, 'When my country takes her place amongst the nations of the earth'?

(d) From this speech, can you explain why Emmet is seen to be a very romantic [filled with passionate, if maybe impractical, idealism] Irish patriot?

Key Terms to Summarise Chapter 9: Age of Revolutions

American Revolution

Absolute monarchy When a monarch (king or queen) has complete control of all aspects of the country including the right to increase taxes and sentence people to death.

Limited monarchy When a monarch must consult with a parliament before new taxes can be introduced.

Contractarians Philosophers who believe there should be a 'contract' between the monarch and the people of the country outlining the rights and responsibilities of both.

Governor The monarch's representative in a colony who has the power to enforce laws.

Stamp Act (1765) A tax imposed on all documents in the American colonies by the British, e.g. wills and even newspapers.

Townshend Acts A tax imposed on American colonies by the British on items such as glass and paints.

Tea Act (1773) A tax imposed on American colonies by the British that allowed tea from the British East India Company to be sold in colonies without tax, thus undercutting local tea prices.

Boston Massacre When British soldiers killed five protestors following a riot in Boston.

Boston Tea Party When American colonists managerd to throw 45 tonnes of tea into Boston Harbour to protest at the Tea Act.

United States of America The name given to the newly independent American Colonies.

French Revolution

Ancien régime Literally means 'old system'. In France this term referred to the old political system under which the king ruled the country.

Bourgeoisie French word for the middle-class or Third Estate.

Estates-General The meeting of representatives of all three Estates to discuss the issue of taxation in France.

National Assembly The alternative meeting of the Third Estate when they left the Estates-General.

The Bastille The Parisian prison stormed on 14 July 1789.

Sans-culottes Name given to the Parisian poor, tradesmen and workers who supported the revolution. Literally means 'without trousers' as they did not wear the silk knee-length stockings fashionable among the rich.

National Guard An armed force of the ordinary people of Paris headed by the Marquis de Lafayette

Tricolore A flag with three colours. The French flag represents the blue and red of Paris and the white of the Bourbon (French) kings appears in the middle.

Republic A form of government with an elected head of government rather than a monarch.

Legislative Assembly The French parliament established in 1791.

Constitutional Monarchy A form of government in which there is a monarch but he/she has no political power.

Émigrés The name for the many French who fled France for other European countries out of fear for their lives.

September Massacre Over 1,000 people were executed in September 1792 on suspicion of not supporting the revolution.

Jacobins An important political party of radical politicians who believed it was necessary to execute anyone who opposed the revolution.

Committee of Public Safety A 12-man group created to remove anyone whom they thought opposed the revolution.

Reign of Terror The period from 1793 to 1794 during which over 40,000 people were executed on suspicion of being enemies of the revolution.

The Directory A five-member group that was set up in 1794 to rule France.

Conscription When a government forces all able-bodied men of a certain age to join the army.

Irish Revolution

Battle of the Boyne The battle in 1690 that took place between Catholic James and Protestant William for the throne of England.

Anglicans Members of the Church of Ireland, which is a branch of the Church of England, who view the monarch of England as the head of the Church.

Protestant Ascendancy A term used to describe members of the Anglican community in Ireland who enjoyed great political and economic power and privileges in the eighteenth century.

The United Irishmen An organisation established in Belfast in 1791 which fought for political reform by bringing Irishmen of all religions together.

Catholic Committee A group set up to campaign against the Penal Laws.

Catholic Emancipation The right of Catholics to vote in elections and to be politicians.

Peep-o-Day Boys Protestant vigilante group who protected Protestants using violence.

Orange Order Organisation established to protect the Protestant population from Catholics.

The Act of Union (1800) The law that dissolved the Irish Parliament and merged it with the British Parliament in London.

The Liberator The name given to Daniel O'Connell after he successfully campaigned to allow Catholics become MPs.

Web References

For further reading on topics mentioned in this chapter, view the following websites:

American Revolution

www.whitehouse.gov/history/presidents/gw1.html

www.bbc.co.uk/history/british/empire_seapower/rebels_redcoats_01.shtml

www.ourdocuments.gov/doc.php?flash=true&doc=2

French Revolution

www.fordham.edu/halsall/mod/modsbook13.html

eudocs.lib.byu.edu/index.php/France:_1789_-_1871

Irish Revolution

www.iol.ie/~98com/english.htm

www.nationalarchives.ie/pdf/1798.pdf

www.ulstermuseum.org.uk

Women in History

▲ Mary Redmond in action during the Wexford Uprising.

Mary Redmond

Mary Redmond was immortalised in a print on her horse firing at the British troops. Born in Gorey, she was heavily involved in the Wexford Uprising. During this time she gave evidence against a number of people even going as far as to insist on the execution of one man. During the trial she attacked the man with a rock shouting, 'You Orange rogue!' The picture shows her at the Battle of Wexford on the 20 June 1798. She was described as, 'The lovely and accomplished Miss Redmond, a leader of the rebels, on her hunter, she is ever fighting where the battle is most violent.' Captured by British troops at Vinegar Hill, the next day she was sentenced to death by hanging. However, as she had three children she was let off and instead deported to Botany Bay in Australia.

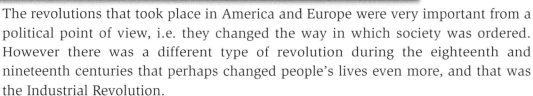

SOCIAL CHANGE IN BRITAIN AND IRELAND 1750-1850

Chapter 10

 Causes of Industrial Revolution in Britain

The revolutions that took place in America and Europe were very important from a political point of view, i.e. they changed the way in which society was ordered. However there was a different type of revolution during the eighteenth and nineteenth centuries that perhaps changed people's lives even more, and that was the Industrial Revolution.

This revolution changed the way they farmed (agriculture), the way they worked (industry) and the way in which they travelled from one point to another (transport). The transformation was known in general as the Industrial Revolution. It began in Britain and it took place between 1750 and 1850.

The Industrial Revolution began in Britain for a number of reasons:

● 1. An Increase in Population

Britain's population grew from roughly 5.5 million in 1700 to 18 million in 1841. This increase was due to a number of factors:

(a) The improvement in **farming methods** meant that more food was produced. This increase in food production meant more people could be fed. There were also different varieties of food being imported from the British colonies. Potatoes, maize and rice were grown and provided a more varied diet than ever before.

▲ Edward Jenner who discovered the cure for smallpox.

(b) There was an improvement in **medical knowledge.** This knowledge meant that the diseases and plagues that had been so common across Europe in the Middle Ages declined. One important discovery was made by Edward Jenner.

Smallpox was a terrible disease. Thousands died from it and if they survived they were left with scars on their faces. Edward Jenner noticed that milkmaids never got smallpox. Instead they got a much milder version called cowpox. He decided to inject a boy with cowpox and then placed him with people suffering from smallpox. The boy did not develop smallpox. The **vaccination** of cowpox made the boy immune from smallpox. Soon, most people were vaccinated and smallpox was eliminated.

2. Migration

The increase in population meant more people had to be fed and clothed. It also meant that there were more people looking for work because there was not enough work on farms in the countryside so people came to towns and cities to look for work.

▲ Jenner vaccinates a boy using cowpox. 'Vaccination' comes from *vacca*, the Latin word for cow.

3. Access to Raw Materials

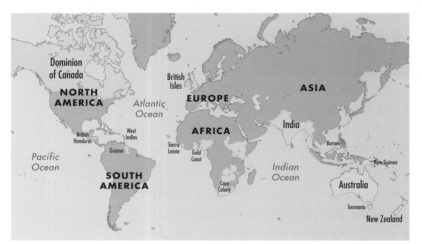

▲ A map of British Colonies in 1800. The British Empire stretched across the world. It was claimed that the sun never set on the British Empire. From this map can you work out why?

Britain had a large empire that stretched across the world. Raw materials like **cotton**, **sugar**, **rubber** and **tobacco** were brought from the colonies into Britain. These materials came from places like Canada, India, New Zealand and Australia and were then made into products in factories throughout Britain. The products were sold either in Britain or sent back to the colonies to be sold there. This trade made some people in Britain very wealthy.

4. Access to Coal and Iron

Factories were set up using coal to power machines with engines. These engines were made from iron. Both coal and iron were plentiful in Britain. Large mines were built in Wales and Yorkshire to dig coal and iron to keep factories supplied. Britain's access to cheap and plentiful supplies of coal and iron was a major reason why the Industrial Revolution happened there first rather than in Germany, France or any other European power at that time.

5. British Inventors

During the Renaissance, Italy produced more artists than any other country. Similarly, Britain produced more inventors during the Industrial Revolution than anywhere else. Perhaps the most important of those inventions was the steam engine. This was invented by Thomas Newcomen in 1712 and improved by James Watt in 1763. It powered trains and ships and also machines in factories.

6. New Banks, More Loans

The huge amounts of money made by British people living in the colonies and trading in raw materials resulted in new banks in Britain. These banks provided loans for many of the new businesses in Britain.

Questions

1. How did improved farming methods help increase the population of Britain in the eighteenth and nineteenth centuries?
2. What is vaccination and how was it invented?
3. Name two raw materials that were imported into Britain from its colonies.
4. What two materials were mined in Yorkshire and Wales?
5. Name a British inventor and his invention.

Changes in Agriculture

Medieval System of Farming

During the Middle Ages, farmers used the open-field rotation method of farming (see Chapter 4, The Middle Ages, page 81) Even by the middle of the eighteenth century, this method still had not changed. This method of farming had a number of disadvantages:

1. To allow the soil to regain its nutrients, every year a third of the land was left fallow. This was a great waste of land.

2. The three fields were unfenced so anyone or any animal could wander into the fields and destroy or eat the crops.

3. The three fields were divided into strips. This meant that if one person did not clear away weeds, they spread to the rest of the field very easily.

4. Disease often spread among the animals as they mingled on the commons (a grassy area in the village/town where the animals grazed). The commons was also not big enough to keep the animals there throughout the winter. Many of the cattle and sheep were killed every winter to feed the farmers' families.

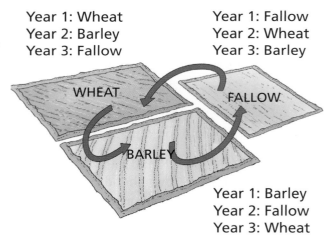

Year 1: Wheat
Year 2: Barley
Year 3: Fallow

Year 1: Fallow
Year 2: Wheat
Year 3: Barley

Year 1: Barley
Year 2: Fallow
Year 3: Wheat

▲ Crop rotation did not allow farmers to produce enough food for the increasing population.

These factors meant that as the population grew, farmers were not able to produce enough food. Farmers looked for new methods. These changes are called the **Agricultural Revolution**.

• Improvements in farming

ENCLOSURE:

1	Hedges & fences
2	Individual fields
3	Fewer labourers needed
4	Animals in fields

▲ How farmland looked before enclosure - see pages 78 – 81 for a reminder of medieval farming.

▲ How farmland looked after landowners began 'enclosing' fields.

1. Landowners began to 'enclose' fields with fences and hedges. Farmers no longer had to move from one field to the next in the open-field method. Instead they brought all their land into individual fields.

2. Weeds and disease from other farmers' strips were reduced.

3. Farmers who wanted to introduce new farming methods found it easier to do in one enclosed area.

4. Animals could no longer wander into fields and eat the crops.

AGRICULTURAL INVENTORS

1. **Charles Townshend** of Norfolk came up with a much better system than the open-field rotation system of the Middle Ages. He divided his land into four fields. Wheat was grown in one field and oats or barley in a second field. Instead of leaving the third field **fallow** (no crops), he planted the third field with turnips. These turnips cleared the field of weeds and gave nutrients back to the soil. The turnips could be used to feed the animals throughout the winter. Therefore, the cattle were much healthier and he did not need to kill his cattle in the winter. In the fourth field he planted grass and

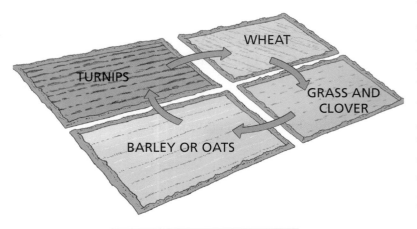

▲ The **Norfolk Crop Rotation System**

clover. Clover is full of nutrients (in particular nitrogen) and so helped the soil to recover. The grass could also be used as hay to feed the cattle in the winter. This four-field method became known as the **Norfolk Crop Rotation System**. The Norfolk System produced a much bigger harvest and the number of healthy cattle also increased.

2. In Leicestershire, a farmer named **Robert Bakewell** introduced a new method of cattle farming. Instead of letting his cattle breed as they wished, Bakewell used selective breeding. He would choose only his biggest and best animals

▲ A painting showing the impressive results of Bakewell's selective breeding policy.

to breed and the small and weak animals were killed. The result was that his animals tended to be of much better quality. His sheep produced better wool, his cattle were fatter and bigger and produced more milk. Soon this system of selective breeding was being used across the country. In 1700, the average individual weight of cattle sold for meat was 168 kg. By 1786, that weight had more than doubled to 381 kg.

▲ Jethro Tull

New farming machines were invented that made farming more efficient:

3. **Jethro Tull** invented the seed drill in 1701. Up until then farmers threw their seeds across the field by hand. This is called **broadcasting**. The seeds were not distributed evenly and birds could eat the seeds as they lay on the ground. Tull's drill made a hole in the ground and dropped a seed into it. A blade at the back of the drill covered the seed. Less seed was wasted and the crop grew in neat straight rows.

4. Up to this point, farmers used scythes to cut the crops at harvest. This required a lot of labour and it was very hard work. To reduce this expensive labour, **Cyrus McCormick** invented the **mechanical reaper** in 1834. This machine followed the neat rows of the seed drill and cut the crop. Using this machine, crops could be harvested far quicker and with much less effort.

The seed drill, invented by Jethro Tull in 1701. ▶

Agricultural Inventors	
Inventor	**Invention**
Charles Townshend	Norfolk crop rotation system
Robert Bakewell	Selective breeding
Jethro Tull	Seed drill (1701)
Cyrus McCormick	Mechanical reaper (1834)

MC CORMICK.

▲ Cyrus McCormick: This picture shows the inventor and his invention – the mechanical reaper (1834).

Questions

1. List four disadvantages of the open-field rotation method of farming.
2. Why did farmers want to enclose their land? Give two reasons.
3. What was the Norfolk crop rotation system?
4. Why was Charles Townshend known as 'Turnip' Townshend?
5. How did selective breeding improve the quality of meat in Britain?
6. Name two inventors of agricultural machines and name the inventions.

RESULTS OF CHANGES IN AGRICULTURE

1. Much more food was produced. As farmers produced more food, prices fell. People could eat meat far more often than before.

2. As a result of greater food production, cheaper food became widely available across Britain. This allowed families to feed their children and so the mortality rate decreased.

3. These changes were of great benefit to larger farmers. There was an increase in crops and cattle and sheep. The large farmers became much richer. There were, however, some problems with these changes:

   (a) As a result of enclosure, the land was divided and some areas of land were of better quality than others. Small farmers could only afford the poorer land. The commons was necessary for their animals to graze, but this was now enclosed. They could not afford the new farming methods that the richer farmers used. Over time they had to sell their pieces of land to bigger farmers and move to the towns and cities to find work.

   (b) The farm-labourers owned no land and were dependent on the bigger farmers for work. Their animals used the commons and they used the forest for wood. With enclosure, the commons and forest were now fenced off. The larger farmers began to use the new inventions so they needed far fewer farm-labourers. Soon, these farm-labourers were unemployed and had no land. Just like the small farmer, they had to move to the cities to seek work.

4. More and more poor people from the countryside moved to the cities. They had no money and therefore needed to find work. Most of these people ended up working for very little money in the new industries and factories in the towns and cities of Britain.

Questions

1. How did the Agricultural Revolution affect the growth of the British population?
2. Write a paragraph on the effects of the Agricultural Revolution on each of the following:
   (a) The landlord   (b) The small farmer   (c) The farm-labourer

Industrial Developments

● Textile Revolution

Before the Agricultural Revolution, most of the population lived in the countryside. People grew their own food and made their own clothes. Cloth was made from wool or the fibres of plants like flax (used for making linen). The process involved spinning wool or fibres of flax into long strands called yarn (thread). This yarn was then made into textile (cloth) by weaving it using a **loom**. The cloth was then cleaned and dyed. Spinning and weaving were the two main parts of the process of making cloth.

Practically every cottage had small looms. The weaving process was very slow and only produced a small amount of cloth. With the increase in population, more cloth was needed. So people began to think of ways in which to speed up cloth-making, resulting in the invention of new machines that helped to produce more textiles.

▲ The Flying Shuttle, invented by John Kay in 1733.

NEW MACHINES

1. **The Flying Shuttle** (1733): **John Kay** invented a small device for the hand loom that could speed up the production of cloth. It took three people working on three spinning-wheels to keep pace with the rate of the flying shuttle.

2. **The Spinning Jenny** (1764): **James Hargreaves** designed a machine that was able to spin eight times more yarn than the traditional method.

3. **The Water-Frame** (1769): It was now possible for large amounts of textile to be produced.

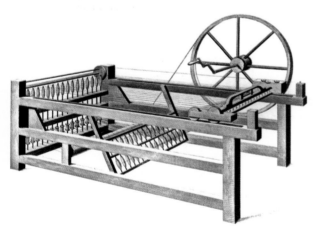

▲ The Spinning Jenny, invented by James Hargreaves in 1764. The machine was named after his wife, Jenny.

This mass production of cloth was helped by **Richard Arkwright's** invention. His spinning machine was powered by water from a river beside the building. This yarn was of better quality. Soon Arkwright was employing large numbers of people to work in his **mill** (factory). Other businessmen followed Arkwright and built mills to produce cloth.

4. **The Spinning Mule** (1779): The Spinning Mule was made by **Samuel Crompton**. This machine was even better than the Water-Frame. It was a mixture of the Water-Frame and the Spinning Jenny. The Spinning Mule became very popular in the new factories built at this time.

5. **The Power Loom** (1785): The Spinning Jenny, Water-Frame and Spinning Mule speeded up the production of yarn. So the process of weaving had to catch up. In 1785, **Edmund Cartwright** invented the Power Loom. This machine used the power of the steam engine to weave yarn into cloth. Its enormous size and its cost meant that these power looms could only be housed in factories.

▲ The Water-Frame, invented by Richard Arkwright in 1769.

▲ The Spinning Mule, invented by Samuel Crompton in 1779, is a mixture of the Water-Frame and the Spinning Jenny. A mule is a cross-breed of a horse and a donkey.

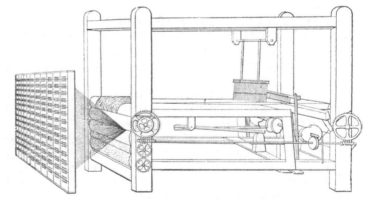

▲ The Power Loom, invented by Edmund Cartwright in 1785, used a steam engine to weave yarn into cloth.

Inventor	Invention	Year	Purpose
John Kay	Flying Shuttle	1733	Weaving cloth on loom
James Hargreaves	Spinning Jenny	1764	Spinning yarn
Richard Arkwright	The Water-Frame	1769	Spinning yarn
Samuel Crompton	Spinning Mule	1779	Spinning large amount of yarn
Edmund Cartwright	Power Loom	1785	Weaving large amounts of cloth

By the late eighteenth century, almost all of the spinning and weaving in Britain was done in large factories. The wool produced in Yorkshire supplied the factories in Leeds, Halifax and Huddersfield. Raw cotton was shipped into the port of Liverpool from the British colonies. It was then spun and woven in the local towns of Lancashire, e.g. Manchester, Bolton and Blackburn. Cotton became much more popular during the eighteenth and nineteenth centuries. It was more comfortable, lighter and easier to clean than wool. By 1841, there was over 100 times more cotton being imported into Britain than in 1771.

Questions

1. Expain the following words:
   (a) Yarn   (b) Textile   (c) Loom   (d) Linen   (e) Mill
2. What are the two main tasks required to make cloth?
3. Name two inventors of the textile revolution and explain how their inventions helped the textile revolution.
4. Why did Liverpool and Manchester become important towns in the manufacturing of textile?
5. Why did cotton become so popular in Britain in the eighteenth and nineteenth centuries?

By the way . . .

Newcomen's steam engine was very similar to the way in which the Italian espresso coffee maker works!

▲ James Watt whose improvement of the steam engine in 1769 was probably the most important event of the Industrial Revolution.

● Steam Engines

The new factories in Britain were powered by the steam engine. The steam engine was first invented in 1712 by Thomas Newcomen. It involved burning coal to turn water into steam that forced the machine to work.

The Scottish inventor James Watt improved on Newcomen's steam engine in 1769. He made it far more efficient and his engine burnt 75 per cent less coal than Newcomen's. This made it much cheaper to run. Watt also designed the engine so that it turned a fly-wheel so that belts could be powered to turn spinning and weaving machines. It was also able to operate pumps and later to power trains. For this reason, the steam engine was perhaps the most important invention of the whole Industrial Revolution.

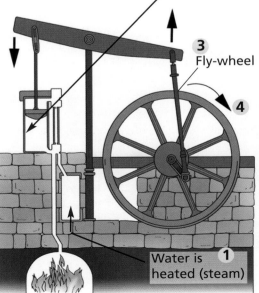

2 Steam pushes piston up, raising the arm which turns the wheel and belt.

3 Fly-wheel

4

1 Water is heated (steam)

▲ James Watt's Steam Engine, 1769

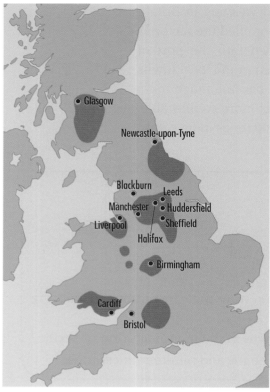

▲ Coal deposits in Britain were plentiful during the Industrial Revolution.

Coal

The steam engine required two things: iron to build it and coal for burning in it. Both of these were plentiful in areas of Britain. Wherever deposits of coal and iron were located, large factories also grew. Coal had many uses during the Industrial Revolution and it was always in great demand.

Uses of coal

1. Coal was used in homes for heating and cooking.

2. Coal was burnt to create steam to power the steam engines in factories.

3. Locomotive trains and steamboats were invented at this time. These trains and boats needed coal to power their engines.

Iron

Iron was made by smelting (heating the rock in a furnace until the iron can be extracted from the rock). Initially charcoal (burnt timber) was used as fuel in the furnaces. As the forests of Britain began to disappear, a new fuel was needed to feed the furnaces. The sulphur in coal made it unsuitable to use as a fuel. However, in 1709, **Abraham Darby** tried to bake coal at a very high temperature and produced **coke**. This method removed almost all of the sulphur from the coal. As coal was plentiful, this discovery meant that iron smelting became far cheaper and so more widespread. Iron could now be used in the making of machines, bridges and trains.

▲ Puddling and rolling – Henry Cort's method of iron production.

Iron and Steel

The iron made by Abraham Darby was called pig-iron and was of poor quality as the metal still had impurities in it, even after smelting. At the end of the eighteenth century **Henry Cort** invented a method of iron production called **puddling and rolling**. This required stirring the iron and then burning off any impurities. The iron was then passed through large rollers. This hardened the iron. Cort's method made better quality iron and it was also cheaper.

Finally in 1856, an inventor named **Henry Bessemer** developed his converter. This machine added a metal called manganese to iron, forced air through the mixture and then burnt off any impurities. The result was a new metal called steel.

Steel has some advantages over iron:

1. It is more flexible than iron.

2. It does not rust as easily as iron.

3. Steel can be sharpened more easily. More precise tools such as cutlery and medical instruments can be made with steel.

4. It costs less to make than iron.

Steel helped to speed up the development of the railways and ship-building industries in Britain. Bessemer had a steel foundry in Sheffield, England. Sheffield was soon the centre for British steel-making. Today, Sheffield is still famous for producing steel products.

▲ The Bessemer converter turned iron into steel, 1856.

Inventor	Invention	Year	Purpose
Thomas Newcomen	Steam engine	1712	Used steam from burning coal to turn engine
James Watt	Steam engine and fly-wheel	1769	Made improvements to Newcomen's engine making it more efficient
Abraham Darby	Smelting of iron with coke	1709	Coke could produce a better, cheaper method of making iron
Henry Cort	Puddling and rolling	1784	Improved the quality and reduced the cost of iron
Henry Bessemer	Bessemer Converter	1856	Turned iron into a higher quality metal called steel

Questions

1. How was Watt's steam engine of 1769 an improvement on Thomas Newcomen's engine of 1712?
2. Name three uses for coal during the Industrial Revolution.
3. (a) Explain the term 'coke'.   (b) Who invented it and what was it used for?
4. Describe one improvement made in the production of iron.
5. Name three advantages steel has over iron.

• Transport Revolution

ROADS

British roads in the eighteenth century were mostly dirt tracks. They were full of potholes and when it rained they became too muddy to use. In 1663, the **Turnpike Trusts** were set up. They maintained certain roads in return for a **toll** (tax) on all carts, carriages and horse-riders that used their roads. By the 1850s the Industrial Revolution had generated a huge increase in traffic on the roads. Raw material and heavy goods were now being transported all across Britain. The turnpike roads were neither wide enough nor good enough to carry this increased load. Luckily two Scottish engineers discovered how to improve the methods used to build a road.

▲ British roads in the eighteenth century were mostly dirt tracks until two Scottish engineers figured out how to improve the methods used to build a road.

MacAdam's road used a layer of small stones topped with gravel ▶

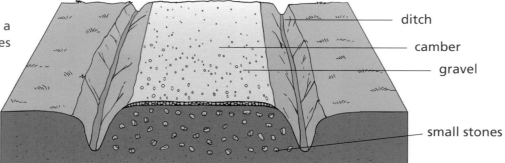

— ditch
— camber
— gravel
— small stones

1. **Thomas Telford** believed that if large stones were placed into the road it provided a firm foundation. Smaller stones were then placed on top of the larger stones. Finally gravel was put on the surface. This gave the road a smooth and firm surface. His roads also had a camber (slope) so that all rainwater would run off the road and into the ditches along the side.

2. **John MacAdam's** design did not require large foundation stones. Instead, a layer of 30 cm of smaller stones was topped with gravel. As the road was used by carriages and carts, the gravel was ground down. This ground gravel worked as a sort of cement. He also proposed that the roads would have a camber and ditches for rainwater along the side.

These improvements meant that by the 1830s, Britain had over 225,000 kilometres of road. These linked the coal mines, factories, towns and cities. The time taken to get from city to city was reduced. In 1794, it took four days to get from London to Manchester. By 1830, the journey took only 18 hours.

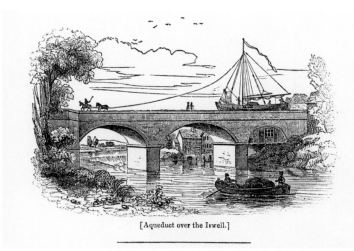

[Aqueduct over the Irwell.]

▲ The Bridgewater canal, 1761, was a huge success.

CANALS

The Duke of Bridgewater transported large amounts of coal to Manchester from his coalmines in Worsley. In 1759, he received governmental approval to build a canal and he employed engineer **James Brindley** to design the canal. The Bridgewater Canal was a huge success. A canal barge required only one horse to pull it and the barge could carry ten times more coal than horse-drawn carts. The increase in the amount of coal coming into Manchester soon meant that the cost of coal dropped by 50%. Many new canals were built in the following years with almost 6,500 kilometres built by the middle of the nineteenth century. The canals were a huge success, but horse-pulled barges were very slow. The barge's top speed was only about five kilometres per hour. By the mid 1800s, a new method of transport had replaced the canal.

RAILWAYS

James Watt's steam engine was used in many of the new inventions of the Industrial Revolution. And his steam engine was just as important in the Transport Revolution. **Richard Trevithick** adapted Watt's steam engine to power a wheeled carriage along iron tracks in 1804. His steam locomotive inspired **George Stevenson** to build his **Rocket** in 1830. Stevenson's Rocket was able to reach speeds of almost 50 kilometres per hour. This method of transport was faster and cheaper than any other. Soon, over 12,500 kilometres of railway track had been laid. The railways had a huge impact on Britain:

▲ Stevenson's Rocket, 1830, reached speeds of almost 50 kilometres an hour.

1. Transport of goods, including farm produce, became quicker and cheaper.

2. The iron, steel and coal industries were helped by the lower costs of transport.

3. People were able to move around more easily. Holidays to coastal towns across Britain became more common.

4. Railways became the main method of transport. Canals and road transport were less and less popular.

STEAM SHIPS

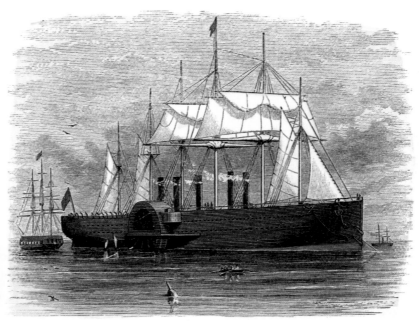

The Great Eastern, capable of carrying over 4,000 passengers from Britain to America, was launched in 1860. ▶

▲ Isambard Kingdom Brunel launched the first ship to sail from Britain to America non-stop.

Large iron ships powered by steam engines began to replace sail-powered wooden ships. These new ships were able to travel against the wind and could carry greater number of passengers. In 1860, Isambard Kingdom Brunel launched his 211-metre long ship, *The Great Eastern*, on its first trip to America. It was capable of carrying over 4,000 passengers from Britain to America non-stop under its own steam power. It crossed the Atlantic in 10 days. Although not all ships were of this size, steamships slowly replaced wooden sailing ships.

Inventor	Invention	Year	Purpose
James Brindley	Canals	1761	Designed the building of the Bridgewater canal into Manchester to transport coal.
Thomas Telford	Improved roads	1803	Created roads that were smooth and durable.
John MacAdam	Improved roads	1800s	Created roads that used crushed stone to give a well-drained, smooth road surface.
George Stevenson	The Rocket	1830	Adapted Watt's steam engine to make a fast locomotive train to carry goods.
Isambard Kingdom Brunel	The Great Eastern	1860	Launched the first large steam-powered iron ship capable of carrying over 4,000 passengers across Atlantic.

Questions

1. Why were the roads in Britain in the 1800s not suitable for transporting heavy goods?
2. What was the Turnpike Trust?
3. Name two inventors who helped improve the standard of roads in Britain in the nineteenth century.
4. Why did the Duke of Bridgewater want to find a new method of transportation for his coal?
5. What advantages did the Bridgewater Canal have over roads?
6. What were the advantages of trains for the transportation of heavy goods?
7. Why were steam-powered ships better for long journeys than sail-boats?

Society in Industrial Britain

The Agricultural Revolution forced many farm labourers into the cities. Furthermore, since the textile revolution, the domestic production of cloth was too slow to compete with the large textile factories. These factors forced millions of people into the cities to look for work. By 1850 almost half the population of Britain lived in the towns and cities. Industrial towns grew in size. For example, Manchester's population grew from 25,000 in the early 1770s to 350,000 in 1850. People came to these cities to find employment in the mines or factories that were springing up during this period.

▲ Newcastle upon Tyne, one of many industrial cities in Britain.

● Living Conditions

The sudden increase in population in the cities caused overcrowding. There were not enough houses for people to live in. Some factory owners built small houses near the factory for the workers. Otherwise people would have to find shelter in the existing houses of the town. It was common for one or even two families to live in a single room of a house. They would sleep on straw on the ground. There were no toilets so any human waste was dumped into the rivers or simply in the yard outside. There was no running water, so drinking water was drawn from the rivers nearby. It was expensive and difficult to heat these houses so many families lived in very cold and damp conditions. The areas where these living conditions existed were known as **slums**.

▲ The slums of London

● Health

1. With large numbers of people living so closely together, it was not surprising that there was much disease. Life expectancy was very low with few people living beyond the age of 40.

2. The drinking water was very polluted from the human waste and rubbish dumped into the rivers. This dirty water caused diseases like typhoid and cholera. In 1832, a cholera outbreak in Britain killed 56,000 people.

3. The coal that was burnt in people's homes and in the factories also caused problems. The smoke from the coal caused smog (a mixture of smoke and fog). This smog contained sulphur and many other harmful particles which could cause asthma.

4. The damp conditions and poor diet also resulted in consumption (tuberculosis).

5. Due to the large numbers of people living so closely together, any disease like smallpox could spread very quickly.

Questions

1. Why did the population of the industrial towns like Manchester grow during the early 1800s?
2. Explain the following terms: (a) Slum (b) Smog.
3. Give one consequence of overcrowding in towns such as Manchester.
4. What diseases were found in the poor areas of the towns and cities of Britain at this time?

● Working Conditions

There were many people looking for employment in the factories and mines. Often they became so desperate to find work that they were ready to work for very low wages rather than not have any work. This also meant that employers were able to replace anyone whom they wanted to sack. The working day started at about 5:30am and lasted for 12 to 16 hours. The only day off was Sunday and there were no holidays. If a worker missed a day at work they did not get paid and were often fired.

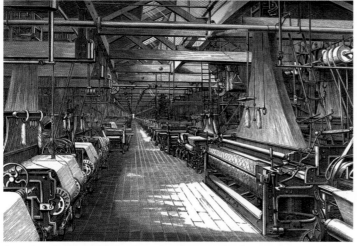

▲ The factory floor in a large textile factory

FACTORIES

The conditions inside a textile factory were very unpleasant. The machines were deafening and the dust from the thread and cloth caught in the workers' throats. The air became very warm and damp from the machines and cloth. However, the windows were kept shut at all times to keep the thread moist and stop it from breaking. The only breaks the workers were allowed were 40 minutes for dinner and three toilet breaks during the day.

Workers were fined if they broke any rules in the factory. Whistling, singing, smoking and bad language were forbidden. The worker also had to pay a fine if any equipment was broken or if he/she was late for work. Workers who did not work hard enough were sometimes beaten by their supervisors.

The machines the workers operated were very large and dangerous. Workers could become over-tired and suffer an injury from one of the machines. It was common for limbs to be lost in the machines and there were often fatal injuries. If a worker could not work due to an injury, they were simply replaced by someone else.

Wages were so low that every member of the family was expected to work. Women usually worked in the textile factories. Employers paid women only half of what they paid men. Children were also expected to work. Their size meant that they could get their hands and bodies into places that adults could not. Beatings were common for children if the supervisor thought that they did not work hard enough. Children often grew up with deformed backs from having to bend over the machines as their bodies grew.

MINING

To get at the coal deposits in the ground, it was necessary to dig **mineshafts** (tunnels). These shafts were supported by wooden beams to stop them caving in. **Colliers** (coal miners) dug the tunnel to find a **seam** (layer) of coal. They then dug the coal out and sent it to the surface using ropes and pulleys.

▲ Child were often crammed into small spaces adults could not reach.

Working in the mines was a very dangerous and difficult job. Men, women and children worked in the mines for 14 hours a day.

From the age of five, children worked as **trappers**. This involved opening and closing trapdoors to allow carts through. This stopped any dangerous gases from building up in the mine.

▲ Children worked in the mines as trappers and hurriers from the age of five.

From the age of eight, children worked as **hurriers**. They were expected to carry coal out of the mine. This required pushing or pulling coal carts through low, narrow mineshafts and carrying the coal to the surface.

Finally when they were old enough, they would work as a collier. They would stand at the coalface and dig out the coal using pickaxes and shovels.

DANGERS

There was always a danger of mines collapsing and trapping the miners or crushing them. Certain gases like methane built up and could cause an explosion if there was a naked flame nearby. **Humphrey Davy** invented the miner's safety lamp which came into use in 1816. This lamp had gauze (thin cloth) around the flame to stop it coming into contact with the gas.

The miner's safety lamp by Humphrey Davy ▲ came into use in 1816.

Mines could easily flood, drowning all the people in the mineshaft. This problem was solved when Thomas Newcomen's steam engine was used to pump water out of mines. The steam engine allowed mine shafts go even deeper under the ground. Later, Watt's steam engine was used to pull the coal up from the mines.

The damp and dirty conditions caused terrible illnesses such as Miner's Lung from inhaling all the coal dust. Colliers also suffered from poor eyesight due to the darkness in the mines.

▲ Football became increasingly popular in Britain during the 1800s.

People working in mines often had bent or misshapen backs due to bending so much.

• Leisure Time

Workers had Sundays off. The terrible conditions in the slums led many people to go to the pubs and drink gin, beer, cider and ale to try to block out the misery of their lives. There were over 1,000 licensed pubs in Manchester in the 1840s and many more illegal bars.

Other workers enjoyed watching and betting on bare-knuckle boxing, cock-fighting, dog-fighting and badger-baiting. Sports such as cricket, soccer and rugby were also played. By the end of the nineteenth century these sports had developed proper organisations, such as the Football Association, to make rules and set up leagues. These sports became even more popular when in the 1850s a half-day on Saturday was introduced.

By the way . . .

Manchester United was originally called Newton Heath Lancashire and Yorkshire Railway Football Club. They were a team made up of workers from the railway station.

Manchester United winning ▲ the European Cup in 2008.

● Life of the Wealthy

The wealthy people in Britain lived very different lives to the factory and mine workers. The factory owners, mine owners and those who owned the iron and steel works became very rich. They were able to pay very low wages to their workers while making enormous profits. These business owners needed to employ doctors, lawyers and accountants. This new rich middle class lived in very large houses in the towns far away from the slums. Sometimes they had houses in the countryside also. Their families were helped in their homes by servants. Their children were educated by private tutors and were well fed. When the children grew up they attended universities such as Oxford and Cambridge. As the popularity of trains grew, holidays were spent at seaside resorts.

Questions

1. List two dangers that workers in a textile factory faced.

2. Why were women and children employed in the textile factories?

3. For what reasons could workers in a textile factory be fined?

4. How many hours a day did people in a textile factory work?

5. Name and describe three different jobs that workers did in a mine.

6. List the dangers faced by workers in mines.

7. What did workers in an industrial town do in their free time? Give two examples.

8. Write an account of either (a) or (b) below:

   (a) The life of a child working in a textile factory during the Industrial Revolution.

   (b) The life of a collier in a mine during the Industrial Revolution.

   Use the following headings as a guide:

   • Your home and neighbourhood   • Your work and the working conditions

   • Your health   • Your free time

WORKERS' RIGHTS! Improvements in Quality of Life

The changes in society that occurred in Britain were not always popular. The poor working and living conditions and the low wages at times made workers very angry. Between 1811 and 1818, a group of people called **Luddites** began to break into factories and smash the machines. They were angry at losing their jobs and being replaced by these machines. The government dealt very harshly with the Luddites and the movement soon died out.

▲ Luddites smashing factory machines in anger.

In the 1830s, a new movement called the **Chartists** attempted to get more rights for workers. They demanded that the right to vote should be given to all men and not just landowners. They also wanted to have fairer elections so that workers could be represented in Parliament. The rich landowners in the parliament did not want to lose their power so they refused all of the Chartists' demands.

In 1825, **trade unions** (organisations made up of workers from a particular industry) were made legal. However, they were not allowed to go on strike (refuse to work). Throughout the nineteenth century many trade unions were established but most failed and many of the trade union members were fired or even sent to Australia. Eventually, workers were given the right to go on strike in 1875. Trade unions then became a powerful force for the improvement of workers' wages and conditions.

● Reformers

ROBERT OWEN (1771-1858)

Robert Owen set up a cotton factory in New Lanark in Scotland. He saw how other employers treated their workers and he was disgusted by it. He decided that if he treated his workers well, they would be happy. Furthermore, if they were happy, then they would work harder and so profits would increase. He built good homes for his 2,000 workers and provided free schooling for their children. There was clean

▲ Robert Owen did not agree with the way in which factory owners treated their workers.

▲ New Lanark, Owen's cotton factory in Scotland, opened in 1816.

running water and there was no overcrowding. The shops at the factory offered their goods at cost price. Later he set up **cooperatives** where the workers owned the shops and the profits were shared out among the workers. His experiment worked. The profits in the New Lanark factory increased. Owen's ideas were not popular among many other factory owners but some of them were influenced by his actions.

OTHER REFORMERS

Others were also influential in the improvement of the workers' conditions. **Edwin Chadwick** wrote a report in 1842 on the appalling conditions of the workers in the slums of the cities. His report forced the government to make changes to improve the sanitation and cleanliness of the towns and cities. **Lord Shaftesbury** forced the government to pass the Factory Act of 1833. This Act made it illegal for children under nine years of age to work in a factory. Any child aged between 9 and 13 could not be forced to work more than 8 hours each day and they must receive 2 hours of education each day. Inspectors were employed to ensure that these rules were followed. Many other Acts followed. The 1844 Factory Act further reduced the hours a child aged between 9 and 13 could work to 6 hours each day. More Acts that sought to improve working conditions for workers were passed between 1847 and 1891. In 1842, it was decided that children and women were not allowed to work in mines.

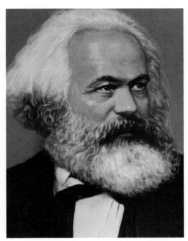

The conditions of the workers of Britain were discussed in books by two German writers – **Karl Marx** and **Friedrich Engels**. In 1867, Marx and Engels wrote *Das Kapital*. In it they stated that the working conditions were so bad that they believed the workers would rise up against their employers. This revolution would mean that the workers would rule instead of the rich employers. This new system was called **communism**. Marx and Engels' ideas were to have a great influence on many people during the following century and a half.

▲ Karl Marx, one of the founders of the political ideology known as communism.

Reformer	Reform	Year	Purpose
Humphrey Davy	Miners' Safety Lamp	1816	Stopped flames from lamp causing explosions in mines.
Charterists	Demanded right to vote and freer elections	1830s	To remove power of rich landowners.
Robert Owen	Working conditions	1816	Improved working conditions in his cotton factory.
Edwin Chadwick	Report on working conditions	1842	To force the government to improve working conditions.
Lord Shaftesbury	Factory Act	1833	Passed a law that made it illegal for a child less than nine years old to work in a factory.
Karl Marx and Friedrich Engels	Wrote *Das Kapital*	1867	Their book suggested that the dreadful working conditions would result in a workers' revolution.

Questions

1. Why were the Luddites angry at the changes occurring in Industrial Britain?
2. List two of the demands of the Charterists.
3. What made Robert Owen's factory in New Lanark so different from other factories?
4. What changes did Lord Shaftesbury's 1833 Factory Act make to the conditions of factory workers?
5. Connect the following names (A–D) with the correct reform (1–4):

   A Karl Marx and Friedrich Engels   1. Report on conditions of slums in British towns

   B Edwin Chadwick   2. Fairer elections

   C Charterists   3. New Lanark factory

   D Robert Owen   4. *Das Kapital*

 # Ireland in the Nineteenth Century

● Politics

Since the beginning of the nineteenth century, Ireland had been part of Great Britain. The Act of Union (see page 255) meant that Ireland was ruled directly by the British Parliament from 1801. Catholic Emancipation (allowing Catholics to vote in elections) had been achieved in 1829. However, the British government insisted that only Catholics who owned land worth at least £10 could vote. This meant that only rich landlords could vote in elections, ruling out the majority of Catholics in Ireland.

Harland & Wolff's South Yard, Belfast

▲ Harland and Wolff in Belfast became the biggest shipbuilding company in the world by the end of the 1800s.

● Industrialisation

Ireland did not experience the Industrial Revolution in the same way as Britain did. The only industrialised area in Ireland was around the city of Belfast. The area of Belfast produced large amounts of linen and cotton. By 1811, there was an estimated 50,000 people employed in the textile industry. During the nineteenth century shipbuilding became very important too. Harland and Wolff in Belfast became the biggest shipbuilding company in the world by the end of the 1800s.

▲ O'Connell Street and the GPO in Dublin in the 1840s

At the start of the 1840s Dublin had a population of 250,000. Its main industries were wool manufacturing and the Guinness brewery. Apart from the towns of Cork and Limerick, most of the rest of the population of 8.2 million lived in the countryside. These were divided up into three different groups:

1. LANDLORDS

Ten per cent of the population owned about ninety per cent of the land. These landowners were descendents of the English and Scottish planters that we looked at in Chapter 8, The Plantations. Their families had lived in Ireland for generations but considered themselves to be still British. Some of these Irish landlords even lived in Britain. These **absentee-landlords** left the running of their estates to middle-men (managers). They cared little for their tenants as long as they received their rents.

▲ Caledon in County Armagh is an example of an estate that had an absentee landlord.

2. TENANT FARMERS

Tenant farmers consisted of about one third of the population. Some of these tenant farmers had over 20 acres and could live reasonably well. Most of them had less than 10 acres and were **subsistence farmers** (they only grew enough food to live). When there was a good harvest they could pay the landlord and feed their families. However, when the harvest was bad it was very difficult to survive.

▲ Cottiers (farm labourers) grew potatoes on their land.

3. FARM LABOURERS

The third group was made up of the farm labourers or **cottiers**. These people rented a plot of land on which they could grow potatoes. This plot was known as a **conacre**. They paid for the use of this land by working a number of days on the farmer's land. One acre of potatoes was able to provide enough food for a whole family for an entire year. Potatoes were an easy food source that had helped support the increase in population in Ireland over the previous 100 years. About three million small farmers and farm labourers depended on the potato as their main food.

● Homes

Housing in Ireland was very wide ranging. The landlords lived in mansions and some wealthy farmers had farmhouses. However, the majority of the population lived in small, one-roomed mud huts with a thatched roof. These huts would have a fireplace and a chimney but there were no toilets. These types of homes were very common in the west of Ireland.

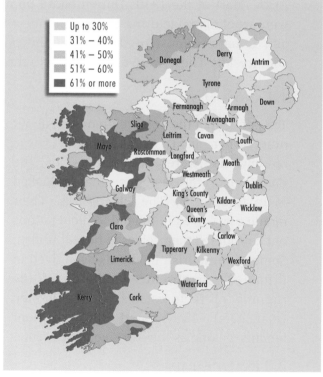

Key:
- Up to 30%
- 31% – 40%
- 41% – 50%
- 51% – 60%
- 61% or more

Donegal, Derry, Antrim, Tyrone, Fermanagh, Armagh, Down, Monaghan, Sligo, Leitrim, Cavan, Louth, Mayo, Roscommon, Longford, Meath, Westmeath, Dublin, Galway, King's County, Kildare, Wicklow, Queen's County, Clare, Carlow, Tipperary, Kilkenny, Wexford, Limerick, Waterford, Kerry, Cork

▲ The percentage of the Irish population living in one-roomed huts in the 1840s.

▲ The small, one-roomed hut of a cottier

Questions

1. Explain the following terms:

   (a) Absentee landlord   (b) Subsistence farming   (c) Catholic Emancipation

2. What were the main industries in Ireland in the nineteenth century?

3. What was the population of Ireland in 1841?

4. Write a short paragraph on the life of a poor farmer in Ireland in 1841. Mention your job, your food and your home.

An Gorta Mór - The Great Hunger

The rise in population in Ireland before 1840 was huge. The population rose from approximately five million at the beginning of the century to over eight million by 1841. As the population grew, land became more scarce.

Apart from Belfast and its surrounds, Ireland had not been industrialised in the same way as Britain. This meant that there were no factories or mines in which people could find work. People depended on farming to survive. Parents had to subdivide their farms among their sons and daughters. The farms, therefore, became smaller and it became more difficult to live off the land.

A family with a small amount of land depended on the potato. It provided a high **yield** (harvest) and potatoes could be eaten all through the winter. Potatoes became the **staple** (the basic and main item) ingredient in the diet of about three million people in Ireland. This dependence on the potato for food for three out of the eight million people living in Ireland

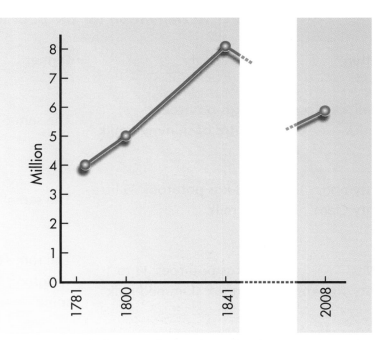

▲ Increase of the population in Ireland up to 1841. The graph also shows that Ireland has not returned to the high of eight million people, even up to 2008.

was very dangerous. In order to get a high yield, Irish cottiers had begun to use a potato called a lumber. The lumber potato produced a large harvest but was of poor quality and was less immune to diseases than other varieties.

▲ Note the store of potatoes in the loft of this hut.

Source A: Daily food for the poor in Ireland in 1840			
Location	**Breakfast**	**Dinner**	**Supper**
Kilmallock, County Limerick	2 kgs potatoes, 1 litre of skimmed milk	The same	The same but often not eaten if food was scarce
Ennistymon, County Clare	2.3 kgs potatoes, ½ litre of milk	The same	The same but often not eaten if food was scarce
Thurles, County Tipperary	2 kgs potatoes, ½ to 1 litre of skimmed milk	The same (herring weighing 110 grammes sometimes used instead)	Only eaten at plentiful times of year

By the way . . .

Potato blight (or *phytophthora infestans*) was introduced to Europe from South America by the importation of guano (bird manure). Guano was used as a fertiliser by farmers to gain better harvests.

Occasionally (for example in 1741 and 1816) there were bad harvests due to poor weather which resulted in thousands of deaths. However, in 1845 a new, more dangerous disease appeared. **Potato blight** was caused by a fungus that attacked the stalks and then the tubers (the actual potato). It liked warm, damp conditions and spread itself by little particles called spores.

▲ Potato blight struck in Ireland in the three years 1845, 1846 and 1848.

● Famine

The potato blight first appeared in Ireland in 1845. While the early summer crop of potatoes was not affected, about a third of the autumn crop was destroyed. The potatoes in the field smelt rotten and when they were dug up they had turned into a black mush. Many died of starvation but overall a full famine was avoided as two thirds of the crop had already been harvested. However, in 1846, blight struck again and this time, two thirds of the crop was destroyed. This caused great starvation throughout Ireland. The blight was not as bad in 1847 but the poor had not planted many seed-potatoes; instead they had eaten them. By now, starvation was widespread. 1848 saw the return of the blight and again, two thirds of the potatoes were destroyed.

A letter in 1846 from Rev Theobald Matthew describing what he saw as he travelled from Cork to Dublin:

I beheld, with sorrow, one wide waste of putrefying (rotting) vegetation. In many places the wretched people were seated on the fences of their decaying gardens, wringing their hands and wailing bitterly the destruction that had left them foodless.

● Disease

It was not just starvation that caused the deaths of so many people during the Famine years. Diseases such as **typhus** and **relapsing fever** were spread by body lice. **Dysentery** (known as 'the bloody flux') was spread by flies, dirty fingers and infected food. These were very easily spread by people crowding into workhouses or waiting in queues for food. Due to the lack of vitamin C from the potatoes, **scurvy** became common. Also, due to the poor health conditions of the starving, they were more likely to die from these diseases. It is estimated that the majority of the million people who died in the Famine died from one or more of these diseases.

▲ Many poor Irish people died from starvation and disease.

The Government Response

▲ Robert Peel imported maize and set up public works schemes to help famine victims.

1. PEEL'S BRIMSTONE

In 1845, the government in Britain under Robert Peel moved quickly to help the starving people of Ireland. Peel imported £100,000 (€127,000) worth of Indian corn (maize) from the United States for sale in Ireland. He also set up the Relief Commission to organise the distribution of the corn. To help provide employment Peel also encouraged **public works schemes** (to build roads, piers and harbours) to be set up. These measures went some way towards avoiding a complete famine in 1845 and 1846. However, the public works schemes failed to provide enough employment and the importation of Indian corn was only partly successful.

The Indian corn was difficult to cook. Notices were put up throughout Ireland explaining how to cook it, but most of these were in English and so many could not read them. The Indian corn was unpopular and gave people bad stomach problems. For this reason, and because of its yellow colour, the Indian corn was nicknamed Peel's brimstone.

▲ Maize – this did not prove popular with Irish people during the Famine.

In 1846, Robert Peel was replaced as British Prime Minister by John Russell. He did not believe the government should interfere in economic matters. This policy is called **laissez-faire**. Therefore, Russell stopped the importation and distribution of cheap Indian corn. Instead, he thought that people should work their way out of starvation and that the Irish were too reliant on charity.

▲ John Russell believed that Irish people relied on charity too much.

2. PUBLIC WORKS SCHEMES

Half of the cost of Peel's public works schemes had been paid for by the British government. The new Prime Minister, Russell, did not believe that the British government should have to pay for these works. The British government believed that 'Irish property must support Irish poverty' and therefore would only offer loans with an interest rate of 3.5 per cent. Furthermore, to ensure value for money, Russell and **Charles Edward Trevelyan** (the British Finance Secretary responsible for Ireland) introduced task-work so that pay would be connected to each individual's work. Despite low pay, the distances people had to travel during the winter and the physically weak condition of most of the population, by March 1847 there were 714,000 people employed. Unfortunately, the food dealers were able to increase their prices and the poor were still not able to buy enough food.

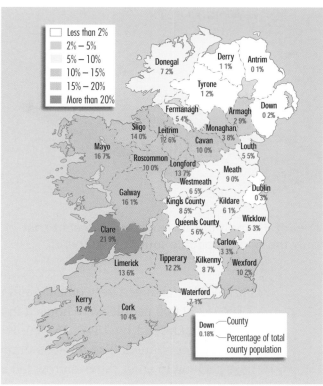

▲ This map shows the percentage of people employed by public works schemes between 1846 and 1847.

3. EXPORTATION OF FOOD

▲ Police in Dungarvan, County Waterford opened fire on protestors who tried to stop a boat full of grain from leaving, 1846.

Under Russell's policy of laissez-faire, the export of food out of Ireland continued despite the starving population. Ships full of agricultural produce were shipped to England during the Famine. This caused great anger among the starving people in Ireland. Riots took place across Ireland, most notably in Dungarvan, County Waterford where people tried to stop a boat full of grain from leaving. The police shot the protesters, injuring several and killing one. People did not forget this British policy of exporting food while Irish people lay dying of starvation. Instead they felt even more angry that Britain controlled Irish affairs. Some became determined to win Ireland's independence.

4. Workhouses

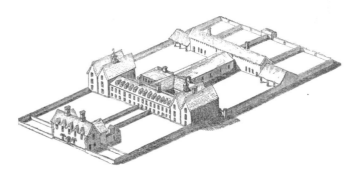

▲ Dreadful conditions in workhouses meant that only the poorest people sought help there.

Workhouses had been set up under the Poor Law Act in 1838. They were very unpopular before the Famine as the conditions were awful. Mothers, fathers, sons and daughters were divided up and made to do very basic work. To discourage too many people coming to the workhouses, the meals provided were very small. The conditions meant that only the very poor sought help in the workhouses. Although the workhouses could accommodate 100,000 people, only 38,000 were housed there at the beginning of the Famine. That changed very quickly and new extensions had to be built. By the end of 1849, 250,000 people were housed in workhouses. Due to overcrowding, disease spread quickly and by 1847, 25 people in every 1,000 were dying each week. In 1847, the government also allowed outdoor relief in the form of soup-kitchens, for those seeking to enter the overcrowded workhouses. By 1849, 800,000 people were receiving outdoor relief.

● Other Help

The **Society of Friends** (also known as the **Quakers**) worked hard throughout the Famine to help the poor and hungry. They opened soup-kitchens throughout Ireland and spent almost €254,000 on aid to Ireland. In 1847, the British Relief Association was set up. It raised €597,000 in aid for Ireland. In today's money, that would be over €20 million. Many Irish people living in other countries also sent money back to their families.

▲ Soup kitchens were opened by Quakers to help the starving.

Questions

1. List the measures Robert Peel introduced to help victims of the Irish Famine.

2. Why was Indian corn also known as Peel's brimstone?

3. Briefly describe the conditions in the workhouses.

4. Why were the Irish angry at the exportation of food out of Ireland?

5. Apart from the government, what other help was given to the Irish victims of the Famine?

6. Explain what the term laissez-faire means.

RESULTS OF THE FAMINE

1. Evictions

During the Famine most poor farm tenants and cottiers were unable to pay their rents. Some landlords reduced their rents or even waived (let them off) their rents altogether. However, others saw this as an opportunity to evict (remove tenants from their home) the poor off the land and replace them with larger, more profitable farms. This meant that during a time of famine and disease many people also became homeless. Landlords arrived with policemen and soldiers to evict tenants.

THE EJECTMENT.

Source A The Quaker, James Hack Tuke describes an eviction:

The policemen are commanded to do their duty. Reluctantly indeed they proceed armed with bayonet and muskets, to throw out the miserable furniture: dirty time-worn stools and bed-frame, if any, ragged cover-lid, iron pot; all must be cast out, and the very roof of the hovel (hut) itself thrown down. But, the tenants make some show of resistance . . . for they know truly that, when their hovels are demolished, the nearest ditch must be their dwelling.

From James Hack Tuke's *A Visit to Connaught in the autumn of 1847*, a letter addressed to the Central Relief Committee of the Society of Friends, Dublin 1847

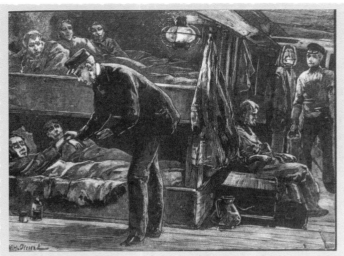

▲ Many people died in boats to Canada, America and Australia, leading to these ships being known as coffin ships.

2. Emigration

During the Famine millions of people in Ireland faced the choice of either starvation or emigration to another country. Most of these people were between 20 and 35 years of age and Catholic. About a quarter of them were Irish speakers. It is thought that between 1845 and 1851 about 1.2 million people emigrated to Britain, the United States, Canada and Australia. The conditions in the ships on the long journeys to Canada, America and Australia were so bad that the boats were known as **coffin ships** due to the large number of people who died on the voyage.

Source B　One witness described the emigrants as,

hundreds of poor people huddled together, without light, without air, wallowing in filth . . . sick in body, dispirited in heart; the fevered patients lying between the sound, in sleeping places so narrow as almost to deny them the power of indulging, by a change of position, the natural restlessness of the diseased . . . dying without the voice of spiritual consolation, and buried in the deep without the rites of the Church.

Source: From a report by Stephen de Vere (*Irish Famine*)

3. Fall in Population

Before the Famine the population of Ireland was 8.2 million. As we have read, 1.2 million emigrated during the Famine and it is estimated that about another million died of starvation and disease. The people who died were mostly the cottiers and the farm labourers from the western half of Ireland. Even after the famine had ended, the population continued to decline. By 1901, the population of Ireland had fallen to 4.6 million.

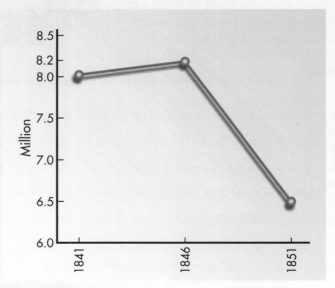

▲ Decline in the Irish population after the Famine

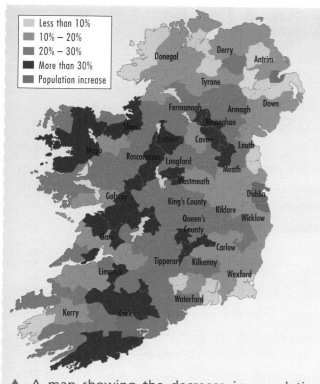

Legend:
- Less than 10%
- 10% – 20%
- 20% – 30%
- More than 30%
- Population increase

▲ A map showing the decrease in population throughout Ireland between 1841 and 1851.

The areas where the Irish language was spoken were worst hit by deaths and emigration. Emigration and decline in the use of the Irish language continued after the Famine.

4. **Politics**

Many people blamed the British government for the Famine. The British policy of laissez-faire and the continued exportation of food from a famine-stricken Ireland were greatly resented. Furthermore, many of the British upper-class did not care about Ireland's difficulties and in some cases even seemed to feel it was deserved. Politicians such as Charles Edward Trevelyan believed that 'the judgement of God sent the calamity to teach the Irish a lesson, that calamity must not be too much mitigated . . . The real evil with which we have to contend is not the physical evil of the Famine, but the moral evil of the selfish, perverse and turbulent character of the people'. The bitter resentment felt by the Irish people would later be seen in the uprisings of the late nineteenth and early twentieth centuries.

Chapter 10 Questions

1. Pictures

(a) What is the name for a building like this in which large amounts of textile were made?

(b) What part of the process of textile manufacturing is being carried out in this picture?

(c) Name one machine that would be used in this process.

(d) Describe the conditions found in a building like this during the Industrial Revolution.

2. Documents

James Hack Tuke describes an eviction of a family in 1847:

Six or seven hundred persons were here evicted; young and old, mother and babe were alike cast forth, without shelter and without the means of subsistence! A favoured few were allowed to remain, on condition that in six months they would voluntarily depart. 'A fountain of ink (as one of them has said) would not write half our misfortunes'; and I feel that it is utterly beyond my power to describe the full misery of this and similar scenes. At a dinner party that evening, the landlord, as I was told by one of the party, boasted that this was the first time he had seen the estate or visited the tenants. Truly, their first impression of landlordism was not likely to be a very favourable one!

(a) How many people were evicted?

(b) On what condition were the people allowed to stay?

(c) Do you think that the author was sorry for the people being evicted? Give reasons for your answer.

(d) Which statement shows how the tenants felt about the situation?

(e) What do you think the author's opinion was of the landlord? Give reasons for your answer.

3. Short-Answer Questions

(a) Name two pastimes of the workers in Britain during the Industrial Revolution.

(b) Name two problems facing workers in the slums of industrialised Britain.

(c) What was a Bessemer Converter and how did it improve iron production?

(d) Who invented the following machines:

   (i)   Spinning Jenny

   (ii)   The seed drill

   (iii)   The Rocket

(e) Name three jobs that people in mines did.

(f) Where was the only place in Ireland that was industrialised at the middle of the nineteenth century?

(g) Explain the following terms:

   (i)   Eviction

   (ii)   Coffin ships

   (iii)   Soup-kitchens

(h) Explain the term conacre.

(i) What food did Robert Peel import into Ireland to help the starving people.

(j) Name one group of people who helped the starving in Ireland during the Famine (apart from the government).

4. People in History

Write about a passenger in a coffin ship from Ireland during the Famine. Use the following headings as a guide:

   (a) Your home and family

   (b) Reasons for leaving Ireland

   (c) Conditions on the ship

   (d) Hopes for your new home

5.

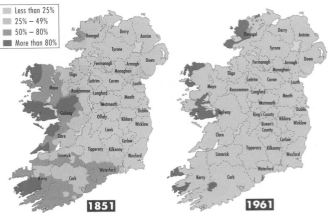

Less than 25%
25% – 49%
50% – 80%
More than 80%

1851   1961

▲ The percentage of people who spoke Irish as their first language.

(a) Why was there such a drop in Irish speakers in Ireland during the Famine and between 1851 and 1961?

(b) How did the rise in the population in Ireland contribute to the Famine in Ireland?

(c) Name three reasons for the drop in population in Ireland in the late nineteenth century.

(d) What were the results of the Irish Famine? Give three results.

(e) Write a paragraph on two of the following:

 (i) Life of a landlord in Ireland during the Famine

 (ii) Life in a workhouse during the Famine

 (iii) Public Works Schemes in Ireland during the Famine

(f) Write about the differences in lifestyle between a rural person living in Ireland and someone living in industrial Britain.

Key Terms to Summarise Chapter 10: Social Change in Britain and Ireland 1750 – 1850

Vaccination The process of injecting people with a small dose of a mild virus to prevent the development of a stronger, maybe lethal virus.

Norfolk Crop Rotation System A system in which the farmer rotates his crops between four fields. The first field could have wheat, the second oats or barley, the third turnip and the fourth clover and grass.

Selective breeding A process of picking only the best, biggest and healthiest of animals to breed in order to produce the best offspring.

Seed drill A machine invented by Jethro Tull that placed the seed into the ground and covered it with soil to ensure the seeds were distributed evenly and protected from birds.

Mechanical reaper Cyrus McCormick's invention that harvested in a faster and more efficient way than harvesting by hand.

Loom Hand-powered or machine-operated machine on which yarn was weaved into cloth.

Mill A factory in which cloth was made using water or steam-powered machines.

Coke Baked coal used to produce iron.

Puddling and rolling Method of making purer iron.

Slum An overcrowded run-down area of a town where poor people live.

Collier Worker in a mine who digs out coal from the rock.

Trade unions Organisations of people from the same occupation that seek better conditions for their members.

Cooperative System of business in which the people who use the service also own and manage it.

Absentee landlords Landowners who did not live on the land and used middle men to run their estates.

Subsistence farmer Farmers who only produced enough food to live on.

Cottier A poor farm labourer in Ireland.

Conacre Rented land on which potatoes were grown.

Potato blight A disease that destroys the potato plant.

Public Works Schemes Building works set up to provide employment for the poor and starving in Ireland during the Famine.

Laissez-faire The belief that the government should not interfere with the economy.

Workhouses Buildings where the poor and starving of Ireland could come and get food and accommodation in return for work.

Eviction The removal of people from their homes due to non-payment of rent.

Coffin ships The term given to the ships that brought emigrants from Ireland to America. These ships had very poor conditions on-board and many people died as a result.

Web References

For further reading on topics mentioned in this chapter, view the following websites:

www.bbc.co.uk/history/british/victorians/

www.womeninworldhistory.com/lesson7.html

www.nationalarchives.ie/topics/famine/famine.html

www.ucc.ie/famine/links/irishfamine.htm

adminstaff.vassar.edu/sttaylor/FAMINE/

Women in History

Elizabeth Garrett (Anderson)
(1836-1917)
Britain's first qualified female doctor

The Industrial Revolution in Britain was a time of great independence but also of great hardship. The needs of families meant that not only men, but also women and children were expected to work in the new factories and mines throughout Britain. Employers did not have to pay women the same wage as men and so by the age of 30, women in factories were earning about one third less than men. Women were generally expected to work in many of the industries and then return home to perform the domestic chores. There was great resentment towards the female workers from their male co-workers who felt women undercut the wage demands of the men. Despite all these obstacles, by 1833 more women than men were employed in factories. The vast majority were girls between the ages of 10 and 20 years old. With this move into the work-force, many women gained an independent wage for the first time. The independence that this gave women resulted in the movement for female equality. One woman who refused to accept the restrictions placed on her by the men around her was Elizabeth Garrett. She was born into a reasonably wealthy family in East London in 1836. After school as a child, she was expected to marry a man and live a quiet life. However, Garrett decided that she wanted to be a doctor which was unheard of at this time. She applied to a number of medical schools and was denied each time due to her gender. She even joined a nursing school in order to attend classes for male doctors. She was barred from doing this after complaints from male students. She managed to sit the exams for the Society of Apothecaries (pharmacists) in 1865 as they did not specifically forbid women. She passed and the Society had to accept her, although they quickly changed the rules to stop any other women trying the same thing. In 1866, Garrett opened a drug dispensary and became a visiting physician to East London Hospital in 1870. She was still determined to receive a medical degree and therefore taught herself French and went to the University of Paris. She earned a degree in Paris but the British Medical Register would not recognise it. She founded the New Hospital for Women which was staffed entirely by women in 1872. Four years later, the government passed legislation allowing women to enter the medical profession. She retired to Aldeburgh in Suffolk, England in 1902. However, she was not finished yet and in 1908 she became the first female town mayor in England. She died in 1917 but her daughter Louisa continued her struggle for women's rights as a prominent suffragette.

World War I and Its Consequences

The twentieth century was the most dramatic and destructive century Europe has ever known. World War II resulted in the deaths of more than 55 million people and it destroyed much of Europe. To understand how such a disaster could happen, it is necessary to briefly examine World War I (1914-18).

● Europe Before World War I

Europe in 1914 – note the size of the Ottoman and Austro-Hungarian Empires. ▶

At the beginning of the twentieth century, Europe contained a mix of large empires and countries. These were divided into two different alliances (countries/empires that agree to cooperate with each other on certain issues).

The Allies (also known as the Entente Cordiale)	The Central Powers
Britain, France, Russia, Italy (joined in 1915). Russia left in October 1917 and the USA joined later in 1917.	**Germany, Austro-Hungarian Empire, Ottoman Empire (joined in October 1914) and Bulgaria (joined in 1915).**

The largest countries in Europe competed with each other for more control over trade and for greater military strength. The tensions that arose from this competition finally resulted in a war between the two alliances. The war was sparked by the assassination of the heir to the Austro-Hungarian throne, Archduke Franz Ferdinand, in Sarajevo (the capital of Bosnia) on 28 June 1914. Soon the great powers of Europe were at war with each other.

● The Great War

The Great War, as World War I is also called, was the most violent and destructive war the world had ever seen. The Central Powers saw the war as a chance to expand their empires west into France and east into Russia. However, the war soon became a **stalemate** (a situation in which neither side wins). At the **Eastern** and **Western Fronts** (the area in which opposing armies face each other), the soldiers dug **trenches** (long deep ditches used by the troops as protection from enemy fire) facing each other with a strip of land in between called

▲ The strip of land between two fronts is called no-man's-land.

no-man's-land. Soldiers were expected to run across no-man's-land and try to push the enemy back. However they were usually killed by machine guns and shelling as they ran towards the opposing army's trench. Battles like those at Verdun (700,000 casualties) and the Somme (600,000 casualties – 19,420 were killed on the first day of the battle) in France and Passchendaele in Belgium (560,000 casualties) were particularly bloody.

> **By the way . . .**
> Armies sometimes used poisonous gas against the opposing trenches but this was not always successful especially if the wind changed direction.

◀ Soldiers dug deep ditches called trenches to protect themselves from enemy fire.

The war dragged on for four years before the arrival of over one million American soldiers in 1917 and 1918 turned the tide. Germany and the Central Powers surrendered to the Allies on 11 November 1918.

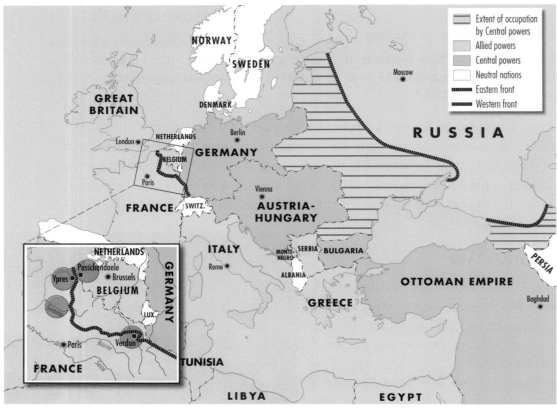

▲ The Western and Eastern Fronts in World War I with some of the key battles labelled.

▲ Leaders at the 1919 Paris negotiations – (from left to right) David Lloyd George (Britain), Vittorio Orlando (Italy), Georges Clemenceau (France) and Woodrow Wilson (USA).

● The Paris Peace Conference

In early 1919, the victorious countries of the USA, France, Britain and Italy met in Paris to create a peace treaty. Each of these countries wanted to achieve different goals in the peace treaty.

1   The American President was **Woodrow Wilson**. He believed that each country in Europe should be allowed to rule itself. In other words, he was not in favour of large empires. This principle was known as **self-determination**. He wrote the **Fourteen Point Plan** listing how Europe could seek peace through friendship.

2. France was represented by **Georges Clemenceau**, the French Prime Minister. The French blamed Germany for starting the war and wanted revenge. Most of World War I was fought on French land and much of their countryside had been destroyed. They lost 12 times more men than the Americans in the war and they felt that the Americans did not really understand how much they had suffered. They also wanted to make certain that Germany could never attack France again. They demanded compensation for the cost of the war from Germany and they wanted to re-take control of the area known as Alsace-Lorraine, which lies between France and Germany.

3. Britain, led by Prime Minister **David Lloyd George**, also wanted Germany to pay for the cost of the war. The British demanded that the German navy be weakened. However, although they understood the French anger, they believed some of the French demands went too far.

4. Italy's leader, **Vittorio Orlando**, hoped to gain large amounts of land from the break-up of the Austro-Hungarian Empire.

> **By the way . . .**
> The ruler of Germany, Kaiser Willem II, was supposed to be tried for crimes against international morality. Before the trial could take place, he fled from Germany and the trial never took place.

Questions

1. Name the countries known as the Allies.
2. What sparked the conflict between the two alliances?
3. Explain the following terms:
   (a) Trenches   (b) No-man's-land   (c) Self-determination
4. Name the leaders of the following countries who negotiated the 1919 peace treaty:
   (a) France   (b) Britain   (c) Italy   (d) The USA
5. What did France hope to achieve with this peace treaty? Give three French demands.

The Treaty of Versailles

The peace treaty, which became known as the **Treaty of Versailles**, was presented to the Germans in June 1919. They were not allowed take part in the negotiations. The Germans were very angry at the Treaty's contents. Initially they refused to sign it but were forced into doing so on 28 June 1919.

Its contents included the following:

1. The Germans had to accept the **War Guilt Clause**. This meant that they acknowledged that the war had been entirely their fault. They were forced to pay **reparations** (i.e. they had to pay for the cost of the war). The amount that was decided was £6.6 billion (which would be almost €300 billion in today's money).

Territory lost by Germany
Territory lost by Russia
Formerly Austria-Hungary
Demilitarised area

to Denmark
DENMARK
Polish Corridor
EAST PRUSSIA
RUSSIA
UK
NETHERLANDS
BELGIUM
GERMANY
POLAND
Alsace-Lorraine to France
CZECHOSLOVAKIA
to Poland
FRANCE
SWITZ.
AUSTRIA
HUNGARY
to Italy
YUGOSLAVIA
ROMANIA
ITALY
SERBIA
BULGARIA
ALBANIA
GREECE
TURKEY
SWEDEN
NORWAY
FINLAND

▲ A map of Europe with post-World War I changes, 1919. Compare the map to the one on page 298.

2. Large amounts of land were taken from Germany. Land was lost to France (Alsace-Lorraine which had been taken by Germany in 1871), Poland (Silesia and Posen) and Denmark (Schleswig). Germany also lost all its colonies in Africa.

3. The German army was limited to 100,000 men and it was not allowed to have an air-force, any tanks or submarines. The German navy was limited to 24 ships and 24,000 naval personnel.

4. To stop Germany launching any surprise attacks on France, Germany was not allowed to station any troops in the Rhineland – the area that bordered on France.

5. The Ottoman and Austro-Hungarian Empires were broken up into different countries.

6. A new organisation called the **League of Nations** was set up. It was hoped that countries in the League would discuss any future disagreements in a peaceful manner.

RESULTS OF WORLD WAR I

It was hoped that the Treaty of Versailles would ensure that there was lasting peace in Europe. In fact, the Treaty became one of the main causes of an even more devastating war two decades later.

1. Resentment

Germans were very angry at the terms of the Treaty. They did not believe they should be blamed entirely for the war and resented the size of the reparations. Many Germans felt betrayed by their government for signing the Treaty. This sense of betrayal resulted in anger towards the German government and also towards the Allied Powers.

Germany was not the only country that felt anger towards the Treaty. The Italian representatives at the negotiations left early in protest at the small amount of land they were to receive under the Treaty. This sense of betrayal by their allies in the war later helped the rise to power of a new leader in Italy – Benito Mussolini.

2. Unemployment and Poverty

The size of the reparations, the loss of land and the failure of many industries made it very difficult for Germany to rebuild its economy. Many people across Europe were unemployed and this poverty led many in Germany to blame the Treaty for their economic difficulties.

3. New Countries

New countries were formed from the Ottoman, German, Russian and Austro-Hungarian Empires. For the first time, nations got the opportunity to govern themselves. Hungary, Poland, Estonia, Lithuania, Latvia and Finland all benefitted from Wilson's belief in self-determination. Other new countries such as Czechoslovakia and Yugoslavia were created by the Allies although they broke up again 70 years later.

▲ Women in Munich, Germany queue outside a building hoping to fill a single job vacancy.

4. Rise of the USA

The entry of the USA into the war in 1917 ensured victory for the Allies. As Europe fought an expensive and damaging war, the USA became one of the most powerful economic countries in the world. Europeans bought weapons and goods from the USA. After the war, the Americans followed a policy of **isolationism**. This meant that they did not want to get involved in the problems of the European countries.

5. The League of Nations

There was great hope that the League of Nations would mean the end of conflicts between countries. However, neither Russia nor Germany was allowed to join the League and the USA's policy of isolationism meant they chose not to join. Without three of the world's most powerful countries, the League found it difficult to operate successfully.

6. The Rise of Communism

Russia withdrew from World War I in 1917 due to the rise to power in Russia of Vladimir Lenin's **Bolshevik Party**. The rise of Russia as the leader of the communist movement in Europe had great consequences for the whole world over the rest of the twentieth century.

Questions

1. What was the War Guilt Clause?
2. What does reparation mean?
3. List the lands that Germany lost following the Treaty of Versailles.
4. What happened to the Ottoman and Austro-Hungarian Empires after the Treaty of Versailles?
5. What did the Allied Leaders hope the League of Nations would achieve?
6. Why were people in Germany angry with the terms of the Treaty of Versailles? Give three reasons.
7. List three countries that were created after the Treaty of Versailles.
8. What is meant by isolationism?
9. Why did the League of Nations find it difficult to operate successfully?

Changes in Russia

During the Great War, Russia was on the side of the Allies. The Russians fought the Central Powers all along the Eastern Front. This Front stretched from the Baltic Sea in the north all the way to the Black Sea in the south. The Russians suffered the deaths of more than three million soldiers and civilians during the war. The effort required to fight this war meant that there was widespread food shortages. For these reasons, the war was very unpopular with the common people of Russia.

▲ Tsar Nicholas II was overthrown in the February Revolution of 1917.

In the February Revolution of 1917, the Tsar (Emperor) of Russia, Nicholas II was overthrown. A new provisional (temporary) government was put in place but it decided to continue the war against the Central Powers. The common people were still suffering and so they turned to the Bolshevik Party led by **Vladimir Lenin**. The Bolshevik party promised to withdraw from the war and to give the people 'Peace, land and bread'. The Bolsheviks were supporters of the ideas of Karl Marx and believed in **communism**. As the war continued to go badly for the Russians, support for the Bolsheviks increased.

▲ Vladimir Lenin, leader of the Bolshevik Party.

● The October Revolution

In October 1917, Lenin and the Bolsheviks led a successful revolution in Russia. Lenin became the leader of the country and began to make drastic changes.

1. He signed the **Treaty of Brest-Litovsk** with Germany in March 1918, taking Russia out of World War I. The Germans won many new territories along the Russian border but Lenin saw this as a small price to pay for peace.

2. The Bolsheviks were the only political party allowed in Russia, therefore making it a one-party state.

▲ Leon Trotsky, Commander of the Red Army.

3. The Bolsheviks believed that the wealth of the country should not be owned by just a few people. Instead, they believed that the country's wealth should be divided between all the people equally. Land was divided up and given to landless peasants. They took over all the factories and **nationalised** them (in other words, they were now owned by the people of the country).

4. The Bolshevik Red Army under **Leon Trotsky** fought any opponents of communism. The Russian Civil War between the Red Army and their opponents (including their old allies of Britain and France as well as Russian supporters of the Tsar) lasted from 1918 until 1921. After millions of deaths, the Red Army defeated their rivals.

5. As a result of the Civil War and the nationalisation of the factories, food production fell. Famine was initially widespread throughout Russia but in 1921 Lenin introduced the **New Economic Policy**. This gave bonuses to workers to produce more. Furthermore, any surplus produce could be sold by the farmer. Soon food shortages ended and general conditions for ordinary Russians improved.

6. In 1922, the Communist Government changed the name of Russia to the Union of Soviet Socialist Republics (USSR).

▲ The Russian Royal family, the Romanovs, were executed in 1918.

● Josef Stalin

After Lenin's death in 1924, there was a power struggle between Leon Trotsky (the leader of the Red Army) and **Josef Stalin** (Bolshevik Party Secretary). Stalin used his influence in the Bolshevik Party to gain power and by 1927 he had control over the government. He expelled Trotsky from Russia in 1929 and began to concentrate on

industrialising the USSR. He claimed that, 'we are 50 or 100 years behind the advanced countries. We must make good this gap in 10'.

By the way . . .

After being expelled from Russia, Trotsky continued to criticise Stalin. In August 1940 he was assassinated in Mexico City by a Soviet agent from Spain using an ice pick.

◀ Josef Stalin became General Secretary (i.e. leader) of the USSR after Lenin's death in 1924.

Questions

1. Who was the Tsar of Russia and why was he overthrown in the February Revolution?
2. What three things did the Bolshevik Party offer the people of Russia?
3. What does nationalise mean?
4. Who was Leon Trotsky?
5. What did Lenin introduce to help solve the famine that developed in 1921?
6. Who became General Secretary following Lenin's death?

● Industrialisation of the USSR

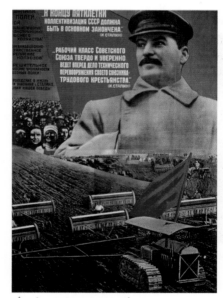

▲ A poster promoting collectivisation of farms.

Stalin introduced his first Five-Year Plan for the USSR in 1929. This plan demanded that industries doubled or trebled their production of goods. Workers were encouraged to work harder and people were punished if targets were not met. The first Five-Year Plan worked very well and two more followed in 1933 and 1938. Soon the USSR was one of the most industrialised and powerful countries in the world.

Stalin also wanted to modernise agriculture. He did this by nationalising all the farms in the USSR. Small farms were merged to create large **collective farms** that used modern farming methods. He hoped that this would increase agricultural productivity and reduce the risk of another famine. Some farmers continued to work on these new large farms. The rest were brought to the cities and given jobs in the new factories and industries. However, many medium-sized farmers (known as Kulaks) did not want to move to the cities and resisted the **collectivisation** of their farms. Stalin dealt with this resistance very harshly. It is estimated that five million Kulaks were killed or sent to prisoner camps called **gulags**. The actions of the Kulaks and Stalin's response to it led to food shortages and a further five million people died as a result. Eventually the collectivisation of the USSR farms was achieved but at the cost of over 10 million lives.

● The Great Purges

Stalin's policies were unpopular with many people inside the USSR. However, anyone thought to be against his policies was arrested by the country's secret police, NKVD. Millions of people were arrested and many were executed or sent to the gulags. Stalin worried that members of the Communist Party might plot against him. From 1936 onwards, thousands of Communist Party members were put on trial for conspiracy. These **Great Purges** (to purge means to get rid of something impure) resulted in many deaths, including seven of the country's leading army commanders and many of Stalin's political rivals.

RESULTS OF STALIN'S POLICIES IN THE USSR

1. By 1939 Stalin had achieved what he had set out to do: to industrialise the USSR in a matter of a decade. The USSR was now a major industrial, economic and political power. It had created the first-ever communist country in the world and millions of people had homes, jobs and a country at peace. Extreme poverty had been largely eradicated (removed) and the USSR was an economic success.

2. Its success was envied by many of the poor and unemployed throughout Western Europe. Communist parties were set up throughout Europe. Communism was particularly strong in Spain, Italy and Germany as well as in Britain.

3. However, others disliked communism. People with wealth, property or political power saw communism as a threat. Some of these people turned to a new political idea called **fascism** which was strongly opposed to the spread of communism.

4. The governments of Britain, France and the USA feared communism and therefore refused to have diplomatic relations with the USSR although they continued to have economic relations. Many people in the Western world were also concerned about the Great Purges and the lack of democracy. The Communist Party was still the only political party allowed in the USSR so voters could not choose to elect a different party to govern, even if they were unhappy with the current government.

5. It was very difficult to get accurate reports of what was happening in the USSR. Many people were unaware of the numbers killed or else dismissed it as Western propaganda against communism. This made it tricky for the outside world to guess how bad things were for some Russians. Details about gulags and purges were almost impossible to obtain outside of the USSR. Even within the USSR, Stalin did not admit to the numbers killed. He was obsessed with secrecy and with ensuring he kept control of all information. For this reason, it is still difficult to provide accurate figures for the number of deaths during this period.

6. The isolation of the USSR and the fear that other countries might interfere in its activities meant that Stalin began to focus on its military defence. In the years leading up to World War II, the USSR increased its number of tanks, aircraft, guns and ammunition. Stalin's fears of a foreign invasion of its borders were proved correct in 1941. The only surprise was the identity of the foreign invader.

Questions

1. What did Stalin hope his Five-Year Plan would achieve?
2. What were collective farms?
3. What happened to the farmers if they refused to participate in collectivisation?
4. Explain the following terms:
   (a) NKVD   (b) Gulag   (c) Great Purges   (d) Kulaks
5. Why did the governments of Britain, France and the USA refuse to have diplomatic relations with the USSR?

Fascism in Italy and Germany

● Italy

The rise of fascism in Italy can be traced back to a number of causes.

By the way . . .

The word fascist comes from the Latin word **fasces.** A fasces was a symbol that showed the authority of ancient Rome. The rods represented the right of the authorities to punish and the axe represented the right of the government to execute by beheading any wrongdoers.

▲ After World War I, Italy gained control of the port city of Trieste and land in the Trentino area. In 1924 it forced the Yugoslavian government to give up the town of Fiume/Rijeka.

1 TREATY OF VERSAILLES

During World War I, Italy lost over 600,000 men fighting the Austro-Hungarian Empire. When the Allies won the war, Italy hoped to gain large amounts of Austrian and Hungarian land at the Treaty of Versailles. When they received much less than they hoped, the Italian delegation stormed out of the negotiations.

2 MEMORIES OF ITS PAST

Italians thought that they were badly treated by their allies at the Treaty of Versailles. They saw Italy as a great country and wanted to see the Italian nation revive its glory. The Roman architecture and art that existed in Italy only served to remind Italians how great their country once was.

3 ECONOMICS

Italy spent huge amounts of money fighting World War I and was heavily in debt. The economy was in trouble and there was high unemployment. The prices of goods had gone up and soldiers returning from fighting were unable to find any work. This caused further anger. People wanted the government to solve these problems.

4 DEMOCRACY

Between 1918 and 1922, five different governments tried to solve the economic problems of Italy. Each failed and many Italians thought the system of democracy was at fault. They wanted a strong and powerful government to provide leadership. Many people turned to extreme political parties on the left and on the right.

Many of the lower-paid workers and the poor saw Lenin's communist Russia as the answer. These people believed that communism would give Italy strong leadership and also solve its economic difficulties, just as Lenin and Stalin had done in Russia. When agricultural and industrial workers went on strike throughout 1920 and 1921, it seemed likely that a communist revolution would take place in Italy.

These strikes frightened many of the wealthier Italians. Landowners, business people and members of the Catholic Church all feared communism. These people turned to a new political party to provide strong leadership: the Fascist Party.

▲ Benito Mussolini founded the Fascist party in Italy.

● Mussolini and the Fascist Party

Benito Mussolini was born in central Italy in 1883. His mother was a teacher and his father was a blacksmith. His father believed in Marxism and his influence meant that Benito Mussolini became a **socialist** (a belief that wealth and power should be shared equally amongst all members of society – it shares some of its core beliefs with communism) in 1912.

> **By the way . . .**
> Mussolini used to leave the light on in his office at night so that people would think he was working until very late.

However, he did not remain one for long. He supported Italy's entrance into World War I – unlike the Socialist Party – and was removed from his position as editor of the socialist newspaper *Avanti!* and then expelled from the Socialist Party. He founded a new paper called *Il Popolo d'Italia* (The People of Italy) before enlisting in the army.

Mussolini was injured in an accidental grenade explosion during training for the war and returned to Italy to continue his newspaper. He was now a strong supporter of Italian **nationalism** (strong respect and love for your nation). In 1919 he established his own party: **Fasci Italiani di Combattimento** (Italian Combat Leagues). Its members became known as fascists. He organised young fascists into armed groups who wore black shirts to provide security at fascist meetings and rallies. In that year, Mussolini and his party ran for parliament but they did not win any seats.

During 1920 and 1921, the economic situation got worse and strikes broke out throughout Italy. Mussolini offered his armed groups of **Black Shirts** to business owners to break the strikes. He also used the Black Shirts to disrupt socialist and communist rallies and meetings. He renamed the party the **National Fascist Party** and promised to bring glory, law and order to Italy. In 1921, he and 34 other Fascists were elected to parliament.

In 1922, the government of Italy collapsed again. Mussolini told King Victor Emmanuel III of Italy that his party should be asked to form the next government. To show how serious he was, he asked tens of thousands of party supporters to march to Rome to show how popular the National Fascist Party was. This **March on Rome** made Victor Emmanuel panic and he chose not to use the army to stop the Fascists. Instead, in October 1922, Benito Mussolini was made prime minister of Italy even though the Fascists had no more than 15% of seats in the Italian parliament.

▲ Mussolini with the Black Shirts

▲ King Victor Emmanuel III

▲ The March on Rome with Mussolini in the centre, 1922

Questions

1. Why did the Italian delegation storm out of the negotiations at Versailles?
2. What economic difficulties did Italy face after the end of World War I?
3. Why did many Italians turn to extreme political parties after World War I?
4. Name two extreme parties in Italy during this time and who supported them.
5. Who were the Black Shirts and what did they do?
6. What was the March on Rome and what did it result in?

• Mussolini in Power

When Mussolini became prime minister he introduced new fascist policies.

1. He created the **OVRA**, a secret police force, to silence any opponents of the Fascist Party. This force used intimidation and violence to disrupt anyone who criticised either Mussolini or his policies.

2. He passed the **Acerbo Law** in 1923. Under this law the party with the greatest number of votes automatically won two thirds of the seats in the Italian Parliament. Mussolini claimed that this would bring an end to the instability of the previous weak governments.

In 1924, Mussolini's National Fascist Party won the general election using violence and intimidation to persuade people to vote for them. This violence became so bad that in June 1924, an important member of the Socialist Party Giacomo Matteotti was kidnapped and murdered. His murder caused a great public outcry and Victor Emmanuel almost removed Mussolini from power. Fearing further political instability, the king chose not to and Mussolini was able to continue with his reforms.

▲ A picture of Mussolini on the wall of Fascist headquarters in Italy. The background says 'si' meaning 'yes'.

3. In 1925 and 1926, Mussolini removed the King's power to dismiss government ministers, banned any other political party and established complete **censorship** (control of the media by the government) of the press.

Using these new powers, Mussolini had created a one-party state where he was **dictator** (had absolute and complete power). He now referred to himself as simply, **Il Duce** – the leader.

● Mussolini's Fascist Policies

Now that Mussolini had established himself as dictator of Italy, he turned his attention to other areas.

1. THE ECONOMY

He tackled the problems in the economy by creating the **Corporate State**. This means that each area of the economy was divided up. Government officials, employers and workers now decided how to run each area. Trade unions were banned and it was illegal to go on strike.

To solve the high unemployment rate, Mussolini began massive public projects:

(a) *Autostrada* (motorways) were built throughout Italy.

(b) The Pontine Marshes just outside Rome were drained and turned into agricultural land.

(c) Grain production was encouraged to help feed the Italian population.

These projects did provide employment but many of these jobs were very low paid.

2. POLITICAL OPPOSITION

Mussolini managed to win over many of the Italian people using a variety of methods.

(a) The OVRA and Black Shirts used intimidation and violence against any opponents of the government.

(b) The Fascists used **propaganda** (spreading rumours and lies about something or somebody to either promote or harm a person, organisation or thing) to gain support. Posters, films and newspapers all portrayed Mussolini working hard for the nation. The government also censored all media to stop any negative information about Il Duce. In this way, the population only ever heard or read good things about the government and their leader. This helped Mussolini's popularity to grow.

▲ Propaganda pictures of Mussolini showing Il Duce working in the fields and a line of cyclists 'wearing' their support.

(c) Young people were targets of **indoctrination** (teaching a biased view to people). Teachers and schoolbooks now had to be approved by the Fascists and after-school clubs called *balilla* were set up for children aged 8 to 14 years. At these clubs, young people would learn how to be a good fascist and to admire Il Duce.

3. RELIGION

Italy's population was 98% Catholic so it was important for Mussolini to have good relations with the Pope. Since 1870, there had been a dispute between the Vatican and the Italian government over the independence of the Pope in Rome. Mussolini agreed to create an independent Vatican state and to recognise Catholicism as the state religion of Italy. This **Lateran Treaty** of 1929 was a huge success for Mussolini who gained great popularity with Catholics all over the world and especially in Italy.

▲ Children were sent to after-school clubs (*balilla*) to learn how to be good fascists.

4. ITALIAN FOREIGN POLICY

(a) Mussolini's **foreign policy** (dealings with other countries) sought to make Italy a great international power again. In 1924, Mussolini forced the Yugoslavian government to give up the town of Fiume (modern Rijeka). Its ownership had been in dispute since the Treaty of Versailles and gaining it made Mussolini very popular with the Italian people.

(b) In 1935, Italy invaded Abyssinia (modern Ethiopia) seeking revenge for the 1896 defeat of the Italians by the Africans. Although this invasion was popular among Italians, Abyssinia was a member of the League of Nations. Abyssinia's leader, Emperor **Haile Selassie**, pleaded with the League to stop the Italians. The League

demanded that Mussolini withdraw his troops. However, Mussolini ignored the demand. The League condemned the Italian invasion and attempted to organise a ban on trade with Italy.

▲ Emperor Haile Selassie, ruler of Abyssinia (now known as Ethiopia)

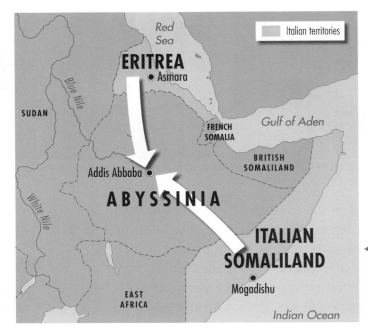

◀ Abyssinia (now known as Ethiopia) was invaded by Italy in 1935.

▲ General Franco, the fascist dictator of Spain

(c) This dispute with the democracies of Europe such as France and Britain resulted in Mussolini becoming closer to the countries in Europe that had followed the fascist model of government – Germany and Spain. During the Spanish Civil War of 1936-1939, Mussolini provided troops and support for the fascist dictator General Franco.

(d) Also in 1936, Mussolini joined in an alliance with Germany's Adolf Hitler called the **Rome-Berlin Axis**. Although he did not particularly like Hitler, Mussolini's alliance with the German leader would lead to Italy's involvement in World War II.

By the way . . .

Emperor Haile Selassie is regarded as a god by the Rastafari movement in Jamaica.

Hitler and Mussolini joined in an alliance called the Rome-Berlin Axis. ▶

Questions

1. What was the Acerbo Law?
2. (a) Explain the term intimidation. (b) Give an example of how Mussolini used intimidation.
3. Explain the following terms:
   (a) Dictator   (b) Censorship   (c) *Balilla*   (d) Propaganda
4. What does Il Duce mean?
5. How did the Corporate State work?
6. How did Mussolini solve the problem of unemployment?
7. What problem did the Lateran Treaty solve and how?
8. How did the Italian invasion of Abyssinia highlight the weakness of the League of Nations?
9. In what way was Mussolini involved in the Spanish Civil War?
10. Which two countries signed the Rome-Berlin Axis?

Germany

When Germany was defeated at the end of World War I, a new government was forced to sign the humiliating Treaty of Versailles. Some people in Germany believed that the democratic politicians who surrendered in 1918 were responsible for Germany's defeat. They thought that these **November Criminals** (so-called because the peace treaty was signed on 11 November 1918) had surrendered too easily and that Germany could have won the war if it had held out for longer.

The Versailles Treaty was also hated by many Germans as the terms seemed unfair, especially the size of the reparations and the War Guilt Clause. Many within Germany blamed the Treaty for many of the problems that Germany faced after World War I, e.g. high unemployment. Many people turned to communism as an answer to their problems. As with Italy, there were some who wanted to find a solution other than communism to Germany's difficulties. One such person was Adolf Hitler.

Adolf Hitler

Born in Braunau am Inn, Austria on 20 April 1889, Hitler spent his early life in Vienna as an artist. After unsuccessful attempts to be accepted at the Vienna Academy of Fine Arts, Hitler moved to Germany to join the army in August 1914. He was decorated for bravery a number of times and served in the army for all of World War I. He strongly believed that Germany had been let down by the November Criminals and that the Treaty of Versailles was too humiliating.

▲ Adolf Hitler disliked the Treaty of Versailles and believed it humiliated Germany.

After the war he worked for the army keeping an eye on some of the political parties that existed in Munich. One such small group was the nationalist and racist German Workers' Party. Hitler soon became a member of this group. Although Hitler was supposed to merely observe the activities of these parties, he realised that one of them, the nationalist and racist German Workers' Party, had ideas with which he strongly agreed. His ability at public speaking meant that he first became their spokesman and then the leader of the party. He renamed the party the **National Socialist German Workers' Party** (NSDAP or **Nazi** Party). Hitler's public speaking and organisational skills were very successful. By the time he was discharged from the army in 1920 more than 2,000 people attended the party's official outlining of its ideas.

Hitler and the Nazi Party

Hitler and the Nazi Party believed in pride in the German people and hatred of France and any people the Nazis considered un-German living in Germany. One group in particular were hated – the Jews. Hitler believed Jews were responsible for the defeat of Germany in World War I and that it was necessary to remove them from society if Germany was to become great again.

To achieve this, Hitler believed that, like Italy, Germany needed a strong leader. He did not believe that the democratically elected government Germany had at the time was strong enough to solve Germany's problems. Hitler also adopted other ideas from the Italian Fascist Party.

▲ The Brown Shirts on the right and the SS on the left are shown here standing over the slogan, 'The New Germany'.

▲ The Nazis used a one-armed salute to show their loyalty to Hitler.

(a) The **Sturm Abteilung (SA)** was created. Its members wore brown shirts and were thus known as the **Brown Shirts**. They did the same job as the Black Shirts in Italy, i.e. using intimidation and violence against opponents of the Nazi Party, in particular communists. Hitler also created his own personal bodyguard called the **Schutzstaffel (SS)**.

(b) Hitler also took the name **Der Fürher** (the leader), just like Il Duce.

(c) The Nazis liked large military rallies with marching and a one-armed salute. Instead of the fasces, Hitler began to use an old Hindu symbol called a swastika.

Hitler Begins His Rise to Power

In November 1923, Hitler and the Nazi Party attempted a revolution in Munich. Hitler hoped that this would be similar to Mussolini's March on Rome but it ended badly. The **Beer Hall Putsch** (so-called as it began in a beer hall in Munich and a putsch is a small revolt) was easily put down by the government. Hitler and the other organisers of the putsch were sent to prison. It was here that Hitler, along with his friend Rudolph Hess, wrote a book called *Mein Kampf* (My Struggle). This book outlined Hitler's views on the world and his plans for the future of Germany.

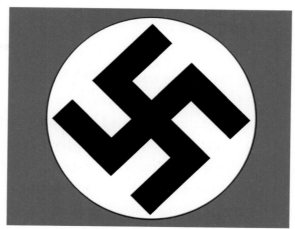

▲ The Nazi symbol of the swastika is a reversed version of a Hindu symbol for good luck.

(1) The German people known as Aryans were a master race (herrenvolk), superior to all other races in the world.

(2) All German Aryans should unite inside one great country. This meant that Germany should unite with Austria and with any other areas where German speakers lived.

(3) This new Germany would require raw materials and living-space **lebensraum**. This could be achieved by expanding east.

(4) Anti-Semitism (hatred of Jews)

(5) All non-Aryans, such as Jews or Gypsies, living in Germany should be removed.

(6) Communism and socialism should be destroyed.

(7) Anything that stops Germany from achieving its destiny as the master-race should be removed. The Treaty of Versailles was one of these obstacles.

Hitler was released early from prison in 1924 but over the next number of years, the Nazi Party failed to gain much support. Germany was actually improving economically and unemployment decreased. **Gustav Stresemann** led the German government and managed to renegotiate the repayment of the reparations. Furthermore, America had financially benefitted from World War I and offered loans to Germany to rebuild its economy.

Questions

1. Who were known as the November Criminals?
2. In which country was Hitler born?
3. Give the full name for the Nazi Party.
4. Why did Hitler hate the Jews so much?
5. Give four similarities between the Nazi Party and the Italian Fascist Party?
6. What was the Beer Hall Putsch?
7. Explain the following terms:
   (a) *Herrenvolk*   (b) *Lebensraum*   (c) Aryan
8. What groups did Hitler target as obstacles to a greater Germany?

● Growth of Nazism

THE ECONOMY

By the way . . .

In 1920 4.2 Papiermark (the name of the German currency) were worth $1. By December 1923 that had risen to 4,200,000,000,000 to $1. Prices were doubling every second day. Soon it became cheaper to burn the money than to buy firewood with it!

Unfortunately, in October 1929, America suffered a great economic downturn. People could not pay back loans and the banks had very little money. This sudden downturn was called the **Wall Street Crash**. This led to the **Great Depression** all across America. American banks that had lent money asked for their money back from German businesses and government. Without this money, German businesses could not function and so they closed. Unemployment rose rapidly and the government could not pay their reparations. By 1932 almost six million people (a quarter of the labour force) were unemployed and **inflation** (when the value of money becomes less and so goods cost more) rose.

▲ Paper money was almost worthless in Germany by 1932. In this photograph the woman is using paper money to light the stove.

DEMOCRACY

After Germany was defeated in World War I, a new democratic government was established in 1918. This government and the period of time between 1918 – 1933 became known as the Weimar Republic. Weimar was an important cultural centre in central Germany and the new German constitution was written there in 1918. The democratic governments of the Weimar Republic faced a number of problems:

(1) The democratically elected members of the Weimar government were held responsible by Germans for their country's defeat in World War I. They were

seen as traitors and were referred to as the November Criminals. These politicians were also blamed for the Treaty of Versailles and its harsh terms.

(2) Since the start of the Weimar Republic, the democratic system had failed to produce a strong and stable government. Extreme parties on the right and on the left made it difficult to form a strong government. Many in Germany regarded the democratic system as contributing to the problems facing Germany. They wanted a new system that would provide strong leadership.

(3) Violence between communists and right-wing groups broke out all over Germany. Communist risings in Munich, the Ruhrland and Hamburg were put down by the army and right-wing militia. In 1920, a right-wing rising called the Kapp Putsch was only defeated after a communist-led general strike across Germany. This showed how divided German society had become.

▲ Weimar, an area in central Germany, became the seat of Government from 1918 to 1933.

(4) The democratic government was also blamed for the economic difficulties faced by Germany.

The communist uprisings throughout Germany caused great fear among many Germans. Hitler's Nazi party played on this fear. They blamed the communists and the Jews for Germany's defeat in 1918 and promised to defeat the communist threat. Hitler also promised to solve the country's economic problems. In 1930 Hitler's Nazi party won 103 seats in the **German Reichstag** (parliament) and in 1932 the Nazi party became the largest party in the Reichstag with 230 seats. President von Hindenburg was persuaded to make Hitler the **Chancellor** (prime minister) of Germany in January 1933.

● Hitler Becomes Dictator

As soon as Hitler became Chancellor, he immediately used the SS and the SA to ensure any opposition was silenced through violence and intimidation. He also created the **Gestapo** (secret police) to keep an eye on the population and any potential threats to his government. The Gestapo was run by **Hermann Göering**, a trusted Nazi official.

In February 1933, a Dutch communist named **Marinus van der Lubbe** was accused of burning down the Reichstag. Hitler used this incident to ban the Communist Party and arrest leading communists.

▲ Hermann Göering was in charge of the Gestapo (secret police) in Nazi Germany.

▲ The burning of the Reichstag in 1933. This incident prompted Hitler to pass the Enabling Act.

Hitler also passed the **Enabling Act** in March 1933. This gave him the right to pass any law he wanted without getting approval from the Reichstag for four years.

Hitler used his new powers to ban all non-Nazi trade unions and political parties. He replaced all those in power with members of the Nazi Party and he put the media and any cultural activities under the control of the Nazis.

When President von Hindenburg died in August 1934, Hitler took the position of President as well. Der Führer was now dictator with absolute power in a one-party state.

Hitler now decided to deal with any potential threats from within his own party. The SA had about two million members and their leader **Ernst Röhm** was becoming increasingly powerful and ambitious. Hitler's personal bodyguard, the SS, were used to deal with this threat. On 30 June 1934, the leader of the SS, **Heinrich Himmler**, arranged for Röhm and many of the leading members of the SA to be arrested and some even murdered. This bloody event became known as the **Night of the Long Knives**.

▲ Himmler, the leader of the SS, organised the Night of the Long Knives.

The SS and the Gestapo were used to keep control of any opposition to the Nazi Party. Opponents were arrested and many were sent to **concentration camps**. Life in these camps was very harsh and torture and murder were common. The first camp of many was built in Dachau in the south of Germany.

Questions

1. What economic difficulties did Germany face at the beginning of the 1930s?
2. What were the reasons for the German people's dislike of democracy as a political system?
3. Who did Hitler blame for the German defeat in World War I?
4. How many seats did the Nazi Party get in the 1930 and 1932 elections?
5. What was the Gestapo and who was its leader?
6. Why was the Communist Party banned in 1933?
7. What did the Enabling Act of 1933 allow Hitler do?
8. What name did Hitler give himself when he became President in 1934?
9. What happened on the Night of the Long Knives?

● Nazi Germany after 1934

Like Mussolini, Hitler recognised the need to indoctrinate the German population.

PROPAGANDA

Josef Goebbels was made Minister for Propaganda and National Enlightenment. He was in charge of all newspapers, radio, cinema and theatre. He ensured that he controlled all parts of the media and used them to show Hitler in a positive light. He had movies made that depicted the German people as a superior race and the Jews as sub-human. Huge rallies such as those at Nuremberg were organised and filmed so that everyone in Germany could see them. Radio stations broadcasted Hitler's speeches at these great rallies.

▲ Josef Goebbels controlled the media in Germany.

▲ A propaganda poster for a film showing Jews as untrustworthy. The title is *The Eternal Jew*.

INDOCTRINATION

▲ Tens of thousands of Germans attended Nazi rallies, such as the Nuremberg rally which was the annual rally of the Nazi Party. These rallies were designed by the German architect Albert Speer.

The Nazi government rewrote school textbooks and teachers were expected to tell pupils about Germany's glorious past. At age 14 boys joined the **Hitler Youth** and girls joined the **League of German Maidens**. These organisations taught boys the skills needed to be soldiers, while the girls learned how to be good German mothers. At all times, children were taught loyalty to Hitler and hatred of the Jews.

▲ A poster advertising the League of German Maidens

▲ The Hitler Youth organisation taught boys how to be soldiers.

ECONOMICS

Hitler came to power with the promise to solve the economic problems facing Germany.

(1) As in Italy, large public works schemes such as the motorway network (autobahn) were organised to provide employment.

(2) Although forbidden by the Treaty of Versailles, Hitler began to re-arm the German army. New factories were opened to provide new military materials and weapons.

(3) Hitler encouraged the building of a new car that was affordable to everyone. This car was called a Volkswagen (people's car).

(4) Married women were paid an allowance to encourage them to stay at home and have more children.

By 1939, Germany had virtually no unemployment.

▲ A Volkswagen, the 'people's car'

ANTI-SEMITISM (HATRED OF JEWS)

All aspects of Nazism encouraged the hatred of Jews. The Jewish community only made up about 500,000 people in Germany, but they were blamed for Germany's defeat in World War I, the Treaty of Versailles and all the wrongs in Germany. Propaganda made the Jews look like greedy, rich enemies of Germany. Hitler believed that it was necessary to protect the Aryan race by getting rid of any Jews from Germany. This was to be done in a number of ways:

(1) All Jews were banned from government jobs.

(2) A boycott of all Jewish shops was organised.

(3) Films were made in which the Jewish community was made to appear ugly, dirty and evil (see poster on page 321).

▲ A Jew wearing a Star of David.

The **Nuremberg Laws** were passed in 1935. These laws were designed to 'protect the pure German blood'. No Jew was allowed to be a citizen of the German state. They were not allowed to vote, marry German citizens or own any property. After 1941 they were also required to wear a yellow Star of David on their clothes so that Germans could immediately recognise them.

In 1938 a German diplomat was killed by a Polish Jew named **Herschel Grynszpan** in Paris. The Nazis took revenge on the night of 9 November. Jewish shops, businesses and **synagogues** (Jewish places of worship) were attacked and destroyed. More than 90 Jews were killed, hundreds were injured and over 30,000 were arrested and sent to concentration camps. The event became known as **Kristallnacht** (the Night of Broken Glass) because of all the damage done to the shops. In addition to the horrors of that night, the Jewish community was forced to pay a fine to cover all the damage that had been done. This fine was paid by taking 20% of all Jewish property.

▲ Germans look at the damage done to a Jewish shop after Kristallnacht.

After Kristallnacht, Jewish children were forbidden to attend German schools.

Almost half of Germany's Jewish population fled to other countries such as Switzerland, Britain or the USA. Those who remained in Germany were to suffer even more over the following seven years as Hitler put his **Final Solution** into place. This 'solution' was the total destruction of all Jews in lands under Nazi control. Hitler put Himmler in charge of this operation and Himmler began to set up concentration and, later, extermination camps all across Nazi-controlled Europe.

1. Who was Josef Goebbels and what was he responsible for?
2. What methods of indoctrination did the Nazis use on young people?
3. Why do you think the Nazis wanted to indoctrinate young people?
4. What economic policies did the Nazis introduce?
5. What does the term 'anti-Semitism' mean?
6. What changes did the Nuremberg Laws make?
7. What was Kristallnacht?
8. What was Hitler's Final Solution?

Tensions Rise Across Europe

Countries drifted towards World War II between 1933 and 1939 due to Hitler's aggressive foreign policy and the British and French policy of **appeasement** (agreeing to unjust demands in the hope of peace). Europe was still recovering from the results of World War I and most politicians were anxious to avoid any future conflict. However, Hitler had made no secret of his future plans when he outlined his beliefs in *Mein Kampf*. As soon as Hitler had complete control of Germany in 1933, he began to put his plans for expansion into place.

The Destruction of the Treaty of Versailles

Hitler's policies in Germany broke the terms of the Treaty of Versailles. He had begun to re-arm the German military, he had introduced **conscription** (forced enrolment into the army) and he had increased army numbers from 100,000 to 550,000.

In March 1936 Hitler marched German troops into the demilitarised area between Germany and France called the Rhineland. Hitler was not sure what the international reaction would be to this move. He ordered his troops to withdraw immediately if the French took any action. Neither the French nor the British did anything more than condemn the Germans for taking such an action. The German troops were greeted by cheering crowds who were delighted that the Treaty was being **dismantled** (broken). Hitler's confidence grew and he

▲ The arrival of troops into the Rhineland. Note the cheering crowds.

was now prepared to take more drastic action. He correctly believed that the Allies were anxious to avoid conflict at all costs.

● Allies' Inaction

The Allies had not done anything to stop Hitler for a number of reasons.

(1) France

The French were reluctant to attack Germany as they were not entirely sure how large Hitler's army was. The French army spent time building a line of defence along the German border called the **Maginot Line** and were not ready for conflict. Also, they were not prepared to attack Germany without the support of the British.

(2) Britain

The British had some sympathy for the Germans. Many saw the Treaty of Versailles as unfair and harsh. The Rhineland was part of Germany and so they saw it as a domestic issue. Also, the British were simply reluctant to begin any conflict so soon after World War I. Their army, navy and air-force were unprepared for any large war and so it was thought best to appease Germany's demands rather than risk another war. The British were also more worried about the threat posed by Stalin and the USSR. For these reasons, Britain's Prime Minister **Neville Chamberlain** chose to follow a policy of appeasement with Germany.

(3) The USA

The Americans were also reluctant to get involved. They had decided on a policy of isolationism and even passed a neutrality law that outlawed any American assistance in foreign conflicts.

▲ Neville Chamberlain decided to appease Germany rather than risk another war.

● The Creation of a Greater Germany

Hitler now turned his attention to the expansion of Germany. He used Mussolini's disagreement with the Allies after Italy's invasion of Abyssinia to forge closer links with Italy. In 1936 Hitler and Mussolini signed the **Rome-Berlin Axis**. This alliance of fascist countries helped the fascist dictator General Franco defeat the Spanish Republicans in the Spanish Civil War (1936-39). Hitler tested his new German air force (the Luftwaffe) during this conflict. By 1938 Hitler was far more confident. He was certain that the German army and air force were well prepared for conflict. He had gained an ally in the Rome-Berlin Axis and he realised that Britain and France either could not or would not attempt to stop his plans for expansion.

Early in 1938 Hitler put pressure on the Austrian Chancellor to resign and he was replaced by the leader of the Austrian Nazi party. Hitler was immediately 'asked' to unite the two countries. Austria became a province of a larger Germany. This unification was known as the *Anschluss* (joining together) and was prohibited by the Treaty of Versailles. Again, Britain and France did nothing.

13·MÄRZ 1938
EIN VOLK EIN REICH
EIN FÜHRER

▲ A postcard celebrating the annexing of Austria, 1938 – it states: one people, one nation, one leader.

▲ The arrival of troops into Czechoslovakia. The weeping woman was said to be weeping 'tears of joy'.

Hitler was encouraged by the ease of the *Anschluss* so he now turned his attention to an area in Czechoslovakia called the **Sudetenland**. This part of Czechoslovakia contained about 3.5 million German speakers and Hitler encouraged them to seek unification with Germany. Tensions rose as Hitler accused the Czechs of mistreating the ethnic Germans. As the situation got worse, a conference was organised in September 1938 between Britain, France, Germany and Italy in Munich. It was hoped that the situation could be solved by peaceful means.

▲ Chamberlain waving the document signed by Hitler in 1938 promising not to demand any more land.

The Czech government was not asked to this conference. Instead, Britain, France, Italy and Germany agreed to give Germany the Sudetenland in return for Hitler's promise not to demand any further land. Chamberlain returned from the Munich Conference to London and declared to the media that he had secured 'peace for our time'. Unfortunately, Chamberlain's optimism was proved wrong.

● Germany's Expansion in the East

In March 1939 Hitler sent his troops into the rest of Czechoslovakia. Britain knew that appeasement had failed and they now offered France and Poland support if Germany attacked them. Poland lay between Germany and the USSR, and the Polish Corridor lay between East Prussia and the rest of Germany. Many Germans were angry at the loss of these lands at the Treaty of Versailles so it seemed obvious where Hitler would strike next. There was one problem that Hitler had to deal with first: the USSR.

Hitler's objectives had always been the creation of *lebensraum* for the German people and the destruction of the USSR. He still hoped to achieve this but he knew that his army was not ready to take on the strength of the USSR. He also did not want to risk fighting a war on two fronts: Britain and France in the west and the USSR in the east.

▲ The areas of German expansion between 1936 – 1939.

Stalin was aware of Hitler's plans and had spent the previous years building up the Soviet military. He had even offered military help to the Czechs in 1938 but had not been invited to the Munich Conference. He was disliked and distrusted by the leaders of the Western democracies (e.g. France, Britain, USA). So in August 1939 Germany and the USSR signed a treaty. The **Nazi-Soviet Non-Aggression Pact** agreed that neither country would attack the other for ten years. Secretly the leaders also agreed to divide Poland up between themselves. Hitler had succeeded in gaining more land and ensuring that the USSR would not attack it, leaving Germany free to deal with any British or French attacks. Stalin also succeeded in giving the USSR more time to build up its defences and military for the war against the Germans which he knew was inevitable.

▲ Stalin and Hitler's Foreign Minister shake hands after signing the Nazi-Soviet Non-Aggression Pact in August 1939.

Hitler now invaded Poland without any fear of retaliation from the USSR. Britain and France demanded that Germany retreat but Germany refused. Finally, on 3 September 1939 Britain and France declared war on Germany and World War II began.

Questions

1. What does appeasement mean?

2. In what ways did Hitler dismantle the Treaty of Versailles?

3. Explain why the following countries did nothing to stop Hitler from dismantling the Treaty of Versailles:

    (a) France   (b) Britain   (c) the USA

4. Give three reasons why Hitler felt he was ready to expand German territory.

5. What does *Anschluss* mean?

6. What reason did Hitler give for his desire for the unification of the Sudetenland?

7. What deal was agreed at the Munich Conference in 1938?

8. Why did Chamberlain claim that he had secured 'peace for our time'?

9. What did the Nazi-Soviet Non-Aggression Pact agree?

10. Why did Stalin agree to make a deal with Hitler?

11. Put in the correct order of German expansion:

    (a) Poland   (b) Czechoslovakia   (c) Rhineland   (d) Sudetenland   (e) Austria

World War II

On 3 September 1939, World War II began. The two groups of countries that fought against each other included:

The Allies	The Axis Powers
Britain, France	Germany, Italy
USSR (joined in 1941)	Japan (invaded China in 1937)
China (invaded by Japan in 1937)	Romania (joined in 1941)
USA (joined in 1941)	Hungary (joined in 1940)

There were many other countries involved in this war, some of which were invaded and occupied by the Axis powers but continued to fight. In countries such as Yugoslavia, Greece, France and Holland, groups of soldiers within these countries fought the invading forces throughout the entire war. These soldiers were known as **resistance fighters**.

This war was the most devastating war ever known. It is estimated that between 50 and 60 million people died during the 6 years of the war. Sixty-one countries and 1.7 billion people had been involved in it. By the end of World War II, the world had changed completely.

● 1939

GERMAN ADVANCE

Germany's invasion of Poland gave Hitler a chance to show off the capability of the German army. The type of warfare he introduced was called **Blitzkrieg** (lightning war).

▲ Hitler introduced Blitzkrieg (lightning war) during Germany's invasion of Poland.

1. First the **Luftwaffe** bombed all roads, bridges and military centres in an area, causing a disruption to the organisation of the defence of the country under attack.

2. Next Germany's **Panzer** (tank) divisions broke through any defences and destroyed any further defences.

3. Then the German **infantry** (foot soldiers) mopped up any resistance and secured the newly-won area.

The Polish army was unprepared for this new tactic. Their air force and armoured divisions were no match for the German **Wehrmacht** (army). The Germans were able to drive through to Warsaw (the Polish capital) within weeks. On 17 September, the Soviet troops also invaded, sealing Poland's fate. Britain and France offered no help to Poland as it was too far away and their armies were not yet prepared for serious conflict.

The six-month period following the invasion of Poland became known as the **Phoney War** because little happened. Hitler did not want to expand his war with the winter coming and the Allies had to work hard to rebuild their military strength. Britain began to evacuate children from the cities, distribute gas-masks and organise underground shelters in preparation for the war.

1940

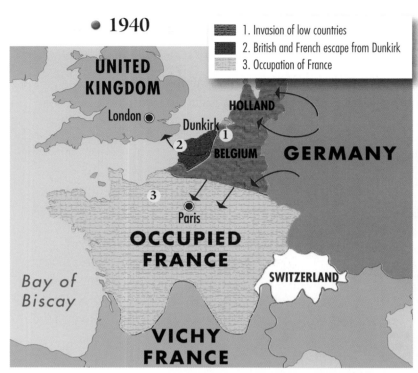

Legend:
1. Invasion of low countries
2. British and French escape from Dunkirk
3. Occupation of France

▲ A map of Western Germany, France, Belgium, Holland and Dunkirk

Hitler's plan was always to expand eastward. He did not wish to fight the Western Allies but he knew that Germany could not fight a war against the USSR in the east whilst also fighting the Allies on the west. For this reason, in the spring of 1940, Germany turned westward. In April 1940 the Germans invaded Denmark and Norway. In May they invaded Holland, Luxembourg and Belgium. These countries' armies resisted but were easily overrun.

France had hoped that the Maginot Line would provide a strong defence against any German invasion. Germany's invasion of Holland and Belgium meant they could simply bypass these defences and invade through the north of France. The French had no answer to Germany's Luftwaffe and the speed of the invasion. By 22 June, France had surrendered.

In May 1940, Neville Chamberlain resigned as British Prime Minister. He was replaced by Winston Churchill. Churchill immediately sent a British Expeditionary Force (BEF) of 250,000 men to help the French. This force arrived in northern France but was taken by surprise at the speed of the German advance. The BEF and over 100,000 French troops were forced to retreat to the port of Dunkirk. With the German army closing in around the troops, thousands of British ships, private yachts, trawlers and boats crossed the English Channel and rescued over 330,000 men.

▲ Hitler in Paris following the surrender of France in 1940.

France was divided into two parts: the north of France was occupied by the Germans while the

▲ Winston Churchill was Prime Minister of Britain during World War II.

southern half was governed by a French government that was loyal to Germany. This half of France was known as Vichy France because the government, led by Marshal Pétain, was based in the town of Vichy.

Germany had managed to conquer most of mainland Europe within the first year of the war. From June 1940, Britain stood alone against Germany. Britain's Prime Minister, Winston Churchill addressed the British parliament in a famous speech in which he said,

> **By the way …**
>
> The German Commander, Gerd von Rundstedt, would have captured all the troops at Dunkirk if he had not decided to rest his Panzer divisions in preparation for the next phase in the war.

> 'We shall fight in France, we shall fight on the seas and oceans, we shall fight … in the air, we shall defend our island, whatever the cost may be, we shall fight on the beaches, we shall fight on the landing grounds, we shall fight in the fields and in the streets, we shall fight in the hills; we shall never surrender.'

Questions

1. Name the countries that were part of the Axis powers.
2. Explain *Blitzkrieg*.
3. Match each item in Column A with the correct item in Column B.

Column A	**Column B**
A German Army	1. Luftwaffe
B German Tank Division	2. Wehrmacht
C German Airforce	3. Panzer

4. Why were the six months after the invasion of Poland called the Phoney War?
5. Why did Britain and France not come to the aid of Poland?
6. How did the German army avoid the Maginot Line?
7. Who was Marshal Pétain?
8. How did the British Expeditionary Force (BEF) manage to escape across the English Channel?
9. How many men were saved from the port of Dunkirk?

BATTLE OF BRITAIN

Now Hitler focused on defeating Britain. He planned two operations:
(1) **Operation Eagle**: The defeat of the **British Royal Air Force (RAF)** by the Luftwaffe.
(2) **Operation Sealion**: After defeating the RAF, the German navy would launch a sea invasion of Britain.

▲ A German Messerschmitt fighter plane in action during Operation Eagle.

Operation Sealion was dependent on the success of Operation Eagle and so on 13 August 1940, the Luftwaffe began to attack British RAF bases. The German Messerschmitt, Heinkel (larger bomber) and Stuka fighter planes were more numerous but the British Spitfires and Hurricanes were more suitable for air-to-air combat. The aerial **dogfights** between the two sides resulted in severe German losses. The British also used a new device, radar, which greatly helped them to pinpoint when and where attacks would take place.

Due to the large number of losses and Hitler's desire to destroy British morale, the Germans changed to night raids on the cities of Britain in September. Between September 1940 and May 1941, London had 71 major attacks This period of time became known as **the Blitz**. There were 56 attacks on other major British cities including Belfast. The Blitz killed over 40,000 people and caused great damage to the cities that were attacked. In September 1941, Hitler postponed Operation Eagle. The Battle of Britain had been won by the RAF.

Hitler also hoped to besiege Britain by cutting off their sea supplies. **The Battle of the Atlantic** involved large numbers of German U-Boats (submarines) sinking British supply ships. The U-Boats used ports in Norway and France to attack British ships throughout the war.

▲ The Blitz forced many Londoners to sleep in air raid shelters such as disused Underground stations.

This resulted in over 5,000 ships being sunk. Britain may have avoided being invaded but they were still exposed to great danger.

In 1940, Italy began the invasion of Yugoslavia and Greece in Europe and into British-controlled Egypt in Africa. Mussolini's troops immediately ran into trouble and asked the German army for assistance. By 14 April 1941, Yugoslavia had surrendered and Greece followed soon afterwards. The German General **Erwin Rommel** (known as the Desert Fox) then pushed the British back in Africa.

▲ General Erwin Rommel, also known as the Desert Fox.

1941

OPERATION BARBAROSSA

After the success of the German army across Europe, Hitler now turned to his primary aim: the invasion of the USSR. The invasion of the USSR was known as **Operation Barbarossa** and began on 22 June 1941. Hitler's plan was to push the Soviet army back and capture Moscow and also USSR's rich oil and wheat reserves in the south near the Caucasus Mountains. To achieve this, a huge army of three million men and four thousand tanks were assembled. The force was divided up into three main armies.

- Army Group North was to attack towards Leningrad (St. Petersburg).

- Army Group Centre drove towards the capital Moscow.

- Army Group South aimed to secure the oil and wheat fields of the Ukraine.

Strangely, even though Hitler had made no secret of his preparations, Stalin was taken by surprise by Operation Barbarossa. The German Blitzkrieg was able to strike deep into Soviet lands. By the beginning of August the Germans were two thirds of their way to Moscow. Stalin had told his infantry to counterattack but this proved impossible. He then refused to let his armies retreat. This meant that by December about four million Soviet soldiers had been captured. By the beginning of December, the German advances were impressive.

In the North, the Germans had reached Leningrad and were besieging the city. In the centre the German commander, Field Marshal **Fedor von Bock**, brought his troops to within 32 kilometres of Moscow. The southern drive had achieved great victories and had reached as far as Stalingrad (modern day Volgograd).

By the end of 1941 the German army had achieved stunning successes across Europe. Almost all of Western Europe was under Hitler or his allies' control and he had managed to push the Soviet Army back to within a few kilometres of Moscow.

Questions

1. What were the two operations that Hitler planned for the invasion of Britain and what did they involve?
2. How did the Germans attack Britain?
3. Name the type of aeroplanes that the British had during the Battle of Britain.
4. What advantages did the British airforce have over the Luftwaffe planes during the Battle of Britain?
5. What was the Blitz?
6. Why did Hitler want to invade the south of the USSR towards the Caucasus Mountains?
7. What cities in the USSR did the Germans try to capture?

▲ Germany's plans to invade the USSR were codenamed Operation Barbarossa.

The Tide Turns

The Germans were very close to capturing the capital of the USSR. However, they now faced a problem that proved too powerful to defeat: the Russian winter.

Operation Barbarossa was delayed by three weeks due to the need to help the Italian offensive in Greece and Yugoslavia. This three-week delay was to prove vital for the Soviet defence.

On 5 December the German offensive was halted. Temperatures of -40°C froze the petrol in the German tanks and machines.

The German soldiers were losing the will to fight. They had not been given the correct clothing to endure the freezing temperatures and many died of frostbite.

The Soviet army used a **scorched earth policy**. This meant that as they retreated, they destroyed anything that might be of use to the German army. Food, buildings, roads, bridges and railways were burnt or destroyed to make life as difficult as possible.

Stalin and his commander, **General Zhukov**, held their reserves back until the German offensive had stopped. On 6 December, the Soviet Army launched its counterattack around Moscow. This counterattack soon turned into a counter-offensive along the entire front.

PEARL HARBOUR

While the American people supported the Allies, the USA had officially remained neutral throughout the war. This changed when Germany's ally Japan launched a surprise attack on the American Pacific military base in Pearl Harbour in Hawaii. Just before 8 a.m. on Sunday, 7 December 1941, the Japanese air force bombed the American navy, destroying 8 battleships and 13 other naval ships. It was a huge success for Japan but it brought the USA into the war. On 8 December the American President, **Theodore Roosevelt**, declared war on Japan. Germany then declared war on

▲ Pearl Harbour came under surprise attack from Japan in December 1941.

the USA. The war had truly become a world war. While the USA prepared to go to war against the Japanese in the Pacific Ocean, they also began to send troops and weapons to Europe to help the British continue their fight against Germany.

• 1942

At the beginning of 1942, Hitler's German army had control over most of Europe and were deep inside Soviet territory. However, by the end of 1942, the war had begun to turn in favour of the Allies. Three major victories by the Allies marked the turning point:

▲ American President Theodore Roosevelt

1 STALINGRAD

Perhaps the most heroic of all the decisive battles of World War II took place in Stalingrad. With the arrival of better weather in the USSR, the German army began to push into Soviet territory again. Leningrad in the north was still being besieged and Moscow was also still under attack. Stalin's decision to remain in Moscow throughout the war seemed to inspire the army to repel the German attacks on the city. The Germans had much more success in the south and pushed through to Stalingrad. Under General

▲ The city of Stalingrad during its siege by the German army in 1942.

Friedrich Paulus, the Germans were able to conquer large areas of land. By August 1942 they were at the gates of Stalingrad. The speed of their advance meant that Hitler needed to use his Hungarian, Italian and Romanian troops to protect the newly-won land. The German troops now tried to take the city. Stalin had ordered his troops to take 'not a step back' and the battle became a street-to-street battle. The German tanks were not suitable for the hand-to-hand fighting that took place in Stalingrad. By the end of October, the German troops were exhausted and running low on ammunition and supplies.

▲ Map of Battle of Stalingrad: The Soviet counter-attack in November 1942 cut General Paulus' Sixth Army off. Within three days the Russians surrounded the Germans trapping them in the city.

In November 1942, the Soviets launched their counter offensive known as **Operation Uranus**. They realised that the Axis allies (e.g. the Hungarian, Italian and Romanian troops) were not as strong as the German troops, so the Soviet army attacked on the south and west sides of the city. They easily cut through the Axis defensive lines and soon encircled the city. General Paulus, the German Sixth Army and half of the Fourth Panzer Division consisting of 290,000 soldiers were caught inside the city. Hitler refused to let Paulus retreat and promised to supply the soldiers by air. The air relief did not succeed and neither did the proposed relief army. The Germans fought on until 31 January 1943 when Paulus finally surrendered. Over 200,000 Axis troops had been killed or wounded during the battle for Stalingrad. Soviet casualties were over one million men with almost half a million killed. While the Battle of Stalingrad cost the Soviet Army a huge loss of lives, the victory proved that the Wehrmacht was not invincible and gave a confidence boost to the USSR.

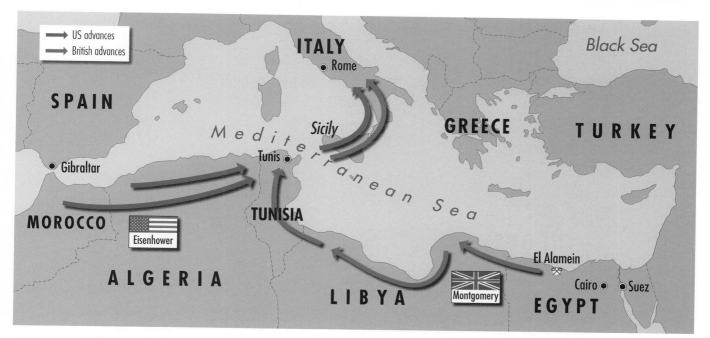

▲ A map of El Alamein where the British General Montgomery managed to halt the progress of the German Afrika Corps.

2 EL ALAMEIN

The German Afrika Corps under Rommel managed to push the British deep inside Egypt. They reached as far as the town of El Alamein before the British General **Bernard Law Montgomery** halted them. On 23 October 1942, aided by the arrival of new American tanks, Montgomery launched an attack on Rommel's troops at El Alamein. The battle was fierce and for two weeks the armies fought each other. Rommel eventually retreated westward into Libya. At the same time, American forces under General **Dwight Eisenhower** landed in Algeria and Morocco and pushed eastward. The German Afrika Corps was forced to retreat to Tunisia where they were surrounded by American and British troops. In May 1943, 275,000 German and Italian soldiers surrendered. Africa was now under the control of the Allies and this would be important when the Allies tried to invade Europe.

▲ General Montgomery managed to push the 'Desert Fox' into surrender.

3 THE BATTLE OF MIDWAY

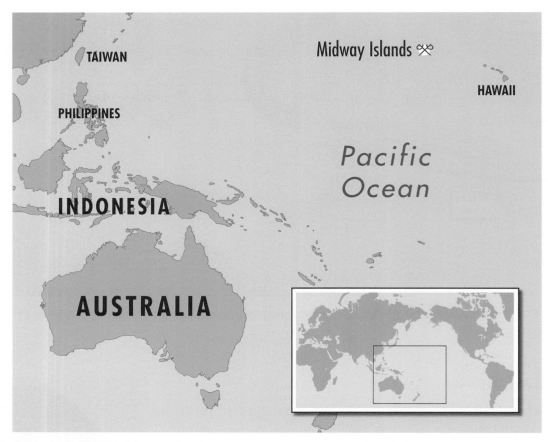

▲ A map of the Midway Islands where an important sea battle between America and Japan took place.

▲ A Japanese cruiser is filled with smoke after being bombed by American aircraft in June 1942.

In June 1942, a sea battle between the Japanese navy and the American navy took place at the Midway Islands. Although outnumbered, the American fleet was able to destroy four Japanese aircraft carriers, two cruisers and three destroyers while only losing one carrier and one destroyer. The loss of the aircraft carriers was a huge blow to the Japanese who were unable to hold onto the islands that they had conquered. The Americans slowly advanced on Japan.

Questions

1. Give four reasons why the German advance into the USSR failed in 1941.
2. What is meant by 'scorched earth policy'?
3. What occurred in Hawaii just before 8 a.m. on Sunday, 7 December 1941?
4. How did the involvement of the USA in the war help the Allies in Europe?
5. Match the following leaders with the correct countries:

   Leader

   A Theodore Roosevelt

   B Josef Stalin

   C Winston Churchill

   Country

   1. Britain

   2. USA

   3. USSR

6. Write a short paragraph on one of the following:

   (a) Battle of Stalingrad   (b) Battle of Midway   (c) Battle of El Alamein

7. Who were the following people:

   (a) Bernard Law Montgomery   (c) General Zhukov

   (b) General Friedrich Paulus   (d) Erwin Rommel

8. What was Operation Uranus?

● 1943

The surrender of the German and Axis troops at Stalingrad and in Africa in 1943 was reinforced by more successes for the Allies.

ITALIAN INVASION

Following the victory of the Allies in Africa in May 1943, British and American troops landed and captured the island of Sicily. By September they had landed in Italy and were moving northward. The Italian population overthrew Mussolini's government, arrested Mussolini and surrendered to the Allies. Mussolini was rescued by German SS commandoes but was finally captured by Italians in 1945 and executed. The Italian invasion was important as it marked the first invasion of the land of the Axis Powers.

▲ After Mussolini (centre) was executed his body was left hanging on display in Milan.

THE EASTERN FRONT

The Soviet army began to push the Wehrmacht back. By 1944 the Soviet army had reached Poland and Romania.

OPERATION OVERLORD

In November 1943, Roosevelt, Churchill and Stalin travelled to Tehran in Iran to make plans for the western invasion of Europe. Stalin hoped that the creation of a Western Front would take the pressure off the Soviet army on the eastern front. **Operation Overlord** was planned for June 1944. The day of the invasion was to be codenamed **Deliverance Day (D-Day)** and was to be led by Generals Montgomery and Eisenhower.

1944

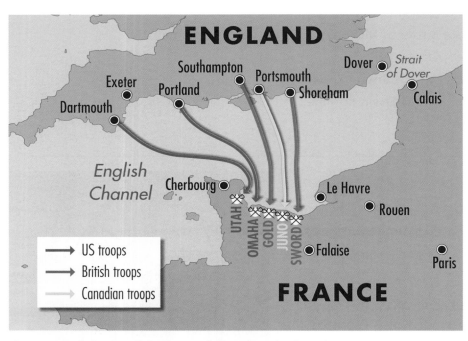

▲ A map of the English Channel showing the beaches.

D-DAY:

The invasion force on the first day consisted of 120,000 Allied troops supported by 20,000 **paratroopers** (soldiers who are dropped behind enemy lines using parachutes). The Allies pretended to be launching their attack at Calais and so Hitler put most of his troops there. The real intended locations were the beaches of Normandy. Each beach was given a code name: Utah, Omaha, Juno, Gold and Sword. On 6 June 1944, under the protection of aeroplanes, the Allied soldiers landed on the beaches. Hitler had built a line of defences called the Atlantic Wall along the French coast. The Allied soldiers had to deal with heavily-mined beaches, heavy gunfire and steep cliffs.

After 18 hours of fighting on 6 June, the Allies had gained a foothold along the French coast. The German resistance to the Allied invasion never really happened as Hitler still believed that the invasion in Normandy was a trick and that the main invasion was going to be at Calais. Over one million troops landed in France by the end of June and by 23 August, Paris had been liberated.

◀ Scene from the beaches in Normandy on D-Day, 6 June 1944.

With the vast numbers of troops and equipment pouring into Europe from Britain and America, Germany stood very little chance of victory. Hitler continued to hope for a change in fortunes and began to use his new long-range rocket, the V-2, to bomb Britain. In December 1944, the Wehrmacht was able to halt the Allied push towards Berlin for a short time. The Battle of the Bulge took place between December 1944 and February 1945 and was the last attempt by Hitler to push back the Allied armies. The battle was a success for the Wehrmacht but it was not enough to halt the Allied advance.

▲ The liberation of Paris, August 1944.

● 1945

The Allies continued to bomb German cities throughout this period. In February 1945 135,000 civilians were killed in the German city of Dresden. The Allied troops crossed the River Rhine in March 1945 and the Soviet Army reached Berlin by April. On 30 April 1945, Hitler married Eva Braun and then committed suicide in his bunker in Berlin. Just before his death he appointed Grand Admiral Karl Doenitz as head of government. Doenitz agreed to an unconditional surrender on 7 May and the next day was declared **VE Day (Victory in Europe Day)**.

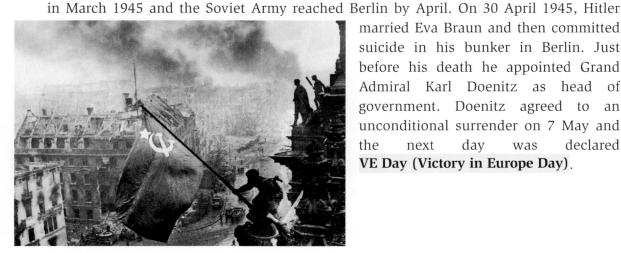

▲ A Russian flag is raised over the rooftops in Berlin.

WAR IN THE PACIFIC

▲ An American soldier stands beside the flag on the island of Iwo Jima, June 1945

Victory had been achieved in Europe but World War II was not over. Japan continued to resist American attempts to push them out of the Pacific. The Japanese navy was badly damaged and would not fight another battle for the rest of the war. However, Japanese soldiers occupied many of the islands in the Pacific and they were determined to cause the American troops large casualties. One new method that the Japanese used was **kamikaze** (divine wind) pilots. These were pilots who flew old planes full of explosives directly into ships in the hope of sinking them. These pilots knew they would not survive the explosion. Between 4 and 13 January 1945, 17 US ships were sunk and 50 more damaged by kamikaze pilots. After heavy fighting, the Americans took the islands of Iwo Jima and Okinawa in April and June 1945. The Japanese fought to the death with many committing suicide rather than surrender. The USA was concerned that defeating Japan would cost a lot of American lives so a new method of warfare was introduced: the atom bomb.

HIROSHIMA AND NAGASAKI

President Roosevelt died in April 1945 and was replaced by Vice-President Harry Truman. Truman decided that in order to ensure maximum impact, two atomic bombs were to be dropped in Japan. On 6 and 9 August 1945 atomic bombs were dropped on the cities of Hiroshima and Nagasaki. It is estimated that between 60-70,000 people were killed by the bomb in Hiroshima and another 40,000 in Nagasaki. On 8 August, USSR declared war on Japan. Japan's position was impossible to maintain and they surrendered on 14 August 1945. That day was named **VJ Day (Victory over Japan Day)**. Finally, World War II was over across the globe.

▲ The destruction caused in Hiroshima by the atomic bomb which was dropped in August 1945.

So how did the Allies win?

(a) The sheer number of countries at war with Germany proved too much. Germany was forced to fight on the Eastern and Western Fronts and its resources were overstretched. The size of the armies and the resources available to the USSR and the USA were massive. The populations of the USSR and the USA dwarfed the Axis populations and they also had almost 400 times more oil reserves than Germany.

(b) Furthermore, Germany had to rely on its Axis allies who had inferior armies. The need to help the Italians in Greece, Yugoslavia and Africa meant that large amounts of men and supplies were diverted from the main German fronts.

(c) Some of Hitler's military decisions were very unwise. For example, his decision not to allow Paulus to retreat at Stalingrad proved to be a major mistake. Perhaps his greatest mistake of all was the invasion of the USSR. The Red Army was larger in number and ultimately had more military equipment.

▲ A mushroom cloud caused by the explosion of an atomic bomb.

Questions

1. Who attended the conference in Tehran and what was decided?
2. How many troops were involved in Operation Overlord?
3. Name the codenames for the beaches in France where the Allied troops landed.
4. What was the Atlantic Wall?
5. When was Paris liberated by the Allies?
6. On which date did Germany surrender?
7. What was the name given to 8 May 1945 and why?
8. What did kamikaze pilots do?
9. Where were the atom bombs dropped?
10. Do you think that the dropping of the second atomic bomb was justified?
11. Give three reasons why the Allies won World War II.

● The Holocaust

One of the most horrific aspects of the Nazis' policies was their attempts to destroy all Jews living in Nazi-controlled lands. Since the Nuremberg Laws of 1935 and Kristallnacht in 1938, Germany's Jewish Community had lived in fear of their lives. Himmler was put in charge of the operation to exterminate all Jews living under Nazi control. As Germany expanded into Czechoslovakia, Poland and the USSR, millions of Jews came under Nazi control.

By the way ...

The term 'ghetto' comes from the name of an island off Venice where Jews were forced to live in the sixteenth century.

Jewish families being arrested and removed from a ghetto. ▶

▲ Millions of Jews were sent to concentration camps where many were killed or died of disease or starvation.

At first, Jews were forced to move into areas of cities called ghettos. The ghettos, like those in Budapest and Warsaw, were surrounded by walls and had terrible living conditions. In 1941, the **Einsatzgruppen** (action groups) were formed with the objective of eliminating all Jews within the USSR. Jews were rounded up and shot and their bodies dumped into mass graves that they had been forced to dig before their execution.

Concentration camps were also set up throughout Germany for the detention of Jews and enemies of the Nazis. In these camps, prisoners were forced to work and were treated very badly. Many of the prisoners were killed or died of disease and starvation.

▲ Adolf Eichmann was in charge of implementing the 'Final Solution'.

▲ The location of some of the concentration and extermination camps in Germany and Poland.

In 1942, the Nazis placed **Adolf Eichmann** in charge of what became known as the 'Final Solution'. This involved gathering all Jews across Europe and transporting them to the extermination camps built for this purpose in Poland and the western USSR. Camps at **Sobibor**, **Auschwitz-Birkenau** and **Treblinka** used **Zyklon-B** gas to kill large numbers of Jews whose bodies were then cremated (burnt).

Due to the enormous numbers, it is difficult to be exact about how many people died in these camps. However, it is estimated that up to six million Jews died in what has become known as the **Holocaust** (the destruction of the Jewish community during World War II).

Corpses from extermination camps ▶

◀ The furnaces in which Nazis cremated their victims.

OTHER VICTIMS

The Jews within Europe were not the only people the Nazis attacked. Communists, socialists, Roma (Gypsies), anyone with mental or physical disabilities and homosexuals were also killed in these camps. For example, it is thought that about 200,000 Roma were killed as the Nazis believed them to be sub-human (i.e. an inferior type of human).

LOCAL ACTIONS

Anti-Semitism, a fear of the Nazis and lack of interest among the populations meant very little help was given to the victims. Some people risked their lives to help the victims and in places like Denmark, Holland, Poland and Belgium, many Jews were helped to escape to neutral countries. In other countries, like the Fascist Ustaše government in Croatia, there was support for the Nazi actions. At the extermination camp at Jasenovac estimates vary greatly, but between 50,000 – 600,000 people were killed, mostly Serbs, Roma and Jews.

Questions

1. What were ghettos?
2. What happened at concentration camps?
3. Name two locations of extermination camps.
4. What was the purpose of extermination camps?
5. What is Zyklon-B?
6. Apart from the Jewish community, who else did the Nazis wish to get rid of?
7. What does Holocaust mean?

Results of World War II

1. LOSS OF LIFE

World War II was the most bloody and costly war the world has ever seen. It is estimated that over 55 million people were killed during the war. The largest number of people killed came from the USSR. About 20 million Russians were killed during the war, far more than from any other country.

2. DESTRUCTION OF EUROPE

By 1945 most of Europe lay in ruins. Cities, railways, roads and industries had been destroyed by bombs and battles. To ensure that Europe did not suffer the same economic difficulties of the inter-war period, the USA government gave large loans called **Marshall Aid** to help rebuild Europe.

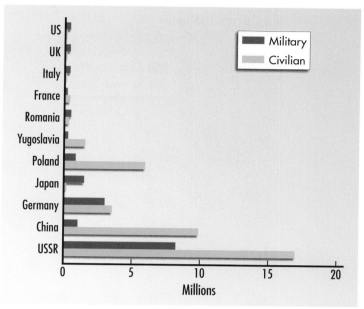

▲ Graph of deaths around the world during World War II.

▲ The utter destruction of Cologne, Germany. The Cathedral took about 70 direct hits but remained standing in an almost flattened city.

3. END OF EUROPEAN POWER AND RISE OF THE SUPERPOWERS

After the war, the European countries were no longer as powerful as before the war. The USSR and the USA had risen in economic and political power. This meant that these two countries would dominate world politics for the rest of the twentieth century.

4. EUROPE DIVIDED

▲ Europe became divided after World War II into Western Europe (democratic, capitalist) and Eastern Europe (one-party states, communist).

The USSR took control of most of Eastern Europe. Countries such as Poland, Czechoslovakia, Bulgaria and Romania became **puppet states** (countries with gvernments who followed orders from another country) of the Soviet Union. Even Germany was divided up. The eastern part of Germany was given to the USSR to control while the western half was controlled by the Allies.

5. THE COLD WAR

The tensions between the USSR and the Western Powers grew after the end of the war. The USSR installed communist governments in the eastern countries it controlled. This raised the Allies' fear of the spread of communism. These tensions between the East and the West resulted in what is known as the Cold War. We will look at the Cold War in Chapter 13, International Relations, 1945–2000.

6. European Unity

Western European powers wanted to ensure that there would never be another war in Europe. To help ensure this, efforts were made to create better relations between countries. This process would eventually lead to the creation of the EEC and later the European Union which we will look at in Chapter 13.

7. The United Nations

Even though the League of Nations had failed, a new organisation was created to help promote peace throughout the world. The United Nations was established and its headquarters are located in New York.

The United Nations building in New York ▲

Chapter 11 Questions

1. Pictures

(a) Name the three people marked A, B and C.

(b) State which countries they governed.

(c) Explain the principal reason why these countries became allies during World War II.

(d) Write a short paragraph on the contribution one of these people made to their country.

2. Documents

The following is a personal account of a concentration camp by a survivor, Alice Lok Cohana:

> Several days later we arrived to Bergen-Belsen. And Bergen-Belsen was hell on earth. Nothing ever in literature could compare to anything what Bergen-Belsen was. When we arrived, the dead were not carried away any more, you stepped over them, you fell over them if you couldn't walk. There were agonizing cries . . . people begging for water . . . They were crying, they were begging. It was . . . hell. Day and night. You couldn't escape the crying, you couldn't have escaped the praying, you couldn't escape the [cries of] "Mercy," . . . it was a chant, the chant of the dead. It was hell.

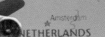

(a) Where was the concentration camp that Alice Lok Cohana arrived at?

(b) Where were the dead lying?

(c) What were the people who were alive doing?

(d) What did Alice Lok Cohana think the camp was like?

(e) Name the Nazi who was in charge of the concentration camps.

(f) What was the purpose of these camps?

3. Short-Answer Questions

(a) What was the name of the political party that Mussolini founded?

(b) Name the African country that Mussolini invaded in 1935.

(c) What does anti-Semitism mean?

(d) What country did Hitler invade first?

(e) What are U-Boats?

(f) Explain the following terms:

   (i) Dogfights   (ii) Radar

(g) Who was known as the Desert Fox?

(h) What was the codename given to Hitler's invasion of the USSR?

(i) Where did the Allied invasion of France take place?

(j) What was Operation Overlord?

(k) In which city did the Allied leaders meet in 1943?

(l) Who was Eva Braun?

(m) Name the two cities on which the Americans dropped the atomic bombs.

4. People in History

(a) Write an account of a Russian soldier fighting on the Eastern Front. Use the following headings as a guide:

- Name of the city or location of the battle
- The conditions in which they were fighting
- The weapons and type of warfare used in the battle

5.

(a) Write a paragraph on three of the following topics:

   (i) The Battle of Britain

   (ii) The Battle of Stalingrad

   (iii) Pearl Harbour

   (iv) The D-Day landings

(b) Outline the contribution the USA and the USSR made to the winning of the war by the Allies.

(c) Give reasons for and against the American decision to drop two atomic bombs on Japan in 1945. State which reasons you support.

Key Terms to Summarise Chapter 11: International Relations in Twentieth Century Europe

Alliance An agreement between countries to cooperate on certain issues, often military issues.

Entente Cordiale Military alliance between Britain, France and Russia during World War I.

Central Powers Military alliance between Germany and the Austro-Hungarian and Ottoman Empires.

No-man's land The area of land between the two opposing trenches during World War I.

Self-determination The idea that every nation should have the right to choose its own government.

Treaty of Versailles The settlement agreed in the Palace of Versailles in 1919 by the victorious powers after World War I.

Reparations Financial compensation imposed on Germany to pay for the cost of World War I.

League of Nations International organisation set up after World War I to help cooperation between countries. The absence of Russia, Germany and the USA meant it lacked credibility.

Isolationism American policy during the inter-war period not to involve itself in European affairs.

Bolshevik A member of the Russian Bolshevik Party who believed in the overthrow of the monarchy and the creation of a communist system of government.

Communism The idea of organising society so that all industry and land is owned and controlled by the State rather than private individuals, for the benefit of the workers.

Nationalisation Changing an industry from private ownership to state-ownership, e.g. electricity companies owned by private individuals are taken over by the government and become state-owned.

Collectivisation The merging of smaller farms to create larger, more productive farms.

Gulag Forced-labour camps in the USSR.

Great Purges The system of removing all Soviet individuals whom Stalin believed were opposed to his policies and whom he suspected wished to overthrow him.

Fascism A political system that promoted a totalitarian, one-party state and followed anti-communist, racist, pro-Church, right-wing policies and used violence and intimidation of political opponents to achieve success.

Socialism The idea of organising society so that all industry and land is owned and controlled by all of society equally rather than private individuals.

Black Shirts Group of Italian fascists who wore black shirts and were used by Mussolini to intimidate political opponents.

March on Rome Event in 1922 when Italian fascists marched to Rome in an attempt to pressurise King Victor Emmanuel III to create a Fascist government.

Acerbo Law Law passed by Mussolini in 1923 stating that any party that received the largest number of seats would automatically gain two thirds of seats in the Italian parliament.

Censorship Control by a government or organisation of the media.

Dictator Person who has absolute and unrestricted control in a government.

Corporate State Italian Fascist system of organising the economic system under which each area of the economy is divided into groups made up of government officials, employers and workers.

Propaganda Spreading rumours, lies and ideas about something or somebody to either promote or harm a person, organisation or thing.

Indoctrination Teaching a biased view to people, e.g. in Nazi Germany school children learned only good things about Hitler and the Nazi party. Information that was critical of Hitler or the party was not allowed to be taught.

Lateran Treaty (1929) An agreement between Mussolini and the Pope in which the Vatican was recognised as an independent state and Catholicism was recognised as the Italian state religion.

Rome-Berlin Axis (1936) Agreement between Hitler and Mussolini.

Nazi Shortened name given to the members of the National Socialist German Workers' Party which was the Fascist party established by Hitler.

Brown Shirts Name given to the SA in Germany who used intimidation and violence against opponents of Nazism.

Mein Kampf The name of Hitler's book where he outlined his views and his plans for the future of Germany.

Lebensraum Literally 'living space', it was the name for the expansion of Germany into the east in search of raw materials.

Inflation The increase in prices resulting in a drop in the value of money.

Gestapo The secret police of the Nazi Party.

Enabling Act (1933) Law passed by Hitler allowing him to pass any law without the approval of the German Parliament.

Night of the Long Knives (1934) The arrest and murder of many of Hitler's political opponents.

Concentration camps Labour camps where political opponents and enemies of Nazism were sent.

Nuremberg Laws (1935) Racist laws designed by Hitler to 'protect the pure German blood'.

Kristallnacht (1938) Event where Jewish places of worship, homes and businesses were attacked.

Final Solution Nazi plan to get rid of all Jews in areas controlled by Germany.

Appeasement Agreeing to unjust demands in the hope of peace.

***Anschluss* (1938)** The unification of Germany with Austria.

Nazi-Soviet Non-Aggression Pact (1939) Agreement between the USSR and Germany not to attack each other for ten years.

Blitzkrieg 'Lightning war' that used air power and speed to defeat opposing armies.

Phoney War The six months after the outbreak of World War II when there was no conflict.

The Blitz The period when German planes were bombing London between 1940-1941.

Scorched earth policy Tactic in warfare whereby an army destroys all resources of use to the opposing army (e.g. food, buildings, roads).

Operation Overlord The codename given to the Allies plan to lead a western invasion of Europe. The first day of this invasion was codenamed D-Day.

D-Day (June 1944) The name given to Deliverance Day when the Allied troops invaded France.

VE-Day (May 1945) The name given to the day of victory over Germany by the Allies.

VJ-Day (August 1945) The name given to the day of victory over Japan by the Allies.

Holocaust The name given to the extermination of up to six million Jews during World War II.

Web References

For further reading on topics mentioned in this chapter, view the following websites:

history.sandiego.edu/gen/text/versaillestreaty/vercontents.html

www.calvin.edu/academic/cas/gpa/

www.pbs.org/wgbh/amex/holocaust/peopleevents/pandeAMEX99.html

www.ushmm.org/wlc/en/

fcit.coedu.usf.edu/holocaust/

www.holocaustsurvivors.org/

www.the-map-as-history.com/demos/tome03

www.worldwar-2.net

www.bbc.co.uk/history/ww2children

video.google.com/videoplay?docid=-6229070629122885245

Women in History

Odette Brailly
(1912 – 1995)

During World War I and World War II, women were expected to perform work previously done by men. During World War I women were asked to volunteer their services to help with the war effort. This movement away from the 'traditional' female jobs gave women great freedom. Although these women were replaced by returning soldiers after World War I, some advances in women's rights had been made.

In 1928 in Britain, everyone above the age of 21 was given the right to vote irrespective of gender.

During World War II, the National Service Act of 1941 made conscription of women legal in Britain. Initially only women aged between 20 and 30 years of age were called up. However, by 1943, almost 90% of single women and 80% of married women were employed in essential work for the war. Many women had already joined the Auxiliary Territorial Service (ATS) formed in 1938. The ATS went to France in 1939 as part of the British Expeditionary Force and was involved in particular with searchlights and anti-aircraft guns, even though members were not allowed to fire the guns.

A number of women became involved in the British Special Operations Executive (SOE). One woman named Odette Brailly was particularly famous. Born in Amiens, France in 1912, she married an Englishman and moved to London in 1931. She offered her services to the War Office in 1942 and was sent to Antibes, France. She was supposed to set up a resistance group in Burgundy but ended up working with a spy named Peter Churchill. Soon

▲ Odette Brailly pictured here with Peter Churchill who was also a spy.

after arriving, both Brailly and Churchill were caught and arrested by the German army. They were both tortured horribly by the Gestapo but did not reveal any information about the work of the other spies.

She was then sent to the concentration camp at Ravensbrück. She spent the rest of the war either in solitary confinement or in the Commandant's quarters. The German Commandant wrongly thought that she was married to Peter Churchill and that he was, in fact, Winston Churchill's cousin. At the end of the war, the German Commandant tried to escape through the American lines by travelling with Odette, but she quickly informed on him and gave evidence against him and many other Nazis from the camp. On her return to Britain, she was awarded an MBE in 1945 and became the first woman to receive the George Cross for her courage in the war.

Chapter 12

IRELAND IN THE TWENTIETH CENTURY

Ireland in 1900

● Irish Politics

▲ All decisions about Ireland were made in the British parliament in Westminster, London.

Since the 1801 Act of Union, Ireland had been part of the United Kingdom (UK). All decisions about Ireland were made in the British parliament in Westminster, London. Politically the Irish population was divided into two main groups: **nationalists** who wanted more independence for Ireland and **unionists** who wished to remain part of the United Kingdom.

NATIONALISTS

The British government's failure to help Ireland during the Famine in the late 1840s and early 1850s convinced many Irish people that complete independence from Britain was necessary in order to improve the lives of Irish people. The Young Ireland Movement attempted a rising in 1848. The Irish Republican Brotherhood (IRB – also known as the Fenians) attempted another in 1867. For various reasons, both of these risings failed but the IRB continued to exist as a secret society and hoped to organise another rising in the future. Organisations such as these wanted to create an Irish Republic (a country where all representatives are elected by the people and there is no ruling monarch) and some were prepared to use violence to achieve independence. Members of these

▲ Charles Kickham, member of the Young Irelanders and a leader of the IRB.

organisations therefore became known as **republicans**.

Other nationalists wanted to win more independence using peaceful political methods. These constitutional nationalists supported the **Irish Parliamentary Party (IPP)**. The IPP was a political party made up of Irish MPs who attended the British parliament. Members of the IPP were happy to remain within the UK but wanted an Irish parliament in Dublin that could pass laws on issues relevant to Ireland. An Irish parliament could pass laws on agriculture, health and education while foreign matters like defence and trade would be dealt with by Westminster. This idea was known as **Home Rule**. The IPP came very close to winning Home Rule for Ireland in 1886 and 1894 but they were narrowly defeated in the British parliament. The IPP in 1900 was led by **John Redmond** who still hoped to achieve Home Rule.

▲ John Redmond, leader of the IPP, who hoped to win Home Rule for Ireland peacefully.

UNIONISTS

▲ Edward Carson, leader of the Unionist Party, was strongly opposed to Home Rule.

Most Irish Catholics supported some form of independence from Britain, but most Irish Protestants wished to remain part of the United Kingdom. These unionists (so-called because they wanted to keep the 'union' between Ireland and Britain) were mostly located in the north east of Ireland. Ulster was the only area in Ireland that was industrialised and its ship-building, linen manufacturing and rope-making industries were very economically successful.

Ulster Protestants worried that 'Home Rule meant Rome Rule'. This meant that they believed an Irish Parliament dominated by Roman Catholics would religiously discriminate against them. They also feared that Home Rule could harm industries in Ulster which depended on open access to the markets in Britain. If Ireland was no longer a part of Britain, trade between the two countries would become more expensive.

The **Unionist Party** in Westminster was led by **Edward Carson** and **James Craig**. Many in the Unionist Party were confident that there would never be Home Rule but the unionist **Orange Order** was prepared to resist Home Rule by force if necessary.

▲ James Craig also opposed Home Rule. He organised massive unionist rallies to show their loyalty to the 'union'.

Questions

1. Where was the British Parliament located?
2. Explain the following terms: (a) nationalist (b) unionist.
3. What was the Irish Republican Brotherhood and what did its members want to achieve?
4. What was Home Rule?
5. Why did Ulster unionists believe that Home Rule would mean 'Rome rule'?
6. Match the following to the correct term:

	Unionist (U)	Nationalist (N)
(a) Irish Parliamentary Party		
(b) Orange Order		
(c) Edward Carson		
(d) Fenians		
(e) Irish Republican Brotherhood		
(f) John Redmond		
(g) James Craig		

● Social Life

▲ Michael Cusack helped to found the GAA in 1884.

At the beginning of the twentieth century, Ireland was an agricultural country. Half of all industrial jobs were located in Ulster and 40% of these were in Belfast alone. Farming was still the main occupation throughout the rest of Ireland. Emigration to America and Britain was still common for young people in search of work. To help them find jobs in Ireland or abroad, parents encouraged their children to speak English instead of Irish. English sports like soccer or rugby also became more popular throughout Ireland. This process of **anglicisation** (in this case, imitating the English in their literature, music, games, dress and ideas) led to a decline in the use of the Irish language and other Gaelic customs. In response to this, new cultural organisations were established to protect the Irish identity.

THE GAELIC ATHLETIC ASSOCIATION (GAA)

The **GAA** was founded in 1884. Its founding members included **Michael Cusack** and **Maurice Davin**. They wanted to:

* Promote traditional Gaelic games such as hurling, Gaelic football and handball.

* Help establish Gaelic football and hurling clubs throughout the island of Ireland.

The GAA proved to be a very successful organisation and soon there were GAA clubs throughout the country. Local parishes took great pride in their teams and the first All-Ireland club tournament was played in 1887.

▲ Douglas Hyde helped to found the Gaelic League.

THE GAELIC LEAGUE

In an attempt to halt the decline of the Irish language, Eoin MacNeill and Douglas Hyde established the **Gaelic League** in 1893. They did this by:

1. Establishing a newspaper called *An Claidheamh Solais* (the sword of light).

2. Sending **timirí** (travelling teachers) throughout the country to teach Irish.

3. Having St Patrick's Day designated as a national holiday.

4. Organising an annual cultural festival called the Oireachtas for Irish dancing and music.

In a similar way to the GAA, the Gaelic League was very successful and by 1905 it had 550 branches throughout Ireland.

▲ Eoin MacNeill was also a respected historian and linguist (person skilled in foreign languages).

By the way . . .

Pádraig Pearse, who became one of the leaders of the 1916 Rising, was an editor of *An Claidheamh Solais.*

Both the GAA and the Gaelic League were **infiltrated** (to join an organisation in order to secretly gain influence over its members) by members of the IRB who hoped to use these two organisations to promote independence for Ireland. Many of the leaders and members of the GAA and the Gaelic League would later participate in the 1916 Rising.

A poster advertising the annual Seachtain na Gaeilge (Irish week), c.1915-1916. ▶

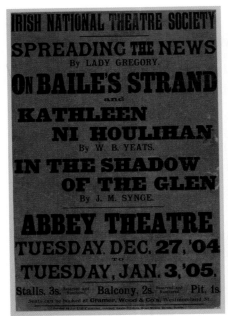

▲ A poster for the opening night of the Abbey Theatre at which Yeats's play *Kathleen Ní Houlihan* was presented.

ANGLO IRISH LITERARY REVIVAL

Another movement led by **WB Yeats**, **JM Synge** and **Lady Gregory** focused on traditional Irish stories and legends. They wrote plays and poetry in English that celebrated the Irish nation and its people. Yeats and Gregory founded the Abbey Theatre in 1903 to promote Irish writers. Famous plays such as *Playboy of the Western World* by Synge and *Kathleen Ní Houlihan* by Yeats were first performed here.

> **By the way . . .**
>
> *Playboy of the Western World* was so controversial that there was a riot on its opening night in Dublin in 1907!

▲ WB Yeats, one of Ireland's most famous poets, was part of a movement to promote Irish culture.

▲ Lady Gregory, a close friend of Yeats, co-founded the Abbey Theatre with him, 1903.

● The 1913 Dublin Lockout

Most of the people living in cities at the beginning of the twentieth century lived in awful conditions. Large parts of Dublin, Cork and Limerick were slums and unemployment was high. The jobs that did exist were often badly paid. In 1908, **Jim Larkin** founded the **Irish Transport and General Workers' Union (ITGWU)** to improve the wages and conditions of the workers. The Belfast branch was run by **James Connolly**. The ITGWU soon had 10,000 members and its growth caused concern among Irish employers. **William Martin Murphy**, owner of the Dublin United Tramways Company, the *Irish Independent*, the Imperial Hotel and Clery's department store, opposed the ITGWU.

▲ Jim Larkin worked hard to improve the working conditions and wages of workers in Ireland.

In 1913, Murphy demanded that all of his workers leave the ITGWU or else they would be fired. When Larkin called a strike in protest, Murphy **locked out** all members of the Union (he would not let them enter their workplace). This **Lockout** continued for five months. During the strike the workers were helped financially by trade unions in Britain and wealthy supporters. Eventually the workers gave up, left the ITGWU and returned to work.

Larkin left for America but Connolly remained in Ireland. He established the Irish Labour Party in 1912 to support Irish workers. During the 1913 Lockout, Connolly organised the **Irish Citizen Army** to protect workers from attacks from gangs

▲ Boys selling newspapers in Nassau Street outside a shop offering penny dinners.

hired by the employers and also from the police. He believed that a socialist revolution should be organised in Ireland to create an Irish Socialist Republic. As we will see, he hoped that this could be achieved through the 1916 Rising.

> **By the way...**
> The ITGWU continued to exist until 1990 when it joined with the Workers' Union of Ireland to form SIPTU.

▲ The Irish Citizen Army gathered outside Liberty Hall, which is the headquarters of SIPTU today.

Questions

1. What does anglicisation mean?
2. What were the aims of the GAA?
3. Why was the Gaelic League established?
4. Which methods did the Gaelic League use to achieve its aim?
5. Who set up the Abbey Theatre and why?
6. Which trade union did Jim Larkin establish and what was its aim?
7. Who was James Connolly? Give three points about him.
8. Write a paragraph about the 1913 Dublin Lockout. Give 5 points.
9. Why was the Irish Citizen Army established?
10. Match the following people to the correct organisation:

Leaders	Organisation
A Jim Larkin	1. The GAA
B W B Yeats and Lady Gregory	2. The Gaelic League
C William Martin Murphy	3. ITGWU
D Eoin MacNeill and Douglas Hyde	4. Dublin United Tramways Company
E Michael Cusack and Maurice Davin	5. The Irish Citizen Army
F James Connolly	6. The Abbey Theatre

Home Rule for Ireland

In the early twentieth century in Britain there were two main political parties:

▲ Herbert Asquith promised the Irish Parliamentary Party that he would introduce a Home Rule Bill.

1. The **Liberals (Whigs)** were led by **Herbert Asquith**. They had supported Home Rule for Ireland in the late nineteenth century but it had almost split the party. They were reluctant to propose Home Rule again in case the same problem arose.

2. The **Conservatives (Tories)** were led by **Andrew Bonar Law**. They opposed Home Rule and supported the Protestant Unionists in Ulster.

● Changes to the House of Lords

In 1909, the Liberals, who were in government at the time, proposed a budget that increased taxes. It was passed by the British House of Commons but was **vetoed** (rejected) by the House of Lords. The House of Lords was made up of rich landowners and Protestant clergy who did not want to increase taxes. Asquith called a new election and King George V threatened to install new Liberal Lords to replace the stubborn Conservative Lords if the House of Lords interfered with a law passed by the Commons.

The 1910 election produced a very exciting result:

Party	Number of Members of Parliament (MPs)
Liberal Party	273 seats
Conservative Party	252 seats
Irish Parliamentary Party (IPP)	84 seats
Labour Party	42 seats
Unionist Party	19 seats

This meant that the IPP held the balance of power. Asquith promised to introduce a Home Rule Bill if the IPP would support the Liberals. Redmond, leader of the IPP, agreed and Asquith passed the Parliament Act in 1911. This Act meant that the House of Lords could only veto a bill twice before they had to allow it through. In 1912, Asquith passed the Home Rule Bill which – even with two vetos by the House of Lords – would become law in 1914.

● Unionist Reaction

▲ The signing of the Solemn League and Covenant. Edward Carson is the man leaning on the table.

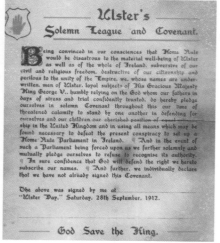

▲ The Solemn League and Covenant

The leader of the Unionist Party, Edward Carson, was determined to oppose Home Rule.

To show the strength of the unionists, he organised huge demonstrations. In September 1912, over 400,000 people signed a document called the **Solemn League and Covenant** stating that Ulster unionists would never accept Home Rule.

> **By the way . . .**
> Many of those who signed the Solemn League and Covenant used their own blood to sign their names.

In 1913, Carson and **James Craig** (a Unionist Party MP who later became Northern Ireland's Prime Minister) encouraged unionists to set up the **Ulster Volunteer Force (UVF)**. This organisation was prepared to oppose Home Rule with force if necessary. Soon they had almost 100,000 members. In 1914, the UVF managed to smuggle 24,600 rifles and 3 million rounds of ammunition from Germany into Larne, County Antrim. They also had the support of Bonar Law, leader of the British Conservative Party, who stated that there was 'no length of resistance to which Ulster can go in which I would not be prepared to support them'.

▲ Irish Volunteers marching on St. Patrick's Day, 1916 in Cork.

Nationalist reaction

Nationalists were delighted to have achieved Home Rule through peaceful methods, but were concerned at the reaction of the unionists. In 1913, Eoin MacNeill, founder of the Gaelic League, now set up the **Irish National Volunteers** in response to the UVF. They soon had almost 160,000 members but their attempt to import guns into Howth, County Dublin in 1914 was not as successful as the UVF. They managed to import just 900 rifles and 25,000 rounds of ammunition. Nevertheless, it appeared that Ireland was sliding towards civil war.

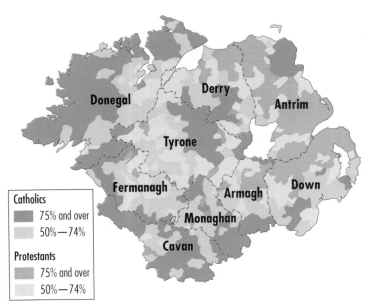

Catholics
- 75% and over
- 50%—74%

Protestants
- 75% and over
- 50%—74%

▲ The percentage of Protestants and Catholics in Northern Ireland, 1911.

By the way . . .

The British Army officers located in the Curragh Army Barracks in Kildare told the British Prime Minister, Asquith, that they would rather resign than force Home Rule on Ulster. This was a major problem because Asquith knew he needed the support of the British army to enforce Home Rule in Ulster. This event was known as the **Curragh Mutiny**.

Partition

Asquith now tried to compromise with Redmond (who had taken over from MacNeill as leader of the Irish National Volunteers) and Carson.

Asquith proposed to **partition** (divide) Ireland. The area in the north where the majority of unionists lived would remain in the United Kingdom while the rest of Ireland would have Home Rule. The only problem between Redmond and Carson was where to draw the line of partition. Carson wanted to include six counties while Redmond thought that only the four counties with unionist majorities should be included.

● World War I

These arguments were put to one side when Germany invaded Belgium in August 1914 and World War I broke out. All sides agreed to postpone Home Rule until after the war. Both Carson and Redmond called on the Ulster and Irish Volunteers to fight against Germany for the freedom of small countries such as Belgium. The vast majority of the Irish Volunteers agreed with Redmond and they formed the **National Volunteers**. A much smaller group of about 10,000 Irish Volunteers led by Eoin MacNeill refused to join the British Army.

▲ John Redmond inspects the National Volunteers.

Questions

1. Explain the following words:
   (a) Veto   (b) MPs   (c) Westminster
2. Name the two main political parties in Westminster and their leaders in 1909.
3. What was the Solemn League and Covenant?
4. Why was the UVF established?
5. Why did the British government suggest the partition of Ireland?
6. Why did Redmond think that only four counties should form Northern Ireland?
7. What event caused the postponement of Home Rule?
8. Who formed the National Volunteers and why?
9. Write an account of a unionist who opposed Home Rule in 1912. Use the following headings as a guide:
   (a) Family background
   (b) Reasons for opposing Home Rule
   (c) Political parties and leaders
   (d) Methods of opposition

1916

▲ Pádraig Pearse believed the only way Ireland could achieve independence from Britain was by force.

Just as the IRB had secretly joined other organisations such as the GAA and the Gaelic League, it now infiltrated the Irish Volunteers without MacNeill's knowledge. They believed that 'England's difficulty was Ireland's opportunity'. The British government did not have the resources to keep watch on well-known Irish rebels as it had to withdraw many of its troops from Ireland to fight in World War I. To the IRB this seemed to be the perfect time to organise a rebellion to gain full independence from Britain. In 1915, a five-man IRB **Military Council** was set up. Its members were **Pádraig Pearse**, **Thomas Clarke**, **Seán MacDiarmada**, **Joseph Plunkett** and **Éamonn Ceannt**. They began to plan a rebellion. MacNeill remained unaware of their plans. The Military Council discovered that James Connolly was also planning a socialist rebellion using the Irish Citizen Army. Members of the Military Council explained their plans to him and in 1916, both he and **Thomas MacDonagh** were included in the planning of the rebellion. They decided that the rebellion would take place on Easter Sunday 23 April, 1916.

If the Military Council was successful, MacNeill had to be persuaded to let the Irish Volunteers join the rebellion. The IRB achieved this by tricking him. Plunkett wrote a letter pretending to be from the British authorities in Dublin Castle declaring the Irish Volunteers to be illegal and ordering its leaders to be arrested. This letter became known as the *Castle Document* . The Council let MacNeill believe this letter was from the British government. MacNeill agreed to put the Irish Volunteers on full alert.

The IRB asked Germany to provide support for their rebellion. The Germans would not send soldiers but offered a shipload of rifles and machine guns. **Roger Casement** was sent to Germany to bring the ship back to Ireland. On 20 April 1916 the ship, called the *Aud*, was captured by the British navy off the coast of Kerry and Casement was arrested.

When MacNeill found out that the *Aud* had been captured and that the *Castle Document* had been written by Plunkett, he cancelled all involvement in the rebellion. He put a notice in the newspapers alerting Irish Volunteers that all plans for the rebellion on Sunday 23 April were cancelled.

▲ Roger Casement was found guilty of treason and hanged in August 1916.

NO PARADES!

Irish Volunteer Marches Cancelled

A SUDDEN ORDER.

The Easter manoeuvres of the Irish Volunteers, which were announced to begin to-day, and which were to have been taken part in by all the branches of the organisation in city and country, were unexpectedly cancelled last night.

The following is the announcement communicated to the Press last evening by the Staff of the Volunteers:—

April 22, 1916.

Owing to the very critical position, all orders given to Irish Volunteers for to-morrow, Easter Sunday, are hereby rescinded, and no parades, marches, or other movements of Irish Volunteers will take place. Each individual Volunteer will obey this order strictly in every particular.

EOIN MACNEILL,
Chief of Staff,
Irish Volunteers.

GRUESOME STORIES

Result in a Girl Killing Her Lover and Attempting Suicide.

To remove her lover from the further dangers of the war, a Prague servant girl named Erna Putzmann shot him and then tried in half a dozen ways to commit suicide. The young man, the son of a Prague professor, had been fighting in the Carpathians and Serbia, and had written the girl most gruesome stories of seeing prisoners' heads chopped off and like horrors.

These tales seemed to have preyed on the girl's mind, and when her lover's leave was expiring she was unable to bear the thought of his going back to the trenches, so she killed him, and then tried to shoot herself, but failed. Next she made two

ARMS SEIZED

Collapsible Boat on Kerry Coast

"MAN OF UNKNOWN NATIONALITY."

A collapsible boat containing a quantity of arms and ammunition was seized at Carrahane Strand, Tralee Bay, on Friday morning.

A man of unknown nationality found on the shore close by was arrested and kept in custody.

It is not known where the boat came from or for whom the arms were intended.

TWO MEN ARRESTED.

Realm Act Case in Kerry—Well-Known G.A.A. Man in Custody.

(From Our Correspondent.)
Tralee, Saturday.

During last night the rooms of Mr. Austin Stack, Tralee, were searched by the police and some time afterwards himself and Mr. Cornelius Collins, a Post Office official, Dublin, and a native of Abbeyfeale, were arrested and kept in the police barracks overnight.

They were charged to-day, before Mr. Wynn, R.M., under the defence of the Realm Act, and remanded for eight days, without bail.

The Irish Volunteers had a special mobilisation last evening, and marched to Mr. Stack's lodgings. They afterwards proceeded to their headquarters, where an armed sentry was posted, and relieved at intervals during the night.

WANTED UNITY AT HOME.

THREE DROWNED

Tragic Motoring Affair in Kerry

A WRONG TURNING.

Tralee, Saturday.

A sensation was caused in Tralee to-day by the news of a tragic motor accident at Killorglin, which resulted in the deaths of three men unknown.

Details to hand indicate that a party travelling in a Limerick registered motor car from Killarney to Tralee stopped en route at Killorglin for a supply of petrol. On leaving the town the chauffeur inquired as to the Tralee road. He was told to take "the first turn on the left." He unfortunately obeyed the direction to the strict letter, and turned the car down towards Ballykissane quay, which is locally regarded as a "bohereen." His informant was under the impression that he would continue until meeting the main road and overlook the "bohereen."

The car, which was occupied by three passengers and the chauffeur, sped down the by-road and plunged into the River Lane, which at that point is of great depth. In some unexplained fashion the driver extricated himself from the steering wheel and got safely ashore, but the other occupants of the car were not so fortunate.

Contradictory rumours are afloat as to the identity of the unfortunate passengers, the chauffeur, it is alleged, disclaiming all knowledge of who they were.

The chauffeur gave the alarm to people living in the vicinity, and dragging operations immediately stated for the recovery of the bodies.

ALLEGED SHOPBREAKER.

Jumped Through a Plate Glass Window to Evade Arrest.

How a young man jumped through the

▲ This page from the *Sunday Independent* on Easter Sunday, 23 April 1916, shows MacNeill's notice cancelling the Rising (referred to as a 'march') as well as news of Casement's arrest (Arms Seized) and the accidental drowning of three men on their way to meet the *Aud*.

The IRB Military Council faced great difficulties. Without the guns from the *Aud* and the support of the Irish Volunteers, it appeared that the rebellion was doomed. Nevertheless, they decided to continue with the rebellion. Even though the leaders knew that the chances of success were small, they hoped that their **blood sacrifice** (heroic deaths) would inspire future generations to fight for independence.

Questions

1. What was meant by 'England's difficulty is Ireland's opportunity'?
2. Name the members of the IRB Military Council.
3. What was the *Castle Document*?
4. Why did MacNeill decide not to support the rebellion?
5. What is meant by blood sacrifice?

Easter Rising

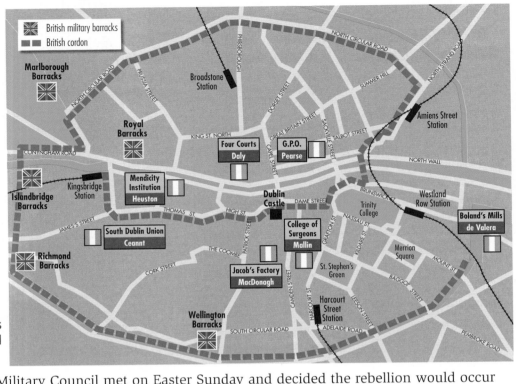

The key locations in Dublin occupied by the rebels. ▶

The Military Council met on Easter Sunday and decided the rebellion would occur on Bank Holiday Monday instead. Those members of the Military Council who were also members of the Irish Volunteers, such as Pearse, called their members out to fight. Due to the cancellation notice in the newspapers by MacNeill it was mostly Volunteers in Dublin who responded. In total 1,500 members of the Irish Volunteers and the Irish Citizen Army took control of key buildings throughout Dublin.

Most of the leaders were located at the General Post Office (GPO) on Sackville Street (now O'Connell Street). From the steps, Pádraig Pearse read out the **Proclamation of the Irish Republic** to rather shocked passers-by. The British were unprepared and only 400 troops were on duty. Soon reinforcements arrived and within two days they outnumbered the Irish rebels 20 to 1. Furthermore, a gunship called the *Helga* had begun shelling the GPO from the River Liffey. By the Friday, the GPO was in flames and Pearse moved the rebels into Moore Street. On Saturday 29 April, Pearse surrendered and soon all other rebel positions followed.

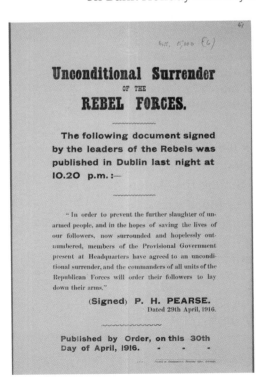

▲ Surrender notice issued by Pearse

> **By the way . . .**
> As Connolly marched out to occupy the GPO he said 'we are going to be slaughtered'.

REACTIONS TO THE RISING

▲ A view of Sackville Street (O'Connell Street) and Eden Quay after the 1916 Rising. The O'Connell Monument is visible in the top left-hand corner.

The Rising caused great devastation in the city: 230 civilians, 64 rebels and 132 British soldiers were killed. Most of Sackville Street (now O'Connell Street) was destroyed and there was widespread **looting** (theft). The citizens of Dublin were not happy with the destruction caused to their city, and the republican prisoners were jeered at as they were marched through the city to prison. Almost 3,000 people were arrested and half of them were sent to prisons in Britain. Ninety of the leaders of the Rising were tried in courts and sentenced to death. Between 3 and 12 May, 15 leaders were shot including all the members of the IRB Military Council. These executions began to turn the public's opinion of the Rising against the British. The last execution was of James Connolly who had to be shot while sitting in a chair due to his injuries.

> **By the way . . .**
>
> Éamon de Valera took over Boland's Mill in Dublin during the Rising. He was not shot because the British ceased executing the leaders due to the change in public opinion at home and abroad.

Questions

1. Write a paragraph about the 1916 Rising. Give at least six points.
2. Why was Sackville Street so badly damaged?
3. Why did the people of Dublin jeer the Irish rebels as they marched through the city?
4. What happened to the leaders of the Rising?

● Change in Public Opinion

Over the following months, the public view changed from anger towards the rebels to admiration for their bravery and sacrifice. The imprisonment of thousands of innocent people also increased public sympathy for the rebels. Those who had been sentenced to death were sent to Britain to **internment camps** (prisons for those imprisoned without trial) but were released within a year. The British government became increasingly aware of the growing support in Ireland for the Rising. They realised that executing more of the Irish prisoners could lead to the rebels being regarded as **martyrs** (a person who dies for the cause she/he believes in).

During the time these prisoners spent in the internment camps, many of them became strong supporters of Irish independence through violent means if required. People like **Éamon de Valera** and **Michael Collins** returned from these camps with far greater determination to achieve independence from Britain.

● Sinn Féin

▲ Arthur Griffith, leader of Sinn Féin.

Sinn Féin, a political party, had been set up by **Arthur Griffith** in 1905. He believed in seeking full independence from Britain through peaceful methods but had not achieved large support. However, after the 1916 Rising, the party's popularity grew because:

1. Due to a lack of accurate information, the British thought the 1916 Rising had been organised by Sinn Féin. Arthur Griffith was arrested and sent to the internment camps in Britain. He became close friends with other leaders of the Rising in the camp. This mistaken connection between the Rising and Sinn Féin meant that most nationalists now supported Sinn Féin rather than the Irish Parliamentary Party (IPP).

2. Arthur Griffith resigned as leader of Sinn Féin in 1917 to allow Éamon de Valera, one of the leaders of the 1916 Rising, take over.

3. In 1918, it seemed very likely that the British government would introduce conscription into Ireland to get more troops to fight in World War I. Sinn Féin along with all other Irish political parties opposed this idea. When the plan was dropped, it was Sinn Féin that got the credit for this opposition.

4. The British then arrested de Valera and Griffith among others on suspicion of organising another rebellion. This increased Sinn Féin's popularity among nationalists even further.

▲ Crowds welcoming home family and friends who had spent time in British internment camps.

RETURN OF I.R.A. PRISONERS, JUNE, 1917. (June 21st)
COUNTESS MARKIEVICZ ARRIVES AT LIBERTY HALL, DUBLIN.

▲ Countess Markievicz's return from a British internment camp (1917).

● 1918 General Election

After the end of World War I, the British Prime Minister called a general election. For the first time since 1910, people were going to vote for a new government. Furthermore, women were given the vote for the first time. Very few people in Ireland supported Home Rule anymore and so people voted in massive numbers for Sinn Féin. While the Unionist Party continued to have strong support in Ulster, the results showed a massive change in the nationalist parties. Sinn Féin won 73 seats in comparison to the IPP who gained a mere 7 seats. This made Sinn Féin the biggest political party in Ireland by far.

By the way . . .

Countess Markievicz was arrested for her part in the 1916 Rising but she was not executed because she was a woman. She spent 13 months in prison. Later she became the first woman to be elected as a member of Parliament (MP).

Questions

1. Give two reasons why public opinion towards the 1916 rebels changed.
2. Name the founder of Sinn Féin.
3. Why did the popularity of Sinn Féin grow after 1916? Give four reasons.
4. In your opinion, was the 1916 Rising a success? Give reasons for your answer.
5. Do you agree with the idea of blood sacrifice? Give reasons for your answer.

Irish War of Independence

● Dáil Éireann

▲ The First Dáil met in January 1919. This picture from later that year includes Collins (second from left sitting down), Brugha (beside Collins), Griffith (to his left) and de Valera in the middle. Markievicz is not present in the photograph.

Sinn Féin won 73 seats in the 1918 general election. They promised that they would not go to Westminster, but would set up an Irish government instead. On 21 January 1919 they did this by establishing Dáil Éireann (dáil means 'meeting' in Irish). Members of the Dáil were referred to as teachtaí dála (TDs), which means representatives of the Dáil. Many of the elected TDs were still in prison in Britain so they were not able to attend, but 27 TDs did attend the first meeting. They elected Cathal Brugha as President in the absence of de Valera who was still in prison. This first Dáil declared that Ireland was a republic and sent delegates to the Paris Peace conference (see Chapter 11, International Relations in Twentieth Century Europe, page 300) to gain recognition for Irish independence.

In February 1919, Michael Collins organised de Valera's escape from Lincoln Jail in Britain. The second meeting of the Dáil was on 1 April and de Valera was voted in as President of the new government. Other members of the government included:

Arthur Griffith	Vice-President and Minister for Home Affairs
Countess Markievicz	Minister for Labour
Cathal Brugha	Minister for Defence
Michael Collins	Minister for Finance (also in charge of organising a military campaign if Britain tried to prevent Irish independence)

• Sinn Féin Government in Ireland

De Valera then travelled to America to try and persuade the American President, Woodrow Wilson, to support Irish independence. He failed but managed to raise over $4 million (almost €30 million in today's money) to help run the new government. In addition to these funds, the Dáil raised over £300,000 (just over €10 million in today's money) from the Irish people. With this money they put in place some reforms.

1. New Sinn Féin law courts were created instead of the British courts.

2. The Irish Volunteers acted as policemen instead of the British Royal Irish Constabulary (RIC).

Many town and county councils supported the new Irish government. However, these peaceful changes in the running of Ireland were not to last. The British government declared Dáil Éireann illegal in late 1919. It was prepared to stop its activities by force if necessary. Certain members of the Dáil were also prepared to use force to protect the new Irish Republic. These TDs believed violence was now the only way to achieve full independence from Britain.

▲ Éamon de Valera, Michael Collins and Harry Boland – three survivors of the Rising, shown here having a chat between sessions of Dáil Éireann.

All of these political decisions took place against a backdrop of growing violence in Ireland. On 21 January 1919, two constables of the RIC were killed in Soloheadbeg, County Tipperary. This had not been authorised by the Dáil, but had been organised by the Irish Volunteers. The Volunteers were now more commonly known as the **Irish Republican Army (IRA)** and were run by Michael Collins although Cathal Brugha was Minister for Defence. The killings in Soloheadbeg marked the beginning of the Irish War of Independence.

▲ Michael Collins

Questions

1. Explain the following terms:
   (a) TDs   (b) Dáil Éireann   (c) IRA
2. Why did de Valera travel to the USA?
3. What reforms did the Irish Dáil make?
4. What event marked the beginning of the Irish War of Independence?
5. Who was in charge of the IRA?

● The IRA

Michael Collins was Director of Intelligence for the Volunteers. He organised a wide network of spies throughout Ireland. He used information from these spies to arrange for attacks throughout Ireland against the police force, the Royal Irish Constabulary (RIC). Instead of fighting the British army in open warfare, Collins used **guerrilla** (this is the Spanish word for 'little war') warfare. This involved small numbers of volunteers planting bombs and carrying out ambushes and killings. They did not wear uniforms so it was easy for them to mingle and blend in with the population after any attack. These groups of guerrilla fighters were known as **flying columns** due to the speed of their attacks. Collins knew that many rebellions had been defeated due to **British informants** (people who told the British the plans for the rebellions). To avoid this, Collins organised a small group of assassins called the **Squad**. They killed anyone who was thought to be a British spy or informant.

▲ Very few clear photos of Michael Collins were available at this time so he was able to travel around Dublin on his bicycle under the noses of the British security forces who were anxiously trying to find him.

● British forces

In early 1920, the British government decided to deal with the increasing number of attacks by Collins' flying columns. There were a large number of ex-soldiers from World War I in Britain who were unemployed so the British government sent them to Ireland. They did not have proper uniforms, but used khaki (a colour also known as 'tan') uniforms mixed with RIC jackets which were black and green. For this reason they became known as the **Black and Tans**. Later, the British government also sent ex-army officers who were known as **Auxiliaries**. By the end of 1920 there were over 40,000 men in the British army and police force in Ireland.

▲ A group of Black and Tans guarding a street in Dublin after a shooting.

During 1920, 182 policemen, including Black and Tans, were killed by the IRA. The British reacted by:

1. Imposing curfews on towns. If anyone was found on the streets after 10 p.m. they could be arrested.

2. Searching houses for guns and suspected IRA members.

3. Terrorising the local population by shooting at them as they walked down the roads.

MAIN EVENTS

Between 1919 and 1921 a number of incidents occurred to turn the Irish population against the British.

1. The Sinn Féin Lord Mayor of Cork, Terence MacSwiney, was arrested. He was imprisoned in Britain and went on hunger strike. He died after 73 days.

2. On Sunday 21 November 1920 (known as **Bloody Sunday**), Michael Collins' Squad killed 11 British secret service men. In retaliation, the Black and Tans surrounded a Gaelic football match in Croke Park and shot 12 spectators and players.

3. In December 1920, Tom Barry's flying column ambushed Auxiliaries in Kilmichael, County Cork. One week later, much of the centre of Cork city was burnt to the ground by the Black and Tans.

> **By the way . . .**
> The Hogan Stand in Croke Park is named after the Tipperary goalkeeper, Michael Hogan, who was killed on Bloody Sunday, 1920.

◄ Parts of Cork city were burned in 1920 by the Black and Tans in revenge for the ambush of Auxiliaries by a flying column.

TRUCE AGREED

By the summer of 1921 the IRA had run out of guns and ammunition. Meanwhile, the American government criticised the British government for the level of violence they were using in Ireland. Roughly 2,000 British soldiers and members of the RIC and 752 IRA men had been killed, with 866 wounded. Negotiations took place between the IRA and the British government and a truce was declared on 11 July 1921.

Questions

1. Explain the following terms:
   (a) Guerrilla   (b) Black and Tans   (c) Auxiliaries   (d) Flying columns
2. What did Collins use the Squad for?
3. What measures did the British government use to stop the IRA?
4. What happened on Sunday 21 November 1920?
5. Why did the Black and Tans burn down the centre of Cork?
6. Why did the IRA and the British government decide to begin negotiations about a truce?

• The Negotiations

▲ Lloyd George was famous as a skilled negotiator and was known as the Welsh Wizard.

British Prime Minister Lloyd George passed the **Government of Ireland Act** in 1920. This divided Ireland into Northern Ireland and Southern Ireland. Carson (leader of the Unionist Party in Westminister) had agreed to a six-county Northern Ireland which would have its own parliament, while Southern Ireland was to get Home Rule in the 26 remaining counties. James Craig was elected as Northern Ireland's first prime minister.

Sinn Féin would not accept anything less than full independence so negotiations began with Lloyd George. Arthur Griffith, Michael Collins, Robert Barton, Eamon Duggan and George Gavan Duffy led the group to London to negotiate while de Valera remained in Ireland. De Valera believed that because he was President, any final decision would have to be referred back to him before agreement could be reached. He hoped that this would stop the delegates from being rushed by the British into signing anything they did not want. Later historians have argued that de Valera may have chosen not to go to London as he already knew that the British would not agree to a Republic. By not going he avoided being seen by the public as having compromised with the British. He may have also wanted to lessen Collins' growing popularity by having Collins deliver any bad news.

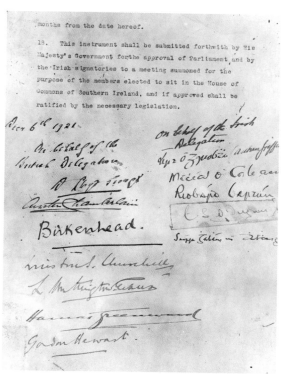

▲ The Treaty signed by the British and Irish delegates.

The Irish delegates' aims were:

- Full independence for Ireland.

- A full 32-county Ireland under Dublin rule.

The British wanted:

- Ireland to remain within the British Commonwealth (independent but still with the King as the head of the country).

- The partition of the island between Northern Ireland and Southern Ireland.

The negotiations continued for two months before Lloyd George put pressure on the delegates to sign an agreement. He told them that if they did not sign, he would begin an 'immediate and terrible war'. On 6 December 1921 the delegates signed the **Treaty**.

The Treaty

1. Southern Ireland would now be called the **Irish Free State**.

2. The Irish Free State would have control over many aspects of government but would not become a republic.

3. The Free State would remain part of the **British Commonwealth**. The British King would continue to be head of the state and all TDs would have to swear an **Oath of Allegiance** (loyalty) to him.

4. The British would have three naval ports within Ireland: Lough Swilly, Queenstown (Cobh) and Berehaven.

5. Northern Ireland would remain part of the United Kingdom

6. A **Boundary Commission** would be set up to decide where the border between Northern Ireland and the Irish Free State would be placed. The Commission would have one member from the Free State, one from Northern Ireland and an independent chairman.

▲ Under the terms of the Treaty, Southern Ireland was called the Irish Free State and Britain kept three naval ports within it.

● Irish reaction

When the delegates returned to Ireland, they found that the Treaty had caused a huge split among the people. De Valera, Brugha and others believed that the delegates had sold out to the British. Others saw this as the best deal possible. On 14 December, the Dáil met to begin a very bitter debate about the Treaty.

ARGUMENTS FOR THE TREATY

- Ireland had much more freedom under the Treaty than it would have under Home Rule.

- While it was not full independence, it would now be easier to achieve it. Collins believed that it gave Ireland the 'freedom to achieve freedom'.

- Peace had been achieved and just in time as the IRA no longer had the resources to continue fighting.

ARGUMENTS AGAINST THE TREATY

- The Free State was not free as it still had the British King as head of state.

- TDs could not be loyal to the republic while also swearing an Oath of Allegiance to the King.

- Too many people had died in the quest for a fully-independent Ireland for the Dáil to accept anything less.

● The Dáil Vote on the Treaty, 7 January 1921

After a long and very angry passionate debate, the Treaty was voted on.

For the Treaty   64 votes

Against the Treaty   57 votes

The Treaty was narrowly passed by the Dáil. De Valera resigned his position as President in protest and Griffith was elected President instead, with Collins as his deputy.

> ### By the way . . .
> After signing the Treaty, Lord Birkenhead said, 'I may have just signed my political death warrant' to which Collins replied 'I may have signed my actual death warrant'.

Questions

1. What did the Government of Ireland Act of 1920 create?
2. Why did de Valera not want to be part of the negotiating team?
3. Do you think de Valera was right not to go? Give reasons.
4. What were the two aims of the Irish negotiating team in London?
5. What were the two aims of the British negotiating team in London?
6. Why did the Irish TDs have to swear an Oath of Allegiance to the King of England?
7. What was the Boundary Commission?
8. Give the arguments for and against the Treaty.
9. In your opinion, were Collins and the other negotiators right to sign the Treaty?

The Irish Free State

The **Provisional** (temporary) Government of Ireland was led by Arthur Griffith. They oversaw the withdrawal of British troops from Ireland and the creation of a new Irish government. The Treaty divided Sinn Féin into pro-Treaty and anti-Treaty groups and this was the case for the IRA too. IRA supporters of the Treaty were known as the Free State Army or **Regulars** and the anti-Treaty IRA were the **Irregulars**. In April 1922, Irregulars led by Rory O'Connor occupied the Four Courts and other buildings throughout Dublin as a protest against the Dáil's acceptance of the Treaty.

Collins was reluctant to attack any of his former colleagues in the IRA so he waited to take action until after the general election of June 1922. The election was based on support for the Treaty with both sides putting forward candidates. The results were very clear:

• Irish General Election, June 1922

Pro-Treaty Sinn Féin candidates	58 seats
Anti-Treaty Sinn Féin candidates	35 seats
Other candidates (all of whom were pro-Treaty)	35 seats

During this time, two Irregulars assassinated a leading British unionist named Henry Wilson. Later, General O'Connell of the Free State army was kidnapped and Collins was forced to act. On 28 June, Collins began his attack on the Four Courts. The Civil War had begun.

▲ On 28 June Collins began shelling the Four Courts, which was occupied by Anti-Treaty forces.

• The Civil War

After two days of bombardment, the Irregulars in the Four Courts surrendered. The fighting continued in and around O'Connell Street before the Irregulars were defeated on 5 July. Sixty-four people had been killed including Cathal Brugha. Collins' close friend, Harry Boland, was shot on 31 July in Skerries by Free State soldiers.

The Irregulars were now outnumbered and out-gunned. Slowly the Free State Army pushed the Irregulars further south towards Munster. Limerick was captured on 20 July. Cork city fell to the Free State army on 12 August. From this point on, the Irregulars began to use guerrilla warfare.

By the way...

Unfortunately, before the Irregulars surrendered, the Four Courts caught fire. The Public Record Office and its collection of historical records were destroyed.

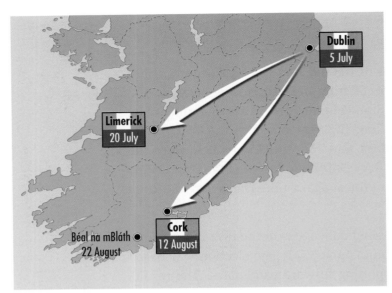

▲ Dublin, Cork and Limerick were under the Free State's control by the end of July 1922.

On 12 August, Griffith died and on 22 August Michael Collins was killed in an ambush by Irregulars at **Béal na mBláth**, County Cork. Collins' death was mourned by both sides of the Civil War. William T Cosgrave replaced Griffith as President in September and immediately brought in tough new laws. The **Special Powers Act** allowed Irregulars to be arrested, tried and executed for a number of new offences including carrying an unlicensed gun.

These new laws made it impossible for the Irregulars to continue fighting. In April 1923 their chief of staff (leader) Liam Lynch was killed. In May, de Valera and the new chief of staff, Frank Aiken, agreed to a ceasefire with the Free State Army.

By the way . . .

Kevin O'Higgins ordered the execution of Rory O'Connor who was his best man at his wedding.

RESULTS OF THE CIVIL WAR

1. The Civil War cost 927 lives including 77 people who were executed by the Irish government. At the beginning of 1923, 12,000 anti-Treaty soldiers were in prison.

2. The country was deeply divided. Families and friends had been split into either pro-Treaty or anti-Treaty supporters. This divide shaped the politics of Ireland for many years. Some say it still influences the politics of the country.

3. The damage done to the country's cities, roads and railways came to £30 million (over €1 billion today).

Questions

1. Looking at the results from the 1922 General Election do you think the Irish population supported the Treaty or not?

2. What events finally began the Irish Civil War?

3. When and where was Michael Collins killed?

4. What did William T Cosgrave's Special Powers Act allow the Free State government do?

5. Outline the results of the Irish Civil War.

● Cumann na nGaedhael

In 1922 the main political party was Sinn Féin. After the Treaty and the Civil War, the party was split in two. The pro-Treaty supporters formed a new party called **Cumann na nGaedhael** (Union of the Irish) while the anti-Treaty side kept the name Sinn Féin. The new Cumann na nGaedhael government was led by **William T Cosgrave** and **Kevin O'Higgins** as the Minister for Justice. This government set about creating a new state.

▲ William T Cosgrave and Kevin O'Higgins were pro-Treaty supporters who founded a new political party called Cumann na nGaedhael.

ACHIEVEMENTS

1. New Constitution and Oireachtas

Cumann na nGaedhael wrote a new **constitution** (rules on how to run the state). They established the **Oireachtas** (houses of parliament). The first house was named Dáil Éireann. Its members are directly elected by the people. The second house was the Seanad (senate). Its members are appointed from different parts of Irish society. Sinn Féin refused to attend the Dáil because of the Oath of Allegiance to the King.

2. New Police Force

Kevin O'Higgins set up a new police force (**An Garda Síochána**) to replace the RIC. After years of living with security forces armed with guns, the population was happy to accept these new unarmed police officers.

3. Irish Versions of Currency

Although Ireland continued to use the same currency as Britain, it issued its own Irish versions of coins, stamps and notes.

4. Teaching of Irish

The government also insisted that the Irish language was to be taught in schools.

These achievements were important to create a sense of normality in the country and soon law and order returned.

▲ An Irish stamp worth two pence.

PROBLEMS

The Cumann na nGaedhael government also faced some difficulties.

1. Army Mutiny

The army was far too large for a country at peace. O'Higgins decided to reduce the numbers in the army from 60,000 to 20,000. In March 1924, army officers who did not like this proposal demanded that the government abandon its plans. O'Higgins saw this as a mutiny and arrested those opposing the plans. Other officers were forced to resign but were given pensions or found work in the Garda Síochána.

2. Law and Order

Many people in Ireland still disliked the Treaty and the new government. IRA Irregulars still had guns and posed a threat to peace in the state. O'Higgins introduced **Public Safety Acts** in 1923 and 1924. These allowed the government to arrest and imprison members of the IRA. In 1926 the Public Safety (Emergency Powers) Act was passed which allowed for internment.

3. Assassination of O'Higgins

Even with all these new powers of arrest and imprisonment, a threat remained. In July 1927 Kevin O'Higgins was assassinated by three members of the IRA while on his way to mass. Another Public Safety Act was passed that created special criminal courts and banned membership of a number of organisations.

4. The Boundary Commission

During the negotiations in London on the Treaty, Collins and Griffith were led to believe that Tyrone and Fermanagh, Derry city and Newry would be transferred to the Free State. When the Boundary Commission was established in 1924 it decided that the border had been in existence for a number of years and so it was reluctant to change it greatly. Cosgrave was very disappointed by this decision. However, there were so many other problems requiring the government's attention that Cosgrave decided to put the issue to one side until more urgent problems had been resolved. As a result the border remained as it was in 1920.

THE GREAT TURBINES, SHANNON HYDRO ELECTRIC SCHEME, ARDNACRUSHA, LIMERICK.

▲ The Great Turbines stand at the Shannon Hydroelectric Scheme in Ardnacrusha, Limerick, Ireland.

The Economy

After so many years of fighting, the Irish economy was in a bad state. There was very little industry in Ireland at the time, so the government focused on agriculture instead.

- The **Agricultural Credit Corporation** (ACC) was created to provide loans to farmers to improve their produce (e.g. beef, milk, wheat). Tax cuts encouraged farmers to produce more food to feed the population and to export the surplus to Britain.

- The government also created the **Shannon Scheme**. This scheme involved building a hydroelectric power station on the River Shannon at Ardnacrusha. It was completed in 1929.

- The **Carlow Sugar Company** was set up to produce sugar from local sugar beet.

- The **Electricity Supply Board (ESB)** was established in 1927 to distribute electricity throughout Ireland.

While there was a slight increase in the number of people employed in industry during these years, over 50% of the population still relied on agriculture as their main source of income. About 20,000 people left Ireland each year to look for work in Britain and the USA. Despite the high unemployment rates in America as a result of the Great Depression, the numbers of Irish people emigrating to the USA continued to rise as they tried to escape the poverty in Ireland.

● Political Developments

In 1923 a general election was called. Even though Sinn Féin refused to recognise the Free State, they still contested the election.

RESULTS OF THE IRISH GENERAL ELECTION, MAY 1923	
Cumann na nGaedhael	63 seats
Sinn Féin	44 seats
Labour	14 seats

Sinn Féin's refusal to attend the Dáil because of the Oath of Allegiance meant that Labour was the main opposition party to Cumann na nGaedhael. In 1926, de Valera proposed to the Sinn Féin *ardfheis* (annual conference) that the party could take its seats in the Dáil if the Oath was removed. His proposal was rejected and de Valera resigned from Sinn Féin. He established a new party called **Fianna Fáil** (warriors of destiny) with a number of other Sinn Féin members including Frank Aiken and Seán Lemass.

After Kevin O'Higgins was killed in 1927, Cosgrave introduced the **Electoral Amendment Act**. This stated that all elected TDs had to take the Oath of Allegiance or give up their seats in the Dáil. Faced with losing all their seats, de Valera and Fianna Fáil decided to take the Oath and enter the Dáil.

Cumann na nGaedhael continued in government between 1927 and 1932 but became increasingly unpopular. This was because:

1. The worldwide Great Depression caused an increase in unemployment and emigration.

2. Ireland had still not developed much industry and continued to be heavily reliant on agriculture.

3. Fianna Fáil became very good at organising its support. De Valera set up *The Irish Press* in 1931 so that Fianna Fáil's views could be spread throughout Ireland via articles in this newspaper.

4. In an attempt to save money, Cumann na nGaedhael reduced teacher's salaries, making the party very unpopular amongst teachers.

By the way . . .
The atmosphere was so tense among the various political parties (mainly due to bitterness created by the divisive Civil War) that Fianna Fáil TDs brought guns – hidden under their coats – into the Dáil as they were unsure of what might happen when they tried to take their seats.

5. The Public Safety Acts of 1923, 1924 and 1927 were very unpopular and Cumann na nGaedhael was blamed for them.

In 1932, a general election was called by Cosgrave. For the first time, all the political parties of Ireland would contest an election to the Dáil.

Questions

1. What does Cumann na nGaedhael mean?
2. Outline the main achievements of the Cumann na nGaedhael government.
3. Give one reason why the Gardaí were accepted by the population.
4. What policy did the Irish Army officers want O'Higgins to change?
5. What did Kevin O'Higgins' Public Safety Acts of 1923 and 1924 allow the government to do?
6. What law was passed in reaction to the assassination of O'Higgins?
7. What happened to the border as a result of the Boundary Commission's establishment in 1924?
8. What economic changes did Cumann na nGaedhael introduce and were they successful? Give reasons for your answer.
9. Why did de Valera leave Sinn Féin?
10. What did the Electoral Amendment Act force all TDs to do?
11. Why did Cumann na nGaedhael lose popularity?

De Valera and Fianna Fáil in Power

● Results of Irish general election, February 1932

Fianna Fáil	72 seats
Cumann na nGaedhael	56 seats
Labour Party	7 seats
Others	18 seats

Although Fianna Fáil did not get a majority, the Labour Party agreed to support them in government. De Valera immediately set out his aims:

1. To **dismantle** (break up) the Treaty.

2. Put **tariffs** (taxes) on imported goods so that it was cheaper to buy Irish produce.

3. To build new houses for those living in slums.

4. Give better pensions to poor people.

● Relationship with Britain

In 1931, Britain passed the **Statute of Westminster**. This stated that any country in the British Commonwealth was allowed to pass any law they wanted to without British interference. De Valera now began to use this Statute to dismantle the Treaty.

- One of the first things Fianna Fáil did was to remove the Oath of Allegiance. Although many feared that this would damage the relationship with Britain, the Oath was officially abolished in May 1933.

- The British monarch's representative in Ireland was called the Governor-General. De Valera ignored the position whenever possible and soon the Governor-General, James MacNeill, resigned in protest. The position was later abolished.

- The Seanad protested at the treatment of the Governor-General and so de Valera abolished it too.

- When the British King, Edward VIII, resigned to marry a divorced woman, de Valera passed the External Relations Act, 1936. This removed all references to the British monarch in the Irish Constitution.

With all these changes in the Constitution, de Valera now decided to produce a new one. The new Constitution, **Bunreacht na hÉireann** was passed in 1937. Some of its main points were:

1. The name of the country is Ireland or Éire.

2. Irish is the first official language.

3. Articles 2 and 3 of the Constitution claim control over all of the island of Ireland.

4. The head of the country is a President elected directly by the people.

5. The prime minister of the country is called the Taoiseach.

▲ Éamon de Valera used the Statute of Westminster to gradually dismantle the Treaty.

Questions

1. What were de Valera's main aims when he entered government?
2. What was the Statute of Westminster?
3. Outline the changes de Valera made to the Irish relationship with Britain.
4. Why do you think de Valera included Articles 2 and 3 in Bunreacht na hÉireann?

● The Army Comrades Association (Blueshirts)

When Fianna Fáil came into government in 1932, de Valera released many of the IRA members who had been imprisoned by Cumann na nGaedhael. Their release led to a revival of the tensions between the two sides of the Civil War (i.e. pro-Treaty and anti-Treaty). A group of ex-army members called the **Army Comrades Association** (ACA) was set up in 1932. They were originally set up to campaign for army pensions but soon began to offer protection against IRA attacks on Cumann na nGaedhael meetings.

When de Valera took power, he dismissed the head of the Garda Síochána, Eoin O'Duffy. In 1933, O'Duffy became the leader of the ACA. He changed its name to the **National Guard** and adopted some of the characteristics of fascists. They wore blue shirts, were anti-Communist, organised marches and even used the fascist salute.

▲ Eoin O'Duffy became leader of the ACA after de Valera dismissed him as head of the Garda Síochána.

▲ Eoin O'Duffy (centre) at a rally of his blueshirts. Once O'Duffy accepted de Valera's ban, support for the Blueshirts began to fade.

In August 1933, O'Duffy organised a march in Dublin close to the Dáil. De Valera was worried that this would be similar to Mussolini's March on Rome (see page 310) and so he banned the march and outlawed the National Guard.

Ex-Taoiseach William T Cosgrave believed that de Valera was being too easy on his old colleagues in the IRA and so he arranged for Cumann na nGaedhael to join the National Guard. This new party was called **Fine Gael**. O'Duffy was appointed leader. However, he let the 'blueshirts' get into clashes with the Gardaí and in 1935, Fine Gael replaced him with the previous Cumann na nGaedhael leader, William T

Cosgrave. In 1936, O'Duffy independently led 600 blueshirts to fight for the fascist leader General Franco in the Spanish Civil.

De Valera also banned the IRA in 1936 and imprisoned over 500 members after they began a bombing campaign in Britain in 1939.

The Economic War (1932-1938)

In the late 1800s Britain loaned a large amount of money to Irish farmers to enable them to buy their farms. The repayments of these loans were called **land annuities**. De Valera decided to stop these repayments estimated to be worth £3 million in 1932 (roughly €166 million in today's money). The British government was angry at this and in response placed a 20% tariff on all agricultural goods from Ireland. This meant there was a much higher price in Britain for Irish goods and people stopped buying them. As 83% of all exports from Ireland went straight to Britain, this caused great hardship to Irish farmers. De Valera decided to retaliate by placing a 5% tariff on all British goods coming into Ireland. This increased the cost of 65% of all goods in Ireland. This Economic War with Britain ended in 1938 with the **Anglo-Irish Agreement (1938)**.

This agreement stated that:

1. Land annuities were abolished and the Irish government paid a once-off fee of £10 million (about €497 million in today's money) to the British government.

2. The British and Irish governments reduced their tariffs on each other's produce.

3. With the increased likelihood of a war with Germany, Britain wished to keep Ireland on friendly terms. The ports that the British had kept after the Treaty (Cobh, Berehaven and Lough Swilly) were returned to Ireland. This would prove very important for Ireland's neutrality during World War II.

The Economic War hurt the agricultural industry in Ireland very badly. Irish cattle sales to Britain dropped by 33% and many more people were now unemployed. The investment in Irish industries was more of a success. Between 1931 and 1938 the number of people employed in industry rose from 162,000 to 217,000. This success was undermined by the numbers who had to emigrate or who became unemployed in agriculture.

Fianna Fáil introduced welfare payments for widows and orphans in 1933 and gave unemployment assistance in 1935. Between 1931 and 1942, 12,000 new houses were built each year as opposed to 2,000 per year between 1923 and 1931.

Questions

1. Who were the ACA and why were they set up?
2. What aspects of fascism did the National Guard adopt?
3. Why did de Valera ban O'Duffy's march into Dublin in August 1933?
4. Why was O'Duffy replaced as leader of Fine Gael?
5. What were land annuities?
6. Explain the term 'tariff'.
7. How did the Economic War affect Irish farmers?

• The Emergency

World War II (known as the **Emergency** in Ireland) began in September 1939. Ireland chose to remain **neutral** (not support either side in the war) in this conflict. The government chose neutrality for a number of reasons:

1. The majority of the Irish people did not want to fight on the side of the British while Ireland was still partitioned.

2. It showed that Ireland had a different and independent foreign policy to Britain.

3. The economic damage that could be done to Irish industry was huge.

The Dáil passed the **Emergency Powers Act 1939** to ensure the country's neutrality. This Act gave the government the power:

1. To censor all newspapers and private letters.

2. To order farmers to grow crops to feed the population.

3. To imprison any person who was a threat to Ireland's neutrality.

4. To censor weather forecasts in case these forecasts helped another country to plan invasions or bombing operations.

THE THREAT TO IRELAND

Ireland was not well defended and was vulnerable to invasion. Germany had plans to do so but Ireland was too far for their bombers to fly without defeating Britain first. German planes bombed Ireland in May 1941. Thirty-four people were killed when bombs were dropped on North Strand, Dublin. Some believe that this was in retaliation for the help given to Britain by de Valera's government a few weeks earlier when fire brigades from the south of Ireland were sent to Belfast to help fight fires caused by German bombs.

The greatest threat of invasion came from Britain. This never happened partly because of Ireland's pro-British form of neutrality and partly because Northern Ireland was involved in the war.

This pro-British form of neutrality was evident from the following:

1. The British and Irish military leaders met to discuss plans if Germany invaded.

2. Weather forecasts and other information were given to the British army.

3. Any Allied pilots who landed in Ireland were released but German pilots were not.

4. Belfast was bombed by Germany in April 1941 and again two weeks later. On both occasions fire brigades from Dublin and Dundalk in Southern Ireland travelled to Belfast to put out the fires.

▲ In May 1941, German bombs killed 34 people in North Strand, Dublin.

5. Roughly 43,000 Irish men and women joined the British army.

In preparation for any invasion of Ireland, the size of the Irish army was increased from 19,000 to 42,000. In addition to the army, the **Local Defence Force** (LDF) was set up. By August 1940, the LDF had about 148,000 members but they were given only very basic training and were poorly armed.

SHORTAGES

Food and raw materials were difficult to get during the Emergency. De Valera appointed **Seán Lemass** as Minister of Supplies to deal with these shortages.

- Lemass established Irish Shipping Limited to bring essential materials into Ireland from abroad. Although 15 ships were purchased, travelling through seas during a war was not easy. In 1942 the *Irish Pine* was sunk by a German U-Boat killing 33 sailors.

- Rationing was introduced. People were given ration-books to ensure everyone got an equal share of goods like tea, flour, butter and sugar.

- Gas was also rationed. The government appointed inspectors called **glimmer-men** to check that people did not use more than their ration of gas and electricity.

- Due to the food shortages, farmers were forced to grow wheat under the **Compulsory Tillage Scheme**. This more than doubled the amount of wheat produced in Ireland between 1939 and 1944.

- **Petrol** was only available to doctors and priests.

▲ Seán Lemass, Minister of Supplies, introduced several measures to deal with food shortages.

> **By the way . . .**
> The glimmer-man was sent to houses to check that gas was not being used outside the appointed hours.

▲ People gathering turf in Connemara during the Emergency.

• **Coal** was very scarce so Irish people began to use **turf** (peat from the bog). Most homes used turf as fuel and some trains even used turf instead of coal to power the engines. Without coal and petrol, many factories had to close. This meant that more people had to emigrate to Britain to find work.

RESULTS OF THE EMERGENCY

1. Ireland was spared the destruction and great loss of life that the rest of Europe experienced. Apart from the rationing, life was reasonably unchanged.

2. The decision to remain neutral had shown that Ireland was independent of Britain.

3. However, the Irish economy suffered greatly as a result of World War II. Irish industry took many years to recover from the Emergency and rationing continued for a number of years after the Allied victory.

4. The partition between Northern Ireland and the South became more definite. The British government felt grateful to Northern Ireland for its support in the war. After the war they were more likely to support unionist wishes to remain part of the United Kingdom.

By the way . . .

De Valera was criticised when he sent condolences to the German embassy in Dublin on the death of Hitler.

Questions

1. Why did Ireland choose to be neutral during World War II?

2. What did the Emergency Powers Act of 1939 permit the Irish government to do?

3. Do you think that Ireland was fully neutral during the war? Give reasons for your answer.

4. What measures did the Irish government take to protect the country from invasion?

5. Explain the following terms:

   (a) Glimmer-man   (b) Rationing

6. Outline the measures that Lemass introduced to deal with shortages of goods during World War II.

7. Do you think Ireland was correct in remaining neutral during World War II? Give reasons for your answer.

Chapter 12 Questions

1. Pictures

Examine the picture and answer the following questions:

The picture shows three leaders from the Irish War of Independence, 1919-1922.

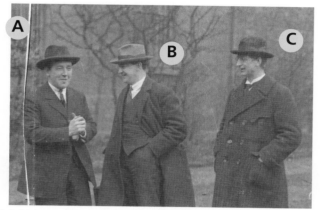

(a) Name two of the leaders in the picture.

(b) State one major contribution which any one of these made to the War of Independence.

(c) Describe how Leader A and Leader B were killed.

2. Documents

H. Q. [Headquarters] Moore Street

Believing that the glorious stand which has been made by the soldiers of Irish freedom during the past five days in Dublin has been sufficient to gain recognition of Ireland's national claim at an international peace conference, and desirous [wanting] of preventing further slaughter of the civil population, and to save the lives of as many as possible of our followers, the Members of the Provisional Government here present have agreed by a majority to open negotiations with the British commander.

P. H. Pearse,
Comandant General,
Commanding in Chief,
Army of the Irish Republic.
29 April 1916.

(a) Where was this document written and who wrote it?

(b) How long had the soldiers been fighting?

(c) What did the author believe the 'glorious stand' had been enough to gain?

(d) What two other reasons does the author give for agreeing to open negotiations with the British Commander?

3. Short-Answer Questions

(a) Who founded Sinn Féin?

(b) Which political party in Britain supported Home Rule?

(c) Name the founder of the ITGWU.

(d) What was the Curragh Mutiny?

(e) Why was the IRA interested in negotiating a truce by 1921?

(f) Who was the leader of the Irish Volunteers after their split with Redmond?

(g) How did the capture of the *Aud* contribute to the failure of the 1916 Rising?

(h) Who wrote the *Castle Document*?

(i) Who was elected President of the first Dáil?

(j) Give three reasons why people opposed the Treaty.

4. People in History

Write an account about a Black and Tan in Ireland during the War of Independence, 1919-21. Use the following headings as a guide:

• Reasons for coming to Ireland

• Activities in Ireland during the war

• Opinions and feelings towards the Irish people and the IRA

• Reasons for leaving Ireland

5.

(a) Give two reasons why the 1916 Rising was a failure.

(b) Give two reasons why the opinion of the 1916 Rising among the Irish population changed after the end of the Rising.

(c) Explain three of the following terms:

(i) Flying Columns

(ii) The Anglo-Irish Treaty, 1921

(iii) The Government of Ireland Act, 1920

(iv) The Boundary Commission

(v) The Oath of Allegiance

(vi) The Statute of Westminster

(d) Write an account of three of the following:

(i) The Irish War of Independence, 1919-21

(ii) The Irish Civil War, 1922-23

(iii) Cumann na nGaedhael in government, 1923-32

(iv) Fianna Fáil in government, 1932-48

(v) The Emergency

Key Terms to Summarise Chapter 12: Ireland in the Twentieth Century

Nationalists Those in Ireland who wanted to gain more independence for Ireland from Britain.

Unionists Those in Ireland who wanted Ireland to remain within the United Kingdom of Great Britain.

Republicans Those in Ireland who wished to gain full independence for Ireland, did not want a king to rule over them and were prepared to use force if necessary.

Home Rule The policy followed by the Irish Parliamentary Party that offered a parliament in Ireland that could pass laws on areas that affected Ireland like agriculture and health while leaving other matters such as foreign affairs to Britain.

Gaelic Athletic Association (GAA) Sporting organisation set up by Michael Cusack and Maurice Davin in 1884 to promote traditional Gaelic games such as hurling and football.

Gaelic League An organisation set up by Douglas Hyde and Eoin MacNeill in 1893 to promote the Irish language.

1913 Dublin Lockout Industrial conflict between the Irish Transport and General Workers' Union and William Martin Murphy, the owner of the Dublin Tramways Company that resulted in a five-month strike.

Irish Citizen Army A military group set up by James Connolly to defend workers during the 1913 Lockout.

Solemn League and Covenant An agreement signed by unionists in 1912 that they would never accept Home Rule.

Ulster Volunteer Force (UVF) A military group set up to oppose Home Rule in Ireland.

Irish Volunteer Force A military group set up by Irish nationalists in response to the creation of the UVF.

National Volunteers A group within the Irish Volunteers that fought alongside the British Army during World War I.

Castle Document A letter written by Joseph Plunkett that led Eoin MacNeill to believe that the Irish Volunteers were going to be made illegal by the British authorities.

Sinn Féin A political party set up by Arthur Griffith in 1905 that sought full independence for Ireland.

Irish Republican Army (IRA) The name given to those members of the Irish Volunteers who answered to Michael Collins.

Flying columns The name given to Collins' IRA troops who used guerrilla tactics to attack British troops during the War of Independence.

Black and Tans The name given to the groups of ex-World War I British soldiers sent to Ireland to fight the IRA. They were recognised by the colour of their uniforms: khaki (tan) and a black and green jacket.

Bloody Sunday (21 November 1920) 11 British secret service men were killed by the IRA and later 12 spectators and players at a match in Croke Park were killed by the Black and Tans in retaliation.

The Treaty The agreement between the British government and representatives of the Irish government that ended the War of Independence.

Irish Free State The title given to the new government of southern Ireland after the passing of the Treaty.

Regulars and Irregulars Regulars were the soldiers who supported the Free State government, while the Irregulars were those who were against the government.

Cumann na nGaedhael Pro-Treaty political party set up in 1922 and led by William T Cosgrave.

Fianna Fáil A political party set up by Éamon de Valera in 1926.

Shannon Scheme A government project which involved building a hydroelectric power station on the River Shannon. Completed in 1929.

Statute of Westminster (1931) A law passed by Britain that allowed any country in the Commonwealth to pass any law that it wished. This meant that Ireland could use it to dismantle the Treaty.

Bunreacht na hÉireann The Irish name for the Constitution of Ireland passed in 1937.

Army Comrades Association (also known as the Blueshirts). A fascist organisation set up in 1932 by Eoin O'Duffy. It later changed its name to the National Guard.

Fine Gael A political party created in 1933 by merging Cumann na nGaedhael, the National Guard and the Centre Party.

The Emergency The name de Valera gave to World War II (1939-1945) in Ireland.

Glimmer-man Inspectors who checked that gas was not being used outside the rationed hours. The term comes from the glimmer of gas that remained in the pipes after the gas had been turned off.

Web References

For further information on topics mentioned in this chapter, view the following websites:

www.nli.ie/en/homepage.aspx
www.nli.ie/1916/biblio.html
www.bbc.co.uk/history/british/easterrising/index.shtml
www.fiannafail.ie/
www.finegael.org/
www.ardfheis.com/
www.labour.ie/party/history.html
www.waterfordcountymuseum.org/exhibit/web/Display/article/22/?lang=en

Women in History

Countess Constance Markievicz

(1868 – 1927)

(Revolutionary, Labour Activist and First Female MP)

Constance Gore-Booth was born in 1868 in Lissadell House, County Sligo. She was one of the wealthy Gore-Booths of London and Sligo and enjoyed a privileged childhood. At the age of 19 she was brought to the court of Queen Victoria in London. She was tall, attractive, multilingual and was both an excellent shot and horse-rider. In 1893 she enrolled in London's Slade School of Fine Art before moving to Paris in 1897. In Paris she fell in love with a Polish artist named Count Casimir Markievicz. In 1900 she married Casimir and had a daughter, Maeve Alys in 1901. They moved to Dublin in 1903.

In 1908 Constance joined the revolutionary women's group *Inghínidhe na hÉireann* (Daughters of Ireland) and contributed to their magazine *Bean na hÉireann* (women of Ireland). As she involved herself more in the revolutionary movement, she established Fianna Éireann (soldiers of Ireland), loosely based on the boy-scout movement. She joined the Irish Women's Franchise League (IWFL) in 1910 and helped distribute food to the poor of Dublin's slums. During the 1913 Lockout she helped in a soup kitchen set up to help feed workers and their families. She was also a regular presence at political rallies, even getting punched and kicked at one such rally.

As Ireland moved towards open revolt, she joined the Cumann na mBan and also Connolly's Irish Citizen Army, being the only woman to be a member of both organisations. During the 1916 Rising, she was second in command of the regiment at St Stephen's Green and was arrested and imprisoned for her role. She was sentenced to death but this was changed to life imprisonment 'on account of her sex'. After

spending time in prison in England, she returned to Ireland to a hero's welcome in 1917. She was elected to the first Dáil in 1918, becoming the first woman to be elected as an MP. Appointed Minister for Labour in 1919, she spent the War of Independence either on the run or serving prison sentences in Cork and in Dublin. Countess Markievicz sided with de Valera against the Treaty and was re-elected in 1923. She was imprisoned a number of other times, spending more than three full years in jail between 1916 and 1924.

In her later life, she helped the poor of Dublin and campaigned for de Valera's Fianna Fáil. In 1927, she died of cancer aged only 59 and is buried in Glasnevin cemetery.

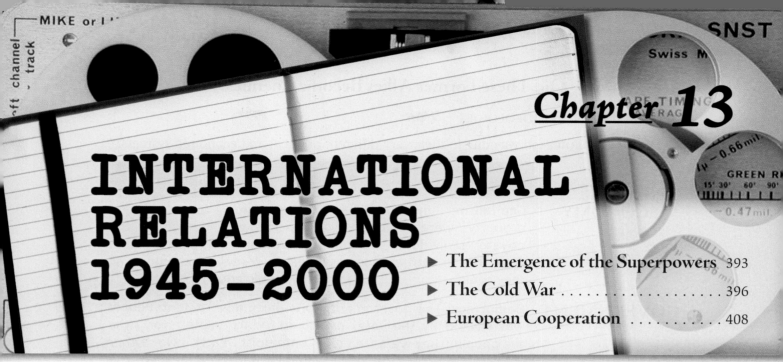

INTERNATIONAL RELATIONS 1945–2000

The Emergence of the Superpowers

As we learnt in Chapter 11, Europe lay in ruins after World War II. Britain, France, Germany and Italy were economically weak. The two countries that emerged from the war in strong positions were the USSR and the USA. Both countries had large populations and strong economies as both had benefitted from supplying arms and munitions during World War II.

▲ The flag of the USSR with the hammer and sickle to represent agriculture and industry.

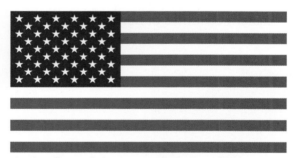

▲ The flag of the United States of America.

In fact, they became so powerful that they were known as **superpowers**. Over the next fifty years these two powers competed with each other both economically and politically. The conflict between these superpowers was known as the **Cold War**.

By the way . . .

The Union of Soviet Socialist Republics (USSR) was sometimes referred to as Russia even though it contained up to 16 different Soviets (Republics) and Russia was only one of these.

By the way . . .

This ongoing conflict was called the Cold War because the two countries never fought each other directly. The term was first used by author George Orwell in 1945.

● Why Did These Former Allies Become Enemies?

1. DIFFERENT IDEOLOGIES

The main reason was due to their very different political and economic systems:

	USA	USSR
ECONOMY	**Capitalism:** Industry and property were owned by private individuals. People were free to earn as much as they could.	**Communism:** Industry and property were owned by the government. Property and wealth were divided among all the people equally.
GOVERNMENT	**Democracy:** The government was elected by the votes of the people. They were free to vote for any political party they wished.	**One-party government:** People could only vote for the Communist Party. No other political party was allowed. The government could do anything it wished. This is a dictatorship.

Different views on how a society should be run are called **ideologies**. Both the USA and the USSR believed that their ideology was the correct one and wanted to defeat the other.

2. LEGACY OF WORLD WAR II

The alliance between the USSR and the USA during World War II had been for one purpose: to defeat Hitler. Now that this aim had been achieved, they grew increasingly suspicious of each other. The negotiations after World War II highlighted the differences between the two countries. The USA wanted Europe to have democratic governments while the USSR wanted the eastern countries of Europe to have communist governments.

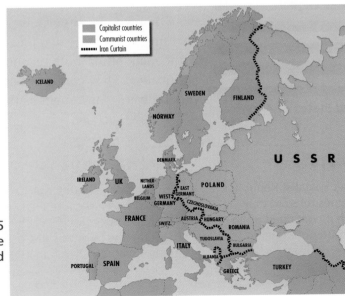

A map of Europe in 1945 showing the divide between capitalist and communist countries. ▶

3. USSR's 'BUFFER ZONE'

The USSR believed it had suffered most during both World War I and World War II. It had been invaded twice by Germany and had lost the greatest number of lives of any country. For this reason, the USSR wanted to create a 'buffer-zone' around its borders. After World War II, Stalin's armies occupied most of Eastern Europe. Stalin installed communist governments in these countries. As a result, they became known as **puppet-states** (they did what they were told to do) of the USSR. Winston Churchill described this divide between East and West Europe as 'an **Iron Curtain** descending across the continent of Europe'.

4. TRUMAN DOCTRINE

▲ Harry Truman introduced a policy of containment during the Cold War.

The USA was extremely worried about the spread of communism. It may be difficult to understand now but in the post-war world, the USA, along with other Western countries, regarded communism as the greatest threat to world peace. In 1946, a civil war broke out in Greece between the government and communist rebels. The President of the USA, Harry Truman, decided to support the Greek government. He promised to give aid to any country that fought against communism. This policy was called the **Truman Doctrine**. Truman made this policy of **containment** (stopping the spread of communism) the basis for American foreign policy during the Cold War.

5. THE ATOMIC BOMB

America's development and use of the atomic bomb against Japan at the end of World War II meant that the USA was the only country with this powerful technology. They refused to share this information with the USSR. Stalin immediately began to develop the USSR's own atomic weapons and it tested its first atomic bomb in 1949. The possession of such weapons increased tensions as any war between the two countries would have devastating consequences, such as destroying the entire planet.

▲ The USSR tested its first atomic bomb in 1949.

6. MARSHALL AID V COMINFORM

Europe was economically destroyed after World War II. High unemployment, homelessness, poverty and hunger made communism attractive to many. To prevent this, the US Secretary for State, George Marshall, proposed to provide billions of dollars to rebuild Europe. This **Marshall Aid** was offered to all the countries of Europe. Stalin forced the Eastern European countries to refuse. Instead, he established the Communist Information Bureau **(Cominform)** to organise the communist countries in Eastern Europe.

For these reasons, both the USA and the USSR were in conflict with each other after World War II. Although they never actually fought directly against each other, there were many minor conflicts that could have led to large-scale war. Over the next 40 years, the world lived with the constant threat of an all-out atomic war between the two powers. Any event, no matter how small, could spark off a major war.

Questions

1. Explain the following terms:

   (a) Ideology   (b) Communism   (c) Capitalism   (d) Puppet-state

2. Why did the USA and the USSR become known as superpowers?

3. What does 'Cold War' mean?

4. Explain the differences between what the USA wanted and what the USSR wanted during the negotiations over Europe after World War II.

5. Why did Stalin wish to have puppet states along the USSR's western borders?

6. What did Churchill mean when he said that an Iron Curtain was descending across Europe?

7. What was the Truman Doctrine?

8. Why do you think Stalin would not allow the countries in Eastern Europe to accept Marshall Aid?

The Cold War

● Germany After World War II

One of the biggest problems facing the Allies after the war was what to do with Germany. Stalin wanted to keep it weak and divided. The USA wanted to introduce democracy and make Germany a peaceful ally. The Allies came to an agreement:

1. Germany would be divided into different Allied sectors: British, French, American and Soviet.

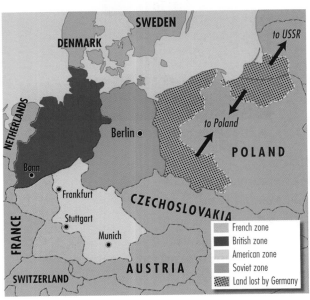

▲ Germany was divided into four sectors.

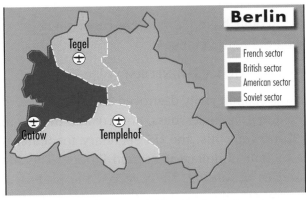

▲ Berlin, which was within the Soviet sector, was further divided into four sectors: British, French, American and Soviet.

2. Berlin was in the Soviet sector but, as it was the capital of Germany, it also was divided into four sectors: British, French, American and Soviet.

3. Large parts of Germany were given to Poland. A small area north of Poland was given to the USSR.

▲ An aerial view of the destruction of Wesel in the north-west of Germany, post World War II.

Germany was totally destroyed during the war. Millions were homeless, very few people were employed and approximately 12 million German refugees returned from Czechoslovakia and Poland. In the years immediately after the war, very few people in the Allied countries had sympathy for the German people. They were not allowed to rebuild their industries and so there was little hope for employment. Disease and starvation caused millions to die. However, by the time the Marshall Plan was introduced, public opinion in the Western countries had changed. To avoid the spread of communism, the USA wanted to ensure that Germany became economically, although not militarily, strong.

The Berlin Blockade

In 1948, a new currency called the **Deutschmark** was introduced into the three western sectors of Germany. The USSR refused to let it be used in their sector because they knew this new currency would help Germany's economic recovery. To stop it being used in the western sectors of Berlin, the USSR decided to block all road and rail links into Berlin. The only way to get into Berlin was by plane. Stalin hoped that this **blockade** would force the Western powers to give up their sectors of Berlin and as a result the USSR would have complete control over the city.

▲ The Western Allies flew supplies into Berlin during the Berlin Blockade.

In accordance with the American policy of containment, the Western Allies decided to fly supplies into West Berlin. **Operation Vittles** began in June 1948. Over 2 million tonnes of food, clothing and fuel were delivered by 270,000 flights into Berlin during the 321 days of the blockade. As the USSR had not yet developed the atomic bomb, Stalin was reluctant to attack any of the planes in case it caused a war. In May 1949, Stalin realised the Western Allies were determined to keep their sectors of Berlin so he lifted the blockade and allowed supplies to be brought in by land.

RESULTS OF DIVISION OF GERMANY

▲ Germany was divided into the Federal Republic of Germany (West Germany) and the German Democratic Republic (East Germany).

1. Britain, France and the USA decided to unify their sectors into one country called the Federal Republic of Germany (West Germany). The USSR decided not to let its sector join and declared its sector was also a country, which it called the German Democratic Republic (East Germany). East Germany had a communist government loyal to the USSR installed. Berlin was also divided into West and East.

2. The Marshall Aid helped West Germany to prosper economically. East Germany was far poorer; as a result many people decided to escape to West Germany. To stop this happening, the East German government, closed the border with the West in 1952. However, it was still possible for East Germans living in Berlin to escape to West Berlin. To prevent any further escapes, the East German government decided to build a wall between both parts of Berlin in 1961. During the Cold War, the Berlin Wall became a symbol of the conflict.

3. In 1949, the Western Allies created the **North Atlantic Treaty Organisation (NATO).** This organisation was a military alliance aimed at containing the spread of communism. West Germany was allowed to have an army and joined NATO in 1955, alarming the USSR. It responded by establishing a military alliance called the **Warsaw Pact.** This included all the communist countries that the USSR controlled.

The Berlin Wall was built to stop East Germans escaping to the wealthier West Germany. ▶

Questions

1. Why was the economic situation so bad in Germany after World War II?
2. Why did the USSR decide to block all the roads and railways into Berlin?
3. What was the Allied response to this blockade?
4. Why was Stalin reluctant to attack any of the Allied planes?
5. Why did the East German government decide to build a wall across Berlin in 1961?
6. What is NATO?

By the way . . .

Ireland refused to join NATO because it did not want to be part of any organisation that included Britain, which was still occupying Northern Ireland.

● The Korean War

Korea had been a colony of Japan since 1910. After World War II, Korea just like Germany, was divided among the Allies. The north of Korea was controlled by the USSR while the south was controlled by the USA. The border between the two lay along the **38° north parallel (38th Parallel),** which is the line of latitude encircling the globe at that point.

After World War II, both sides agreed to hold free elections. As relations between the two superpowers got worse, the elections never took place. Instead, in 1947, two new countries were created:

1. The Communist People's Republic of Korea (North Korea) led by **Kim Il Sung.**

2. The Republic of Korea (South Korea) led by **Syngman Rhee.**

▲ 38th Parallel Sign

Kim Il Sung wanted to unite the whole country under communist control. Stalin reluctantly agreed to support him and on June 25 1950 the North Korean army invaded South Korea. Within three days it had captured the entire peninsula except for a small area around the city of Pusan. However, President Truman was determined that Korea would not become communist. He asked the United Nations (see Chapter 11, International Relations in Twentieth Century Europe, page 349) to support an invasion of South Korea to combat the North's aggression.

▲ Kim Il Sung, leader of North Korea, wanted all of Korea under communist control.

▲ Syngman Rhee, leader of South Korea, did not support communism.

● UN Intervention

The UN was set up in the aftermath of World War II to ensure disagreements between countries could be resolved without conflict. However, as the world increasingly divided into communist and non-communist countries, the five main victors (the USA, China, the USSR, Britain and France) who made up the Security Council, became similarly divided in their aims. The USA, Britain and France wanted to halt the spread of communism while the USSR and China, both under communist rule, did not.

▲ In June 1950 North Korea invaded South Korea and captured the entire peninsula within three days except for one small area around Pusan.

Each of the five countries on the **Security Council** could **veto** (stop) any decision made by the UN to involve itself in military situations around the world. In 1949, the communists won the Chinese Civil War and took control of the country. The Western Allies believed that the communists had not allowed free and fair elections in China and so they refused to let the new communist leaders take their seat at the Security Council. In protest, the USSR refused to attend any further meetings of the Council. Without China or the USSR to veto any decisions, the Security Council agreed to send troops to Korea. Stalin removed all Soviet advisors from Korea as he did not want war to break out between the USSR and the USA.

UN and Chinese offensives

▲ General MacArthur led the multinational UN army in the Korean War.

Truman sent **General Douglas MacArthur** to lead the multinational UN army. On September 15 1950, MacArthur daringly landed his troops at Inchon, behind North Korean lines. After heavy fighting, the UN troops won back all of South Korea by early October.

Truman ordered MacArthur to continue into North Korea. China warned Truman not to advance further, as they did not want an American-controlled North Korea on their border. However, by the end of October, MacArthur had advanced as far as the Yalu River (the border between China and North Korea).

On October 25 almost 300,000 Chinese People's Volunteers attacked the UN troops. The Chinese pushed the UN forces across the 38th parallel and into South Korea. MacArthur wanted Truman to use nuclear weapons to stop the Chinese advance but Truman refused. Instead, MacArthur launched a counter-attack in February 1951. This pushed the Chinese back to the 38th parallel.

MacArthur now wanted to invade China but Truman again refused. When MacArthur openly criticised President Truman, he was dismissed and replaced by General Ridgway.

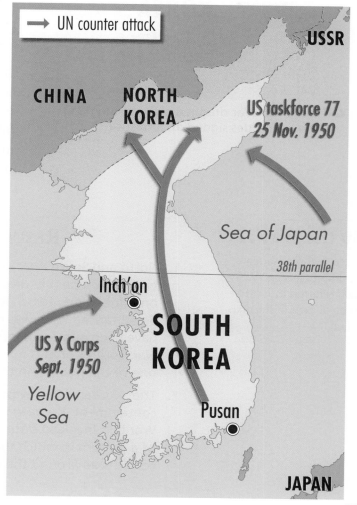

UN forces led by General MacArthur won back all of South Korea and pushed forward to the border between North Korea and China. ▶

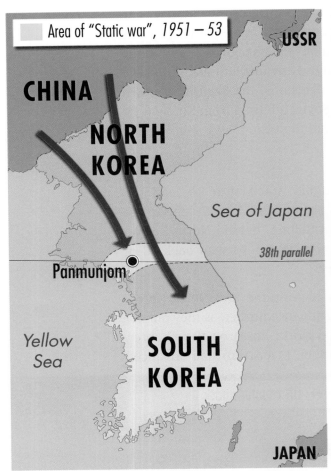

Area of "Static war", *1951 – 53*

CHINA

NORTH KOREA

USSR

Sea of Japan

38th parallel

Panmunjom

Yellow Sea

SOUTH KOREA

JAPAN

▲ The Korean War dragged on until July 1953 when both sides signed an armistice.

Both sides dug in on either side of the 38th parallel and for some time there was no more movement. The USA used bombers to attack North Korean cities and industrial sites, causing large numbers of civilian casualties. The USSR and China continued to supply weapons and men to North Korea. Negotiations on a truce began in June 1951.

▲ UN troops walk past local women collecting water during the Korean War.

The peace talks dragged on for two years, and so the fighting also continued. Stalin was happy to let the USA continue a war that would cost millions of dollars. When Stalin died on 5 March 1953, both sides of the conflict took the opportunity to sign an **armistice** (ceasefire). It was signed on 17 July 1953 at Panmunjom.

By the way . . .

In 2002, the American President George W. Bush referred to North Korea as part of the Axis of Evil.

RESULTS OF KOREAN WAR

1. North and South Korea continue to be very hostile to each other. Over two million people died in the Korean War and both sides remained on high alert for a long time afterwards in case of attack. A demilitarised zone was created between the two countries and there have been numerous incidents but luckily none has resulted in another war. South Korea is now a very wealthy country while North Korea is one of the poorest in the world.

2. The Korean War was seen as a success for America's policy of containment. Korea was the first major conflict since the end of World War II. It involved both superpowers in a war. This was the beginning of a pattern in which the superpowers involved themselves in various conflicts all around the world.

Questions

1. Where did the border between North and South Korea lie?
2. Why did Stalin support North Korea?
3. How come the UN was able to participate in the invasion of South Korea?
4. Why did China send the Chinese People's Volunteers into Korea?
5. Why was General MacArthur replaced?
6. Why was Stalin happy to allow the war to drag on?
7. In your opinion, was the Korean War a success for the American government's policy of containment?

● The Cuban Missile Crisis

CUBAN REVOLUTION

In 1959, communist rebels successfully overthrew a corrupt dictatorship in Cuba. Led by **Fidel Castro** and **Ernesto 'Che' Guevara**, they established a communist country only 160 kilometres from the USA. The American government reacted by banning all trade with Cuba. Castro turned to the new leader of the USSR, **Nikita Khrushchev**, for help. The USSR agreed to buy all of Cuba's main export – sugar. This agreement angered the Americans. In 1961, the American government gave their support to an invasion of Cuba. The invasion was badly organised and was defeated at the **Bay of Pigs**. This attempted invasion forced Castro to ask Khrushchev for more help in protecting the country.

▲ Fidel Castro (top) and Che Guevara established a communist government in Cuba, prompting the USA to ban all trade with it.

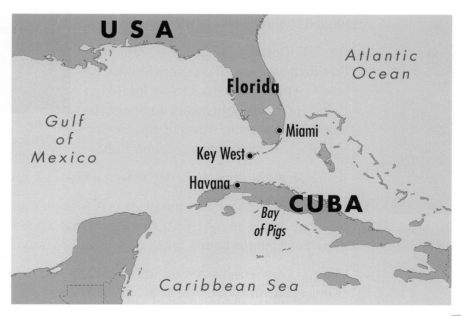

SOVIET ASSISTANCE

▲ Khrushchev, leader of the USSR, agreed to buy all of Cuba's main export, which was sugar.

▲ Pictures from an American U-2 spy plane clearly showed that missile sites had been constructed in Cuba.

Khrushchev sent military equipment and advisors to Cuba. Meanwhile, the new American President, **John F. Kennedy**, quickly became concerned that Soviet missiles were being secretly located in Cuba. He ordered spy-planes, called U-2s, to monitor any work being done in Cuba. Photos taken by the U-2s revealed that the USSR was building launching sites for Intermediate Range Ballistic Missiles. These missiles would be able to hit the USA within three minutes of launch and could destroy whole cities.

JFK'S RESPONSE

At first, Kennedy was unsure how to respond without causing war with the USSR. After meeting with senior American advisors, he responded in the following ways:

▲ John F. Kennedy delivered a speech on 22 October 1962 stating that Cuba had become a Soviet base.

1. On 22 October 1962, the American President announced on television that he could not allow missiles to be located in Cuba. He asked Khrushchev to 'move the world back from the abyss of destruction' by withdrawing the missiles from Cuba.

2. Using US Navy ships, Kennedy placed a blockade around Cuba.

3. He announced that if any missile was fired from Cuba, the USA would launch a full-scale attack on the USSR. This meant that a full-scale nuclear war was likely if the Soviet ships bound for Cuba forced their way through the blockade.

4. The US Army was placed on full alert for a war. American B-52 bombers with atomic weapons were in the air in case of an attack.

THE WORLD WAITS FOR WAR

For two days Khrushchev ignored Kennedy's statement and the Soviet ships continued on their way to Cuba. The world tensely waited. World War III seemed very close. As both countries had nuclear weapons, a war could lead to the destruction of the entire planet.

Finally on 24 October, Khrushchev ordered the ships to stop as they neared Cuba. Negotiations between the two countries ended on 28 October with the announcement that a compromise had been reached:

1. The USSR would withdraw its missiles from Cuba.

2. The USA promised not to attack Cuba.

3. Secretly the USA also agreed to withdraw its missiles in Turkey which lay on the border with the USSR.

▲ American navy vessels such as the *USS Barry* (front of photo) shadowed Russian ships bound for Cuba in the tense days when World War III seemed very possible.

RESULTS OF CUBAN MISSILE CRISIS

1. A full-scale nuclear war had only just been avoided. The two superpowers were shaken by these events. Cooperation between the two countries improved afterwards.

2. A hotline between the two leaders was set up to help communication. This hotline came in the form of a telephone linking the offices of the President of the USA and the President of the USSR.

3. A Test Ban Treaty was signed between the superpowers in 1963. This banned testing of nuclear weapons on land or sea.

● End of the Cold War

Further conflicts occurred over the next 25 years.

1. America involved itself in a war in **Vietnam**. The war lasted from 1959 until 1975 and resulted in a humiliating defeat of the USA by the Soviet-backed communist North Vietnamese. Over four million people died during this conflict.

▲ The Vietnam War lasted for 16 years. The USA used its superior aerial power to carpet bomb large areas of Vietnamese jungle in an attempt to destroy enemy camps.

2. The USSR fought a war in **Afghanistan** between 1979 and 1989. The USSR tried to install a communist government in Afghanistan but faced resistance from the mujahideen guerrilla fighters. The mujahideen fighters were financially and militarily supported by the USA among other countries.

▲ Mujahideen soldiers celebrate destroying a Soviet helicopter during the war in Afghanistan from 1979 to 1989.

3. The USSR also had to deal with revolts against the communist governments across Eastern Europe. In 1956, **Hungarians** staged an uprising against Soviet interference in its affairs. The Hungarians called on the West to support them in overthrowing the Soviet occupation but after 13 days, Soviet tanks and troops crushed the uprising.

4. Throughout the Cold War, both countries tried to build more weapons and bombs than the other superpower. This was called the **arms race**.

● Reform of the USSR

Even though there were many close calls, the superpowers never actually went to war. In 1985, a new Soviet leader was elected. His name was **Mikhail Gorbachev**. He wanted to create a better relationship between the USSR and the West and to reorganise the Soviet economy.

▲ Russian tanks arrived in Budapest to crush the Hungarian revolt in 1956.

1. The economic reforms that Gorbachev began were known as **perestroika** (the Russian word for 'restructuring'). These reforms created more private ownership of industry, which was a move towards a capitalist form of economy.

2. He also believed in a more open discussion on the USSR's policies. This policy was known as **glasnost** (the Russian word for 'openness'). Political prisoners were released and censorship of the media was relaxed.

▲ Gorbachev brought many dramatic changes to the USSR.

3. He wished to stop the arms race. He agreed to reduce military spending and withdrew missiles from Eastern Europe.

4. Borders between Eastern and Western Europe were opened and on 9 November 1989 the hated Berlin Wall was torn down by rejoicing crowds.

5. Free and democratic elections were called throughout Eastern Europe.

Soon, countries within the USSR wanted to declare independence from the Soviet Republic. The Baltic countries (Estonia, Latvia and Lithuania) declared independence in 1991. Others followed and on 8 December 1991 the USSR ceased to exist.

▲ People tore down the Berlin Wall in 1989 using chisels, hammers, axes and their bare hands.

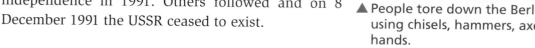

Questions

1. Name two locations where the superpowers involved themselves in conflict.

2. What was the arms race?

3. Explain the following terms: (a) Perestroika   (b) Glasnost

4. In your opinion, why was the fall of the Berlin Wall such a symbolic moment? Give reasons for your answer.

5. Using other sources, write a page about one of the other conflicts that took place during the Cold War.

European Cooperation

After World War II, the governments of Europe looked for ways to avoid another conflict. They realised that competition for resources (e.g. land) and power between different European countries had caused many deaths and led to much destruction.

Europeans needed to feel a greater sense of unity amongst each other in order to prevent future conflicts. Such unity would:

1. Create more **cooperation** between countries. If countries were working together there was less likelihood of another war.

2. Spread **democracy** and **human rights** throughout Europe. This would reduce the appeal of dictatorships and political extremism such as fascism or communism.

3. Improve the **economic conditions** of the people of Europe. Employment could increase if countries worked together rather than competed with each other.

By the way . . .

Ironically, just as European governments worked out ways to avoid competing amongst each other for land or power, the USA and the USSR entered their Cold War phase, during which time they competed incessantly against each other. This competition ranged from (a) who had the most weaponry (e.g. atomic bombs, missiles) to (b) who had the most ideological influence over other countries (e.g. capitalism v communism) throughout the world.

Early European Cooperation

- Belgium, the Netherlands and Luxembourg created the first economic organisation in 1948. The **Benelux Union** abolished most of the tariffs on goods traded among these countries.

- To distribute the billions of dollars coming into Europe as part of the Marshall Plan, a new organisation was set up. The **Organisation for European Economic Cooperation (OEEC)** helped to distribute the money throughout Western Europe.

- **The Council of Europe** was set up by ten countries including Ireland. The Council agreed to meet regularly to discuss ways of cooperating and helping each other.

● The Beginning of the EU

▲ Robert Schuman helped to establish the ECSC in 1952.

Robert Schuman, the French Foreign Minister and his economic advisor, **Jean Monnet**, recognised the success of the Benelux Union. They proposed that France and West Germany could cooperate with each other in the production of coal and steel. Both coal and steel were very important in rebuilding European industries. They invited any other European country who wished to join to do so. In April 1952, France, West Germany, Italy and the Benelux countries formed the **European Coal and Steel Community (ECSC)**. The ECSC abolished duties (taxes) on coal and steel products between the members. This resulted in cheaper steel and coal which further helped production of other goods.

> **By the way...**
> Coal and steel are also vital goods for warfare. It was hoped that if countries were dependent on each other for coal and steel, they would be less likely to go to war.

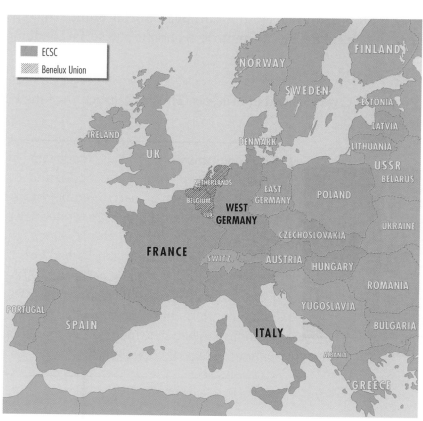

▲ A map of Europe in the 1950s showing the countries belonging to the Benelux Union and the countries belonging to the European Coal and Steel Community (ECSC).

The Treaty of Rome

▲ Members of the European Coal and Steel Community signed the Treaty of Rome in March 1957.

The ECSC proved to be such a success that more ways of cooperation were explored. In March 1957, the members of the ECSC signed the Treaty of Rome. This Treaty created the **European Economic Community (EEC)** and **(European Atomic Energy Community) EURATOM**. The main aspects of the Treaty were:

1. Customs duties between these countries were abolished.

2. Goods, services, money and people could now travel freely between the member countries. This was called the **Common Market**.

3. The **Common Agricultural Policy (CAP)** offered farmers a guaranteed price at a high level for their produce. This encouraged European farmers to produce as much as possible.

4. The members also promised to create the **European Social Fund**. This gives money to the poorer parts of the EEC to improve economic and social conditions.

The EEC

The headquarters of the EEC was located in Brussels. The basic structure of the EEC is the same as the EU now:

▲ EU Commission in Brussels, Belgium

The Commission: This is made up of commissioners – politicians appointed by the governments of each member state. Commissioners draft proposals for new laws and present them to the Council of Ministers and the European Parliament. If these proposals are accepted, the Commission is then responsible for implementing these new laws. The first Commission had nine members in charge of different areas of cooperation.

The Council of Ministers: This is made up of national government ministers who are in charge of that area in the member state. For example, agricultural ministers from all the member states meet at the Council if a new agricultural proposal is being discussed. The Council decides which policies (proposed by the Commission) to accept or reject.

The European Parliament: This is made up of a number of directly elected (since 1979) representatives from each country, depending on the size of the population. The number of Members of the European Parliament (MEPs) is now at 785. The Parliament provides a democratically elected forum that can discuss political issues and develop laws.

▲ MEPs attend the European Parliament.

The European Court of Justice: This ensures that all the member states obey the laws made by the EU. This means that the law is equal for everyone in the EU.

The European Court of Auditors: This institution checks that all the funds the EU receives (from taxpayers in the EU) is spent correctly and legally. It also carries out checks on EU budgets.

◄ The European Court of Justice ensures all laws made by the EU are obeyed by member states.

Questions

1. Why did people wish to have greater cooperation between European countries?
2. Explain what the following stand for and why they were set up:
   (a) ECSC (b) OEEC
3. What influence did Robert Schuman have on the creation of the EU?
4. What did the Treaty of Rome establish?
5. What is the CAP?
6. What does the term 'Common Market' mean?
7. Explain the purpose of the following institutions of the EEC/EU:
   (a) Parliament (b) Court of Justice (c) Commission (d) Council

● Enlargement of the EEC

▲ Jack Lynch (Taoiseach), second from left, brought Ireland into the EEC in 1973.

The United Kingdom (UK) decided not to join the ECSC in 1951 or the EEC in 1957. Instead it helped set up the **European Free Trade Association (EFTA)** in 1959. The UK, along with Switzerland, Austria, Denmark, Norway, Sweden and Portugal agreed to create an economic alliance. It was not as successful as the EEC which was now the second biggest producer of steel in the world.

In 1961, the UK chose to apply to join the EEC. Ninety percent of all Ireland's trade was with the UK and so Ireland, under Taoiseach Seán Lemass, also applied. The French President, Charles de Gaulle, blocked the application of the UK as he thought the British were politically too close to America. De Gaulle did not trust the Americans and also believed that the UK would try to dominate the EEC.

De Gaulle resigned from the French Presidency in 1970. This allowed Ireland (now under Taoiseach Jack Lynch), the UK and Denmark to apply for membership of the EEC. On 1 January 1973, the EEC increased its membership from six to nine.

● Further European Integration

EUROPEAN MONETARY SYSTEM

To further strengthen the economic cooperation between member states, the European Monetary System (EMS) was introduced in 1979. This was intended to keep the value of member states' currencies stable and free from fluctuations or sudden changes.

SINGLE EUROPEAN ACT

In 1986, the President of the European Commission, Jacques Delors proposed greater integration between member states. The Single European Act abolished all other restrictions on trade and the movement of people in the EEC. The EEC was renamed the European Community (EC) to show that it was more than simply an economic alliance.

THE MAASTRICHT TREATY

In December 1991, the EC member states signed the Treaty on the European Union in Maastricht, the Netherlands. This Maastricht Treaty came into force in 1993 with the following results:

1. The EC was renamed the European Union (EU).

▲ Jacques Delors, President of the Commission in 1986, wanted to make the EEC more than just an economic alliance.

2. Closer political ties were agreed, making the EU more of a political union of member states rather than just an economic union.

3. A new European currency called the **Euro** was introduced. It became the currency of 12 of the member states, including Ireland, in 2002.

4. A **Social Charter** created new laws about the standards of working conditions and pay.

5. The **Common Foreign and Security Policy (CFSP)** was introduced to help create a more common policy on foreign affairs among the member states. This would help the EU to speak on issues with a single voice.

THE AMSTERDAM TREATY

The Amsterdam Treaty was signed in 1997. It strengthened the laws on employment and on discrimination within the EU. It also prepared the EU for further expansion eastwards (i.e. Eastern European countries who had been anxious to join the EU for some time but had been unable to do so until the fall of communism).

The Amsterdam Treaty also created the position of High Representative for the Common Foreign and Security Policy. This person speaks on behalf of the EU on foreign policies agreed among the member states.

● Future for the EU

New treaties and constitutions have been created since 2000. They have tried to simplify the complicated number of treaties that govern the EU. Some of these have been rejected by countries such as Ireland, France and the Netherlands. Throughout all this time, the EU has continued to enlarge. In 2010, the population of the EU stood at about 490 million people.

CRITICISM OF THE EU

Some people think the European Parliament should have more power as it is the only directly elected part of the EU. They believe that this is the only way to solve the EU's **democratic deficit** (lack of democracy).

The creation of European military capabilities has worried some that the EU will begin to involve itself in wars both inside and outside Europe.

Critics also believe smaller countries must fight to ensure that they are not dominated by the larger, more powerful countries in the EU.

▲ The Anti-Lisbon campaign in 2007 was very successful in the first referendum on the Lisbon Treaty. However, the Irish people voted in favour of the Lisbon Treaty in the second referendum in 2009.

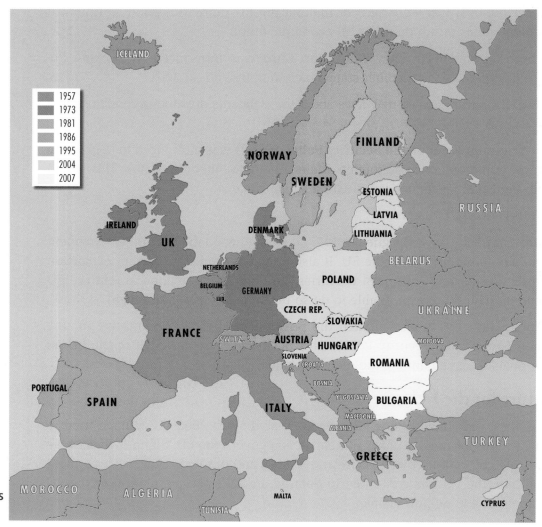

There are currently 27 member states in the EU. ▶

▲ The European anthem is Beethoven's Ode to Joy.

RESULTS OF EUROPEAN INTEGRATION

1. There has been peace among all the member states of the EU for the last 60 years.

2. Democracy and human rights have been helped as a result of laws enforced by the European Court of Justice.

3. The EU has become far wealthier through cooperation. The EU is now the most powerful trading bloc in the world.

4. The European Social Fund has helped poorer areas of Europe, such as Ireland, to become wealthier.

5. The CAP has maintained and benefitted the farming communities around Europe.

Questions

1. How many members does the EU now have?
2. Name the original six members.
3. Outline the main aspects of the Maastricht Treaty. Give five points.
4. What were the main aspects of the Amsterdam Treaty? Give three points.
5. What job does the High Representative for the Common Foreign and Security Policy have?
6. In your opinion has the EU been a good or bad thing for:

   (a) Europe   (b) Ireland

   Give reasons for your answers.

Chapter 13 Questions

1. Pictures

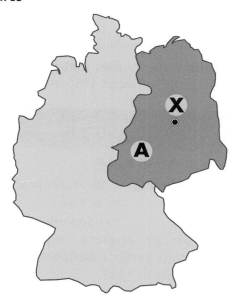

Examine the map above and answer the following questions:

(a) Which four countries had control over the different sectors of Germany after World War II?

(b) Which of the four was in charge of the country marked 'A' on the map?

(c) Which city is marked 'X' and why was it also divided after the War?

(d) Name the two countries that emerged out of East and West Germany after 1949.

2. Documents

> From Stettin in the Baltic to Trieste in the Adriatic an iron curtain has descended across the Continent. Behind that line lie all the capitals of the ancient states of Central and Eastern Europe. Warsaw, Berlin, Prague, Vienna, Budapest, Belgrade, Bucharest and Sofia, all these famous cities and the populations around them lie in what I must call the Soviet sphere, and all are subject in one form or another, not only to Soviet influence but to a very high and, in some cases, increasing measure of control from Moscow. Athens alone – Greece with its immortal glories – is free to decide its future at an election under British, American and French observation.
>
> -Winston Churchill, 1946

(a) Between which two cities does Churchill believe the iron curtain has descended?

(b) Name three of the capitals and the countries that lie behind that line.

(c) Under whose influence does Churchill fear that these capitals have come?

(d) Which city, according to Churchill, will still have free elections?

(e) Which political parties took over the governments in the countries behind the iron curtain?

3. Short-Answer Questions

(a) What was Operation Vittles?

(b) What caused the Soviets to blockade Berlin?

(c) Name three leaders involved in the Cuban missile crisis.

(d) Give two results of the Cuban missile crisis.

(e) Name the leaders of North and South Korea during the Korean War.

(f) Give two differences between capitalist and communist societies.

(g) What countries are involved in the Benelux Union?

(h) What does EFTA stand for?

(i) Name two politicians who encouraged closer European cooperation.

(j) Which treaty established the European Coal and Steel Community?

4. People in History

Write an account of a German citizen living in Berlin during the Berlin blockade, 1948-49. Use the following headings as a guide:

- The political situation after World War II
- The blockade by the Soviets
- The airlift by the Allies
- The results of the ending of the blockade

5.

(a) Give two reasons why the Cold War began after World War II.

(b) Write an account on one of the following crises and how it affected relations between the USA and the USSR:

The Korean War, 1950-1953

The Cuban Missile Crisis

OR

(c) Give two reasons why there was a desire for European unity after World War II.

(d) Outline the main treaties that have developed European unity between 1950 and 1997.

Key Terms to Summarise Chapter 13: International Relations 1945 – 2000

Superpower The term given to both the USA and the USSR after World War II due to their strong economic and military power.

Cold War The conflict between the USA and the USSR from 1945 to 1989. While there was no direct conflict or war between the two superpowers, they competed economically, politically and militarily.

Ideology A set of beliefs about how society should be organised, e.g. communism, capitalism.

Iron Curtain The phrase used by Winston Churchill to describe the divide in Europe between communist and capitalist countries.

Truman Doctrine The policy of the USA to stop the spread of communism throughout the world by offering financial and military aid to countries under threat of a communist takeover.

Containment Term used for policy of American government to stop the spread of communism around the world.

Marshall Aid Money offered to all European countries by the USA to help rebuild their economies post-World War II.

Blockade Surrounding a location with military forces to prevent any entry or exit.

Operation Vittles The codename given for America's airlift of essential supplies to the population of West Berlin in defiance of the Soviet blockade of the city in 1948.

North Atlantic Treaty Organisation (NATO) A military organisation of some western countries aimed at limiting the spread of communism.

Warsaw Pact A military alliance set up by the Soviets in response to the creation of NATO.

Arms race The competition between the USA and the USSR to build more and better weapons than each other.

Perestroika Russian word for restructuring. Part of the economic reforms of Soviet leader Gorbachev.

Glasnost Russian word for openness. The term given to the policy of increased political freedom in the USSR begun by Gorbachev.

Organisation for European Economic Cooperation
An organisation set up to distribute Marshall Aid.

European Coal and Steel Community (ECSC) An organisation set up in 1952 with six members. It eventually became the EU.

Common Market The creation of an area within Europe in which people, goods, services and money can move around as freely as within one country.

Common Agricultural Policy (CAP) A programme set up by the EEC to guarantee a high price to European farmers for their produce. This helped to increase productivity and also helped increase farmers' incomes.

Democratic deficit Some believe that the EU suffers from a democratic deficit. They feel the political systems of the EU are not democratic enough and the populations of the EU should have a more direct say in the running of the EU.

Web References

For further information on topics mentioned in this chapter, view the following websites:

europa.eu
www.un.org
www.bbc.co.uk/history/worldwars/coldwar
Watch footage of Hungarian Uprising or the fall of Berlin Wall on youtube.com

Women in History

Eleanor Roosevelt

(1884 – 1962)

Political Activist and Chair of United Nations Commission for the Declaration of Human Rights

Anna Eleanor Roosevelt was born in New York in 1884. Born into a wealthy family, she was sent to 'finishing school' in England at the age of 15. She returned to America in 1902 and fell in love with Franklin D Roosevelt whom she married in 1905. Franklin Roosevelt was inaugurated as President of America in 1933 and died in 1945. During her time as First Lady, she used her position to raise awareness of civil rights issues.

After her husband's death she became chairperson of the Human Rights Commission that drafted the UN Declaration of Human Rights, adopted in December 1948. It is the most translated document in the world and is the foundation for human rights around the world.

Roosevelt resigned as American delegate to the UN in 1953 and volunteered her services to the American Association of the United Nations. She was reappointed to the United States Delegation to the United Nations by President Kennedy in 1961. Kennedy also appointed her as a member of the National Advisory Committee of the Peace Corps and chairperson of the President's Commission on the Status of Women. She died in 1962 and is buried alongside her husband.

Chapter *14*

IRELAND SINCE 1948

Post-Emergency Ireland: 1948-1957

The Emergency, as World War II was known in Ireland, had been very difficult. High unemployment levels and rationing of food and clothes forced people to leave Ireland and search for work in Britain and America. By 1948, Fianna Fáil had been in government for 16 years and they were blamed for the country's poor economic situation. Some nationalists felt that Fianna Fáil should have taken World War II as the chance to declare Ireland a republic. Britain was in the midst of fighting and could not pay great attention to events in Ireland. The British may not have had the resources to react if a republic had been declared.

Unemployment levels grew after World War II, creating long queues at local post offices where people collected their dole payments. ▶

418

So it was not surprising that in the general election of 1948 there was a change of government:

Irish General Election, February 1948	
Fianna Fáil	67 seats
Fine Gael	31 seats
Labour Party	14 seats
Clann na Poblachta	10 seats
Others	24 seats

▲ John A Costello was Taoiseach of the first coalition government in Ireland, 1948–1951.

● The First Inter-Party Government

Even though Fianna Fáil was still the largest party in the Dáil, the other parties formed a **coalition** (alliance). As Fine Gael was the largest party in the coalition, it appointed **John A Costello** as Taoiseach. Labour's **William Norton** became Tánaiste and the leader of Clann na Poblachta, **Seán McBride**, was appointed Minister for External Affairs.

> ### By the way . . .
> Seán McBride was the son of Maud Gonne, the woman about whom WB Yeats wrote many poems.

ACHIEVEMENTS

1. On 18 April 1949, the Irish government declared Ireland to be a republic. It was no longer part of the British Commonwealth.

2. Éire was now to be known as the Republic of Ireland.

3. Costello maintained Ireland's neutrality by refusing to join NATO.

4. The Industrial Development Authority (IDA) was set up to help new industries in Ireland. It also hoped to attract companies from abroad to establish industries in Ireland.

John A Costello and Seán McBride giving an interview in 1948. ▶

NOEL BROWNE

Noel Browne was appointed Minister for Health in the Inter-Party government. He was a member of Clann na Poblachta. His main objective was to eradicate tuberculosis (TB) which killed 3,000 people in Ireland each year. He achieved this by:

▲ Noel Browne led a successful campaign to eradicate TB from Ireland.

By the way . . .

Noel Browne had first-hand experience of TB: three of his family died from it.

- Setting up special hospitals called **sanatoria** to deal with sufferers of TB.

- Introducing new mobile x-ray units to detect TB before it became fatal.

- Introducing a new vaccine called the BCG.

The results were amazing. The number of deaths from TB dropped to about 300 per year.

THE MOTHER AND CHILD SCHEME

▲ Archbishop John McQuaid, pictured here with de Valera, opposed the Mother and Child Scheme.

Following the success of eradicating TB, Browne now proposed the **Mother and Child Scheme**. Ireland at this point had one of the highest rates of death among children. The proposed scheme would give free medical care to all mothers and their children (under the age of 16). Doctors were opposed to the scheme and argued that the scheme would result in the end of doctor-patient privacy. The Catholic Church also attacked the scheme. They believed that the state should not interfere in private family matters. The Catholic Church was very powerful in Ireland and many in the government supported the Church. Costello told Browne that he must drop the scheme. Browne resigned from the government and from Clann na Poblachta in protest. Soon after, Clann na Poblachta withdrew its support for the government and the Inter-Party government collapsed in 1951.

Questions

1. What were the reasons for Fianna Fáil's loss at the 1948 general election?
2. What did John A Costello announce on 18 April 1949?
3. What was the IDA?
4. How did Noel Browne eradicate TB?
5. Who would have benefitted from the Mother and Child Scheme?
6. Who opposed the Scheme and why?

● Fianna Fáil and the Inter-Party Government: 1951-1957

Under de Valera, Fianna Fáil won the next election with the support of Noel Browne (who was no longer a member of Clann na Poblachta) and a number of other independents. The problems facing the country resulted in another election in 1954 which brought in the second Inter-Party government again led by John A Costello.

Irish General Elections:	1951	1954
Fianna Fáil	68 seats	65 seats
Fine Gael	40 seats	50 seats
Labour Party	16 seats	18 seats
Clann na Poblachta	2 seats	3 seats
Others	21 seats	11 seats

A number of challenges faced the two different governments between 1951 and 1957:

1. Ireland's economy was in difficulties due to its **balance of payments**. The country was importing far more goods into Ireland from Britain than it was exporting. As a result Ireland had to borrow money to buy these imports. To pay back this borrowed money, taxes were raised and less money was spent on housing and social welfare. These policies were very unpopular and so McBride withdrew support for the government in 1957.

2. After World War II, there was very little employment in industries or agriculture.

3. Emigration to the UK, Canada, Australia and the USA continued. Between 1951 and 1953 about 39,000 people left Ireland each year. By the time the second Inter-Party government came into power between 1954 and 1957, this figure had reached 42,000 annually. This led to a population of 2.8 million by 1961 – the lowest in the history of the country.

4. 1956 saw the beginning of an IRA campaign of violence in Northern Ireland. The Taoiseach of the Inter-Party government, John A Costello, was very hostile toward the IRA. His hostility was in conflict with many in the population who still had strong republican sympathies.

Another general election was called in 1957.

> **By the way . . .**
>
> Ireland was admitted into the United Nations in 1955 even though its application had been refused in 1945 by the USSR. The Russians disliked the Irish position of neutrality during World War II.

Ireland Changes: 1957-1973

▲ De Valera, pictured here with his wife Sinéad Ní Fhlannagáin, became President of Ireland in 1959 at 77 years of age.

Irish General Election 1957	
Fianna Fáil	78 seats
Fine Gael	40 seats
Labour Party	11 seats
Clann na Poblachta	4 seats
Others	14 seats

The 1957 general election saw Fianna Fáil receive a full majority in the Dáil. In 1959, de Valera resigned from his position as leader of Fianna Fáil and as Taoiseach. He was 77 years old. He was elected as President of Ireland later that year.

Seán Lemass replaced de Valera as leader of Fianna Fáil and as Taoiseach. Lemass immediately gave up de Valera's policy of high tariffs on imported goods. He worked closely with the Secretary of the Department of Finance, **T.K. Whitaker**, to achieve a number of important changes.

Seán Lemass replaced de Valera as Taoiseach in 1959. ▶

● Economics

The **New Programme for Economic Expansion** was drawn up. The main points of the Programme were:

1. Grants were given to farmers and businesses to produce more goods more efficiently.

2. Foreign industries and businesses were encouraged to come to Ireland. This was done by:

   • Offering grants to businesses to help them set up in Ireland.

   • Offering low levels of tax on the profits made by foreign businesses that came to Ireland.

3. Shannon Town and Industrial Estate was established. A new airport was also established to aid economic development.

The Programme was a success. Many firms from the USA, Britain and Japan set up businesses here in the years that followed. The availability of jobs in Ireland led to a drop in unemployment; emigration fell from 43,000 per year to 16,000 between 1956 and 1966.

The **Anglo-Irish Free Trade Agreement** of 1965 allowed Irish industries to export goods without any tariffs into Britain. In return, Ireland had to reduce its tariffs by 10% every year. By 1975, there was total free trade between the two countries.

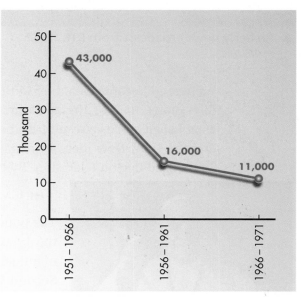

▲ Emigration levels dropped in the late 1950s thanks to the success of the New Programme for Economic Expansion.

● Education

In 1966, the Minister for Education, **Donogh O'Malley**, recognised the importance of a well-educated workforce in Ireland. He hoped that such a workforce would fill the new jobs being created by foreign businesses in Ireland. He tried to achieve this by:

1. Offering free secondary school education to all students.

2. Offering students free transport to and from school.

3. Giving grants to build new schools and improve older schools.

4. Opening new **comprehensive schools** and **Regional Technical Colleges** in 1970.

These changes meant that far more children were able to attend school. Before the offer of free education, many children left school before their Intermediate Examination (now Junior Certificate).

● Social Changes

Telefís Éireann

▲ An early news broadcast from RTÉ, 1962.

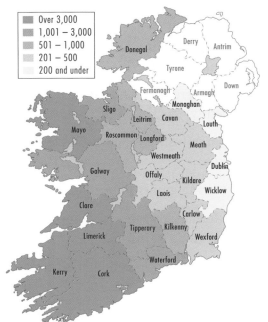

Over 3,000
1,001 – 3,000
501 – 1,000
201 – 500
200 and under

▲ The increase in new TV licences in Ireland between 1965 and 1987.

As Ireland became wealthier in the late 1950s and early 1960s, people began to buy televisions. In 1961, Ireland's first national television service, **Telefís Éireann** was established and as a result Irish people were exposed to new influences from Britain and the USA. New ideas were easily spread and political and church leaders were challenged live on television. By the 1970s, over 50% of all homes had a television.

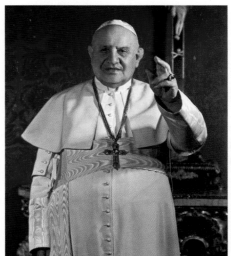

▲ Pope John XXIII called the Second Vatican Council with the aim of modernising the Catholic Church (1958).

The Catholic Church

The population of Ireland was overwhelmingly Catholic in the 1960s. This meant that the Catholic Church had a lot of influence. In 1958, the new Pope, **John XXIII**, called the **Second Vatican Council**. This council of bishops set about modernising the Catholic Church. Mass was allowed to be said in the vernacular (i.e. the local language) rather than in Latin and many other changes occurred. People began to question the power the Church had and even some of its teachings. This led to a gradual lessening of its influence over Irish society.

Northern Ireland

Lemass also began to change Irish policy on Northern Ireland. He accepted an invitation to meet with the Northern Irish Prime Minister, **Terence O'Neill** in 1965. This meeting was the first ever between an Irish Taoiseach and a Northern Irish Prime Minister. O'Neill also visited Dublin and both leaders discussed how they could cooperate in different areas such as tourism and agriculture. While no decisions were made, it was a step towards making relations between North and South more normal.

▲ Terence O'Neill, Prime Minister of Northern Ireland. He met with Seán Lemass several times to discuss cooperation between north and south.

Questions

1. Who did Lemass work with to create the New Programme for Economic Expansion?
2. What were the main points of the Programme?
3. Did Lemass's economic programme work? Give evidence to support your answer.
4. How did the Anglo-Irish Free Trade Agreement help Irish industries?
5. How did Donogh O'Malley hope to create a well-educated workforce?
6. How did Telifís Éireann influence people's lives?
7. Name one change the Second Vatican Council made to the Catholic Church?
8. Why was the meeting between Lemass and O'Neill important?
9. In your opinion, was the Lemass period of government a successful one?

Ireland Since the 1970s

General Elections	Government	Taoiseach
1973	Fine Gael & Labour	Liam Cosgrave
1977	Fianna Fáil	Jack Lynch 1977-79 Charles Haughey 1979-81
1981	Fine Gael & Labour	Garret FitzGerald
1982	Fianna Fáil	Charles Haughey
1982	Fine Gael & Labour	Garret FitzGerald
1987	Fianna Fáil	Charles Haughey
1989	Fianna Fáil	Charles Haughey
1992	Fianna Fáil & Labour (1992-1994)	Albert Reynolds
(No General Election)	Fine Gael, Labour & Democratic Left (1994-1997)	John Bruton
1997	Fianna Fáil & Progressive Democrats	Bertie Ahern

• The 1970s

The EEC

▲ Jack Lynch greeting Jacqueline Kennedy, wife of JFK.

Seán Lemass retired in 1966 and was replaced by **Jack Lynch** as Taoiseach and leader of Fianna Fáil. During Jack Lynch's time as Taoiseach he negotiated Ireland's membership of the EEC in 1973. Membership for Ireland came as a mixed blessing:

Benefits

- The **Common Agricultural Policy** helped farmers almost double their incomes between 1973 and 1978.

- The poorer areas in Ireland, particularly the west, benefitted from the **European Structural Fund** (ESF). The ESF gave money to less wealthy areas in Europe to build better infrastructure (roads, railways and public transport).

- Ireland became part of a free trade area (common market) for its produce.

- Irish citizens could now travel and work freely all across the EEC.

Drawbacks

- Membership of the EEC allowed fishermen from Europe to fish in Irish waters. The Spanish fishermen in particular had better boats and equipment. This allowed them to catch far more fish than Irish boats. This has reduced Irish fish stocks.

- Imports into Ireland were far cheaper as there were no tariffs. This resulted in job losses in Irish industries as people bought imported goods at a cheaper price than Irish goods.

Economics

Liam Cosgrave of Fine Gael was Taoiseach from 1973 until 1977. The economic advances that had occurred in the 1960s and early 1970s were wiped out by the **international oil crisis**. The shortage of oil due to the Arab-Israeli War caused the price of oil to increase. This led to inflation and many Irish businesses had to close. Unemployment and emigration began to grow again.

◀ Liam Cosgrave of Fine Gael was Taoiseach from 1973 until 1977.

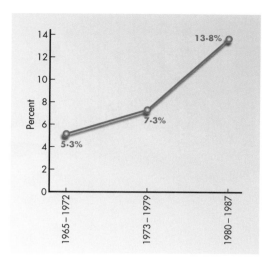

To finance the running of the country, the government borrowed money. The **budget deficit** (money the government had to borrow) almost doubled between 1979 and 1981.

◀ Graph of unemployment in Ireland between 1965 and 1987.

NORTHERN IRELAND

Arms Trial

1969 saw the beginning of the **Troubles** in Northern Ireland (see Chapter 15, Northern Ireland). Catholic communities in Northern Ireland came under attack from Protestants and the B-Specials (a part-time police force). Politicians in the South wanted Lynch to intervene but he refused. Two ministers in his government, Charles Haughey and Neil Blaney, were accused of importing guns using public money. They were tried but found not guilty. This court case became known as the **Arms Trial**.

Sunningdale Agreement

In 1973, Lynch and the British Prime Minister, Edward Heath, signed the **Sunningdale Agreement** creating a power-sharing government (politicians from both nationalist and unionist sides) in Northern Ireland. It was also proposed that there would be a **Council of Ireland** to promote North-South cooperation. Unionist opposition to Sunningdale led by Ian Paisley destroyed the power-sharing agreement and also the Council of Ireland.

▲ Charles Haughey was accused of using public money to import arms in 1970. He became Taoiseach three times between 1979 and 1992.

Representatives from the British government, the Irish government and Northern Ireland political parties meet in 1973 during the Sunningdale talks in London. ▶

The Dublin and Monaghan bombings

The violence that had become so common in Northern Ireland came to the Republic in 1974. Two bombs exploded in Dublin and one bomb in Monaghan within hours of each other on 17 May. The blasts killed 33 people and injured over 300.

▲ This photo of Talbot Street in Dublin shows how much damage the bomb explosion caused in 1974.

● The 1980s

THE ECONOMY

The 1980s were very difficult for the Irish economy. A number of factors contributed to this:

1. The budget deficit forced the government to make cutbacks in spending on education and health.

2. Unemployment levels continued to rise.

3. Emigration to the UK, Europe and the USA increased due to the lack of jobs.

4. Overproduction of agricultural goods in the EEC forced the European Commission to impose quotas (a limit on the amount of a product that can be produced).

These economic difficulties meant that there were many different governments during the 1980s (see table on page 425). This was because no government was able to solve the economic problems.

NORTHERN IRELAND

As the violence in Northern Ireland continued, a new agreement was signed in 1985 between Garret FitzGerald and Margaret Thatcher (the prime minister of Britain). The **Anglo-Irish Agreement** gave the Republic a say in the running of Northern Ireland.

▲ British Prime Minister Margaret Thatcher (centre-right) and Taoiseach Garret FitzGerald (centre-left) during an Anglo-Irish Summit conference in Britain in 1985.

• The 1990s

THE CELTIC TIGER

To deal with Ireland's budget deficit and economic difficulties, a number of governments made severe cutbacks in government spending. They also introduced an agreement between the government, employers and trade unions. This **Social Partnership** allowed for small wage increases for workers in return for lower taxes. This partnership proved to be very successful during the early 1990s.

▲ The arrival of companies such as Intel into Ireland created more jobs.

The arrival of foreign, especially American, computer companies such as Intel into Ireland created more jobs. These companies were attracted to Ireland due to its low tax rates, its well-educated workforce and its location as a base within the EU. With the arrival of jobs into Ireland, unemployment fell and emigration dropped. As people earned money, they were able to spend more money. This created more jobs in services such as restaurants.

RESULTS OF THE CELTIC TIGER

1. Ireland's economy grew faster than any other European country between 1995 and 2000. The economy grew at over nine per cent every year for those five years. By 2005, Ireland was the fifth richest country in the world (based on GDP per head of population).

2. Ireland managed to reach full employment (i.e. an unemployment rate of 4.3%) by 2000.

3. People were no longer forced to emigrate. Instead, people began to immigrate into Ireland looking for work. This led to a rise in population. In 2002, Ireland had a population of 4.2 million, the largest in over a century.

4. Ireland became richer and prices began to rise. By 2008, Dublin was the sixteenth most expensive city in the world.

5. The gap between rich and poor in Irish society grew. In 2006 Ireland had about 30,000 millionaires but its population had the highest risk of falling into poverty in the EU.

6. People in Ireland were working for longer (average age of retirement was 61 in 2001) and dying younger (71 for men and 78 for women in 2001) than others in Europe.

7. The price of houses, especially in the cities, rose steeply. The average house price in Dublin rose from just under €50,000 in 1987 to over €400,000 in 2005. This property bubble would ultimatey result in a banking and economic collapse.

8. Ireland's growth was based on unsustainable borrowing and many of the benefits of the Celtic Tiger years were lost in the years after 2007.

● Northern Ireland

◀ Irish Taoiseach Bertie Ahern and British Prime Minister Tony Blair at the announcement of the Good Friday Agreement in 1998.

New efforts to find peace in Northern Ireland resulted in the signing of the **Good Friday Agreement** in 1998. This was the beginning of the road to peace within Northern Ireland.

Questions

1. Outline the benefits and drawbacks for Ireland of joining the EEC in 1973.
2. Explain how the international oil crisis damaged the Irish economy. Use evidence to support your answer.
3. Explain the term 'budget deficit'.
4. What were Charles Haughey and Neil Blaney accused of importing in 1969?
5. What economic difficulties did Irish governments face in the 1980s?
6. What was the Anglo-Irish Agreement of 1985?
7. Explain the term 'social partnership'.
8. What were some of the factors that created the 'Celtic Tiger' economy of the 1990s?
9. Give examples of how the Celtic Tiger affected Ireland in a positive and in a negative way.

Chapter 14 Questions

1. Pictures

A

B

C

D

Since becoming Minister for Health I have striven [tried] within the limits of my ability to improve the health services of the country. Some progress has been made but much remains to be done. It is perhaps only human that I should wish to have the honour of continuing the work. However that is not to be. To me the provision of a health scheme for the benefit of the mothers and children of our nation seems to be the very foundation stone of any progressive health service without which much of our efforts in other directions would prove fruitless. It seemed equally important to me that any such scheme to be effective and indeed just [fair] should be made available free to all our people who choose of their own free will to use it without the imposition of any form of means test [a test by the government to check if a family can afford to pay for the scheme themselves or if the state should provide it for free].

(a) Name the four politicians in pictures A, B, C and D.

(b) Which parties did they lead?

(c) Which crime was the politician in Picture C accused of in 1969?

(d) Which Agreement did the politician in picture D sign with Margaret Thatcher in 1985?

(e) Explain the term coalition.

(a) Why did Noel Browne make this speech?

(b) What position did Noel Browne have within the government before he resigned?

(c) What scheme does Browne believe is the foundation stone of any progressive health service?

(d) Do you think the scheme should have been free or not? Give reasons for your answer.

(e) What was the name given to the scheme in question?

(f) What disease is Noel Browne credited with eradicating in Ireland?

2. Documents

This is an excerpt from a speech made by Noel Browne to the Dáil in April 1951:

It is fitting and, I am informed, in accordance with usage [what usually happens], that I should explain to the Dáil very briefly the reasons which led me to resign my position in the Government. I am deeply grieved that I have found myself compelled [forced] to take this step.

3. Short-Answer Questions

(a) Give one reason why there was high unemployment in Ireland between 1951 and 1957.

(b) Why was the IDA established in 1950?

(c) Give one method Noel Browne used to eradicate TB in Ireland.

(d) Which party was Noel Browne a member of?

(e) What was the Arms Trial?

(f) What did the Common Agricultural Policy (CAP) do for Irish farmers?

(g) In what year did Ireland join the EEC?

(h) Give one advantage and one disadvantage to Ireland's membership of the EEC.

(i) What was the Sunningdale Agreement?

(j) What change did the Anglo-Irish Agreement of 1985 make in the running of Northern Ireland?

4. People in History

Give an account of a named head of government of Ireland during the period 1948 to 2000 using the following headings as a guide:

- Policies
- Problems
- Successes
- Failures

5.

Write an account of two of the following:

(a) The First Inter-Party Government, 1948-1951

(b) Fianna Fáil in government, 1959-1973

(c) The Celtic Tiger years, 1990-2000

Key Terms to Summarise Chapter 14: Ireland Since 1948

Coalition government When two or more political parties form an alliance in order to achieve a majority within parliament and form a government.

Sanatoria Special hospitals set up to deal with sufferers of tuberculosis (TB).

Mother and Child Scheme A medical scheme proposed in 1951 by Minister for Health Noel Browne to provide free health care to all mothers and their children up to the age of 16.

Balance of payments The difference between how much it costs to import (buy) goods into a country and how much is earned by exporting (selling) goods from the same country.

The New Programme for Economic Expansion A set of economic policies developed in 1959 by the government led by Seán Lemass.

Anglo-Irish Free Trade Agreement (1965) An agreement between Britain and Ireland aimed at eliminating all taxes and tariffs between the two countries.

Telefís Éireann The name of Ireland's first television service which began broadcasting in 1961.

Second Vatican Council (1958) A large meeting of Bishops called by Pope John XXIII to help modernise the Catholic Church.

Common Agricultural Policy (CAP) An EEC policy that provided a guaranteed income for farmers' produce.

European Structural Fund An EEC programme that provided money for the development of poorer regions within the EEC, including parts of Ireland.

Budget deficit When a government spends more than it receives.

Arms Trial The trial of Charles Haughey and Neil Blaney on the charge of attempting to import arms (weapons) using public money.

The Sunningdale Agreement (1973) A political treaty between Ireland and Britain that created a power-sharing government in Northern Ireland. It did not succeed.

The Anglo-Irish Agreement (1985) A political treaty between Ireland and Britain that provided the Republic of Ireland with a say in the running of Northern Ireland.

Social Partnership Economic agreements on taxation and wages between the government, the trade unions and the employers.

Good Friday (Belfast) Agreement (1998) A political treaty between Britain, Ireland and the political parties of Northern Ireland that led to the establishment of peace in Northern Ireland.

Web References

For further information on topics mentioned in this chapter, view the following websites:

www.cso.ie/statistics/
www.taoiseach.gov.ie/index.asp?locID=349&docID=-1
www.president.ie/index.php?section=20&lang=eng
www.rte.ie/laweb/ll/ll_t09_main.html

Women in History

Mary Robinson

President of Ireland and Human Rights Activist

(1944 –)

Mary Bourke was born in Ballina, County Mayo in 1944. She attended school in Dublin before studying law in Trinity College Dublin. She was appointed to the prestigious position of Reid Professor of Law while she was still only in her twenties. She was a member of Dublin City Council between 1979 and 1983 before being elected by Trinity College to the Seanad. During her time as a senator, she campaigned for women's rights (i.e. equal rights for women), the liberalisation (relaxation) of laws on the availability of contraception and homosexual law reform (i.e. equal rights for homosexuals). She joined the Labour Party in the 1970s and stood for election to the Dáil but was unsuccessful. She did not seek re-election to the Seanad in 1989. In 1990, she was approached by the Labour Party to run for the Irish Presidency.

In the election against Brian Lenihan and Austin Currie, Robinson managed to win and become Ireland's first female president. She was sworn in as the seventh president of Ireland on 3 December, 1990. Her time as president saw the role of the Irish presidency grow. She worked hard to bridge divides within Ireland. She became the first Irish President to meet the British monarch, Queen Elizabeth, at Buckingham Palace. She also met leaders of many of the major parties in Northern Ireland. She resigned as President in 1997 to take up the position of High Commissioner for Human Rights in the United Nations. When she resigned as president, the Taoiseach at the time, Bertie Ahern, described her as a 'woman of exceptional talent and charisma'.

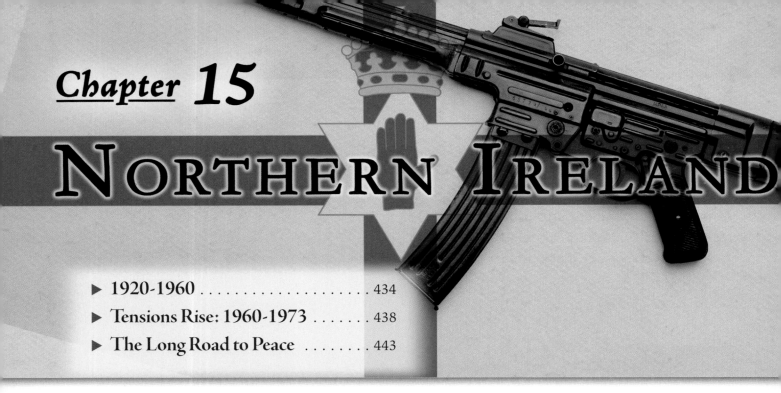

Chapter 15

NORTHERN IRELAND

 ## 1920-1960

In 1920, the British government passed the **Government of Ireland Act** which created the state of Northern Ireland. This state contained six of the nine counties of Ulster. There were majorities of unionists in four of these counties, while Fermanagh and Tyrone contained large unionist minorities.

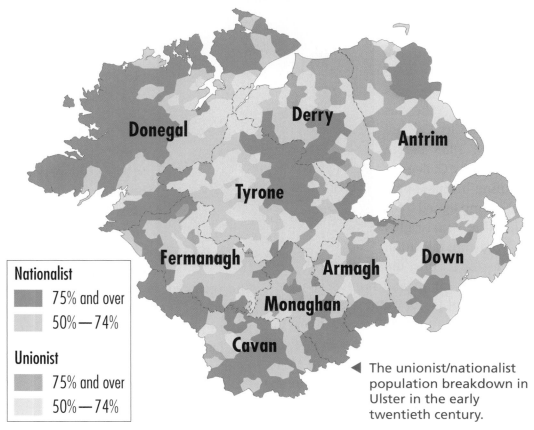

Nationalist
75% and over
50%—74%

Unionist
75% and over
50%—74%

◀ The unionist/nationalist population breakdown in Ulster in the early twentieth century.

Unionists in the 1920s

Following the Government of Ireland Act, Northern Ireland remained part of the United Kingdom and had its own parliament in **Stormont**. This parliament was dominated by the Ulster Unionist Party (UUP). **James Craig** was chosen as Prime Minister in 1920.

Unionists were delighted when the **Boundary Commission** decided in 1925 to keep the six counties within Northern Ireland. Craig said, '. . . we are a Protestant parliament and a Protestant state'. Northern Ireland was still represented by 13 MPs (11 of whom were members of the UUP) in the British parliament, Westminster.

▲ James Craig became Prime Minister of Northern Ireland in 1920.

Nationalists in the 1920s

Nationalists in Northern Ireland were generally Catholic. Due to their position as a minority population within Northern Ireland, they had little hope of getting into power. In 1921, nationalists won only 12 seats in Stormont in comparison to the 40 seats that unionists won. Nationalists wished to become part of the Irish Free State and were hostile to British involvement in Ireland.

Unionist Control of Power

This hostility toward British involvement meant that unionists saw nationalists as a threat to the state of Northern Ireland. The unionists used a variety of methods to ensure that they kept their power:

1. The police force in Northern Ireland was the **Royal Ulster Constabulary (RUC)**. They were backed up by a part-time police force called the **B-Specials**. Both these forces were almost exclusively Protestant and they discriminated against nationalists.

2. Sectarian violence broke out in Northern Ireland. Between 1921-1922, about 11,000 Catholics were forced from their jobs and many Catholic shops and houses were burnt. Overall almost 60% of casualties during the violence were Catholic although they only made up one third of the population.

3. The **Special Powers Act 1922** allowed the government to **intern** (imprison without trial) nationalist suspects.

4. To ensure that nationalists had very few people to represent them in the Northern Ireland parliament, Craig abolished the system of **proportional representation** (PR). PR allows smaller political parties to be represented by MPs in parliament and gives a fairer representation of the population. The system **introduced by Craig** was called the **first-past-the-post-system** and it meant that bigger parties got more representation, i.e. more MPs. This system favoured the larger unionist parties such as the UUP.

5. Where there were nationalist majorities, the government changed the borders of the **constituencies** (areas represented by MPs) to ensure that unionists still had

a majority. For example, Derry City had an overwhelming nationalist majority yet unionists still controlled the town corporation. This is called **gerrymandering**.

Sectarianism

Sectarianism (discrimination due to religious beliefs) was also a problem. Poor Protestants were given local authority housing before poor Catholics who were equally in need of housing.

Protestants were hired to work in the civil service and in private businesses (mostly owned by Protestants). Catholics, in general, were not employed by the civil service and they rarely found work in businesses owned by Protestants. If they found employment it was unlikely that Catholics would be promoted over a Protestant.

For these reasons, Catholics had very little chance of finding work. By 1932, unemployment in Northern Ireland was at 28%. This was made worse due to the poor economic situation that existed worldwide after the Wall Street Crash of 1929 and the Great Depression that followed.

World War II

Northern Ireland was still very much part of the UK during World War II. It played an important role in the British war effort but it also benefitted economically from it:

1. Shipbuilding in **Harland and Wolff's** shipyards and plane manufacturing at the **Short Brother's** factory ensured that there was plenty of work for the population (although the vast majority of it was given to the Protestant workforce).

2. The linen industry also benefitted as it supplied uniforms and parachutes for the British Army.

3. From 1942 until 1945, 300,000 American soldiers were based in Northern Ireland. These soldiers were customers for local businesses, e.g. cinemas, cafes, pubs, shops.

4. Roads and ports were improved to help transport large amounts of goods and American soldiers travelling through the North.

By the end of World War II, unemployment had dropped to only five per cent.

▲ An assembly line in Short's factory in Northern Ireland

Because Northern Ireland was not neutral, it was a target for attack by Germany. In April and May 1941 the Luftwaffe bombed Belfast. This bombing killed 745 people and destroyed more than 3,000 houses. This common suffering strengthened the link between Britain, who endured The Blitz during the same year, and Northern Ireland. For some people, the peaceful neutrality of the Irish Free State only reinforced the differences between the North and the South of Ireland (See Chapter 12, Ireland in the Twentieth Century, page 386).

▲ A view of Bridge Street in Belfast following the 1941 bombing of the city by the Luftwaffe.

● The Welfare State

After the war, the Labour Party was elected in Britain. It wanted to improve the lives of its citizens by introducing what became known as the **Welfare State**.

1. The **National Health Service (NHS)** was set up. This offered free healthcare to everyone and new hospitals were also built.

2. The **Education Act** of 1947 gave free secondary education to all children regardless of religion.

3. Better pensions and unemployment assistance were provided.

These social improvements gave unionists another reason to want to remain part of the UK. They also offered poorer Catholics an opportunity to attend schools which produced a generation of educated Catholics who were determined to stop the discrimination and who pushed for equal rights in the late 1960s.

Questions

1. List the six counties that make up Northern Ireland.

2. What measures did the newly-formed unionist government in Northern Ireland take to ensure that the nationalists could not get into government?

3. Explain the following terms:
   (a) Gerrymandering
   (b) Constituencies
   (c) Sectarianism

4. Give two examples of how Northern Ireland was able to aid the British war effort.

5. What economic benefits did Northern Ireland gain during World War II?

6. In your opinion, why did the Irish Free State's neutrality reinforce partition?

7. Outline some of the improvements to people's lives that the Welfare State introduced.

8. How did the Welfare State help Catholics in Northern Ireland?

Tensions Rise: 1960-1973

● The 1960s

▲ Terence O'Neill introduced reforms to help Catholics.

Terence O'Neill became prime minister of Northern Ireland in 1963. He wanted to introduce reforms to help Catholics. He was the first Northern prime minister to invite the Taoiseach, Seán Lemass, to Northern Ireland. O'Neill travelled to Dublin a few weeks later. This worried extreme unionists, such as members of the sectarian protestant **Orange Order** and **Ian Paisley** (founder of the strongly anti-Catholic Free Presbyterian Church), who thought that O'Neill was being far too friendly to nationalists.

● The Northern Ireland Civil Rights Association

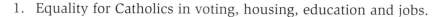

The **Northern Ireland Civil Rights Association (NICRA)** was set up in 1967. This movement included both Catholics and Protestants and hoped to end discrimination against Catholics. It demanded:

1. Equality for Catholics in voting, housing, education and jobs.

2. The abolition of the Special Powers Act (see page 435) and the disbanding of the B-Specials.

3. An end to gerrymandering.

▲ Ian Paisley, an extreme unionist, felt O'Neill was too friendly to nationalists.

The leaders of the NICRA – **John Hume**, **Gerry Fitt**, **Austin Currie** and **Bernadette Devlin** – organised a number of peaceful marches to pressure O'Neill to make more reforms. Some unionists disliked the prospect of equal rights for Catholics. Led by Ian Paisley, they organised counter-marches.

▲ John Hume (left), Gerry Fitt (centre) and Ivan Cooper (right) organised marches to demand equality for Catholics in Northern Ireland.

In October 1968, a civil rights march through Derry was planned. A unionist group known as the Protestant Apprentice Boys planned to march on the same day. O'Neill banned both marches but the civil rights march went ahead anyway. Riots broke out and the RUC baton-charged the civil rights marchers, injuring many people including women and children. These clashes were caught on TV and broadcast around the world. The images brought the '**Troubles**' (as the violence became known) to the world's attention for the first time.

Pressure came from the British government to make some reforms. The reforms proposed included equality in the areas of housing, an end to gerrymandering and the disbanding of the B-Specials. However O'Neill faced growing pressure from extreme unionists such as **Brian Faulkner**, Ian Paisley and **Major James Chichester-Clark**, who firmly opposed introducing these reforms. In April 1969, O'Neill resigned and was replaced by Chichester-Clark.

● The Troubles

During 1969 violence erupted throughout Northern Ireland. Bomb explosions damaged electricity and water supplies. Although officially the bombs were blamed on the IRA, they were in fact thought to be the work of the loyalist paramilitary (a non-government military organisation) **Ulster Volunteer Force (UVF)**. In August, a riot broke out in the nationalist area of the **Bogside** in Derry City.

▲ Members of NICRA holding placards stating their demands.

THE BATTLE OF THE BOGSIDE

The Catholic population of the Bogside area in Derry felt particularly discriminated against by the police and UVF. They created barricades around the Bogside to protect themselves from Protestant attackers and the RUC. Following a Protestant Apprentice Boys march through Derry, rioting broke out in the area on 12 August. The RUC clashed with local Catholics in fighting that lasted a week. These scenes of violence were broadcast globally.

At the same time, violence broke out in Belfast. Unionist crowds invaded Catholic areas, and the RUC and B-Specials were sent in to keep control. At least 7 people were killed and 3,500 families were driven from their homes, 3,000 of whom were Catholics.

The Taoiseach, **Jack Lynch**, stated on television, 'it is clear that the Irish Government can no longer stand by and see innocent people injured and perhaps worse'. It appeared that Northern Ireland was on the brink of civil war. The British government decided to send in the army to restore order on 14 August.

▲ The Battle of the Bogside in Derry, 1969

▲ A protestor throws a petrol bomb at members of the RUC during the Battle of the Bogside.

▲ A young boy wearing a gas mask to protect himself from tear gas prepares to throw a petrol bomb.

ARRIVAL OF THE BRITISH ARMY

The arrival of British troops in August 1969 was welcomed by some of the Catholic populations especially in Belfast, who no longer had any trust in the RUC. In fact Catholics hoped that the British army would be able to protect them from both the RUC and the UVF. Violence simmered down for a short while after the arrival of the troops.

Questions

1. What were the aims of NICRA?
2. What sparked the rioting in the Bogside in August 1969?
3. Why do you think Derry City was at the centre of much of the violence which took place in Northern Ireland?
4. Why was the British Army sent into Northern Ireland?
5. Why do you think the British Army was welcomed by some of the nationalist communities?

● Political changes

In 1970, a number of members from the NICRA set up a new political party called the **Social Democratic and Labour Party (SDLP)**. Its leaders included Gerry Fitt and John Hume.

The IRA split during 1969. The Official IRA moved away from violence while the **Provisional IRA** still believed in the use of force. The 'Provos', as they became known, were prepared to attack Protestants, the RUC and the British Army in an attempt to force them into accepting a united Ireland. This brought them regularly into conflict with the UVF.

▲ Members of NICRA founded a new political party in 1970 called the Social Democratic and Labour Party (SDLP). From L-R: Ivan Cooper, John Hume, Paddy Devlin, Austin Currie, Paddy O'Hanlon.

INTERNMENT

▲ Brian Faulkner introduced internment when he became prime minister of Northern Ireland in 1971.

The increasing level of violence resulted in Chichester-Clark's resignation in 1971. Brian Faulkner replaced him and he quickly introduced **internment** (arrest and imprisonment without trial) of IRA suspects. On the first day of internment 342 suspects were arrested. Within 6 months, 2,357 people had been arrested, 1,600 of whom were released without questioning.

Internment was not successful for a number of reasons:

1. Despite the huge numbers of people arrested, the Northern Ireland authorities failed to arrest the leaders of the IRA.

2. Many innocent Catholics were arrested and badly treated by the police force.

3. This mistreatment led to increased support and sympathy for the IRA throughout nationalist communities, sometimes by people who had previously been opposed to IRA activities.

● Bloody Sunday

On Sunday, 30 January 1972, a protest march against internment took place in Derry. The British Army shot and killed 13 unarmed marchers in what became known as **Bloody Sunday**. This event increased support for the IRA. Protests and rioting took place all over Northern Ireland. In Dublin, a crowd attacked and burned the British embassy on 2 February. As a result of this violence, the parliament in Stormont was suspended and direct rule from Westminster was re-introduced.

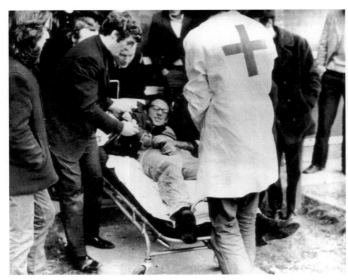

▲ An injured member of the protest march is placed on a stretcher, Bloody Sunday, Derry City 1972.

▲ A British soldier removes a demonstrator on Bloody Sunday, 1972.

● Sunningdale Agreement, 1973

To help solve the violence between nationalists and unionists in Northern Ireland, the British government pushed for a new agreement. The British government, all of the North's political parties and the Irish government signed the **Sunningdale Agreement** in December 1973. This proposed that:

1. A new coalition government would be created between the unionist and nationalist parties. This **power-sharing government** would have Faulkner as Prime Minister. The leader of the SDLP, Gerry Fitt, would be his Deputy Prime Minister.

2. A **Council of Ireland** would be set up. This was a rather symbolic creation but it was seen by unionists as allowing southern influence in Northern policies.

Many **loyalists** (extreme unionists) including Ian Paisley, opposed the Agreement. In an attempt to destroy it, the **Ulster Workers' Council** organised a strike in May 1974. Roadblocks were set up all over the North, and electricity and water supplies were cut. The power-sharing government collapsed and direct rule from Westminster was re-introduced.

▲ British soldiers had to work in businesses, such as this petrol station in Belfast, during the strike by the Ulster Workers' Council in 1974.

Questions

1. What was the difference between the Provisional and the Official IRA?
2. Why did internment help to increase support for the IRA?
3. What was Bloody Sunday and on what date did it take place?
4. What did the Sunningdale Agreement propose?
5. In your opinion, why did loyalists oppose the Sunningdale Agreement?
6. What actions did the loyalists take to destroy the Agreement?

The Long Road to Peace

Hunger Strikes (1981)

Violence continued throughout the 1970s. In 1980, a new crisis occurred. Nationalist political activists in prison had been treated as being a 'special category', that is, different to criminal prisoners. This special status was removed in 1976. IRA prisoners in the Maze prison in Northern Ireland continued to demand special status. They wanted to wear their own clothes and to be treated as **political prisoners**. They believed that they were in prison for political crimes rather than 'criminality'. Protests began in the prisons in 1980 when prisoners wore only blankets rather than prison clothes. When this initial protest achieved nothing, a more serious protest began.

▲ One of the many entrances to the Maze Prison in Northern Ireland.

▲ Bobby Sands was elected as a British MP whilst on hunger strike in the Maze Prison in 1981.

On 1 March 1981, a nationalist prisoner called **Bobby Sands** refused to eat any food. He began a **hunger strike** that was to last 66 days. During his hunger strike he was elected as an MP to Westminster. The new British Prime Minister, **Margaret Thatcher**, refused to negotiate with the strikers. On 5 May, Sands died. A further nine strikers died between May and 20 August. Under pressure from the Catholic Church, the SDLP and others, the strike was called off in October 1981. Shortly afterwards, most of the demands of the strikers were granted. They were not, however, given political prisoner status. The coverage in the media increased support for the IRA.

▲ British Prime Minister Margaret Thatcher refused to negotiate with the hunger strikers.

● Anglo-Irish Agreement (1985)

In 1985, the British and Irish governments met in Hillsborough Castle to create a new agreement on Northern Ireland. **Garret FitzGerald** and Margaret Thatcher signed the **Anglo-Irish (Hillsborough) Agreement** in November 1985. The Agreement stated that:

1. There could be no change to Northern Ireland's position within the UK without the agreement of the majority of the population.

2. The Republic of Ireland would have a limited role in the internal affairs of the North.

Many unionists opposed the Agreement but the British government refused to give in to their protests.

● The Downing Street Declaration (1993)

▲ British Prime Minister John Major (left) and Taoiseach Albert Reynolds announce a joint declaration to bring peace to Northern Ireland in 1993.

In late 1993, British Prime Minister, **John Major** and Taoiseach **Albert Reynolds** issued the **Downing Street Declaration**.

This recognised that:

1. Britain no longer had a strategic or economic interest in Northern Ireland.

2. Self-determination of the populations of the Republic and Northern Ireland was necessary if the unification of Ireland was to occur.

Along with behind-the-scenes talks between the British government and the IRA, this Declaration helped bring about an IRA ceasefire in 1994. The **IRA ceasefire** was followed by some other paramilitary groups such as the UVF. While these ceasefires sometimes broke down and had to be renewed over the next number of years, the **peace process** had begun.

● The Good Friday Agreement (1998)

In 1998, the new Labour Prime Minister in Britain, **Tony Blair,** began to push for a more lasting solution. With Taoiseach **Bertie Ahern**, he persuaded the leaders of the main political parties in the North (**David Trimble** – Ulster Unionist Party, **John Hume** – SDLP and **Gerry Adams** – Sinn Féin) to come to an agreement.

The **Good Friday (Belfast) Agreement** of 10 April 1998 proposed:

1. The creation of a new **Northern Ireland Assembly.** This Assembly would be open to all political parties who accepted democracy and rejected the use of violence.

2. The Assembly would include all political parties in a power-sharing government.

3. The Republic of Ireland would remove **Articles 2 and 3** of the Irish Constitution. These articles claimed control of the entire island of Ireland, including Northern Ireland.

4. **Referenda** (voting on a particular issue) would take place in Northern Ireland and in the Republic on whether or not to accept the Good Friday Agreement.

▲ Gerry Adams (right) and Martin McGuinness met with British Prime Minister Tony Blair as part of the negotiations for the Good Friday Agreement.

▲ David Trimble (UUP) (left) and John Hume (SDLP) onstage with Bono at a concert to promote a yes vote in the peace referenda.

● Northern Ireland at Peace

The Good Friday Agreement was passed in Northern Ireland by 71% and in the South by 94%. Over the following number of years there were many challenges. Several power-sharing governments have collapsed because of unionist demands that the IRA destroy its weapons. In 2005, the **Independent International Commission on Decommissioning** (IICD) stated that the IRA had put all its weapons beyond use. A power-sharing government was established with Ian Paisley (**Democratic Unionist Party**) as First Minister (Prime Minister) and **Martin McGuinness** (Sinn Féin) as Deputy First Minister.

▲ Former enemies Ian Paisley (left) and Martin McGuinness share a joke after being sworn in as ministers in the power-sharing government in 2005.

Questions

1. In your opinion, why did nationalist prisoners not want to be seen as criminals?

2. What effect did the hunger strikes have on support for the IRA among the nationalist community? Give reasons for your answer.

3. What did the Anglo-Irish Agreement of 1985 state?

4. What benefits did the government of the Republic enjoy as a result of the Anglo-Irish Agreement?

5. Outline the main proposals of the Good Friday Agreement.

6. Look at the proposals for the Good Friday Agreement and the Sunningdale Agreement. What are the main differences?

7. Why was it important to unionists that Articles 2 and 3 of the Irish Constitution were removed?

8. Why was Britain's statement that it had 'no strategic or economic interest' in Northern Ireland of great importance to nationalists?

Chapter 15 Questions

1. Pictures

A

B

(a) In picture A, who is the Carson mentioned in this poster and which party did he lead?

(b) In picture A, which Bill is mentioned in the poster?

(c) Look at picture B and name the political leader from Northern Ireland who was against the Sunningdale Agreement of 1973.

(d) From your reading of this chapter, why did the Sunningdale Agreement of 1973 fail?

2. Documents

From the testimony of Betty Curran, given at the Bloody Sunday Tribunal

After they had thrown a couple of stones, the lads turned and walked towards us. As they were coming towards us, I heard a shot. Damien 'Bubbles' Donaghy was shot. I did not know him at the time, but learned his name later. He was only about 14 or 15 years old. I remember he had a lovely head of curly hair. He was wearing jeans. He had only been dandering across the road. He was facing me when he was shot, walking to my right hand side as I was facing him. He had just about reached the footpath on the side where I was standing. I just saw his body falling. He was only a few feet away from me when he fell. I think he fell face down. I remember that he fell onto a piece of ground which had originally been part of a small porch leading into a derelict house because I remember the black and white tiles on which he fell. It had clearly been someone's hallway. I didn't see where the bullet hit him at the time. I saw it bounce off the tiles though, and I realised that it was not big enough to be a rubber bullet. I heard two shots, one straight after the other, and they were the first two I had heard that day. I recognised them as live because I saw one bullet bounce off the black and white tiles and I saw Damien Donaghy fall. I would not have known about the particular type of ammunition otherwise. I heard no further shots after that for 10 or 15 minutes.

I did not see Damien Donaghy throw any stones towards the soldiers and, as he came towards me with his fellows, there was nothing in his hands. I remember this quite clearly because he had his hands down by his sides and not in his pockets. My husband, who helped carry Damien Donaghy into a house in Columbcille Court, told me afterwards that he had been shot in the leg. I cannot remember if I knew this before he told me.

I subsequently heard that Mr Johnston had been hit too. He had been running over to Bubbles when he fell. I did not see Mr Johnston shot and I did not know him.

My husband said to me that we had better get out of there because they were firing rubber bullets but I said "it's not rubber bullets, it's live bullets" – I had seen the long narrow darkish object hit the ground and bounce back up again and at the same time Damien Donaghy had fallen to the ground. I began to tremble, I was very frightened.

SIGNED *Mrs Betty Curran*
Betty Curran

DATED 1 – 6 – 1999

Note: Bubbles is a nick-name for Damien Donaghy

(a) Where was Damien Donaghy shot?

(b) Did Donaghy have any weapons in his hands? Give evidence to support your answer.

(c) What kind of bullets did Betty Curran first think they were shooting?

(d) Why did Betty Curran believe that they were shooting live ammunition?

(e) Was she scared? How can we tell this?

(f) What impact did Bloody Sunday have on support for the IRA? Give reasons for your answer.

3. Short-Answer Questions

(a) In what ways did Northern Ireland contribute to the British war effort during World War II?

(b) Name one leader of the Ulster Unionist Party between 1900 and 1978.

(c) Who were members of the Orange Order?

(d) Where was the Northern Ireland parliament located?

(e) How did the Welfare State help Catholics gain equality?

(f) Which political party did Gerry Fitt, John Hume and Austin Currie help to set up in 1970?

(g) Name the Taoiseach of Ireland and the British Prime Minister who signed the Anglo-Irish Agreement of 1985.

(h) Why did prisoners in the Maze go on hunger strike in 1980-1981?

(i) What did Articles 2 and 3 state and why did the unionists want to have them removed from the Irish Constitution?

(j) What Agreement set up the Northern Ireland Assembly in 1998?

4. People in History

Write an account of a Catholic living in Derry during the late 1960s and early 1970s. Use the following headings as a guide:

- The political situation in Northern Ireland
- Discrimination
- The Civil Rights movement
- Some of the main marches

5.

The following statistics are from the 1966 Cameron Commission's investigation into gerrymandering in Northern Ireland:

City of Derry	Catholics	Protestants	Number of MPs
Total Population	20,102	10,272	
Number of Ratepayers (eligible to vote)	14,429	8,781	
Constituencies			
South Ward	10,047	1,138	8 Nationalist
North Ward	3,946	2,530	8 Unionist
The Waterside	3,697	1,852	4 Unionist

(from *A Story of Ireland* by John McCormack, Mentor Books)

(a) From the statistics listed in the table, answer the following questions:

    (i) How many Catholics lived in the city of Derry?

    (ii) How many Protestants lived in the city of Derry?

    (iii) How many unionist MPs were elected in Derry?

    (iv) How many nationalist MPs were elected in Derry?

    (v) Using this information, explain how gerrymandering worked.

(b) Explain three of the following terms relating to Northern Ireland:

    (i) Internment

    (ii) B Specials

    (iii) Hunger strike

    (iv) Power-sharing

(c) Write an account on two of the following:

    (i) Battle of the Bogside, 1969

    (ii) Bloody Sunday, 30 January 1972

    (iii) The Government of Ireland Act, 1920

    (iv) The Northern Ireland Civil Rights Association

Key Terms to Summarise Chapter 15: Northern Ireland

Government of Ireland Act, 1920 This Act created the state of Northern Ireland containing six of the nine counties of Ulster.

Royal Ulster Constabulary (RUC) The police force of Northern Ireland.

B-Specials A part-time militia-style police force in Northern Ireland that was almost exclusively Protestant.

Gerrymandering Creating election districts that favour one political party over another.

Sectarianism Discrimination based on religious beliefs.

Northern Ireland Civil Rights Association (NICRA) An organisation set up in 1967 with the aim of ending discrimination in Northern Ireland and promoting civil rights for all citizens of the state.

The Bogside A Catholic area in Derry City where violence between residents and the RUC and Protestant attackers broke out in 1969.

Social Democratic and Labour Party (SDLP) A moderate nationalist political party set up by John Hume and Gerry Fitt among others in 1970.

Provisional IRA A nationalist group who believed in the use of force to achieve its aims, unlike the official IRA.

Internment The arrest and imprisonment of suspects without trial.

Bloody Sunday The name given to the violence that took place in Derry City on Sunday, 30 January 1972 between civil rights marchers and the British Army that resulted in the deaths of 13 marchers.

Sunningdale Agreement, 1973 A political treaty between Ireland and Britain that created a power-sharing government in Northern Ireland. It did not succeed.

Loyalists Extreme unionists. Their name comes from their 'loyalty' to the British monarch.

Hunger Strike A political protest by IRA prisoners in the Maze Prison in 1981 demanding to be treated as political prisoners rather than ordinary criminals.

Anglo-Irish (Hillsborough) Agreement, 1985 A political treaty between Ireland and Britain that provided the Republic of Ireland with a say in the running of Northern Ireland.

The Downing Street Declaration, 1993 A joint declaration from the heads of state of Ireland and Britain that recognised self-determination of the populations of Northern Ireland and the Republic as necessary for unification.

The Good Friday Agreement, 1998 A political treaty between Britain, Ireland and the political parties of Northern Ireland that led to the establishment of peace in Northern Ireland.

Articles 2 and 3 Two articles of the Irish constitution that claimed control over the entire island of Ireland.

Referendum (plural referenda) A vote on one particular issue by all those eligible to vote in a country.

Web References

For further information on topics mentioned in this chapter, view the following websites:

museumoffreederry.org/gallery-bsphotos-05.html

www.bbc.co.uk/history/recent/troubles/the_troubles_article_01.shtml

www.bbc.co.uk/history/recent/troubles/fact_files.shtml

www.youtube.com

www.rte.ie/laweb/ll/ll_t11_main.html

news.bbc.co.uk/onthisday/hi/dates/stories/december/9/newsid_2536000/2536767.stm

nobelprize.org/nobel_prizes/peace/laureates/1976/williams-cv.html

Women in History

Betty Williams

(1943 –)

Peace activist and Nobel Prize winner 1976

Betty Williams was born in Belfast in 1943. Like many others in Northern Ireland during the 1950s and 1960s, her family suffered from violence within the community. Two of her cousins were killed by paramilitaries and in 1972 she joined the IRA. A year later, she withdrew from the IRA after witnessing a British soldier being shot in front of her.

On 10 August 1976, a runaway car driven by an IRA member smashed into a family of four killing all three children – Joanne, John and Andrew – and injuring their mother, Anne Maguire. Williams organised a petition against violence and soon had over 6,000 signatures. At the funeral of the children, their aunt, Máiréad Corrigan, met Williams and journalist Ciarán McKeown. The three of them co-founded the Peace People. This organisation was dedicated to bringing peace to all of Northern Ireland and the world. A peace march to the graves of the Maguire children was attended by 10,000 Protestant and Catholic women. The march was disrupted by members of the IRA who accused the organisers of

being sympathetic to the British. In response, another march was organised and this time 35,000 people joined.

In recognition for their work in promoting peace in Northern Ireland and around the world, Williams and Corrigan were awarded the Nobel Prize for Peace in 1976. Since then Williams has also received the People's Peace Prize of Norway, the Martin Luther King Jr Award and many other awards. She is the President of World Centers of Compassion for Children and lectures at Nova Southeastern University in Florida, USA.

Social history examines the way in which people lived in the past: where they lived, what they worked at, how they spent their free time and how they travelled from place to place. In this chapter we will examine the many changes that have occurred during the twentieth century in Ireland.

Rural Life in Twentieth-Century Ireland

● Housing

In 1900, over 60% of the Irish population lived in the countryside or in small towns and villages. Most of these worked in agriculture. Their lifestyles varied depending on how much money they had.

1. THE RICH LANDLORD

There were about 20,000 landlords in Ireland at the beginning of the century. Most lived in large houses. It is estimated that about 1,000 of these landlords owned half the land of Ireland. They lived lives similar to landlords in England. They went shooting, hunting or horse-riding in their spare time. Most of them ran their estates and acted as judges in the local community. They spent very little time with the local people. The vast majority were Protestant and saw themselves as British rather than Irish.

▲ Rich landlords lived in large houses on huge estates. Muckross House in Killarney, County Kerry is a good example of such a house.

2. THE WEALTHY FARMER

▲ An example of the house of a wealthy farmer

A wealthy farmer had roughly 50 to 300 acres of land. These farmers lived in large, two-storey farmhouses with slate roofs. Their farmhouses had stables and courtyards for farmwork at the back of the house. The house had a number of bedrooms, a large kitchen and a **parlour** (like a modern sitting room). The parlour was used only for special occasions. These farmers often employed farm labourers during busy seasons.

3. THE SMALL FARMER

In 1911, 40% of rural dwellers owned 15 acres of land or less. They lived close to the road and often alongside a number of other houses. The houses had whitewashed walls. The windows were small to keep in the warmth. The roof was made of **thatch**. They had three rooms on the ground floor, including the kitchen. Toilets were located outside in the backyard. The children slept upstairs in the loft. The farmer's time was spent working on his/her own land or working for larger farmers.

▲ A small farmer's house in Galway in the early twentieth century

4. The Farm Labourer

In 1901, there were about 260,000 farm labourers in Ireland. The labourers' cottages were on the outskirts of a town or village. These cottages were of the same style as the small farmers' cottages but with only two rooms and a loft. There was little furniture and the houses were often in very bad repair.

◀ Farm labourers gathered outside a cottage in Connemara, County Galway.

● Life in the Home

The kitchen was the centre of the home. A large fire stayed lit throughout the day. This fire was used to heat water for cleaning and cooking and to provide warmth. Evenings were spent talking and telling stories around the fire.

▲ The fireplace was an important part of every home. Fires were used to produce heat and provide hot water for cooking and cleaning.

The rooms were dark because the windows were so small. Furniture was very simple and made from wood. **Súgán** chairs (made from straw ropes) and benches were used to sit on. A wooden dresser held all the crockery (cups and plates).

In the bedrooms, simple beds were made from wood. The children slept in the same beds for warmth and also because there was not enough room for them each to have their own bed. It was quite normal to sleep in the same bed as three or four of your brothers or sisters. Light came from candles, lamps using oil and wicks and later, paraffin lamps.

Running water came from a pump or a well outside the house.

▲ Súgán chairs were made from straw ropes. Because they were quite easy to make many poor families used them in their homes.

Oil lamps were used to provide light in houses. ▶

● Electricity

The biggest change in rural Ireland came with the introduction of electricity in 1946. In the 1950s electricity was supplied to many rural parts of Ireland. Almost 75,000 miles of new electrical lines were put up around the country. Electric lights, washing machines, hairdryers and irons were common by the 1960s. Electrical pumps brought running water into the house and toilets were now built inside the house.

When Ireland joined the EEC in 1973, large amounts of money from the CAP (see Chapter 13, International Relations 1945–2000, page 410) were given to rural communities. Many of the old farmers' houses were abandoned and new larger homes were built beside the old ones. These houses had some of the new appliances such as washing machines, vacuum cleaners and central heating. Televisions also became more popular throughout Ireland in the 1960s and 1970s.

▲ The electrification of rural Ireland during the 1950s was a milestone in Ireland's social history.

● Other Changes

The number of cars in rural Ireland also grew in the 1960s. This meant that rural communities were no longer so cut off from each other. Small villages disappeared as people could travel longer distances. Towns with shops, pubs and even cinemas grew instead.

The Clock Gate in Youghal, County Cork. Note the horse-and-cart on the right. ▶

FARMING

In the early part of the twentieth century, most farming was tillage farming. This required a lot of **manual** (done by hand) work for the farmer. Fields were ploughed, crops were sown and harvests were gathered using horse-drawn machinery. During the busy farming seasons, neighbours helped each other to make sure the harvest was collected. This was called *meitheal*. Farm animals such as sheep, cows, pigs, geese and chickens were used for their meat, milk and eggs.

▲ Rural Ireland in the 1950s: A farmer and his son standing close to their cottage in 1954.

▲ Rural Ireland in 2007: A row of holiday houses in Kenmare, County Kerry.

By the 1950s and 1960s motorised tractors had replaced horses. As a result, ploughing and sowing fields was done much more quickly. Combine harvesters collected the crops without the help of the neighbours. These new methods made farming much more efficient. Farms grew bigger as it was possible for farmers to farm much bigger areas. Many farmers moved away from **tillage** (using their land to grow crops) and into **livestock** (cattle and sheep) farming. The **EEC Social Policy** gave farmers grants to improve their land. The **CAP** also meant that farmers were able to get guaranteed prices for their produce and had a much larger market in which to sell their produce (i.e. all the countries in the EEC). By 1979, 59% of rural homes had a washing machine, 84% had a TV and 76% had a refrigerator.

▲ By the 1950s amd 1960s many farmers began to move away from tillage and into livestock.

Questions

1. Describe where the following people would live:

   (a) Rich landlord   (b) Farm labourer   (c) Small farmer

2. What kind of pastimes did the rich landlord have?

3. Describe a kitchen in a small farmer's house in the early 1900s.

4. In what ways would the life of a person living in the country in 1900 have been difficult? Give three examples to back up your answer.

5. In what ways have the conditions of rural families improved since the 1900s? Give three examples.

6. Did the CAP help Irish farmers to improve their living standards? Give reasons for your answer.

7. Why did smaller villages disappear and bigger towns grow after the 1960s?

8. In your opinion, have the changes in lifestyle of rural dwellers improved or disimproved since the early twentieth century? Give reasons to support your answer.

Urban Life

At the beginning of the twentieth century, only 32% of the population lived in towns of more than 1,500 people. The population of Dublin was 350,000, Cork was 76,000 and Limerick was 40,000. Belfast was the only city in Ireland with heavy industry similar to British cities.

▲ Market day in Limerick City in 1937

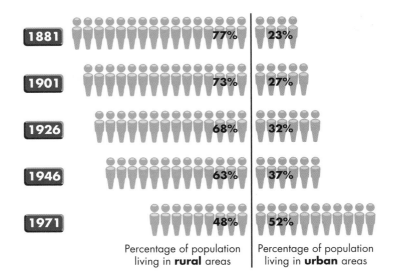

	Percentage of population living in **rural** areas	Percentage of population living in **urban** areas
1881	77%	23%
1901	73%	27%
1926	68%	32%
1946	63%	37%
1971	48%	52%

▲ Between 1881 and 1971 the percentage of Irish people living in cities grew from 23% to 52%.

● Housing

▲ Wealthy families lived in large houses such as these in Merrion Square, Dublin with accommodation for servants.

Rich people like doctors and solicitors lived in large houses, usually on the outskirts of the city. They had large gardens and the houses had accommodation for their servants.

Other less wealthy families rented large houses in the cities. Many tradesmen lived in terraced, red-brick houses called **two up two down**. As the name suggests, these had two bedrooms upstairs with a living room and a kitchen downstairs.

The poor of the cities lived in **tenements**. These were the former houses of the wealthy in Dublin before they moved to the suburbs. The houses had five to seven bedrooms and had been converted into flats in order to fit more people into one house. Families lived in a single room.

▲ Two up two down houses were popular with tradesmen.

◄ Michael's Lane in Dublin with tenement buildings lining the street.

● Conditions

At the start of the twentieth century the living conditions of the poor in the cities were awful. 118,000 of Dublin's poor lived in 5,000 tenement houses and 1,500 of these houses were regarded as being unfit for human habitation (to live in). 22.9% of Dublin's population lived in one-bedroom tenements. Life expectancy was just under 50 years and the child mortality rate (number of children who die aged five years or under) was almost twice that of London. Toilets were outside and running water had to be brought in from pumps on the street.

These conditions produced health problems similar to British towns during the Industrial Revolution. Damp, dirty water and a lack of any sewerage system resulted in **TB** and **cholera**. In 1904, there were 13,000 deaths due to TB in Ireland.

▲ Families gathered outside tenement buildings in Angle Court off Beresford Street.

▲ The interior of a tenement flat. Note the damp on the wall.

In the 1930s, the government began large-scale house-building projects. Local councils re-housed many tenement dwellers in **corporation houses** in the suburbs. Crumlin in Dublin and Gurranebraher in Cork are examples of these suburbs. Between 1926 and 1946 the percentage of families living in homes of one or two rooms decreased:

	Dublin	Cork	Limerick
1926	50%	28%	39%
1946	25%	21%	23%

During the 1960s people began to move out of the city centre and buy or rent homes in the suburbs. Large new housing estates were built to house these people. These new homes all had running water, electricity and central heating.

▲ The government built large-scale housing projects, such as this one in Crumlin in Dublin, in the 1930s.

▲ In 1966, large corporation housing flats were built in Ballymun in Dublin. All but one of these towers were demolished between 2004 and 2008.

▲ In the 1990s many new apartments were built in the city centres of Dublin, Cork, Limerick and Galway.

The city centres became depopulated and were like ghost towns in the evenings. This development was reversed in the last decades of the twentieth century and **urban renewal schemes** were put in place. During the Celtic Tiger years, there was a lack of housing for the population and many new apartments were built in the city centres of Dublin, Cork, Limerick and Galway.

Work

At the beginning of the century most people in Ireland were employed in agriculture, but this has changed. Although Ireland still does not have much heavy industry, the arrival of foreign companies that concentrated on light industry, e.g. computers and technology, from the 1960s onwards resulted in more people working in factories. Many of these factories were built on the outskirts of towns. This meant that there was a further growth of houses built in the suburbs. Large shopping centres and industrial parks were built in these population growth areas. Good examples of these are Mahon Point Shopping Centre in Cork, Shannon Industrial Park in Limerick and Dundrum Town Centre in Dublin. One of the largest growth areas for work has been in services (bars, restaurants, transport, insurance, banks and law). It is possible to see the changes in the chart below:

	% Of Workers Employed In Each Sector		
	Agriculture	Industry	Services
1926	53	13	34
1971	26	31	43
1996	10	27	63

Questions

1. Describe what type of houses the following people would have lived in at the start of the 1900s:
   (a) Wealthy professional
   (b) Poor unemployed person
   (c) Tradesman
2. Explain the term 'tenement'.
3. Describe the conditions in a tenement.
4. How did the government help to reduce bad conditions in the 1930s?
5. Why did city centres become 'ghost towns' in the 1980s?
6. What is an urban renewal scheme?
7. Identify three differences between the life of a rural dweller and an urban dweller in the early twentieth century.
8. Write a short paragraph about life in a Dublin tenement in 1900. Use the following headings to help you:
   (a) the building
   (b) parents' employment
   (c) health risks

Sports and Leisure

● Early Years

ENTERTAINMENT

In the early 1900s people often gathered in each other's houses in the evening. Music was played and songs were sung. Storytellers told myths and legends from memory that could last hours. Wealthier people attended balls, and those invited wore very formal clothes. People also met at local public houses, fairs, markets and mass.

The local GAA club played on a Sunday and many people from the parish attended to play or to support. 'Foreign' sports were also well supported. Rugby became very popular in Limerick – clubs such as Shannon and Young Munster were founded during this time. Soccer was also popular in the towns and cities of Ireland.

▲ Rugby clubs such as Shannon and Young Munster were founded in Limerick in 1884 and 1895.

▲ GAA clubs were founded in every parish.

▲ The Abbey Theatre in Dublin first opened on 27 December 1904.

THEATRE AND MUSIC HALLS

Theatres and music halls across the country presented plays, concerts, variety shows and operas. Domestic and visiting companies performed in the **Cork Opera House** (1877), the **Abbey Theatre** (1904), the **Gaiety Theatre** (1871) and many other theatres. Some theatres lost popularity with the arrival of cinema. In 1909, the first cinema opened in Dublin. By 1916, there were 149 cinemas around Ireland.

> **By the way . . .**
> Over one week, 7,000 people attended the first film (or 'cinematic moving images' as it was known then) shown in Dublin in 1896.

RADIO

In 1926, Ireland's first radio station **2RN** began broadcasting. More people bought radios leading to more music, news and sports programmes. Radio became an important method of keeping up to date with events at home and around the world.

▲ The radio, or 'the wireless' as it was then known, became extremely popular in Ireland during the early part of the twentieth century.

● 1960s Onwards

DANCE HALLS

During the 1960s, **showbands** performed at dancehalls. Bands like The Capitol and The Royal Showband played the music that was heard on the radio. The crowd loved the dances, such as the Twist and the Hucklebuck, that accompanied this music. Rock 'n' roll music became hugely popular in the 1960s producing stars such as Elvis Presley in America and The Beatles in England. By the 1970s discos had replaced dance halls. The 1990s saw the arrival of dance music (also known as rave music or electronic music) in Ireland. Popular DJs from all over the world played to large crowds at venues all around Ireland.

▲ The Royal Showband were one of Ireland's most popular showbands. They're pictured here in Times Square, New York, during a tour of America in the 1960s.

▲ Dance music arrived in Ireland in the 1990s.

TELEVISION

The arrival of television and the establishment of RTÉ in 1961 meant that many big cinemas closed. People watched programmes such as *The Late Late Show* with Gay Byrne on Saturday nights (it later changed to Friday nights). Soap operas such as *The Riordans*, *Dallas* and *Glenroe* became very popular. Video recorders (VCRs) were widely used in the 1980s and allowed people to watch films at home. In the 1990s, videos were replaced by DVDs. By 2002, 54% of people in Ireland watched over two hours of television each day.

The popularity of television resulted in more people being exposed to other cultures, especially British and American. It also meant that Irish people became more aware of world events such as Neil Armstrong landing on the moon, John F Kennedy's assassination and the fall of the Berlin Wall. Important international sporting and political events like the World Cup, the Olympics or foreign presidential elections and revolutions were beamed straight into Irish homes.

Internet

◄ The *Late Late Show* presented by Gay Byrne was very important in raising moral and ethical issues that helped to modernise Ireland.

In 2006, 50% of all homes in Ireland had internet access. Use of the internet grew hugely over the last decade of the twentieth century. Computer consoles such as X-Box and Playstation became very popular among young people. Gamers can play against each other on the internet. Social networking websites such as Bebo, Facebook and Twitter offer new ways for people to keep in touch. People use the internet to book flights, buy products and get information.

▲ Games can be played on video game consoles or personal computers.

Holidays

At the beginning of the century, only the very wealthy went on holidays. By the 1960s, people had more leisure time and people in towns could take the train to the seaside. Places such as Bray, south of Dublin, became a very popular destination for Dublin holidaymakers. By the 1970s and 1980s Irish people were travelling to Spain and other places for sun holidays. Air travel became much cheaper in the 1990s leading to a huge increase in the number of people taking holidays abroad.

Sport

During the second half of the twentieth century, sport had become very popular. In 1911, 10,000 people watched the All-Ireland hurling final. Now Croke Park holds over 80,000 people. Irish teams have done very well at international events such as the World Cup in soccer in 1990, 1994 and 2002. Cyclists such as Seán Kelly and Stephen Roche in the 1980s were among the top cyclists in the world, and athletes

such as Sonia O'Sullivan and Eamon Coughlan achieved great success. Boxing continues to produce the largest number of Olympic medals for Ireland. Ireland's Padraig Harrington has become a Major winner in golf. Sport is now a big industry. In 1995 families, tourists and the government spent almost €900 million on sport in Ireland.

▲ Croke Park was reopened in 2007 after extensive redevelopment. It now holds more than 80,000 people.

▲ Padraig Harrington has won numerous golf tournaments.

Questions

1. Give three examples of how people entertained themselves in early twentieth-century Ireland.
2. Which sports were played in Ireland in 1900?
3. Name three theatres that people might have attended in the early twentieth century?
4. What impact did radio have on people's entertainment?
5. Outline the changes in the dance scene in Ireland over the twentieth century.
6. What kind of programmes did people watch on their television?
7. How has the internet changed people's lives?
8. In your opinion, has the internet changed people's lives for the better? Give reasons for your answer.
9. How has cheaper air travel changed Irish holidays?
10. In your opinion, has sport improved since the beginning of the twentieth century? Give reasons for your answer.

Transport and Communications

● Transport - Early Years

At the beginning of the century, bicycles, donkeys and the horse-and-cart were popular methods of transport, but the main way to travel was on foot.

Roads in Ireland were not very good. They rarely followed a straight path and sometimes they were no more than dirt tracks. Cobblestones were used in the big cities.

▲ A typical Irish road in 1917

In Dublin, Cork and Belfast, **electric trams** were used to travel in the city. Any long distances in Ireland were taken by train. There was over 5,500 kilometres of railway across Ireland. The trains were powered by steam and were very slow. The trains stopped at many towns along the route.

Cars were very rare. In 1945 there were only 7,845 licensed cars on the road in Ireland. However, this number quickly increased after World War II and by 1951 there were 156,000 licensed cars on Irish roads.

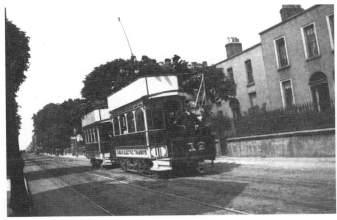

▲ Electric trams were used in cities. The tram in this picture was run by Dublin United Tramways Company on the Dalkey Route.

▲ This steam train was called the *Cork Express*, but journey times were usually the very opposite of express!

Journeys abroad were taken by ship. Ferries from Kingstown (Dún Laoghaire), Queenstown (Cobh) and Belfast connected Ireland to Britain. Huge liners such as the *Titanic* stopped at Cobh before sailing across the Atlantic to the USA. This journey took five days.

So, for many people, long journeys were not possible. Most people lived near to where they had been born unless they were planning to emigrate. Any journeys had to be planned well in advance.

▲ The deep harbour at Queenstown (Cobh) was used by huge ocean liners such as the *Titanic*.

◄ A horse-drawn milk cart in Tipperary.

● Transport - 1960s Onwards

From the 1960s, cars became cheaper due to their mass production. Many middle-income families were now able to buy cars. Cars became the main method of transport and many railway lines closed. All the tramlines in Dublin, Cork and Belfast closed and were replaced by buses.

▲ Ring-roads, such as the M50 in Dublin pictured above, help to reduce traffic levels in the city centre.

▲ The re-introduction of electric trams in Dublin (called the Luas) in 2004 has been a great success. Trams had previously been phased out of use by 1959.

The increase in cars meant that new roads had to be built using tarmacadam. Dual carriageways and motorways were built. The centres of many cities were not suitable for such large numbers of cars and buses. These cities, therefore, suffered from pollution and traffic congestion. New bypasses and ring-roads have been built in the last number of decades to bring traffic out of the cities, helping to some extent to reduce pollution levels. In Dublin, a new electric tramway called the Luas was introduced and has been very successful.

▲ Stena Line ferries bring thousands of holidaymakers from Ireland to Britain or France.

Ferries have improved. They are now quicker and more comfortable. They provide fast journeys to Britain and to mainland Europe from several locations. Car-ferries are particularly popular with holidaymakers travelling to Britain or France.

Air travel boomed over the last 20 years of the twentieth century. Irish airline Aer Lingus offers flights all over the world and private airlines such as Ryanair provide cheap flights to many destinations around Europe. In the 1990s, it became popular to travel to New York, Paris or Rome just for a weekend.

Communications – Early Years

Letter-writing was the main method of communication in the early 1900s. Letters were delivered the next day. In cities, there were three postal deliveries each day.

The **telegraph** was much faster. It was used for business and for emergencies. It was possible to send a telegram by dictating your message to an operator who would then send it by Morse code to another post office. This would then be deciphered and delivered to the intended recipient.

▲ Operators at work in a telephone exchange.

Telephones were rarely used. In order to ring somebody, you had to dial the **telephone operator** and ask to be connected. Using the phone was also very expensive. There were 56 manual **exchanges** in Ireland in 1900. They were slowly replaced by automatic exchanges.

Communications – 1960s Onwards

▲ Laptops, mobile phones and MP3 players have become common in Ireland.

From the 1960s, phones became common in private homes. They were quite large and the line was not always very clear. In the late 1980s/early 1990s **mobile phones** were introduced. By the end of the century, mobile phones were everywhere; people sometimes had a number of phones. By 2000, a third of all people in Ireland had a mobile phone, and the number was still rising.

The **facsimile** (fax) became common in the 1990s. A fax machine sent a copy of a piece of paper through the telephone line and reproduced its image at the other end. The internet has revolutionised communications. **Emailing**, social network sites and Skype allow people to stay in contact more cheaply, faster and more easily than ever before.

1. List three methods of transport used at the beginning of the twentieth century.
2. How would you travel abroad in 1900?
3. What impact did the arrival of cars have on other modes of transport?
4. What problems did the increased use of cars cause in city centres?
5. What solutions have the government introduced to try and solve these problems?
6. Describe how telephones have changed during the twentieth century.
7. Explain the following terms:
   - (a) Facsimile
   - (b) Telephone exchange
   - (c) Telegraph
   - (d) E-mail
8. In your opinion, what impact has the increased number of mobile phones had on Irish society? Give reasons for your answer.
9. Write an account of a person who has lived in Ireland through the twentieth century. Use the following headings as a guide:
   - (a) changes in work
   - (b) changes in leisure
   - (c) changes in transport
   - (d) changes in communications

Role of Women

Women in the early twentieth century had very few rights. Over the last 100 years, there has been a huge change in the position of women in education, politics and employment.

● Access to Education

The **Intermediate Education Act** of 1878 and the **Royal University of Ireland Act** (1879) allowed girls to sit examinations and take university degrees. By 1900, 417 women had arts degrees and 25 had medical degrees. It was not until 1904 that Trinity allowed women into the main male campus. After 1908, all universities accepted women.

▲ Women were not admitted to Trinity College Dublin until 1904.

Statistically, girls now do better than boys in state exams at secondary level. At university, women in 1998 accounted for 55% of all students rather than 25% in 1950.

● Access to the Vote

Women benefitted from the changes in the laws on education in the late nineteenth century. Better access to education resulted in more women demanding **suffrage** (the right to vote). In 1896, the **Dublin Women's Suffrage Association** was set up to fight for the vote for women. In 1908, the Irish Women's Franchise League (IWFL) was established by Hanna Sheehy-Skeffington. The IWFL travelled around Ireland

▲ The arrest of a suffragette by the Royal Irish Constabulary outside the Mansion House in 1914.

trying to gain support. On 8 June 1912, they attacked a number of buildings including the GPO and the Customs House, breaking windows in the process. Sheehy-Skeffington and 36 other women were arrested. Whilst in prison, several women went on hunger strike to gain political prisoner status.

In 1913 Cumann na mBan was set up to help the Irish Volunteers. One of the most famous of Cumann na mBan's members was Countess Markievicz. She was a leading member of Sinn Féin who supported equal rights for women. In 1918, women over 30 years of age received the vote. Sinn Féin was swept into power in Ireland and Markievicz was the first woman to be elected as an MP. She also became a Minister in the first Dáil.

The Constitution of Ireland of 1922 gave both men and women over the age of 21 the right to vote. After the Civil War, there were five women elected to the Dáil but four of these were anti-Treaty so they did not attend. Margaret Collins-O'Driscoll (sister of Michael Collins) was a TD from 1923 to 1932.

▲ Hanna Sheehy-Skeffington campaigned to give women the right to vote. See page 475.

● Employment

At the start of the twentieth century the areas of employment for women were limited. In 1901, one third (193,300) of all employed women worked in domestic service and 45% of all National School teachers were women. During the 1920s and 1930s, several attempts were made to limit the involvement of women in the workplace.

1. In 1932, de Valera passed a law that forced women to give up their jobs in the civil service and national school teaching when they got married. This was known as the **Marriage Ban**.

2. The **Conditions of Employment Act** (1935) gave the government the right to limit the number of women in any industry.

3. Trade Unions often pushed for special wage rates for married men. This was because they thought it was more important for a man to be able to provide for his wife than for a woman to work.

4. The 1937 Constitution supported the traditional view of women's place in society by recognising their special role 'within the home'.

These restrictions meant that by 1946 only 2.5% of married women were employed compared to 25% in Britain. Many women emigrated and between 1946 and 1951, 1,365 women left Ireland for every 1,000 men.

● Employment Equality

Organisations like the National Council of Women and the Irish Women Workers' Union helped to improve women's position in Irish society over the following decades. Ireland's membership of the UN in 1955 and the EEC in 1973 also brought further rights and equality. In 1972, the **Commission on the Status of Women** issued their report. It recommended 49 ways to eradicate inequality. Following these recommendations, the Marriage Ban was lifted and the 1977 **Employment Equality Act** banned any discrimination based on gender or marital status.

Even with these developments, women are still under-represented in positions of authority. In 1998, only 5% of university professors were female and only 16% were judges. Only 12% of the Irish Parliament is female. So far, there has been no female Taoiseach. Mary Harney became the first female leader of a political party when she led the Progressive Democrats in 1993. She also became the first woman to be Tánaiste in 1997.

In 1990, Mary Robinson was elected as President of Ireland. She was followed by Mary McAleese who became president in 1997.

▲ Mary Harney became the first woman to lead a political party when she took over the Progressive Democrats in 1993.

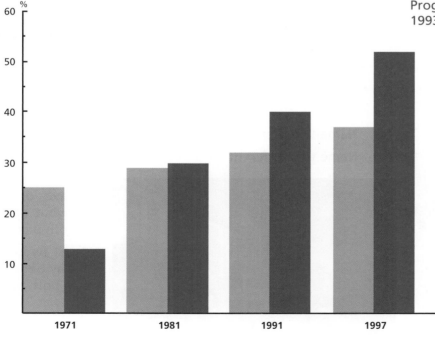

Females at work as a % of total workforce

Married women at work as % of same

Questions

1. What changes in education helped to encourage equality for women?
2. What does the term 'suffrage' mean?
3. How did the changes in education contribute to the women's suffrage movement?
4. When were women first given the right to vote in Ireland?
5. What was the importance of Countess Markievicz's election in 1918?
6. In the beginning of the twentieth century, what were the main occupations of women?
7. What changes in legislation made it more difficult for women to work outside the home?
8. Why do you think more women than men emigrated between 1946 and 1951?
9. What was the 'marriage ban'?
10. List four organisations that pushed for women's equality.
11. List two changes in legislation that gave women equal status in employment.
12. Write an account of the changes that have occurred for a woman living in Ireland during the twentieth century. Use the following headings as a guide:

    (a) Education
    (c) Changes in employment legislation
    (b) Right to vote
    (d) Political status

13. In your opinion, why are women still not represented at the highest levels of authority? Give reasons for your answer.
14. In your opinion, do women now have equality with men in politics and employment? Give reasons for your answer.

Chapter 16 Questions

A.

B.

1. Pictures

Examine the pictures of Dublin and answer the following questions:

(a) Name two methods of transport shown in Picture A.

(b) Name two different methods of transport in Picture B.

(c) List three changes that have occurred in the layout of the streets in both pictures.

(d) List two changes in the way people are dressed in both pictures.

2. Documents

Mary Foran, born 1924, Railway Street

The conditions in the tenements of Railway Street were outrageous. I lived with my Mother, my Granny, my uncle Richard, my brothers Philip, Jamsey and Michael in one room that held four beds. We lived at the top of the house. One of my many memories of the tenements was having to carry two heavy galvanised buckets up and down the seven flights of stairs. Being an only girl I had to do all the work in the house; the boys didn't do anything and were not expected to do anything. I carried the buckets – one was the stinking smelly slop bucket that we used for the toilet and the other was the clean bucket for the water.

(a) How many people lived with Mary Foran?

(b) How many beds were there in the room?

(c) How far up inside the house was their room?

(d) Why do you think the boys did not do any work?

(e) Why did Mary have to go outside with the buckets?

(f) Was there a toilet inside the tenement? Give a reason for your answer.

3. Short-Answer Questions

(a) What role do ferries have for holidaymakers in Ireland today?

(b) Give two examples of methods of communication from today that did not exist in 1900.

(c) Why did cinema decline in popularity in the 1980s?

(d) Give one example of how television has affected Irish society.

(e) Give one example of a woman's suffrage organisation.

(f) Explain the following terms:
   (i) Meitheal   (iii) Combine harvester
   (ii) Tillage   (iv) Livestock

(g) List two diseases that were common in the tenements of Dublin in the early twentieth century.

(h) Give one benefit the internet has had for communications in Ireland.

(i) Explain how by-passes have helped reduce pollution in city centres and towns.

(j) Why was there a reduction in the amount of railway line in the 1960s and 1970s?

4. People in History

Write an account of a rural farmer who was born in Ireland in 1910. Describe the changes that have occurred in his/her life since then. Use the following headings as a guide:

• His/her early life as a farmer

• The farming methods of his or her early life

• The changes in farming methods in the 1950s and 60s

• The changes in the standard of living and housing

• The impact of membership of the EEC

5.

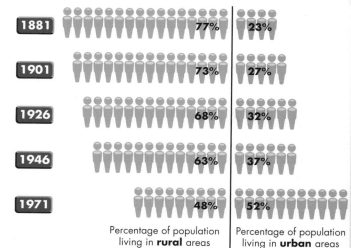

	Percentage of population living in **rural** areas	Percentage of population living in **urban** areas
1881	77%	23%
1901	73%	27%
1926	68%	32%
1946	63%	37%
1971	48%	52%

(i) Give one reason for the high percentage of population in rural areas before the 1970s.

(ii) Give one reason why the majority of the population now live in urban areas.

(iii) Describe the changes that occurred in each of the following areas since the beginning of this century:

(a) Transport

(b) Communications

(c) Housing

(d) Leisure and Entertainment

(e) Services (shops, hospitals, schools, etc.)

Key Terms to Summarise Chapter 16: Ireland: Social History

Thatch A type of roofing that uses straw instead of slate. Typically used in poorer Irish rural homes in the first half of the twentieth century.

Súgán chairs Chairs made using straw ropes, typical in Irish rural homes in the twentieth century.

Tillage Crop farming.

Meitheal An Irish word describing the way in which neighbours helped each other to collect the harvest.

Two up two down A house with two bedrooms upstairs and a living room and a kitchen downstairs.

Tenements Houses in which wealthy people once lived that were divided into cramped flats for poor families.

Corporation houses Houses built by the local town or county councils to replace the tenements. Most of these houses were built in new housing estates in the suburbs of large cities and towns.

Urban renewal schemes Government schemes that encouraged people to invest money in rebuilding and renovating areas of cities and towns by offering tax breaks to build there.

2RN Ireland's first radio station. It began broadcasting in 1926.

Showbands Bands that played at dances during the 1960s in Ireland.

The Late Late Show A television programme presented by Gay Byrne that was very influential in modernising Ireland in the 1960s.

Electric trams A light-rail form of transport that uses electricity fed by overhead lines. Common in the early part of the last century but replaced by buses only to be reintroduced in Dublin at the start of the twenty-first century as the Luas.

Telegraph A method of communication that required an operator to send the message by Morse Code to another post office where it would be deciphered and delivered to the recipient.

Facsimile (fax) A method of communication in which a piece of paper is copied, sent through a telephone line and reproduced on paper at the other end of the telephone line.

Telephone exchange To make a call in the early part of the last century it was necessary to call an operator who would then connect you to the appropriate number.

Intermediate Education Act (1878) This Act allowed women to sit state examinations.

Royal University of Ireland Act (1879) This Act allowed women to take university degrees.

Suffrage This is the right to vote. The term 'suffragettes' was given to women who fought to gain the right to vote in the early years of the twentieth century.

Dublin Women's Suffrage Association An organisation set up in 1896 to seek the right to vote for women.

Marriage Ban This required any woman who worked in the Civil Service or as a National School teacher to give up her job once she got married.

The Conditions of Employment Act (1935) A regressive law that gave the government the right to limit the number of women working in any industry.

Commission on the Status of Women (1972) A committee that issued a report on the position of women in 1972 and offered 49 recommendations to help deal with inequality.

Employment Equality Act (1977) This Act banned any discrimination based on gender or marital status.

Web References

For further reading on topics mentioned in this chapter, view the following websites:

www.nwci.ie

www.nationalarchives.ie/wh/

www.gaa.ie/page/general_history.html

multitext.ucc.ie/d/Housing_Report_Dublin_1913

Women in History

Hanna Sheehy-Skeffington

(1877 – 1946)

Women's Rights Campaigner and Labour Activist

Johanna Mary Sheehy was born in County Cork in 1877. The family moved to Dublin where she was educated at the Dominican convent in Eccles Street and later at the Royal University (later renamed UCD). Her education made Sheehy realise that although highly educated, she had no vote and therefore was in the same category as criminals and lunatics (other groups who were not allowed to vote).

In 1903 she married Frank Skeffington, an academic of similar views. He believed in full and equal rights for women and considered himself to be 'merely the male member of the Sheehy-Skeffington household'.

In 1908, Hanna co-founded the Irish Women's Franchise League (IWFL) to push for women's right to vote. The Sheehy-Skeffingtons set up their own newspaper called *The Irish Citizen* promoting pro-suffrage, pacifist and nationalist views. In 1912, Hanna and members of the IWFL led direct action to promote their views, smashing windows in the Customs House and the GPO. She was arrested and jailed in Mountjoy Prison. During the 1913 Lock Out, she helped in the soup kitchens and was arrested again for assaulting a policeman.

As committed pacifists, the Sheehy-Skeffingtons did not wish to kill for Ireland during the 1916 Rising. Instead, Frank assisted the injured and tried to stop the looting that was taking place. He and two others were stopped and arrested by the army. They were taken to Portobello Barracks and shot without a trial. Hanna only found out about this a number of days later when her house was raided. Hanna decided to go to the USA and managed to meet President Wilson and gave him a petition from Cumann na mBan for Irish freedom and a copy of the 1916 Proclamation. On her return she was arrested but went on hunger strike and was released. Throughout the War of Independence, she acted as a judge in the republican courts. She sided with the anti-Treaty side during the Civil War.

Hanna resigned her position in de Valera's new Fianna Fáil party as she realised that de Valera did not believe in full and equal rights for women. She was very strongly opposed to both the 1935 Conditions of Employment Act and to the 1937 Constitution because of their anti-woman bias. She died in 1946 and was described by Maude Gonne as 'the ablest of all the fearless women who worked for Ireland's freedom'.

EXAM GUIDE
History – Junior Certificate

What To Study

Higher Level

FIRST YEAR:

ALL

SECOND YEAR:

ALL

THIRD YEAR:

ALL

Note: For International Relations 1945 – 2000 (Chapter 13) you only need to study **one** of the following:

- Rise of the Superpowers
- Moves towards European Unity
- African and Asian Nationalism

Ordinary Level

FIRST YEAR:

ALL

SECOND YEAR:
Concentrate on the **Special Study** topics for each section:

- **One** voyage of discovery
- The career of **one** reformer
- **One** Plantation in detail
- The life of **one** revolutionary
- Life in a factory town in England during the Industrial Revolution
- Life in Rural Ireland during the Famine

THIRD YEAR:
One topic from International Relations in the Twentieth Century:

- Peace and war in Europe
- The Rise of the Superpowers
- Moves towards European Unity
- African and Asian nationalism

And **one** topic from the following:

- Political developments in Ireland 1900-2000
- Social History

Topics To Focus On For The Exam

Section I: How we find out about the past

Chapter 1: What is History?

Skills of a historian

Problems with sources – bias etc.

Work of an archaeologist

Methods of archaeology

Primary and Secondary sources

Timelines

Artefacts

Dating artefacts

Chapter 2: Ancient Ireland

<u>Stone Age</u>

Tools and weapons

<u>Bronze Age</u>

Tools and weapons

Burial customs

Food and drink

Role of women

Religion

Monastery

Mesolithic/Neolithic houses

Burial customs

Food

Houses

<u>Celtic Ireland</u>

Political society

Homes

<u>Christian Ireland</u>

Work of monks

Chapter 3: Ancient Rome

Roman Army

Gods and religion

Life in Rome – homes/leisure/clothes/eating/women

Legacy of Rome

Chapter 4: The Middle Ages

Feudal society

Medieval castle: attacking/defending/food/leisure/knight's life

Life in countryside: life of a peasant – food/leisure/clothes

Life in a town: health/churches/monasteries

Ireland in the Middle Ages: Vikings/Normans

Chapter 5: The Renaissance

Why did it start in Italy?

Artists in Italy

Artists outside Italy

Printing Press – Gutenberg

Science and Medicine

Renaissance art

Leonardo/Michelangelo/Raphael

Rembrandt

Writers: Shakespeare/Machiavelli

Vesalius/Galileo

Section II: Studies of change

Chapter 6: Age of Exploration
Causes   Advances in travel
Portugal: Henry the Navigator/Diaz/da Gama
Spain: Columbus
<u>Special study:</u> Magellan
Conquistadores: Cortés/ Pizarro
Results

Chapter 7: The Reformation
Causes   Reformers
<u>Special study:</u> Martin Luther/John Calvin/Henry VIII
Differences between reformed churches and Catholic church
Results and Counter-Reformation

Chapter 8: The Plantations
Surrender and Regrant
Causes and results of each plantation
<u>Special study</u>
One of the plantations: Laois-Offaly/Munster/ Ulster/Cromwellian
Results of Plantations

Chapter 9: Age of Revolutions
American Revolution
Causes   The American War of Independence: battles/Valley Forge
                                        George Washington
Results
French Revolution
Causes: First, Second and Third Estates
The Revolution: Sans culottes/Reign of terror/Robespierre
Results

1798 Irish Rebellion
1798
Causes
United Irishmen   Uprising: Ulster/ Wexford/ Humbert
                                        Wolfe Tone

Results

Chapter 10: Social Change in Britain and Ireland 1750–1850

Agricultural Revolution   Causes

Changes: Enclosure/inventions

Results

Industrial Revolution   Textile: inventions/coal/iron

Transport Revolution   Roads/Canals/Railways/Ships

Society   Living and working conditions/leisure

Reforms and reformers   Irish Famine

Irish society   The Famine and the government response

Results

Section III: Understanding the Modern World

NOTE

Ordinary Level Students will study either Political developments in Ireland and International Relations in the Twentieth Century (i.e. Chapters 11, 12, 13, 14 and 15) OR Social Change in the Twentieth Century and International Relations in the Twentieth Century (Chapters 11, 13, 14 and 16.

Higher Level Students will study ALL topics in Section III.

Chapter 11: International Relations in Twentieth Century Europe

World War I: causes and results

Russian Revolution

Fascism in Italy: causes and characteristics/Mussolini

Fascism in Germany: causes and characteristics/Hitler

Nazi Germany   Causes of World War II

World War II: Battle of Britain/Invasion of USSR/War in Pacific/Holocaust

Results

Chapter 12: Ireland in the Twentieth Century

Ireland up to 1948   Home Rule crisis

1916   War of Independence and Civil War

Irish Free State: problems/de Valera/The Emergency

Chapter 13: International Relations 1945 – 2000

Rise of the Superpowers

Berlin Blockade: causes and results

Korean War: causes and results

Cuban Missile Crisis: causes and results

OR

Moves towards European Unity

Treaty of Rome

Development and growth of EEC (EU)

Chapter 14: Ireland Since 1948

Inter-Party Government   Mother and Child Scheme

Lemass government: Economic and social change

Changes since 1970s: Economic and social

Chapter 15: Northern Ireland

1920-1960s: Unionists versus nationalists

1960s: Civil Rights Movement/Troubles/Bloody Sunday/Internment

Peace Process: Sunningdale/Anglo-Irish Agreement/Good Friday Agreement

Chapter 16: Ireland: Social History

Changes 1900-2000

Early century and changes in following areas:

Rural Life: houses and work

Urban life: houses and work

Transport and Communications

Sports and Leisure

Role of Women

How to study

- **Re-read** the chapters keeping in mind the key areas of study.
- Learn and use the **key terms** at the end of each chapter to help jog your memory about the important parts of the chapters.
- Make **notes** in your copybook as you read the chapter.
- Try to remember the **causes**, **main events** and the **results** of each chapter.
- Use questions from **past papers** and **workbooks** to test yourself.

Structure of the Exam

- HIGHER LEVEL
  You must do Questions 1 to 6.

- ORDINARY LEVEL
  You must do Questions 1 to 4.

Breakdown of the Exam

QUESTION 1: PICTURE QUESTION

Ordinary Level	Higher Level
35 marks	15 marks
Time to spend on question:	10 minutes

- A picture that you probably have not seen before will be given in the exam. It can be from any part of the course. The first two or three questions will relate directly to the picture; the final question(s) will be about background information on the subject.

QUESTION 2: DOCUMENT QUESTIONS

Ordinary Level	Higher Level
35 marks	15 marks
Time to spend on question:	10 minutes

- Usually two document questions are given. The documents can relate to any part of the course. You will be asked to find information in the documents. Keep your answer brief and to the point. Use the space provided in the answer book as a guide for how long your answer should be. Look for key words in the question that are repeated in the text.

QUESTION 3: SHORT-ANSWER QUESTIONS

Ordinary Level   Higher Level
60 marks   20 marks
Time to spend on question: 15 minutes

- Usually 20 questions are given. You must answer 10 correctly. The answers are often just one word; you do not need to give full sentences. Answer as many as you can because you will be given the marks for your best ten answers!

QUESTION 4: PEOPLE IN HISTORY

Ordinary Level   Higher Level
60 marks   20 marks
Time to spend on question: 40 marks

- You must write **two** accounts of people. Read your options carefully – you get many choices so choose the ones you are most happy with. Give as many facts as you can. Do not tell the story of this person. Get straight to the point.

- FACTS, FACTS AND THEN MORE FACTS!

- Ensure you provide at least 10 clear facts per account. Be careful to state the name of the person or the place they come from.

- Clearly state if it is a leader or a follower, e.g. a named reformer (such as Martin Luther) OR a follower of a named reformer (a German living in Saxony who follows Martin Luther). The facts might be very similar but the people are different!

- If the exam asks for a supporter of a reformer or revolutionary then you can start in the following way:

  'My name is Pat, I grew up near Wittenberg in Saxony. I am a supporter of Martin Luther. Luther was born in . . . '

  Then you can begin writing about Luther.

Note: Questions 5 and 6 are to be answered by **Higher Level Students only**.

QUESTION 5: SOURCE-BASED QUESTION

Higher Level
30 marks
Time to spend on question: 25 minutes

- This question is based on topics from Section II: Studies of change. It can be either pictures or documents. There will be either two or three sources given followed by questions on the sources and one question asking you to write a paragraph on the subjects raised in the sources. You must give as many facts as possible.

QUESTION 6: TOPIC-BASED QUESTION
Higher Level
60 marks
Time to spend on question: 40 minutes

- You must answer two questions from the option of four topics.
- There are more marks available for this question than any other question on the paper. In other words: it is the most important question!
- There is a mixture of paragraphs and short-answer questions. Section A can be about anything from Year 1 or Year 2 of the syllabus.
- Sections B and C are usually on Political developments in 20th century Ireland and Social History in Ireland in the 20th century.
- Section D is usually based on International Relations in the 20th Century.
- Use the number of marks awarded for each question as a guide to indicate how long you should spend on each question.

General Guide

- Take five minutes at the beginning of the exam to look over the paper and write down any points or ideas that you might have.
- Take five minutes at the end to re-read the exam paper. You may be surprised at how much you remember when you review the paper.
- Check you have answered all the questions. It is very easy to miss a question.
- Read and then re-read the question before you start.
- Try not to panic. If you are worried, take a moment to calm down and then begin again

Index